MW00806277

CLIMATE, CLOTHING, AND AGRICULTURE IN PREHISTORY

Clothing was crucial in human evolution, and having to cope with climate change was as true in prehistory as it is today. In *Climate, Clothing, and Agriculture in Prehistory*, Ian Gilligan offers the first complete account of the development of clothing as a response to exposure to cold during the ice ages. He explores how and when clothes were invented, noting that the thermal motive alone is tenable in view of the naked condition of humans. His account shows that there is considerably more archaeological evidence for Paleolithic clothes than is generally appreciated. Moreover, Gilligan posits, clothing played a leading role in major technological innovations. He demonstrates that fiber production and the advent of woven fabrics, developed in response to global warming, were pivotal to the origins of agriculture. Drawing together evidence from many disciplines, *Climate, Clothing, and Agriculture in Prehistory* is written in a clear and engaging style, and is illustrated with more than 100 images.

One of the world's leading authorities on the origins of clothing, Ian Gilligan holds university degrees in medicine, psychology, prehistoric archaeology, and biological anthropology, and is an honorary associate in the Department of Archaeology at the University of Sydney. He has authored a book on the clothing of Australian Aborigines, and his work has been published and cited in numerous scientific journals.

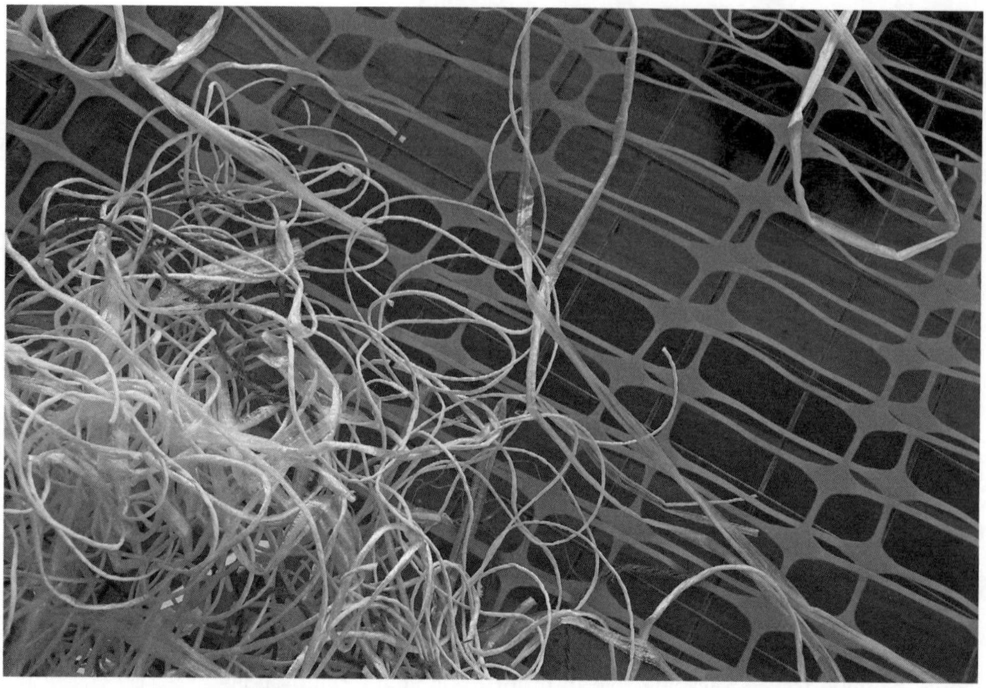

The Unravelling of Form. Textile artwork by Elizabeth Day, using natural and synthetic fibers. Installation detail, mixed media. Displayed in the exhibition *Invisible Words / Invisible Worlds*, Heritage Courtyard Pavilion, Parramatta (Sydney, Australia), November 2017.

CLIMATE, CLOTHING, AND AGRICULTURE IN PREHISTORY

LINKING EVIDENCE, CAUSES, AND EFFECTS

IAN GILLIGAN
University of Sydney

CAMBRIDGE
UNIVERSITY PRESS

CAMBRIDGE
UNIVERSITY PRESS

University Printing House, Cambridge CB2 8BS, United Kingdom

One Liberty Plaza, 20th Floor, New York, NY 10006, USA

477 Williamstown Road, Port Melbourne, VIC 3207, Australia

314–321, 3rd Floor, Plot 3, Splendor Forum, Jasola District Centre, New Delhi – 110025, India

79 Anson Road, #06–04/06, Singapore 079906

Cambridge University Press is part of the University of Cambridge.

It furthers the University's mission by disseminating knowledge in the pursuit of education, learning, and research at the highest international levels of excellence.

www.cambridge.org
Information on this title: www.cambridge.org/9781108455190
DOI: 10.1017/9781108555883

First published 2019

Printed in the United States of America by Sheridan Books, Inc.

A catalogue record for this publication is available from the British Library.

Library of Congress Cataloging-in-Publication Data
NAMES: Gilligan, Ian, author.
TITLE: Climate, clothing, and agriculture in prehistory : linking evidence, causes, and effects / Ian Gilligan, University of Sydney.
DESCRIPTION: First edition. | Cambridge, United Kingdom ; New York, NY : Cambridge University Press, 2019.
IDENTIFIERS: LCCN 2018010096 | ISBN 9781108470087 (hardback) | ISBN 9781108455190 (paperback)
SUBJECTS: LCSH: Clothing and dress, Prehistoric–Environmental aspects. | Textile fabrics, Prehistoric. | Prehistoric peoples–Clothing. | Human beings–Effect of climate on. | Climatic changes. | Agriculture, Prehistoric–Environmental aspects. | BISAC: SOCIAL SCIENCE / Archaeology.
CLASSIFICATION: LCC GN799.C5 G55 2019 | DDC 930–dc23
LC record available at https://lccn.loc.gov/2018010096

ISBN 978-1-108-47008-7 Hardback
ISBN 978-1-108-45519-0 Paperback

WARNING

Aboriginal and Torres Strait Islander people are warned that this book may contain images of people who are now deceased.

CONTENTS

FIGURES

TABLES

PREFACE

For someone who has no interest in clothes at a personal level and virtually no knowledge of fashion, it is strange that I had to write a book about clothing. There are two reasons why this happened. First, my real motivation is trying to understand how humans came to be the most unusual species on this planet. A long time ago, in high school, I was reading the novel *Lord of the Flies* by William Golding when something struck me about that allegorical tale. The fate of the boys marooned on a tropical island during a nuclear holocaust rang true, but I was bothered by something that did not seem to make sense. If we are products of evolution, a tendency toward self-destruction is an unlikely outcome of our evolutionary inheritance. I think Golding, like many others, was inclined to put it down to a conflict between our civilized state and our animal nature. From our origin in the animal world we inherit a taste for aggression, held in check (but perhaps intensified) by the thin veneer of civilization. This made me wonder about that thin veneer: What was this thing called civilization, and where did it come from? The conventional answer – civilization is the end-product of our natural talents such as possessing big brains, language, and so on – seemed only to raise more questions, and contradictions. Then it occurred to me, in one of those revelatory moments when something obvious presents itself. The thin veneer was the very thing that covered the boys when they landed on the island, the actual thing that, in the tropical heat and without the controls of adult society, began to disintegrate as the civilized veneer disappeared and their suppressed hunting instincts resurfaced. So I decided on the spot that clothing was the missing link, and I started to wonder about why we invented clothes.

My revelation about clothing led me to the second reason for this book. It soon became apparent as I began researching the origin of clothing, nothing was really known about its origins, at least scientifically, or its possible repercussions – the existence of clothing was taken for granted. I could not find a single book on the subject. The origin of clothing lay in prehistory, which led me into anthropology and archaeology, where I found there was little factual information. However, I did discover there had been ice ages in the recent past, which seemed to offer a fairly obvious answer, especially given our unusual nakedness – which likewise was largely taken for granted, with its origins shrouded in mystery. I began reading books on anthropology, prehistory, and human evolution, and I was lucky to start with one of those great academic books written for the layperson, an early edition of Brian Fagan's *Men of the Earth* (yes, the title has changed, but that goes to show how long ago it was). Among other things, I learned that virtually nothing was known about clothing in archaeology (and there was no real interest in the subject). I learned too that the advent of agriculture at the end of the last ice age was pivotal in humanity's rise to civilization. And I learned that sheep were the first animal species to be domesticated in the Near East, the world's first major agricultural center (things have changed somewhat since I read Fagan's book). And our first crops were grasses like wheat, which happen to be what sheep like to eat. Sheep produce wool, and so I started to wonder about whether clothing might have played a role in the transition to agriculture – but alas, those first domesticated sheep did not have a woolen fleece, so wool wasn't the reason. Anyway, to cut a long story short, that's how it came about that someone with no interest in clothing at all came to write a book – the first in a series – about why clothing is our most important invention.

In writing this book, I was torn between addressing an academic audience and wanting to make the text accessible to a wide audience, a la Brian Fagan. The solution was an unsatisfactory compromise, with the book written at two levels: the main text is written in an easy style, avoiding academic jargon as far as possible, but with detailed footnotes and referencing for those who may want to delve further. The other reason for doing this is that the subject matter cuts across quite a few scientific disciplines, and specialized terminologies would undermine even academic access to what is essentially an interdisciplinary endeavor. At least that is my excuse for all the generalizations and loose terminology; I hope the benefits outweigh the disadvantages.

ACKNOWLEDGMENTS

Over the years, my work has benefited greatly from the support of many people. However, a few names head the long list: Bill Lyndon, Michael J. Walker, and J. Peter White.

Colleagues who have helped include James Adovasio, Richard Attenborough, Val Attenbrow, Peter Bellwood, Annie Bickford, Robert Boyd, Tony Boyce, David Bulbeck, Steven Churchill, Jean Clottes, Eric Colhoun, Mark Collard, Alan Cooper, Richard Cosgrove, Christophe Darmangeat, Iain Davidson, Robin Dennell, Joe Dortch, Roland Fletcher, Josephine Flood, Gayle Fritz, Richard Fullagar, Jack Golson, Chris Gosden, Colin P. Groves, Brian Hayden, Pat Heslop-Harrison, Peter Hiscock, Ian Hodder, Elizabeth Temple Horton, John F. Hoffecker, Johan Kamminga, Jean Kennedy, Ray Kerkhove, Richard Klein, Marcus Klek, Yaroslav Kuzmin, Colin Pardoe, Dwight W. Read, David L. Reed, Bruce D. Smith, Olga Soffer, Bob Steadman, Robin Torrence, Erik Trinkaus, Nathan Wales, Robert S. Walker, Mark White, and Richard (R. V. S.) Wright.

Many institutions and libraries have assisted with material, but some individuals went above and beyond the call of duty. I want to single out Mark Alvey at The Field Museum, Chicago; Gabrielle Baglione at the Muséum d'histoire naturelle, Le Havre; Zhanna Etsina at The State Hermitage Museum, Saint Petersburg Melitta Franceschini at the South Tyrol Museum of Archaeology, Bolzano; Dianlin Huang at the Hemudu Site Museum, Yuyao City; Richard Ratajezak, Rare Books & Special Collections at Fisher Library, University of Sydney; and Debbie Tanna at the Museum of Sydney.

Special thanks to Bradley Hardy, Brewarrina Aboriginal Cultural Museum, and to Chickasaw Elder Robert Perry.

At Cambridge University Press, this book would not have come to fruition without the enthusiasm and patience of my editor, Beatrice Rehl. In the production team, I am indebted to Sindhujaa Ayyappan, Katherine Tengco Barbaro, and Mark Stein. Also, for more than two decades I have had the privilege of advice and guidance from my literary agent in New York, Bob Roistacher.

Among the many friends and colleagues over the years whose help and encouragement have been so valuable, I thank Greg Been, David Cameron,

Alan Cholodenko, Peter Cohen, John Cottrell-Dormer, Daniel Davenport, Gayle Edwards, Lewis Fung, John Gascoigne, Daniel and Sylvia Gibson, Carl Godfrey, Christopher Gregory, Robin Haig, Sheik Sulaiman Raiz Muthu Ismail, Katia Josua, Gabriel Khouri, Bruce Lachter, Matthew Large, Steven Leffers, Michael Mira, Maryanne O'Donnell, Chester Omana, Gayle Philpott, Kelly Smith, Richard Stone, Donald Toope, Peter Tsathas, Mark Walker, Harry Wark, Richard Wu, Greg Wyncoll, and last but by no means least, my dear friend the late David Leask, to whom this book is dedicated.

PART I

INTRODUCTION

ONE

WHAT SEPARATES US FROM NATURE?

Not so long ago, every human was a hunter-gatherer. A mere 20,000 years ago, people moved around regularly from place to place, carrying few material possessions. Unlike us, they kept in close contact with their natural surroundings. In places such as Australia and in parts of Africa, Southeast Asia and the Americas, the foraging way of life continued until just a few hundred years ago. This mobile hunter-gatherer lifestyle had served our species quite well for a long while, from the time when we first appeared on this earth around 300,000 years ago – just as it had served our earlier hominin ancestors for more than a million years before us.[1]

Not only were humans once all hunter-gatherers; they were naked. Could it be that these two things – adopting clothes and settling down to live in a world set apart from nature – are connected?

One reason why we might fail to notice any connection with clothes is that naked foragers have now gone from the face of the earth. The only exception is a small community comprised of perhaps two hundred people who still survive to this day as humans completely at home in the wild – and totally comfortable within their natural suits of naked skin. They remain hidden in tropical forests on one of the Andaman Islands in the Bay of Bengal, still living in isolation from the rest of humanity – except for sometimes glimpsing a passing ship on the horizon, or an aircraft drifting high overhead.[2]

The first thing we shall look at in this book is the origin of clothing. The subject has long been shrouded in mystery and confusion. Everyone seems to have an opinion about why humans first adopted clothes, but we shall depart from a long tradition here and carefully consider the evidence. There are two kinds of nakedness to think about: one is the absence of clothes, and the other is biological nakedness – our lack of a decent fur cover. Next, we shall look at what happened to the hunter-gatherer lifestyle. For some reason (or reasons), people in some parts of the world started to engage in agriculture – and, well, the rest is history. Again, everyone probably has an opinion about why people would start to plant crops and domesticate animals. Indeed, the answer might seem rather too obvious. However, archaeologists have been looking at the evidence for quite a few decades and, as we shall see, their findings raise some serious doubts about the obvious answer, which is that agriculture started because it was a better way of feeding people. In reality, that answer is more of an assumption, and it actually raises some rather awkward questions. There may be a better answer, though not so obvious. What if clothes played a role in the origin of agriculture?

How might the origin of clothing and the origin of agriculture be connected? The answer is climate change. Actually, two climate changes: global warming – not now, but around the time when agriculture began – and before that, global cooling. Climate change is the common thread that can connect the origin of clothing and the origin of agriculture. Speaking of threads, the agricultural revolution was really two revolutions: a revolution in the food economy and a revolution in clothes – the textile revolution.

A WIDER VIEW

Hunter-gatherers were not the same all around the world, and some changes did occur over time, but nevertheless, the lifestyle of foragers was a fairly stable mode of existence – socially, technologically, and ecologically. Their traditional lifestyle stands in stark contrast to the incredible instability and the extraordinary rate of technological change that has typified the entire span of recorded human history – the last 5,000 years.

We take the opportunity here to view this turbulent trajectory in a longer time frame, the one provided by archaeology. Only archaeology can open up the vast expanse of human existence called prehistory – history before writing. And we adopt the broad view of human society provided by anthropology, in the field called ethnography (which studies traditional premodern societies, including hunter-gatherers). We must take this vantage point if we are ever to make sense of what has happened. We need to stand back and get a truly global view: the widest possible view, stretching all the way to remote places, such as Tasmania and to the farthest tip of South America. And we need to take a longer view than history: the longest possible view, one that goes back all the way into prehistory.

History is too late: most of the big changes – like the advent of agriculture (and clothes) – had already happened by the time history began, with the first writing 5,000 years ago. So by the time history started, the story was over, more or less. One exception is the Industrial Revolution, which, as it happens, had a great deal to do with clothes – textiles in particular. When we take the long view, we soon arrive at a rather awkward fact: we have been hunter-gatherers for most of our existence as a species. That prolonged delay before the rise of civilization raises an obvious question about what happened – and why.

Science generally tries to make sense of our modern maelstrom as an outcome of the usual evolutionary processes: adaptation and natural selection. Our inherited talents – such as possessing a large brain, extraordinary language skills, and a knack for inventiveness – helped us to conquer the environment and make the transition to a more artificial existence (or so the story goes). And these very same talents gave us a competitive advantage over other species – like our poor Neanderthal cousins. This conventional narrative can create the comforting impression that civilization is a predictable product of the same evolutionary processes that largely govern the rest of nature. Alternatively, however, it may be more realistic to see civilized life instead as a rather unusual development that has led humanity in a quite unnatural direction.[3]

One common approach has been to stress how certain human talents, such as having more intelligence than our competitors, helped our ancestors in the never-ending endeavor to extract sufficient food resources from the environment. In this popular scenario, our recent emergence as the dominant species on earth reflects a final success in the food quest.[4]

When Agriculture Once Made Sense

Agriculture is the classic example. Sharing the widely held assumption that the shift from foraging to farming revolved around food, archaeologists have tried to find out why agriculture first began when and where it did. Maybe, according to one way of thinking, agriculture was an adaptive response to uncertainties in food supplies caused by the massive upheavals in global climates at the end of the last ice age. Yet after more than a century of research and digging, we are none the wiser about why hunter-gatherers abandoned foraging in favor of agriculture – and that unshaken faith in the prevailing food paradigm may be largely to blame.[5]

Some archaeologists are now suggesting that we need to think about other things besides food. They say we should think about agriculture not so much as a revolution in the economic sphere but as one facet of a wider phenomenon, a subtle but pivotal change in how people were looking at the world and relating to their surroundings.[6]

Time to Forget about Food – and Remember Naked People

A preoccupation with food can lead to a couple of unfortunate consequences. For one, the emphasis on food will narrow our focus to just one aspect of the struggle for survival, limiting the search for causes. And even to describe our hominin ancestors – or recent peoples who were habitually unclad, such as Australian Aborigines – as hunter-gatherers or foragers is a real issue. By saying they are hunter-gatherers we effectively define their entire existence in terms of the food economy. It is like saying that our entire way of life is essentially agricultural. Are we all happy to be defined as farmers?[7]

The focus on food implies that other features, such as nakedness – whether a lack of clothes or a lack of body fur – were of no consequence. In a similar vein, the old concept of civilization is regarded nowadays almost as a dirty word in anthropology, relegated to the history books and replaced with cleaner terms, such as social complexity, that reflect a narrowing of focus. All of the messy morality – and the colonial savagery – of civilizing those naked peoples by coercing them into wearing clothes can be safely suppressed, superseded by a relatively superficial emphasis on economics and social organization.[8]

AN UNUSUAL EVOLUTIONARY HISTORY

If our modern lifestyle is not really a result of typical evolutionary processes, does this mean that we are not a product of evolution? Have our special human qualities allowed us to rise above the mundane struggle for survival that dictates the destiny of every other species?

Many people do not accept the scientific consensus about the validity of evolutionary theory – or at least they are reluctant to accept that we modern humans are simply a product of evolution. Instead they believe we are a special creation. And despite the mainstream view in science that we are merely sophisticated animals, it is hard to deny that we are a special species – more so perhaps than some scientists would like to admit. Nonetheless, our special status is still a product of evolutionary processes – just not the usual ones.

What might be those unusual processes?

The struggle for survival is not only about finding food. All species must adapt to their environments in various ways – and no natural environments stay the same forever. As we are all made well aware by the specter of global warming, a major aspect of the environment is the climate, particularly its thermal component. Extremes of heat and cold exert strong selection pressures on all living things, and every species must adapt to its local thermal environment or perish. Temperature is in fact more fundamental than food: it affects not only all living things all the time but all matter – nothing escapes its control.[9]

Natural Climate Change

In the case of our own evolutionary past, the science of climatology tells us that the earth's climate was far from stable over the last two million years. Hominins first appeared in Africa around six million years ago, and the last third of hominin evolution took place during a time of great environmental instability dominated by ice ages, known as the Pleistocene epoch. During the coldest phases, ice sheets extended over much of the earth's surface. Places like New York and northern England were hidden under thick layers of ice, while in China the zone of permafrost stretched all the way south to Beijing.

The last of these glacial cycles started 120,000 years ago and reached its coldest point 22,000 years ago – which climatologists call the Last Glacial Maximum (LGM). At that time, the average global air temperature had fallen by between 3° and 5° Celsius (approximately 5–10° Fahrenheit). A few degrees might not sound very significant, but this was just a global average that includes a lesser cooling over the surface of the oceans. Humans at the time would have been more concerned about how much the temperatures fell over the land areas. The terrestrial decline in temperature was most marked in the middle latitudes of the northern hemisphere, where winter temperatures often dropped by amazing amounts – between 10°C and 20°C (~20°F and 35°F).[10]

The evolution of *Homo* took place during these protracted cold spells, the last of which finished only recently – a mere 11,700 years ago.

Naked in a Colder World

What makes our evolution really unusual is that we evolved when the global climate was getting colder, and yet we became more vulnerable to cold. Somehow in the process we lost the natural cover of fur that is one of the main traits of mammals. So it is really quite an enigma: we evolved in a colder world and yet we went naked.[11]

The explanation for this odd situation probably relates to the sequence of events. And human nakedness could reflect the fact that in evolution, not every single trait is necessarily adaptive – and even a successful adaptation can later become maladaptive if the environment changes.

Early *Homo* evolved in Africa, and prior to the onset of the Pleistocene, the global climate was actually a little warmer than it is now. Even when the Pleistocene got started, the main impact of climate change in Africa was not cooler but drier conditions. Local climates became drier as vast quantities of water were locked up in the expanding polar ice caps, and water vapor was lost from atmospheric circulation. Our loss of body fur – together with the evolution of sweating as an adaptation to heat stress – happened within this ecological context.[12]

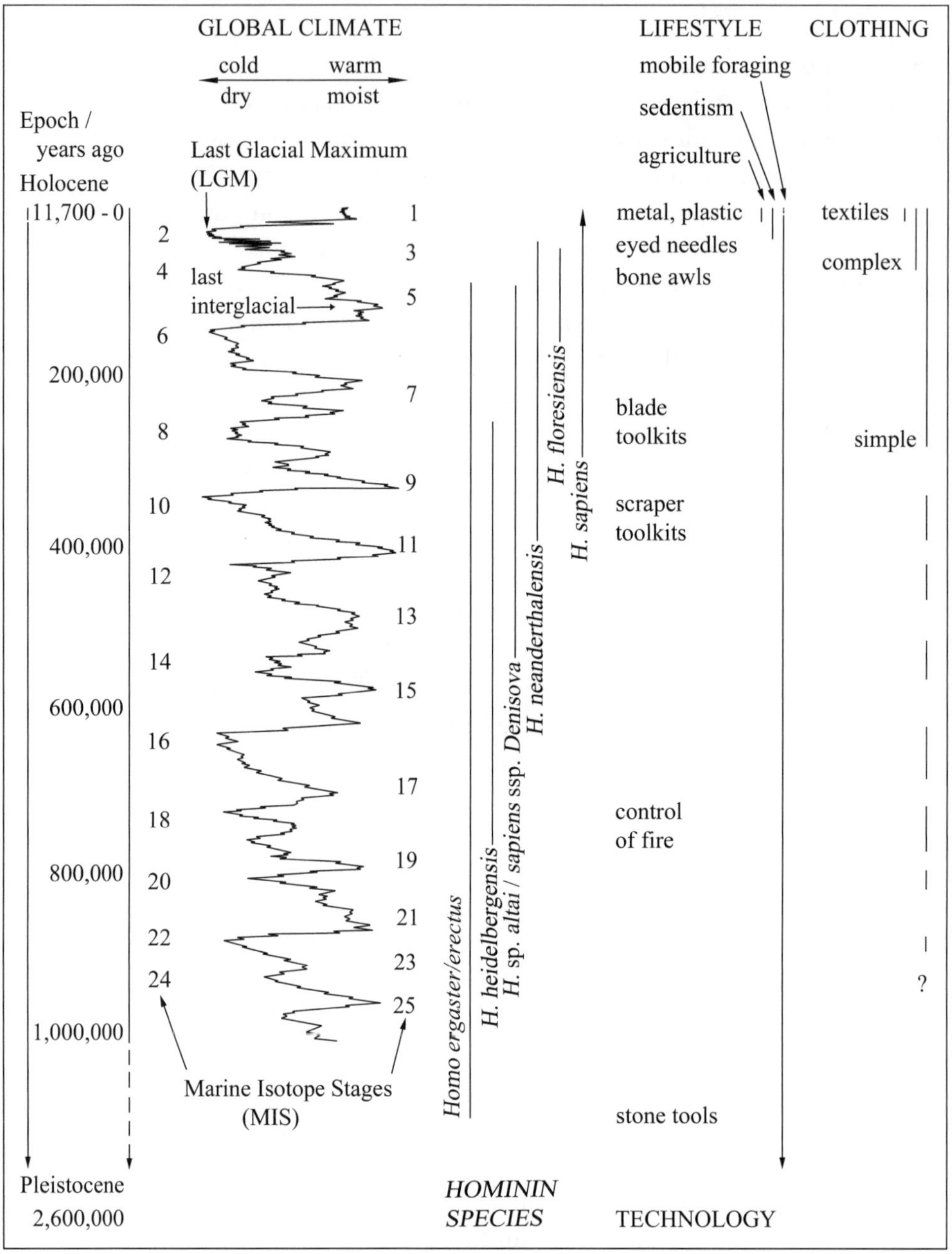

1. **Climate change and human trends over the last million years**
Global climate trends over the last million years, with MIS (Marine Isotope Stage) numbering of the major glacial and interglacial episodes. Shown also are hominin species (and their durations) together with major technological innovations, lifestyle changes, and developments in clothing.

Source: Temperature curve based on proxy data from multiple sources, including the 800,000-year ice core record at Dome C, Antarctica (Jouzel et al., 2007).

Sweating is quite an unusual trait too: sweating only works well as a cooling mechanism in dry conditions – and without a fur cover. The challenge of keeping cool in Africa was made worse by our larger brains: big brains are not just expensive in terms of energy requirements, but they generate a lot of extra heat. Our large brains made us more prone to overheating in the tropics – which probably explains why we have retained some hair cover on our heads, to provide shade. However, the problem with relying on sweating to keep cool was that our need for water increased just as the environment became drier.[13]

2. **Winter landscape in southern Russia**
Even during the present warm interglacial epoch, climates in the middle latitudes of Eurasia pose thermal challenges for humans. Here is a winter scene in the Russian city of Novosibirsk (55°N), southern Siberia.
Source: Photo by Yaroslav Kuzmin, © Yaroslav Kuzmin. Reproduced by permission of Yaroslav Kuzmin.

Clearly, there were competing – and sometimes conflicting – adaptive pressures on *Homo*. Science does not have all of the answers yet, and we shall look at these questions again in more detail later.

When Naked Is Hot – and Not

In contrast to the popular notion that we shed our body fur to cope with heat stress, it turns out that exposing a naked skin surface to the sun probably creates more heat stress. Even in the tropics, having a layer of fur can be quite useful, because it functions as portable shade. Direct exposure of our skin surface to the hot overhead sun led to a higher heat load on the body – and this thermal stress led to that special cooling adaption of sweating. And then there was the opposite problem of cold stress, which became more of an issue when some of our ancestors began to spread into middle latitudes.

No matter how we look at it then, our nakedness is a biological oddity. Whether we consider the risks of heat stress or cold stress, the loss of body fur involved a loss of insulation – from heat as well as from cold. In relation to coping with cold, we may not be the only naked mammal on the planet, but all of the other naked mammals such as elephants and marine mammals seem to have good reasons to dispense with a thick layer of fur. In the case of elephants, their large body mass puts them in constant danger of overheating. But in the case of humans, we have no obvious reason to be naked. Neither have we acquired any compensatory means of coping with exposure to cold. Most other naked mammals stayed in tropical places, while their more adventurous relatives that pushed into colder regions during the Pleistocene often evolved heavy layers of wool – like the woolly rhinoceros and woolly mammoth. Mammals that ventured into the water had to find new adaptations to prevent them getting too cold – like the thick layers of blubber that protect whales and dolphins in their oceanic environments.[14]

Humans relied instead on an inventive mind, starting with fire. Our ancestors discovered how to tame fire by nearly halfway through the Pleistocene. Yet having a warm fire in a cave was of little help when, sooner or later, they had to venture out into the open. On its own, fire could never have allowed our ancestors to live very far from the tropics at the height of an ice age.[15]

We are not sure when our ancestors became biologically naked, but we do know from archaeology that at least some *Homo sapiens* did survive outside of the tropics during the last ice age without a decent coat of fur.

Yet they did have a coat: they invented clothes. And that is not just an unusual adaptation: it is unique.

CLIMATE CHANGE AND CLOTHING

The evolutionary history of humans is most unusual, not with regard to food, but in relation to keeping warm. Our biological inheritance as a naked primate left us vulnerable to cold. So climate change during the Pleistocene posed a special challenge to human survival, and it posed the biggest threat to those of our ancestors who had migrated beyond the tropics during the warm interglacial periods. Our ancestors met the challenge posed by winter cold with a series of behavioral adaptations: they learned how to control fire; they moved into caves or constructed artificial shelters to escape from wind chill; and they invented clothes. These unusual aspects of our evolution may provide us with some unexpected clues about the origins of our modern way of life.

The key assumption here is that clothing first originated as a solution to the problem of cold exposure during the ice ages. In other words, regardless of all the many functions that clothing has since come to serve, our ancestors first adopted clothes to keep warm.

Our Natural Nakedness

Although almost every human being in the world today wears at least some clothing on a regular basis, the habitual use of clothes has not been a universal behavior of humans from the outset. The evidence from science points to the localized origins of clothing in cooler regions of the globe during the latter part of the Pleistocene.

In ethnography, for example, we can see that humans do not always wear clothes. Unlike the rest of humanity, hunter-gatherers in warmer places typically wore no clothes at all. When they did decide to don a garment, the purpose was to ward off the cold. We find this thermal pattern for clothing in Australia, where the Aborigines enjoyed an intimate relationship with their environment. Even in the chilly climate of Tasmania,, they might sometimes tie a loose cape across their shoulders to keep warm, but otherwise they went about their business completely unclad. Aborigines were perfectly happy to stroll naked across the landscape – weather permitting.[16]

3. **Aborigines in the Sydney area, 1803**
In the Sydney area, Aborigines were typically unclad. This 1803 watercolor illustration, attributed to Philip Gidley King, shows a group of Aborigines at their campfire.
Source: Mitchell Library, Banks Papers Series 36a.04 a2225. Reproduced courtesy of the State Library of New South Wales, [IE513073], Sydney.

One of the first Europeans to encounter this casual nakedness in Australia was Captain Cook, who led the British expedition that sailed along the eastern coast of the continent during the autumn and winter of 1770. Cook first stepped ashore at Botany Bay, now surrounded by the suburbs and airport of Sydney, where he reported a total absence of clothing:

> No sort of cloathing or ornaments were ever seen by any of us upon any one of them or in or about any of their hutts, from which I conclude that they never wear any.[17]

4. **Tasmanian dinner party, 1823**
Tasmanians preparing a meal in the vicinity of Lake Echo, March (early autumn), 1823.
Source: An Aboriginal Dinner Party, Ross, 1831:101. Mitchell Library, DSM/986/25A1. Reproduced by permission of the Mitchell Library, State Library of New South Wales, Sydney.

When their ship *Endeavour* was beached for repairs 2,700km (1,800 miles) to the north of Sydney, the white visitors spent two weeks ashore. During this sojourn they enjoyed the close company of Aborigines for the first time, and although they did see a little more in the way of personal ornaments, they failed to see any clothes. Sir Joseph Banks, the botanist on the voyage, was stunned by the total absence of modesty – a supposedly innate human consciousness of being naked. Banks witnessed their nakedness many times, both with his binoculars and with his own naked eyes:

> That their customs were nearly the same throughout the whole length of the coast along which we saild I should think very probable... we saw them either with our eyes or glasses many times... they likewise in the

> same manner went naked... Our glasses might deceive us in many things but their colour and want of cloths we certainly did see...
>
> Of Cloths they had not the last part but naked as ever our general father was before his fall, they seemed no more conscious of their nakedness than if they had not been the children of Parents who eat the fruit of the tree of knowledge...[18]

Casual nakedness was true also for some African forager groups such as the Bushmen of the Kalahari (nowadays generally called San peoples by anthropologists). Some foragers in South America were routinely naked too, like the hardy souls who lived on the windswept tip of South America. On this remote archipelago that almost touches Antarctica, and within sight of snow-capped peaks, Tierra del Fuego is the most southerly location of any human society. Charles Darwin encountered the local Fuegians in 1832 during his famous voyage on the *Beagle*, when he began to formulate his theory of evolution by natural selection. In his journal, Darwin describes the nakedness of the Fuegians in a tone of shock that borders on bewilderment, as though he (like Banks) could hardly believe the evidence before his own eyes:

> But these Fuegians in the canoe were quite naked, and even one full-grown woman was absolutely so. It was raining heavily, and the fresh water, together with the spray, trickled down her body. In another harbour not far distant, a woman, who was suckling a recently-born child, came one day alongside the vessel, and remained there whilst the sleet fell and thawed on her naked bosom, and on the skin of her naked child.[19]

5. **Fuegians wearing guanaco skins**
Fuegians wearing guanaco skins, 1895. Shown here is an Alakaluf (Kawésqar) group, western Tierra del Fuego. Other groups such as the Yaghan (or Yamana) who lived along the shores of the Beagle Channel and on the southernmost islands, often wore even less – to the astonishment of Charles Darwin when he visited Tierra del Fuego in 1832.
Source: Hulton Archive, © Getty Images, # 463956945. Reproduced under license, Getty Images.

The Fuegians did wear simple clothes at times, but only when they felt the need to keep themselves warm. They used the skins of wild animals like the guanaco (ancestor of the llama) and sea mammals such as otters and seals. Yet they were happy to go around naked too, as Darwin witnessed. Lack of clothing is a well-documented fact in ethnography. The simple fact is that many hunter-gatherers were quite happy to stay naked unless the weather got too cold. Their reluctance to wear clothes routinely can easily refute any notion we might harbor that humans have some innate inclination to wear clothes.

THE COMMON THREAD

Among the mysteries with the emergence of our modern lifestyle is not only a connection with clothes but also with climate change. As we shall see later, the early signs of clothing coincide closely with exposure of our ancestors to the changing environments of the ice age. A connection with climate is seen also with the transition to agriculture, which coincided with global warming after the end of the last ice age. Adding to the mystery, these developments did not follow on consistently from the emergence of our species but, instead, they were delayed and limited to only some societies. As well as the strange delay, the restricted pattern alone argues against our modern lifestyle being simply a consequence of universal human qualities such as language or intelligence.

The leading British prehistorian Colin Renfrew, Professor of Archaeology at Cambridge University, describes this strange delay as the "sapient paradox." He wonders how we can attribute the rise of modern life to basic qualities in *Homo sapiens* when we know from archaeology that key aspects such as agriculture and civilization only happened very late in our evolution. And even then, most members of our species were happy to carry on as hunter-gatherers.[20]

Yet as Renfrew points out, one aspect of the paradox is that the main manifestations of this modern trend, including agriculture, began to appear independently at similar times in a number of separate regions. A simultaneous emergence hints at the presence of similar causal processes operating in each of those regions. When we come to consider how clothing might be involved, we shall discover that some new things were happening with clothes in those places, things that might offer us some plausible reasons for the delay, and also for the restricted pattern. And clothing may represent a logical reason to connect the rise of modern life with past climate change.

An Invisible Invention

One problem with claiming that clothing was so important in prehistory is that we have grown accustomed to the role of clothes in history, where shifting fashions serve as mere passive reflections of changing cultural trends. Historically, clothing does not seem to have played any active or decisive role in promoting change – although there is certainly some evidence to the contrary. For instance, among hunter-gatherers who wore clothes, clothing was often their most complex technology – more complex than their food-getting technologies. And in the first farming villages, and in all of the early civilizations, the manufacture of textiles was a major technology and a major industry. As mentioned too, the Industrial Revolution was first ignited in the realm of clothes, with new machines and factories constructed to manufacture cotton fabrics. Beginning with water power and then coal, the Industrial Revolution saw the harnessing of new energy sources (and human labor) to fuel those machines to manufacture cloth. And to make the machines, wood was replaced by metals such as iron and then steel [21]

6. **Industrial Revolution**
At the heart of the Industrial Revolution, the city of Manchester in the English midlands witnessed the first modern factories, filled with machines dedicated to making cotton textiles – hence the city became known as Cottonopolis. Many textile-driven developments in technology have since transformed both the human and natural worlds, leaving behind their historical origins in the realm of clothing manufacture.
Source: World History Archive / Alamy Stock Photo

Clothes have often been at the forefront of technological innovation, right up to the present. The Stone Age came to an end with the advent of agriculture (and to some extent, with the advent of pottery), but stone technology was not widely replaced until another new kind of material – metal – came on the scene, during the Copper, Bronze, and Iron Ages. Among the world's oldest metal artifacts – perhaps the oldest – is a copper awl found in Israel that dates to around 7,000 years ago.[22]

7. **Spinning jenny**
One technological innovation that helped spark the Industrial Revolution was a textile-weaving machine, called the spinning jenny. Invented in 1764 by James Hargreaves, the machine allowed one person to do the work of many; it was followed by water-powered devices that further multiplied the output of cotton cloth.
Source: World History Archive / Alamy Stock Photo

In more recent times, the most significant new material in everyday life has been the development of plastics, beginning early in the twentieth century. The first useful plastics derived from commercial efforts to manufacture artificial textile fibers; nylon was an early success, followed by polyester. The latest technological innovations utilize woven carbon fibers and related composite materials based on combining textile and ceramic technologies, and these are finding applications in many areas – such as replacing aluminum and metal alloys in the structural components and the turbine engines of large aircraft.[23]

Without textiles there might have been no agriculture, no Industrial Revolution, and no plastics. Neither should we forget that in colonial times, the first serious challenge to confront the missionaries who often followed in the wake of explorers such as Cook was the task of educating all those naked indigenous peoples around the world about the urgent moral need to cover themselves with decent clothes.[24]

Still, none of these roles of clothing in history can shake a common misconception that clothing is a relatively irrelevant invention. And whereas the great technological and economic importance of cloth-making was once very visible in Western industrialized nations, in our postindustrial world the cost of fabrics has diminished as production shifts to third-world countries. Most of our clothes are now made cheaply in "faraway factories," and the significance of cloth has been "left out of the broader historical narrative."[25]

To make matters worse, little evidence survives from ancient times since clothes are made from such perishable materials. In archaeology, prehistoric clothing is almost invisible. Yet as we shall discover in the following chapters, we can nonetheless use science to make prehistoric clothes virtually visible.[26]

8. **Teaching Aborigines to wear decent clothes**

In the early days of the Sydney settlement, efforts by the British to encourage the local Indigenous people to adopt decent clothes met with only partial success. This drawing is by Alphonse Pellion, 1819: *Sauvages de la Nouvelle Galles du Sud (d'apres nature dans leur Camp pres de Sidney (20 dec. 1819).*

Source: State Library of New South Wales, SV/118. Reproduced by permission of the State Library of New South Wales, Sydney.

Women's Work Is Never Seen

A tendency to neglect or trivialize clothing reflects the low status of women too, and it reflects a sexist bias in science. In most cultures, making clothes is mainly women's work. So the archaeological invisibility is compounded by the neglected role of women in prehistory. In archaeology, clothing is the invisible invention of the invisible sex – or at least it has been, until quite recently.[27]

Moreover, the academic approach to clothing tends to focus on the appearance of clothing, on clothes as fashion. Social theorists are fascinated by the flamboyant role of clothing in the fashion industry, where the stress is on sartorial display, and by the reflective function of garments as a form of social discourse.[28]

True, the analysis of appearance can be quite revealing from a sociological point of view. The study of clothing (as dress) can certainly help to inform us about power relations and social structures. Yet all of this focus on fashion, appearance, and clothing as dress can make it look like clothes have always been indispensable, since humans have always been concerned with appearance. In this sense, humans are always dressed, and some dress historians are inclined to dismiss a pragmatic purpose, such as protection from cold, as the original cause of clothing.[29]

We should not privilege the role of clothing as dress at the expense of seemingly mundane purposes such as warmth, or even modesty. Leaving aside the sheer absurdity of dismissing thermal insulation, the priority of surface appearance might be fine for historians, but the origin of clothing does not lie in history: it lies in the province of prehistory.

Not that one particular approach is necessarily right or wrong: it is more a matter of horses for courses. The purpose here differs from that of sociologists and historians of dress. The real danger, however, is that focusing on clothing as dress tends to accept the fact of clothing as given – and it is precisely that fact that should be interrogated. Only by doing so can we bring its presence into question.

In the modern world, we are not all slaves of fashion, but everyone is a loyal slave of clothing. The situation is not unlike that little boy in *The Emperor's New Clothes*, though in reverse: so mesmerized are we by the sheer appearance of clothes that we fail to notice the fact that we wear clothes. It is quite a paradox: most of what we see when we look at ourselves is clothing, and yet, scientifically, we fail to notice clothes.[30]

THE DEFINITION OF CLOTHING

This brings us to the question of definition: what is clothing? The emphasis on fashion – on clothes as display – can be misleading and, technically, mistaken.

Clothes may serve this purpose of display but only by default. Since clothes cover the body, the fundamental functions of body decoration and display tend to be displaced onto clothes. This has some important archaeological implications, as we shall see later. Perhaps the most precise definition of clothes is found in the *Concise Oxford English Dictionary*:

> items worn to cover the body.[31]

Regardless of what functions our clothes may or may not serve, clothing always covers. In this sense, clothing is the exact opposite of display: it hides and conceals. The problem with fashion and all the stress on dress is that it can distract from the fact of cover and, in effect, cover the cover. In this way, the phenomenon of clothing remains hidden from view, and we can no longer see ourselves as covered. Fashion can make clothing so familiar that the actual presence of clothing is taken for granted, beyond question, which is probably how we like it.

CLOTHING AND HUMAN UNIQUENESS

The story of clothing echoes some key themes in the biblical story of Genesis – our original nakedness, the sense of shame and guilt, the advent of clothing (in the form of those famous fig leaves) and the separation of humanity from nature. Ancient origins in the ice age can almost invoke a kind of Garden of Eden scenario – although the reason for our eviction from nature was different and so too was the sequence of events. It was hardly our fault that we were born naked, and it was the fickleness of nature itself – in the form of climate change – that finally drove us out of Eden.[32]

The narrative of our separation from nature can be traced back even before biblical times to the dawn of civilization in Mesopotamia, to the Epic of Gilgamesh, written around 4,000 years ago, making it one of the oldest surviving texts. The hero of the story is Gilgamesh, a king who struggles to conquer the sinister natural forces of the forest in order to build the walls and temples of the first great city in Mesopotamia, Uruk. In the process he befriends and civilizes a naked "wild man" of the woods, named Enkidu. Gilgamesh arranges for his friend to have a sexual encounter with a harlot, who teaches him to wear clothes. Afterwards, Enkidu feels shame and remorse for having defiled his pure body. Then he is persuaded to help Gilgamesh destroy the evil-looking guardian of the forest, called Ḫumbaba, who had nurtured Enkidu as a child. Thereafter Enkidu dies, as punishment by the gods for betraying nature, and Gilgamesh is overcome with despair at the loss of his friend. In the end, although Gilgamesh succeeds in creating "civilization from savagery," his life story enacts a tragic "confrontation of the forest with the city, of the tree and the animal with humanity, of primitive man with urban man, of a hunting culture with a farming culture... of instinct with self-control," suggesting that "no city man is wholly happy when he has lost...contact with nature."[33]

Ultimately, we are dealing here with a more fundamental issue: the question of whether we are, or at least have become, so different from all other species that we are effectively unique and qualitatively distinct from every other form of animal life on earth. Technically every species is unique by definition, of course. Yet we have somehow become separated from the rest of evolution and uniquely unique. Science is inclined to deny this truth or minimize it by reductionism since it lacks any really convincing explanation for how this unusual situation could possibly have arisen.[34]

The enduring appeal of stories like Genesis lies in how they readily accept a self-evident truth that science is reluctant to concede: namely, we have somehow become separate from the rest of nature. Genesis also highlights the powerful moral issues involved that science meticulously avoids – like why modesty and the need for cover are so important for our modern sense of being human. Yet the invention of clothing is unique in the whole of nature, and this artificial cover is the scientific key that may allow us to unlock the mystery. Our separation is true not just subjectively, as with our sense of shame: our physical separation is proven by the presence of clothes, and so there may be a sound scientific foundation after all. In which case, the biological basis for our rise to global domination is not brainpower but nakedness. By taking clothes seriously, we can find a scientific alternative to stories like Genesis and render them redundant as reasons for how we came to be what we are.

No Return to Nature

To recognize clothes as the reason for our separation is not to advocate for any return to our former naked state, even if we could somehow dispense with clothes. Most of us look better in clothes, if it comes to that. We should not abandon clothes but appreciate how there is much more to clothing than meets the naked eye. Not that our eyes are naked anymore, regardless of whether we wear sunglasses. Being clothed has become so basic to our being – and so essential for civilized society – that we can barely see ourselves as clothed and our perception of ourselves is always covered, even when we are naked. We are always already covered – and so too is the world we see around us. Clothes may be removable and perishable, but clothing is now a permanent aspect of being human.

Yet at the risk of contradiction, in coming to that realization we should not get too preoccupied with clothes. The focus on clothes in this context is quite accidental. The real question is what separates us from nature. It could just be that the answer is clothing – the actual thing that covers us.

PART II

CLOTHING IN THE ICE AGE

TWO

CLIMATE CHANGE AND THE INVENTION OF CLOTHES

The human need for clothes did not start out from any sense of modesty nor a desire to decorate ourselves: naked hunter-gatherers, such as the Australian Aborigines, can easily disprove those theories. This is likewise for theories of clothing origins that are based on social purposes, such as displaying social roles. Of course, these motives – modesty and display – are often the main reason why we wear clothes in the modern world. And, like a lot of modern things, they are rather contradictory: we like to show ourselves, and we also like to cover ourselves. Clothes embody these ambivalent feelings about our bodies.

Display and modesty make more sense as later motives: they arose as reasons to wear clothes once we had already adopted clothing. And yet, these were the motives that finally made clothes indispensable and permanent. The psycho-social need for clothes played a big role in our modern development – in the emergence of agriculture, for example, as we shall see. So, we should not discount the roles of modesty and display, but in searching for original causes, we have a couple of more respectable candidates.

First, is our biological nakedness: we lack natural body cover in the form of fur. As mentioned in the first chapter, this is an unusual trait for any mammal, though not unique: some other species also became naked. And it is true that our own nakedness varies quite markedly and is never complete: we still retain some body hair – some people more than others – but we are nonetheless naked in a biological sense. In a moment, we shall look at the questions of when and why our hominin ancestors lost their fur cover.

TABLE 1. *Theories of clothing origins*

Physical	Protective: thermal (cold); others (e.g., abrasion, insects)
Psychological	Decoration/display; modesty/shame; protection from evil spirits
Social	Roles/status; luxury value (in complex societies)

The other clue about the origin of clothes is climate change. We know from fossil evidence that our genus *Homo* evolved when the global environment was warmer than it is now. On average, temperatures then were 2°C–3°C (3–5 °F) higher (a fair amount as a global average). But soon after humans arrived, the climate started to get cooler and more unstable. For most of their recent evolution, our ancestors were living through a long environmental epoch – the Pleistocene – dominated by ice ages. Only those who lived in the tropics escaped the colder global climate – except it did impact the higher tropical areas, such as central New Guinea, the Andes, and the highlands of Ethiopia. In the tropics, the main impact of climate change was a drier climate and – more noticeable to coastal people – a dramatic drop in sea levels.

So, we have a couple of good reasons for why our ancestors invented clothes. They were naked, and the world got colder. There is really no mystery about why they invented clothes. We saw in the first chapter how people living on the southern tip of South America were at the limit of our naked capacity to cope with cold. As Darwin described, they would sometimes cover their bodies – but only to keep warm. If we take the trouble to consider all of the evidence, the question of clothing origins becomes almost a no-brainer.

TROUBLE WITH THE TRANSIENCE OF CLOTHING

We do face a challenge though when we look for clothing in the ice ages: there is none – not a stitch. Fortunately, we can make use of science to help defeat this daunting deficit.[1]

The key sciences are climatology and physiology. Climatology can tell us how cold the weather was, while the physiology can tell us about the cold limit for naked humans and how much clothing they would have needed to survive. When we combine data from these two sources, we can discover when – and where – people first had to wear clothes.

Archaeology is not entirely silent on the subject. The archaeological record tells us that humans did survive during the ice ages in certain locations where we can deduce – from the temperatures and the naked limits – that people must have had clothes at the time. Archaeology gives us other kinds of evidence too, such as the tools that people were using to make the garments. Some tools were clearly connected with clothes – notably the slender eyed

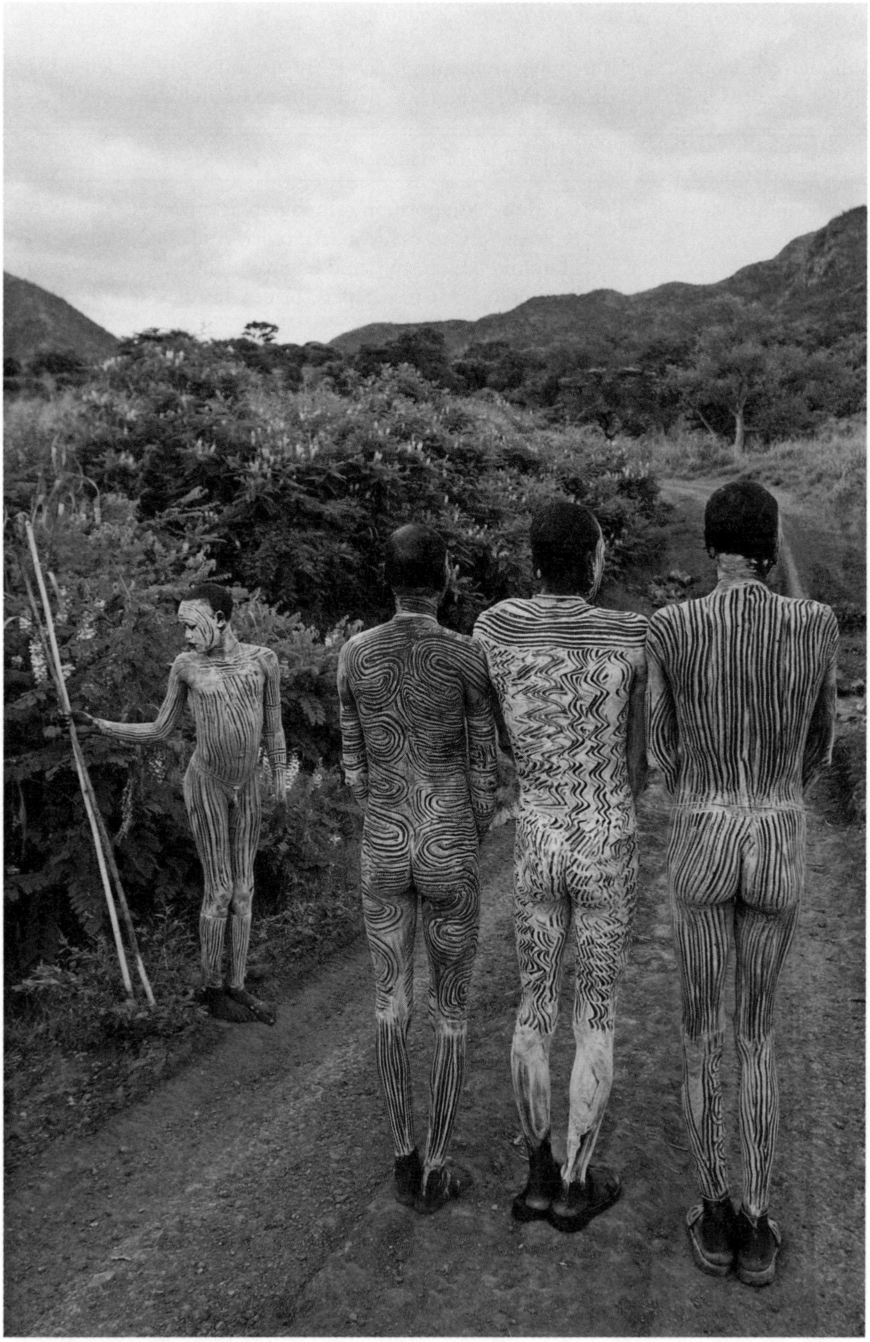

9. **Well-dressed gentlemen, Omo Valley, Africa**
Decorating the body for personal and social display is not a reason for humans to invent clothes. On the contrary, for hunter-gatherers in prehistory who used animal skins, the body could be more easily and elaborately decorated without clothes. Only in recent historical times have garments begun to approach the decorative potential of body painting. Shown here are some well-dressed gentlemen from the Suri agro-pastoral peoples, Omo Valley, southern Ethiopia.
Source: Photo: Piper Mackay, © Getty Images, # 136204396. Reproduced under license, Getty Images.

TABLE 2. *Sources of evidence about Paleolithic clothing*

Although ice age clothing is invisible archaeologically, there are sources of evidence that allow inferences to be drawn about the origin and development of prehistoric clothing.

Discipline	Major lines of evidence
Ethnography	Cautious extrapolation (ethnographic analogy)
	Role of "test cases" (e.g., Australia, Andaman Islands)
Archaeology	Hominin presence in cold environments
	Technologies (e.g., scrapers, blades, needles, spindle whorls)
	Art (rock art, figurines)
Physiology	Limits to cold tolerance (hypothermia, frostbite)
	Clothing physiology
Paleoclimatology	Pleistocene thermal conditions: temperature/wind proxies
	Moisture levels in Holocene
Molecular biology	Dating of human nakedness (body hair reduction)
	Dating of clothing origins (body lice)

needles carved from long animal bones that have been found at many sites of the last ice age. Other tools – stone tools such as scrapers and blades – were used for a range of purposes, including scraping and cutting the skins of animals to make clothes. Archaeologists can use microscopes to study the patterns of wear and tear on the edges of these tools and identify the telltale traces of contact with hide. Moreover, as we shall discover, the human need for clothes may actually have promoted some of these technological innovations during the Paleolithic era. And during the last ice age, we also have works of art that may depict clothes – such as the small figurines found at a site called Malta in Siberia that appear to show people covered by warm clothes.

The Science of Early Clothing

When we bring together these lines of evidence – the climate, the naked limits, and the archaeological evidence of technologies – we can get a surprisingly clear picture of how clothing was developed, despite the fact that the actual garments disintegrated long ago. And if it is indeed true that our ancestors only invented clothes to keep warm, then we should be able to see a pattern in the archaeology: the technologies should accompany the changes in climate quite closely. And regardless of the global swings in climate, whenever we find that humans were present in the coldest regions (like within the Arctic Circle), we should expect to see signs of decent clothing, such as eyed needles. In other words, we can predict a thermal pattern in the archaeological evidence.

Yet as we can ascertain from examples such as the Australian Aborigines, the presence of clothing does not always lead to the habitual or permanent use of clothes: in their case, they stayed routinely naked. The indigenous garments – kangaroo skins and fur cloaks – did not cover their bodies on a regular basis. And in Tasmania, as the local climate got colder toward the height of the last ice age, we can see more signs of technologies linked to making clothes (like hide-scrapers and bone needles). These tools reflect the likely use of sewn garments made from wallaby skins to battle lower temperatures and wind chill. But as we shall see later, those intriguing technological trends were reversed in Tasmania when the climate improved after the end of the ice age – and the Tasmanians were again naked when Europeans arrived.[2]

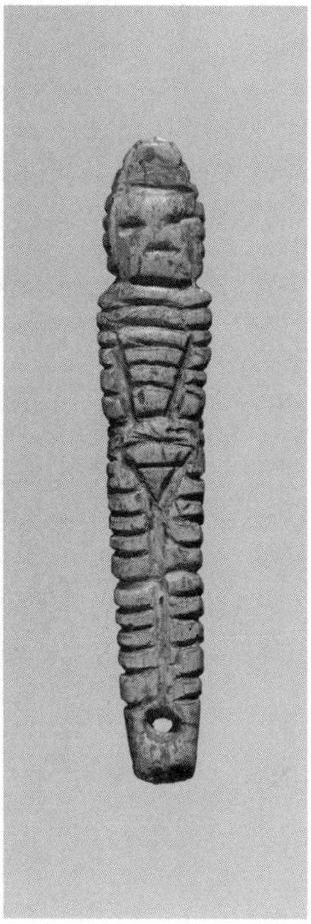

10. **Ice age figurine from the Malta site, Siberia**
Pendant figurine from the Malta site, 80 km (50 miles) east of the city of Irkutsk in southern Siberia. The site was occupied between 24,000 and 15,000 years ago, spanning the LGM. The figurine is made from mammoth tusk, measures 4.2 cm in length, and has carved lines that are thought by Russian archaeologists to depict clothing.
Source: Photo by Vladimir Terebenin, © The State Hermitage Museum, Inventory # 370–753. Reproduced by permission of The State Hermitage Museum, St. Petersburg.

Complex Clothing and Modern Life

There is a crucial step that people must take before clothes become a permanent fixture: the step from simple to complex clothing. The difference between simple and complex clothes relates first to factors affecting the warmth of clothes and, second, to the technology. Simple clothes are loose and only a single layer. Complex clothes are tailored to fit the body and limbs, and complex clothes can also be multilayered. We shall discuss details later, but the difference between these two forms of clothing is profound.

What matters most is whether clothes come to enclose the human body. With complex clothing, the body becomes routinely enclosed and concealed: enclosed from the external environment and concealed from ourselves – a step that has immense psychological significance. For instance, concealing our sexual organs in public on a constant basis has some obvious ramifications. For Aborigines, even when they wore heavy possum cloaks, they still remained open in this regard – and the same was true with the wallaby capes in ice-age Tasmania.

Complex clothing is where things get really interesting: it is not merely clothes but a special kind of clothing that becomes a permanent part of us. Shame and modesty only emerged with the advent of complex clothing, and

11. **Kangaroo skin worn in southwestern Australia** Photograph taken in the 1860s in the Perth area, southwest Australia, of an Aboriginal man wearing a kangaroo-skin cloak and a nose ornament. Kangaroo cloaks are well-documented by early white visitors in the area, beginning when Jacob Pieterszoon landed in Geographe Bay, near Cape Leeuwin, in 1658 (Heeres, 1899:81).

Source: Photo by Alfred Hawes Stone, A. H. Stone Collection of Photographs, The State Library of Western Australia, catalogue # 6923B/26. Donated by Dorothy Croft. Reproduced by permission of The State Library of Western Australia, Perth.

other nonthermal functions got attached to clothes, including the personal desire (and the social need) to adjust our appearance by decorating the visible surface of the self, as a basic kind of screen. For this purpose of display, once the human body was routinely concealed, then the surface of the skin was replaced by the surface of clothes. So, for all of these reasons, with complex clothing there was a transition from thermal to psychosocial necessity. With this transition – which happened only quite late and only in some parts of the world – clothing became imperative for reasons other than climate.

So, there is quite a lot of ground to cover in this clothing narrative – and quite a lot at stake. We should start the story with the physical causes and the changing environments before getting too entangled in all the repercussions. We shall begin with our biological nakedness because that marks the real beginning from an evolutionary perspective. We can then look at how exposure to cold became critical when the climate changed in the Pleistocene. The thermal properties of clothing become relevant then, especially with regard to wind chill, which leads into the thermal benefits of complex clothing. We can then look at the technology of manufacturing the right level of portable protection whilst remembering that we are dealing here with hunter-gatherers who relied on animal skins and furs, not textiles. And finally, we can look at how this scenario for the origin of clothes pans out in relation to the archaeological evidence.

THE ORIGIN OF NAKEDNESS

Various theories have been put forward over the years, but we still do not know why our species became naked. As with another distinctive physical trait – upright posture – scientists have been frustrated in their effort to find a convincing reason for why nakedness first evolved. Some theories have fallen

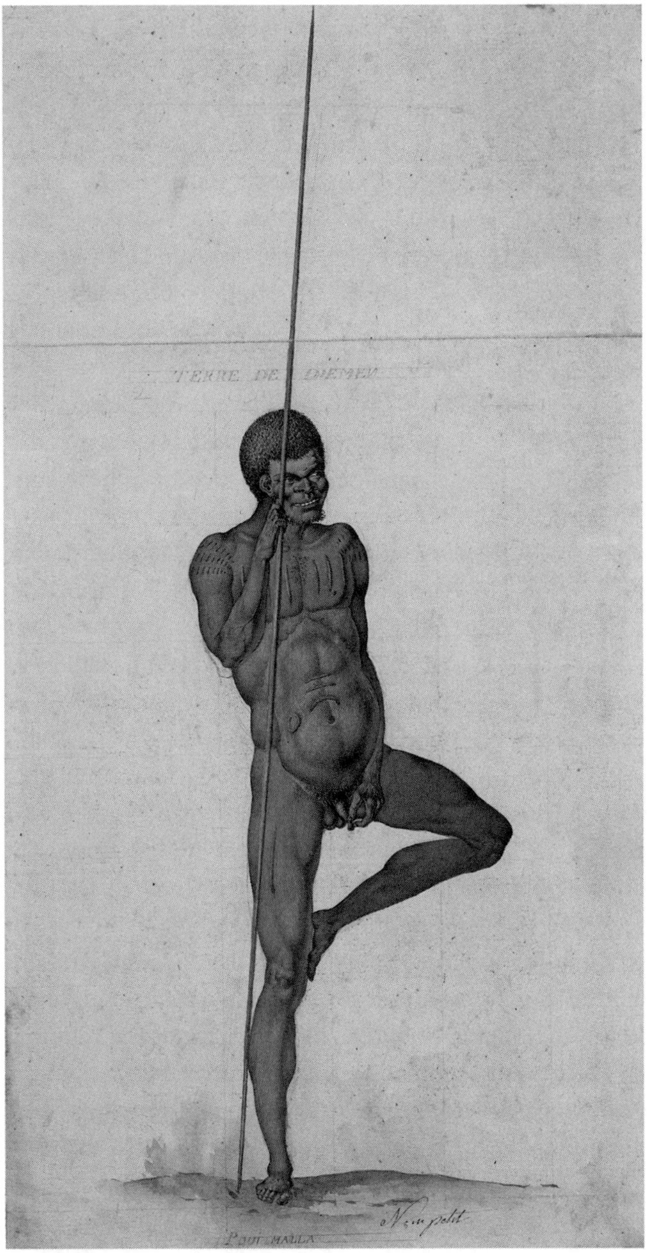

12. **Tasmanian man, 1802**
Tasmanian man, standing in what was described by French visitors in 1802 as a typical pose, on one leg with a spear, holding the tip of his penis between thumb and forefinger. He is adorned (or dressed) with elaborate scarification, or cicatrices.
Source: Nicolas-Martin Petit, gouache, 1802. Muséum d'Histoire Naturelle, Le Havre, Catalogue # 20.023.2. Reproduced by permission of the Muséum d'Histoire Naturelle, Le Havre.

out of favor, such as the aquatic theory (that we evolved in water, not on land) and the possible roles of parasites and clothing. These last two theories suggest we lost our fur to get rid of lice or because we already had clothes, and so having heaps of hair was too uncomfortable.[3]

13. **Aboriginal possum-fur cloaks**
In the cooler southeast of Australia, Aborigines sometimes wore large fur cloaks sewn from multiple possum skins. These garments, while sewn, were still simple clothes – draped, not fitted, and a single layer. Even in the southeast, however, Aborigines often went naked, as described in early journal accounts. This photo – somewhat staged – was taken at the Coranderrk mission (50 km east of Melbourne) established by the white government. The man standing is wearing the cloak with fur outside, while the seated man has the fur inside. On the mission, among other civilizing endeavors, the Aborigines were taught how to become farmers.
Source: Photographer Fred Kruger, 1870. *Natives and Bark Canoe.* Hulton Archive / Getty Images, and Pictures Collection [H39306], State Library of Victoria.

Naked Is Not Necessarily Sexy

Darwin was mystified by nakedness: he could see no obvious advantage in terms of natural selection. Instead, he suggested that nakedness may have resulted from sexual selection: naked skin evolved because we find it sexually attractive. To support his theory, he cited the fact that women are not as hairy as men.[4]

Darwin may have had a point when he said that having naked skin is no great advantage, but he may have been mistaken to see it as an example of sexual selection. For one thing, in most animal species, sexual selection is performed by females and tends to make the males more attractive – as with the feathers of peacocks. So, if having less body fur is sexually attractive for humans and this led to our loss of body hair, then men should be less hairy than women. To explain why women are less hairy than men, the sexual selecting would need to be shifted from females to males. One possibility is that there was a shift from the general promiscuity typical of higher primates to pair-bonding and monogamy among our ancestors, and this may have led to a shift in sexual selection from females to males – in which case, the men would select less hairy women. However, evidence for pair-bonding early in our evolution is contentious. Even among recent hunter-gatherers, stable pair-bonding is far from the norm, and monogamy may have only become more commonplace with the advent of agriculture. In any case, hormonal differences can account for the sex differences in body hair, and there are wide differences – individual and cultural – in preferences for body and facial hair. In the modern world, women often prefer at least some body hair, and men often prefer less hairy women. Whether such preferences were always the case is another matter.[5]

With sexual selection as the reason for nakedness, the main advantage is that if nakedness is due to its sexual appeal, then this could override the disadvantages that otherwise would ensure its removal by natural selection. There is plenty of evidence for sexual selection in other species; the peacock's tail is the classic example. Darwin realized that these elaborate, expensive, but useless traits seemed to contradict natural selection, prompting him to think about

14. **Tasmanian lady with wallaby-skin cape, 1802**
Tasmanian lady wearing a wallaby-skin cape and carrying an infant, 1802. The Baudin expedition visited the southeast of Tasmania during the summer (January to February) of 1802. Wallaby-skin capes were said by the French observers to be used by women, apparently not as garments for warmth, modesty, or decorative display but rather for the purpose of carrying items, including their infants.
Source: Nicolas-Martin Petit, *Femme du Cap Sud*. Reproduced by permission of the Muséum d'Histoire Naturelle, Le Havre. Catalogue # 20.022.3.

sexual selection as an additional factor in evolution. However, Darwin was theorizing about nakedness before much was known about human evolution and climate change in the past. Had Darwin known more about the

Pleistocene ice ages, he probably would have been even more anxious to have a theory to override the obvious thermal disadvantage of being naked. Unless, we are wrong to assume that nakedness offered no advantage in terms of natural selection. If nakedness can be shown to have had an advantage, especially before the Pleistocene began, there may be no need to invoke sexual selection (with all of its problems). As it happens, one recent theory argues that loss of body hair did confer an advantage – a thermal advantage, in fact, but only after our ancestors became bipedal. Before taking a look at that theory, another theory deserves an honorable mention.

Neoteny and Loss of Body Hair

One popular candidate for explaining our nakedness is called neoteny – the general trend over the long course of evolution for hominins to become more childlike in physical form. Quite a few distinctive human traits reflect a general slowing down of development, such as our prolonged lifespan. As a result of this slowing down, we become adults while still retaining relatively juvenile bodies. One of our juvenile features is a large head, another is less body hair. Proponents of this theory point out how we look more like baby chimpanzees than adult chimpanzees – our resemblance to baby chimpanzees is rather disconcerting. The rare bonobo (pygmy chimpanzee) is almost a neotenous version of the common chimpanzee. More striking, perhaps, is how adult chimpanzees who suffer from complete hair loss (alopecia) look even more like humans.

15. **Baby bonobo**
Neoteny is a slowing of body development, and in the case of humans, it would mean we live longer and retain more childlike features – such as having a relatively large head and less body hair. Hence, we look more like the juvenile forms of our nearest evolutionary relatives, chimpanzees, as opposed to looking like adult chimpanzees. The bonobo, or pygmy chimpanzee, is more humanlike in behavior than common chimpanzees, and baby bonobos look even more like us. Shown here is a bonobo infant in the Lola Ya Bonobo Sanctuary, Democratic Republic of Congo.
Source: Nature Picture Library / Alamy Stock Photo

Neoteny is well known as an evolutionary process in other species, and it happens in plants as well as animals. Neoteny involves a change in the timing of gene expression. We have mostly the same genes as chimpanzees and gorillas; however, in our case the activation of certain genes is delayed or switched off. Paradoxically, neoteny requires an opposite process: an acceleration of sexual development (relative to body form). Unless that occurred, we would all be in danger of facing retirement or dementia before reaching sexual maturity. So, in relation to the maturation of our bodies as primates, we humans are hypersexual, or sexually precocious. In terms of body development, neoteny means we become sexually mature without ever growing as old as gorillas.

At the genetic level, neoteny means that a tiny change in the genetic code can lead to a massive change in body form. And it involves a whole package of traits, so all the traits are connected. In terms of adaptation, if natural selection were to favor just one of the traits – a larger brain, for instance – then all of the other traits in the package (like nakedness) could be selected indirectly even if they were not adaptive, or even if they were a little maladaptive. The kind of genetic – and possibly epigenetic – changes associated with neoteny relate to controlling the timing of gene expression, which can affect many parts of the genome, rather than involving many actual changes in the genetic code. The code can remain basically the same, but the sequence of when particular genes are turned on and off is altered. With brain growth, for instance, it means that rapid juvenile expansion of the brain is prolonged – both in real time and in relation to body development. With nakedness, it means that we may still have all the genes that promote the growth of body hair, but these genes are not switched on, or they are delayed, and hence their expression is suppressed. Technically, this change in the timing is called heterochrony, whereas neoteny (sometimes called paedomorphism) refers to the end result – a more juvenile adult. The changes in timing can affect different aspects of bodily development at different rates; certain aspects, such as sexual development, may even be accelerated relative to the rest of the body. In terms of natural selection, this change in when the genes are activated, or expressed, is presumably favored because one or more consequences confer some adaptive benefit. In other words, nakedness might have been carried along passively as a part of the package. If nakedness is due to neoteny, then it does not require any adaptive function in its own right; it could even have

16. **Chimpanzee with alopecia**
Chimpanzees with complete loss of body hair (alopecia) look even more like humans than those with body hair. Hair loss exposes the typical white skin of chimpanzees, which likely results from evolving with a cover of fur. When our hominin ancestors lost their fur cover, the result was black skin – to protect us from harmful ultraviolet radiation. White skin later reemerged in some populations as they moved outside the tropics – and covered themselves with clothes.
Source: Nigel Dowsett/ Alamy Stock Photo

some disadvantages. All that evolution would require is that the whole package was favored, for whatever reason. Neoteny is an attractive theory of nakedness for this reason alone: it does not presume any adaptive benefit for nakedness. Unfortunately though, it turns out that neoteny is not so good at explaining many of our distinctive features.[6]

The Thermal Theory and Its Problems

The most popular theories about nakedness involve thermal factors – the adaptive benefit of keeping cool in the African heat. Yet, as so often happens in science (and as happened with neoteny), the situation is a little more complicated. We now realize that a naked skin surface is actually more exposed to heat stress – which is why most tropical mammals still keep a cover of fur: their fur functions as portable shade. So, we no longer accept the simple notion that our ancestors first shed their fur to keep cool. Current ideas focus instead on a possible connection with upright posture. If there was some connection between standing upright and going naked, then this might help to explain why nakedness became adaptive in the special case of early hominins.

Stand Up and Stay Cool

Upright posture may lower the heat load on the body by reducing how much skin surface is exposed to the overhead sun. In this theory, once most of our surface was more vertical and not baking in the overhead sun, a loss of fur on the body uncovered most of our surface to allow more cooling (while retaining some hair cover on the head, to act as shade). The process is cooling by convection: air moving over the skin carries the body heat away from the surface. A fur cover, on the other hand, will inhibit this kind of cooling.

The cooling effect increases further from the ground – so benefitting from the extra height gained with an upright posture. And it becomes more effective if we develop a greater capacity to sweat – to cool by evaporation. In this theory, developed by Peter Wheeler at the Liverpool John Moores University in England, once our ancestors left the shady forests and started to spend more time out on the open savannah – which might have happened due to climate change and a shrinking of forest habitats – the combination of upright posture and a naked skin (with sweating) was advantageous.[7]

The jury is still out on Wheeler's theory, and it has attracted its fair share of criticism. A lot comes down to mathematical modeling of thermal variables and heat stresses (which are rather complex) and the validity of assumptions. For example, what if our ancestors already had an upright posture before they moved out onto the savannah? Indeed, the latest fossil discoveries show that upright posture evolved very early in our ancestry – bipedalism defines the

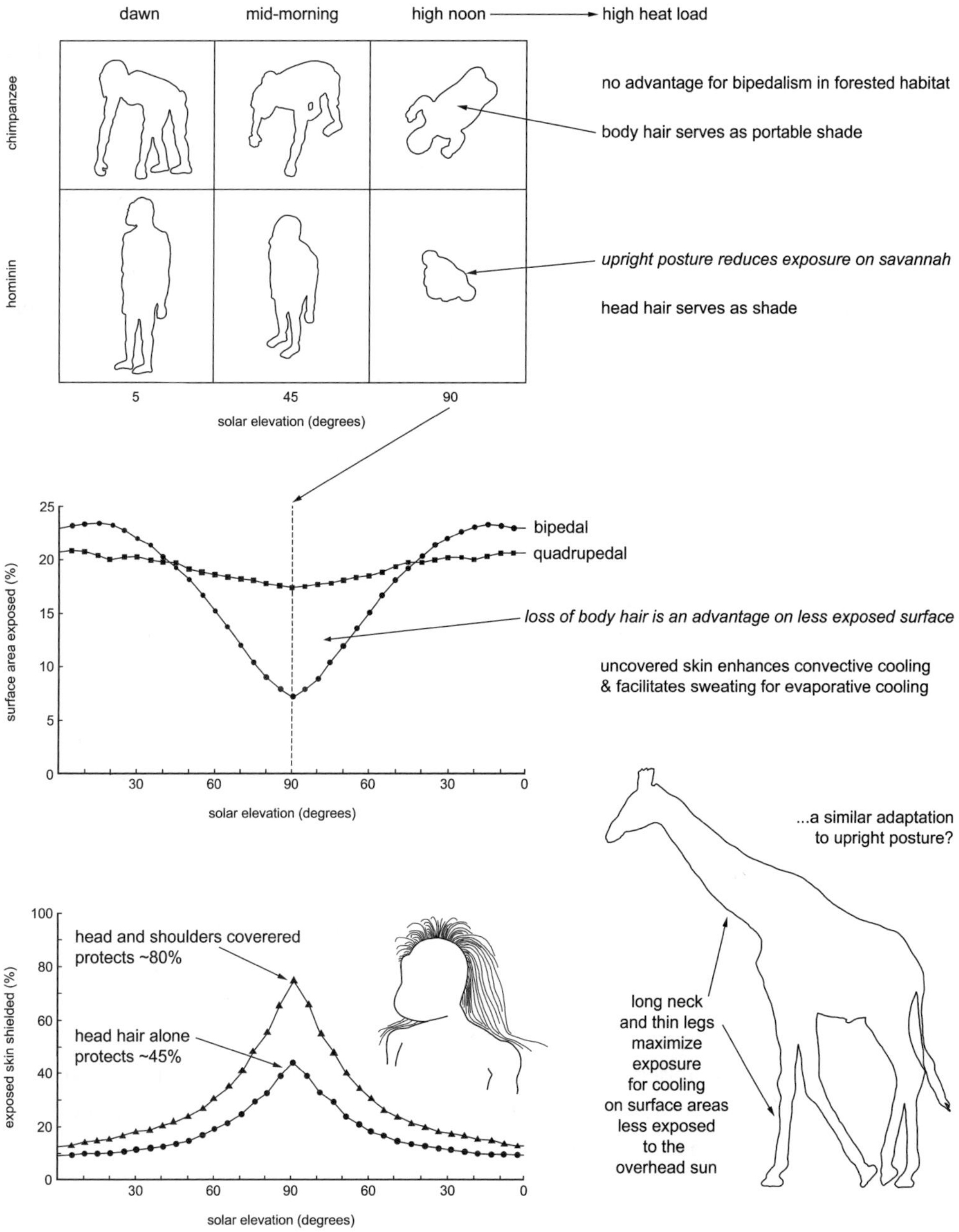

17. **Wheeler's theory of bipedalism and nakedness**
Wheeler's theory claims that upright posture and nakedness evolved as linked adaptations to heat stress. Recent work has refined his theory, suggesting that the loss of body hair evolved when the genus *Homo* spread into more open habitats between two and three million years ago. Another variation on this theme argues that giraffes evolved their long necks for similar thermal reasons, rather than to reach the leaves of high trees, as Lamarck – and many others – have thought.

Source: Redrawn from Wheeler, 1984:94–95, 1985:26, and Mitchell et al., 2017:36. © Elsevier. Reproduced under licenses, Elsevier.

point of departure between hominins and the last common ancestor with chimpanzees. Adopting an upright posture may have first happened in forested environments, not on the open savannah.[8]

If our bipedal ancestors evolved in the shade, then the thermal advantage of having an upright posture – less exposure to the overhead sun – might not apply. Yet, none of the other theories about bipedalism are widely accepted either. Among them we can list popular notions, such as the idea that standing upright helped hominins to carry food, collect fruit from trees, and see predators more easily from a distance – or that walking on two legs freed their hands to make tools. Each theory has its supporters, but none has gained general credence. So, the evolution of upright posture still remains a mystery in adaptive terms. Where does that leave nakedness?

It turns out there might still be a connection between upright posture and nakedness. Even if we cannot blame heat stress for bipedalism, the cooling benefit of nakedness could still apply after our upright ancestors strode out onto the savannah – in fact, it might only have been thermally adaptive after they became bipedal. On four limbs, out on the savannah it is best to retain a fur cover. Walking on two legs though can open up a new adaptive niche for nakedness (and sweating). So, we may have lost our fur to keep cool after all – but only because we were already standing upright.[9]

How Long Have We Been Naked?

No one is really satisfied that we have a good reason for the origin of human nakedness – there is certainly no consensus on the subject. Neither is anyone satisfied that we know when it happened, which is unfortunate since it bears on the need for clothing among our ancestors. If they still possessed a proper coat of fur during the Pleistocene, then they could have survived in colder conditions without much need for an artificial fur coat – which could be relevant to Neanderthals and the mystery of why they went extinct, as we shall see later. However, there are a few methods we can use to help find out when our ancestors became biologically naked.

Nakedness and Dark Skin

One approach is based on the idea that skin color was related to nakedness. Dark skin may have evolved after nakedness, to protect hominins from the harmful effects of ultraviolet radiation in the tropics. Other primates, such as chimpanzees, have a more convincing cover of body fur – and they have a light skin color. A genetic study indicates that darker skin appeared among our ancestors a million years ago (if not earlier), which suggests they had lost their fur cover by then.[10]

Only afterwards, when some of our ancestors migrated out of the tropics, did a lighter skin again become adaptive. In higher latitudes, the dangers posed by strong sunlight are reduced whereas a lighter skin will allow more ultraviolet radiation to penetrate, which helps to prevent the vitamin D deficiency that results from lack of sunlight. The evolution of lighter skin in higher latitudes also coincided with people covering their bodies more with clothes, further favoring white skin.

Another clue about when we lost a fur cover comes from the thermal connection with upright posture. In that scenario, nakedness helped a bipedal hominin to stay cool on the open savannah – which implies nakedness evolved around the time when our ancestors first moved into that habitat. On this ecological basis, the origin of nakedness could be placed between two and three million years ago.[11]

Getting Pubic Lice from Gorillas

Genetic studies of lice also bear on this question of nakedness – not body lice or head lice but a third kind of lice that infest humans and get less publicity: pubic lice. These lice belong to a different species altogether, and their nearest relatives are the species of lice that infest gorillas. In fact, our pubic lice are almost identical to gorilla lice. Genetic analyses estimate that we somehow acquired these critters from gorillas quite recently in evolutionary terms – more recently than the time when we last shared a common ancestor with gorillas. We shall leave aside the tricky question of how we acquired these lice – presumably it required fairly close proximity. Or, maybe some hapless hominin fell into one of their nests.

Pubic lice relate to nakedness because they could only move from gorillas to humans after our own lice had retreated to the head – that is, after we lost the fur on our body. With lice restricted to the scalp, the groin niche was left vacant and available for gorilla lice. The time when this happened should therefore provide us with a proxy for when we became naked. Luckily, the results of this research do not conflict with the estimates derived from other lines of evidence, though the findings could push back the origin of nakedness a little further – to between three and four million years ago.[12]

Naked before the Ice Age

All these ways of looking at when and why we became naked seem to point in one direction: our ancestors probably lost their fur cover a long time ago, before the beginning of the Pleistocene. We will now look more closely at what happened to the climate and how cold the weather was – and what this would mean for a naked hominin.

GLOBAL COOLING

Climate scientists are still searching for the causes of the ice ages. Discovering why the global climate changed back then is important because if climatologists can find out why the climate changed naturally in the past and identify the mechanisms, this could help us to predict how much the climate will change in the future because of human activities – anthropogenic climate change. We want to have more precise estimates about the amount of global warming that will happen by the end of this century – current estimates range widely from 1°C to 6°C. And we need to have a better idea about some of the other ecological consequences, such as rising sea levels. Climatologists say that due to geological movements in the earth's crust and varying thermal expansion of the ocean masses, the rise in sea level will not be the same all around the world. In the New York area, for instance, the mean sea level is predicted to rise between 0.7 and 0.9 meters (between two and three feet) over the course of this century.[13]

On the other hand, we also face the prospect of another ice age in the future – the Pleistocene cycles may not yet have ground to a halt. While we all worry about global warming in coming decades, the onset of another ice age would be catastrophic for civilization. A few centuries ago, there was a Little Ice Age just before the Industrial Revolution, when the world may have made a narrow escape from another full ice age. Some climatologists suspect that higher CO_2 levels from agriculture might have saved us then, which means our future carbon emissions could actually forestall – or prevent – the onset of another ice age.[14]

A Wobbly Theory

The reasons for the cycles of ice ages are rather hard to pin down, but the main factor was first identified in the 1920s by Milutin Milankovitch, a Serbian geophysicist. He theorized that regular changes in the earth's orbit and tilt are the main cause of the cyclic patterns of climate change, and this so-called orbital theory has been largely verified.[15]

For our purposes, it is important to know when these cycles started and to get some idea of the conditions that prevailed for hominins. The evidence is now quite detailed, and the weather conditions can be reconstructed fairly well. Temperatures, precipitation, and seasonal variations can be estimated with some accuracy – more so for the recent cycles – although it is much harder to estimate wind chill levels.

Chilling Out in the Pleistocene

The Pleistocene began around 2.6 million years ago – which is after our ancestors likely became naked. There were many ice ages during this geological epoch. The exact number depends on whether we define an ice age as a glacial advance, a change in sea level, or a fluctuation in the earth's climate – the various aspects of these environmental changes did not always coincide. There have been dozens of major swings in global temperature since the start of the Pleistocene, with around ten major glacial advances over the past million years, and most of these cold epochs lasted for around 100,000 years. They were separated by periods of warmer weather (interglacials), each averaging around 10,000 years. Unless this natural cycle of recurring ice ages has come to an end, and we really cannot be sure, then we are now living at the tail end of an interglacial.

Ice Age or Cold Age?

Two things about the ice ages should be stressed here. The first is that although we cannot be sure when our ancestors became naked, it seems likely they were already naked (or nearly so) when the Pleistocene began. The second point is that while the ice ages were first identified and defined on the basis of geology, ice activity was not the most important feature. In the nineteenth century, the Swiss geologist Louis Agassiz proposed the idea of an ice age based on evidence that glaciers were once more widespread in Europe. Yet, it is mere historical accident that we were first alerted to these past upheavals in climate by geological evidence in the form of heightened ice activity in high latitudes.

The ice ages involved a host of environmental changes on a global scale: the expansion of ice sheets and glaciers was only one of the changes (and quite localized). Perhaps the main impact of ice on humans was in the Americas, where the northern ice sheets may have delayed the southward spread of humans. If we were to pick the most definitive feature of the ice ages, it would have to be either the cooling or the drying of the atmosphere, or perhaps the changing sea levels. Most environmental scientists would agree that on a global scale the single most consistent variable was lower temperatures – which means the ice ages should really have been called cold ages. Renaming ice ages as cold ages would also reflect what was probably the most significant aspect of the Pleistocene for a primate that was biologically naked (or at least on its way to becoming naked). According to the fossil evidence, the earliest members of our own species – who presumably were just as naked as us – appeared around 300,000 years ago. At that time, the global climate was slipping into another full-blown ice age.

Measuring the Cold with Isotopes

Our knowledge of the ice age cycles is based largely on temperature indices – or proxies – which reflect the climatic fluctuations. The main proxy is the oxygen isotope ratio. Molecules of water consist of oxygen and hydrogen atoms, and some water molecules are heavier because they contain a heavier kind of oxygen, or isotope. During an ice age, cooler temperatures will mean that water molecules with the heavier isotope cannot evaporate so easily from the oceans, so the global atmosphere will contain more of the lighter molecules.

Climate scientists have measured the changing ratio of oxygen isotopes in the polar ice caps. By drilling deep into the ice sheets, they can extract cores of ice that preserve a record of past precipitation. From these, they can measure the changing ratio of the isotopes over time, and this gives them a good idea of ancient air temperatures. The past fluctuations are classified into warm and cold stages known as Marine Isotope Stages (MIS).[16]

MIS stages are numbered backwards beginning with our present interglacial, MIS1. In this scheme, the warm periods are assigned odd numbers, and cold periods have even numbers. The very cold LGM (the Last Glacial Maximum around 22,000 years ago) is MIS2, and the last warm interglacial like our own (which lasted from 130,000 to 120,000 years ago) is numbered as MIS5e. The onset of the Pleistocene corresponds to the peak of a warm period, MIS103.[17]

Why It Got Colder in the Northern Hemisphere

During the ice ages, there was a big difference between the two hemispheres: temperatures dropped much more in the northern hemisphere. The reason for the hemispheric difference relates mainly to how much of the earth's surface is covered by the oceans, which have a moderating effect. About 70 percent of the earth's surface is covered by water, but the distribution of surface water is not equal. In the northern hemisphere, water makes up around 60 percent of the surface area whereas in the southern hemisphere the figure is around 80 percent. So, except in the vicinity of Antarctica, temperatures on land in the southern hemisphere tend to be warmer. On average, the seasonal temperature difference on land is larger in the northern hemisphere too, and winter temperatures on land are lower in the northern hemisphere.[18]

We can see this effect by comparing temperatures during the LGM at the same latitude in both hemispheres. For instance, we can compare Sydney, Australia (latitude 34°S), with Osaka, Japan (latitude 34°N). In Sydney, the average temperature dropped by around 4°C during the LGM, but in Osaka, the drop was much greater, around 10°C. The big hemispheric difference means that with the prehistoric development of clothing, we can expect to see more happening in the northern hemisphere – and indeed, as we shall see later when we look at the archaeology, we do find more evidence for clothes in the northern hemisphere.

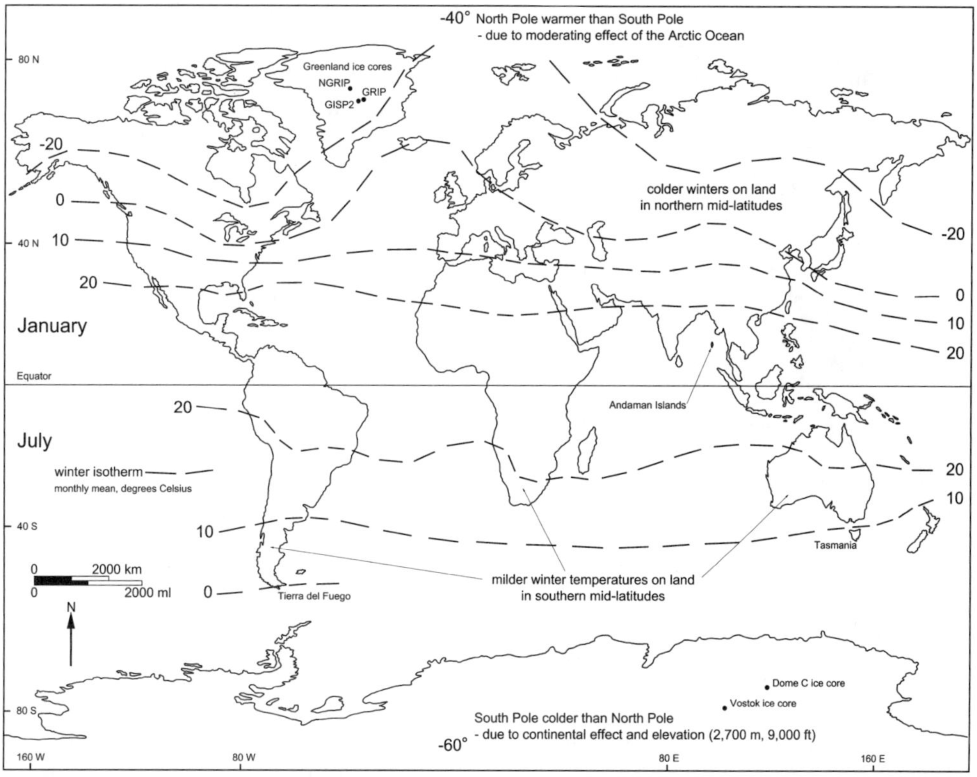

18. **Map of world winter temperatures**
Winter temperatures on land are generally lower in the northern hemisphere than in the southern hemisphere (except in Antarctica), especially in the middle latitudes. During the Pleistocene ice ages, the hemispheric difference was more marked. For this reason, prehistoric developments in clothing were more pronounced in the northern hemisphere. Shown here are present monthly average winter temperatures (isotherms, in degrees Celsius) in the northern and southern hemispheres, for January and July, respectively.

A Bigger Chill in Higher Latitudes

Another difference in the amount of cooling during the ice ages occurred with latitude. Further from the equator, the temperature drop was much greater. Even at the height of an ice age, the tropics stayed fairly warm. For instance, during the LGM when the average global temperature dropped by around 4°C, the temperature drop in the Caribbean was only around 2°C. In northern Florida, the drop was 4°C, but in the vicinity of New York City temperatures dropped by much more, by around 10°C. Further away from the ocean in the Chicago area (42°N), the average temperature fell by 20°C. So, there was a greater cooling with increasing latitude and also a bigger drop further from the oceans – as well as a big difference between the two hemispheres.

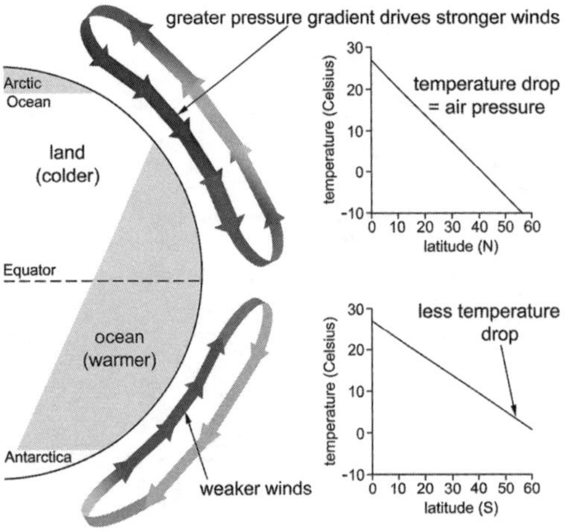

19. **Hemispheric difference in wind strength**
Winds tend to be stronger in the middle latitudes of the northern hemisphere compared to the southern hemisphere. In the southern hemisphere, the greater ocean mass has a moderating effect on temperatures, which reduces the temperature difference – and hence the air pressure gradient – between the equator and higher latitudes. Antarctica is an exception: temperatures are lower than at the North Pole due to the continental effect and also elevation.

Why It Got Windy as Well

The greater cooling at high latitudes during an ice age affects wind speeds and, hence, wind chill. A key driver of global wind is the temperature difference between the equator and the poles. Since warm air has high pressure and cold air has lower pressure, the temperature difference between the equator and the poles translates into a pressure difference: air pressure is higher in the tropics. Air pressure should not be confused with air density: cold air has lower pressure but higher density. And, vice versa, warm air is less dense but has higher pressure. So, warm air in the tropics tends to expand and rise whereas cold air at the poles tends to sink. During an ice age, the greater fall in temperature in higher latitudes creates a greater difference in air pressure between the poles and the equator. Air pressure at the poles gets even lower, which draws in more air, more quickly, from the tropics. Since the pressure difference is greater, winds tend to be stronger in the middle latitudes during an ice age, and the wind chill factor can increase markedly – due to the combined effect of lower temperatures and stronger winds. And because the higher latitudes of the northern hemisphere witnessed a greater drop in temperatures on land compared to the land masses in the southern hemisphere, average wind strength (and hence wind chill) in middle latitudes was often greater in the northern hemisphere.

Measuring Past Wind Chill Levels

Although we have good climate proxies for temperature (like the oxygen isotope ratio), we lack reliable proxies for past wind speeds. The deficit in wind data is disappointing because wind chill is so important for cold stress and for estimating how much clothing people needed. However, there are two methods that can give us some idea about average wind velocities in the past. One is the analysis of dust particles, and the other is a marine phenomenon called oceanic upwelling – and both methods indicate that average wind speeds were higher during the ice ages.

Ice ages were associated with much more atmospheric dust. Geological evidence includes the vast wind-blown loess deposits found in the soil of places such as northwest China – which give a yellow tinge to the Yellow River. However, the difficulty with using dust to measure wind strength is that a major cause of more atmospheric dust is dryness, and we know that aridity was a feature of ice age climates. Fortunately, we can separate the effects of aridity and wind speed by looking at the weight of the dust particles. Dryness on its own cannot cause heavier dust particles to be blown away, but with stronger winds, heavier (generally larger) dust particles can be lifted up and transported over greater distances. Although the task is tedious, by carefully analyzing not just the quantity but the size of dust particles, scientists can gain a fair idea about past wind strengths. These analyses of dust size show not only that the colder phases have more wind-borne (aeolian) dust but they generally have larger dust particles, pointing to stronger winds.[19]

The other wind proxy is oceanic upwelling, which refers to the wind-driven movement of surface sea currents that can cause upwelling of deeper water, especially along the coasts of continents. The deeper water is usually rich in nutrients, and so these areas of upwelling often have more plankton and other marine life; some of the world's richest fishing locations are found in these regions of oceanic upwelling. We can measure the organic remains preserved in sediments below the sea floor, and this will give us a measure of past wind strengths. The results indicate that upwelling increased in many regions during the Pleistocene. Again, the data are consistent with higher wind velocities during the ice ages, and those stronger winds were driven mainly by the steeper temperature (pressure) gradient between the poles and the equator.[20]

So, in terms of the environmental conditions for hominins, lower temperatures are just the tip of the iceberg. Wind chill is the most critical factor, and it looks like the colder air temperatures were often made even worse by stronger winds. And with regard to clothing, there are a couple of other things that we need to consider about the climate.

Rapid Climate Swings

One of the most striking aspects of climate change in the ice ages is that it was sometimes a very sudden event. When we think about how hominins coped with the situation – for instance by making better clothes – we should remember that coming up with new adaptations is not easy overnight. Yet, climate scientists have discovered that in geological terms, some of the enormous swings happened almost overnight.

When we look at charts showing the oxygen isotope ratio, the most distinct trend in the last ice age is how the swings become much more frequent and sharper in MIS3, as we approach the LGM. Some of the big swings are almost

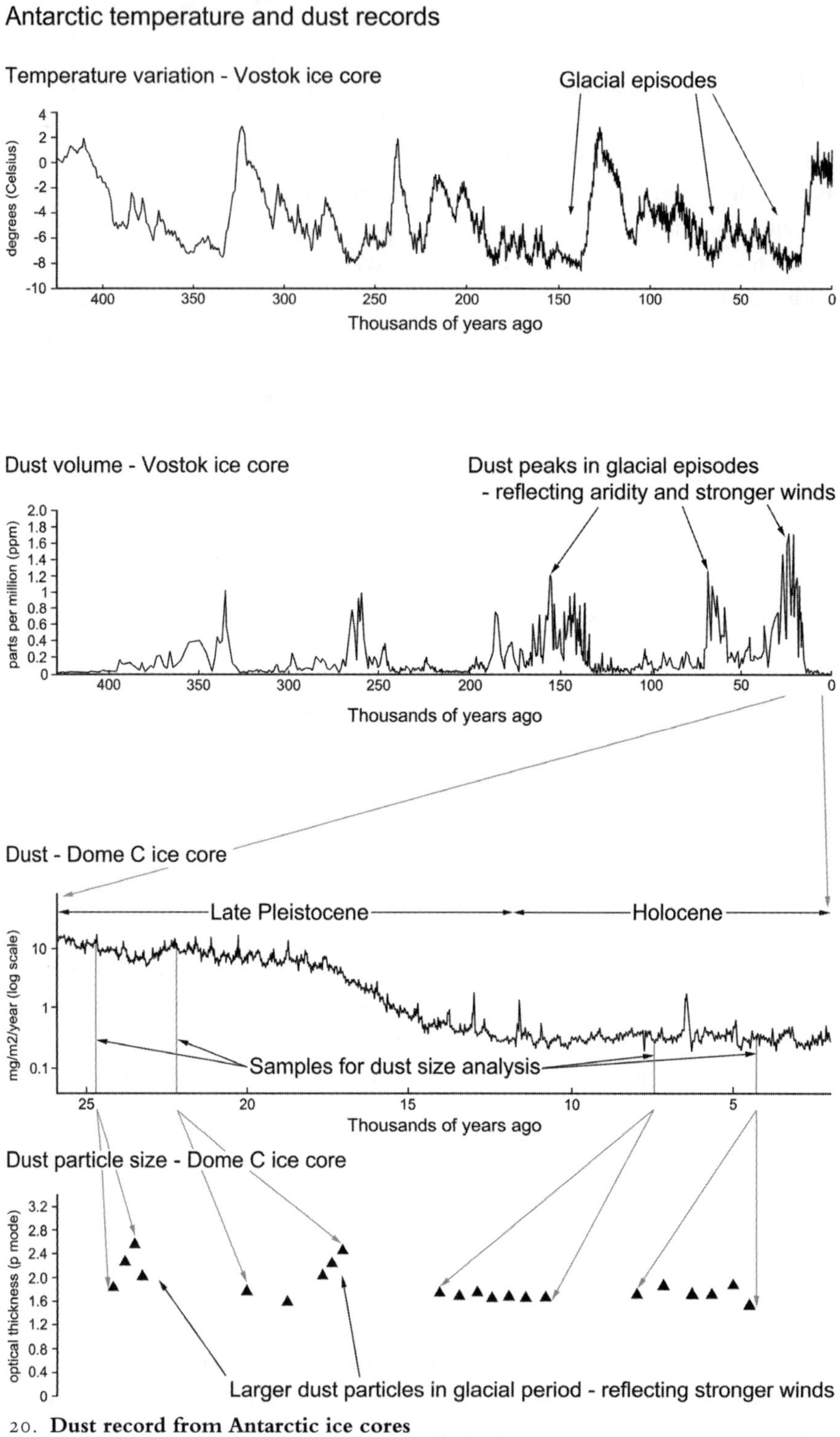

20. **Dust record from Antarctic ice cores**

The upper two graphs show temperature and dust records from the Vostok ice core in Antarctica spanning the past four glacial cycles, from 400,000 years ago. The next graph shows a more detailed record of dust volume over the past 25,000 years, from the Dome C ice core (also in eastern Antarctica), covering the end of the last ice age and the Holocene. To distinguish between the effects of aridity and wind strength, climatologists can measure the size of the dust particles, as shown in the bottom graph. The glacial peaks not only contain more dust (reflecting aridity) but they also contain larger (heavier) dust particles, pointing to stronger winds.

Source: Vostok data from Petit et al., 1999:430; Dome C data from Potenza et al., 2016:5.

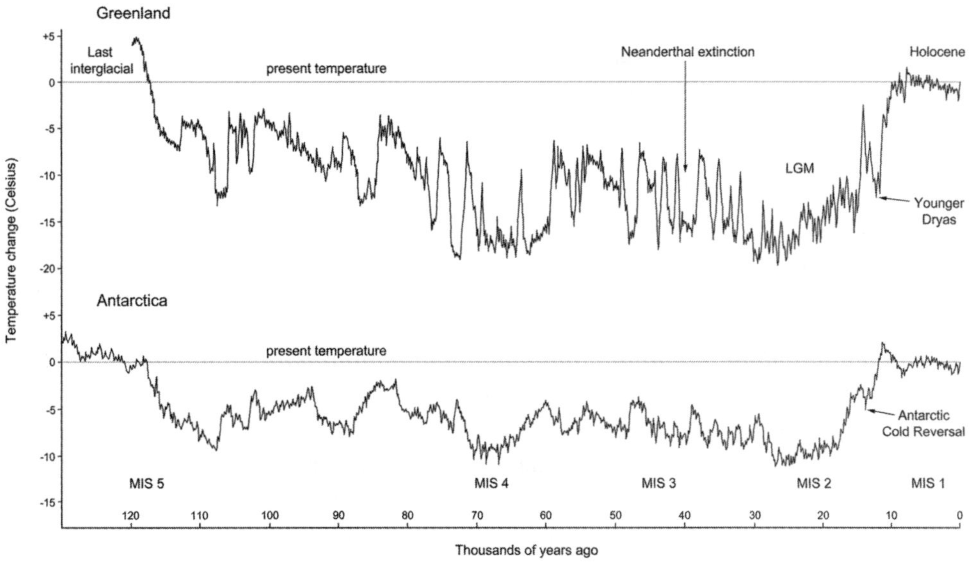

21. **Climate change over the last 120,000 years**
Global temperature trends over the last 120,000 years, spanning the most recent glacial cycle, based on ice core data from Greenland and Antarctica. The magnitude of cooling is greater in the northern hemisphere; note also the series of rapid climate swings during the latter part of MIS3, when Neanderthals went extinct.
Source: Greenland data from the NGRIP ice core (Steffensen et al., 2008); Antarctic data from the Vostok ice core (Petit et al., 1999).

vertical. In terms of magnitude, one of the warming episodes around 38,000 years ago caused average temperatures in Greenland to jump suddenly by 12°C. Quite a few of these swings are too rapid to be measured accurately at present: their rate of change exceeds the temporal resolution of our records (usually one or two millennia at best). Some of the big oscillations in the middle northern latitudes may have happened on timescales as brief as a century, or even less.

At the end of the last ice age in Europe, there were two rapid warm swings separated by one final cold swing – the last flicker of the ice age. This last cold swing is called the Younger Dryas, and its counterpart in the southern hemisphere is called the Antarctic Cold Reversal (ACR), which was much less severe. In the northern hemisphere, these swings were all fairly large (around 10°C) but what is really surprising is their suddenness. The last warm swing around 11,700 years ago – which marks the start of our present Holocene interglacial – happened over a span of just fifty years while the earlier warm swing around 15,000 years ago may have happened over an incredibly short time span: just three years. In comparison, the intervening cold swing (the Younger Dryas) was almost leisurely – it took 200 years for the climate to swing back again to glacial conditions. Those earlier climate swings in MIS3 could have been just as rapid – we cannot be sure until we get more accurate data.[21]

In any case, these last flickers of the Pleistocene prove that the natural ecosystem is quite capable of astonishingly brief and massive climate swings. Scientists suspect, too, that the sheer rapidity and severity of the swings may have caused stronger winds – it was almost as though the earth's atmosphere could hardly keep up with the rapid pace of climate change.[22]

Averages and Extremes

The other point to keep in mind is that our ancestors needed to cope not just with average temperatures (or average wind chill levels) but with actual conditions that varied on a seasonal and daily basis. What determines whether a species can survive is its ability to endure the extremes, not the averages. Our environmental proxies are rather good with generating average figures but not so good when it comes to telling us about the likely range of variation around those averages. In the world today, even mild cold spells – periods of a few days in winter when temperatures are a little lower than average – are associated with significantly higher mortality rates.[23]

For example, it is like trying to take into account the risk of a major flood that happens on average only once a century. Our ability to cope not just with the daily and seasonal variations but with the chance of unusually severe conditions is what will ultimately determine whether our adaptations prove successful or not. In wondering whether a tribe of *Homo sapiens* could survive in central Europe during a certain phase of MIS3, or in northern China during MIS2, what we really need to know is how cold was the coldest night in winter – not the average temperature for the millennium. Alas in this regard, the available data leave us largely in the dark.

Sunny but Freezing

There really are no exact present-day analogs for the ice-age environments. In terms of average temperatures, for example, we might compare northern China in the LGM to a modern-day tundra in northern Siberia. However, some aspects of the prehistoric environment are not replicated. For instance, the difference in latitude means that the intensity of sunlight was different. Compared to present-day tundras in high latitudes, stronger sunlight meant that ice-age environments in middle latitudes were better stocked with plants and animals for hominins, despite the very cold temperatures. So, maybe finding food was less of an issue than in modern-day tundras. Even in the Arctic zone of Siberia during the last ice age, large mammals (such as the woolly mammoth and the woolly rhinoceros) were abundant.[24]

To further complicate matters, the actual strength of sunlight reaching the earth's surface during ice ages also differed from today because of cyclic changes in the earth's orbit and axial tilt. Nonetheless, we can extrapolate from modern meteorological records to get a rough idea of the likely extremes in temperature and wind chill that are masked by the average figures.[25]

Keeping these extremes in mind is more relevant to clothing than it is to food. Although people might not have liked it much, they could survive for weeks without having a full dinner every night. And like all good hunter-gatherers, they could move around, and they had a variety of fallback options. But to cope with cold weather, the options open to hunter-gatherers were more limited – and the dangers of failing to adapt were dramatic. If they were caught off guard by a sudden cold spell without enough clothes, their survival time could be measured in hours.

COLD FACTS AND NAKED TRUTHS

Our species is better adapted to coping with heat than with cold. Primates in general are adapted to life in tropical climates, but we humans have really gone out on a limb. Our responses to heat are rapid and quite effective – in that regard sweating is our trump card. But our responses to cooling are sluggish and relatively ineffective.

The most obvious sign of this human weakness is nakedness. The thermal function of fur can be seen when we look at what happens to other species when they are deprived of their fur. Rabbits, for instance, can cope down to as low as −45°C, but if they are shorn, they begin to struggle at a mere 0°C. Feathers serve a similar function in birds. At −40°C, a dove can live for days, but if we pluck its feathers, it will start to freeze in a matter of minutes. In fact, warmth was the likely reason why the reptilian ancestors of birds evolved feathers in the first place, not because they were trying to fly.[26]

The Limits of Cold Tolerance

We are indeed a tropical species: without any clothes, the human body begins to react to cold once the air temperature falls below 27°C. At 20°C, our metabolic rate begins to climb to generate more heat, and the circulation of blood to our skin starts to shut down to conserve heat. At 13°C, we start to shiver – a sign of failure. For comparison, an arctic fox starts to shiver at −40°C. These figures come from laboratory studies and apply to still air conditions. In the real world, there is usually some air movement, even if only a light breeze.

Soon after the Second World War, American scientists working in Antarctica devised the wind chill index. The index has since been revised a few times, but the basic principle remains the same: with any wind, an unclad body will lose heat quickly due to convection. The scientists actually used a bottle of water hung outside their tent: they simply measured how long it took the water to freeze in different wind conditions. More worrying, they found the chilling effect of wind is almost exponential, especially below 0°C (32°F). For instance, with a moderate wind velocity of 10 m/s (22 mph), the wind chill index shows that even mild sub-zero temperatures can be dangerous for people without clothes.[27]

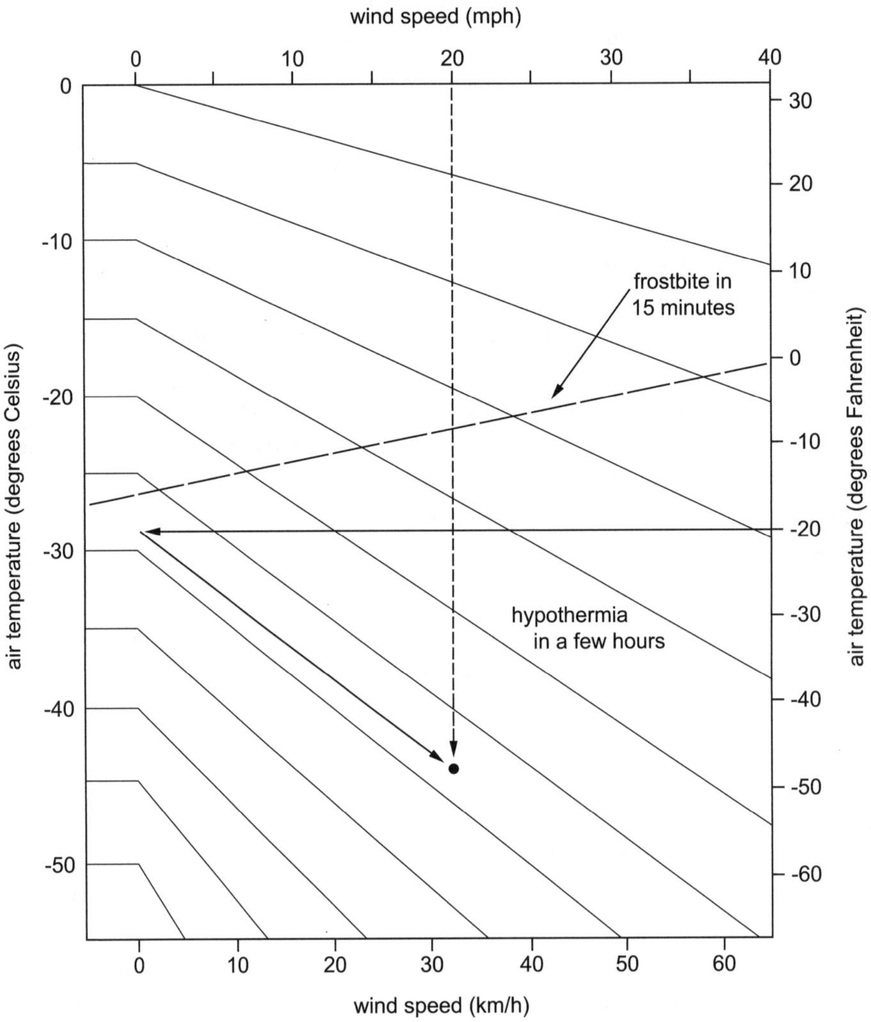

22. **Wind chill chart**

Wind chill refers to the exaggerated cooling effect due to wind at low ambient air temperatures, increasing the risk of frostbite and hypothermia. For example, frostbite can begin in fifteen minutes at a still-air temperature of −20°C, but with a 30 km/hr wind, frostbite can begin in less than fifteen minutes at an air temperature of −10°C. The chart shown here is based on the revised wind chill index adopted in 2001 in the United States and Canada; the example shows an air temperature of −20°F and wind velocity of 20 mph, which results in a wind chill level of nearly −50°F.

Moisture is the other killer. Any water sitting on our body surface will add to heat losses through evaporative cooling. For this reason, sweating becomes an issue. We might think that sweating should be the least of our worries in a cold environment, but that is far from the case. Physical activity generates extra body heat, but it also generates more sweat. Even when we stand still, the sweating mechanism is never completely switched off. Sweating continues at rest and in cold conditions too, though we are not usually aware of it – this is called insensible sweating. And the anxiety caused by cold stress can add even more sweating – a cold sweat. Clothing can make things worse: physical exercise within the warm microclimate of clothes creates more sweat, even when the outside air temperature is low. And as we shall see later when we look at how clothing works, moisture is a big issue with clothing. Once clothes get wet – whether from rain, melting snow, or sweat due to physical activity – the thermal function of clothes as insulation is effectively finished.[28]

Hypothermia

So, what happens when we get too cold? We develop hypothermia, and hypothermia is very scary. Our body core temperature must remain around 37°C, and we can tolerate only a few degrees of variation from that point. Cold-blooded species, reptiles mainly, can allow their core temperature to fall quite a lot (they rely instead on heat from the environment). Warm-blooded species, such as us, use their metabolism to generate body heat and to maintain a constant core temperature.

When our core temperature falls due to a failure of thermoregulation, the human body goes through stages of hypothermia that will lead rapidly and inevitably to death if not reversed. We have learned about these stages of hypothermia from experimental studies on other mammals and from hospital emergency rooms when people are brought in with accidental hypothermia. Shamefully, we also learned about the dangers of cold exposure from the infamous Nazi experiments on humans in the Second World War – and also from medical studies of frostbite in Chinese captives (including children) carried out by a Japanese military unit stationed in Manchuria.[29]

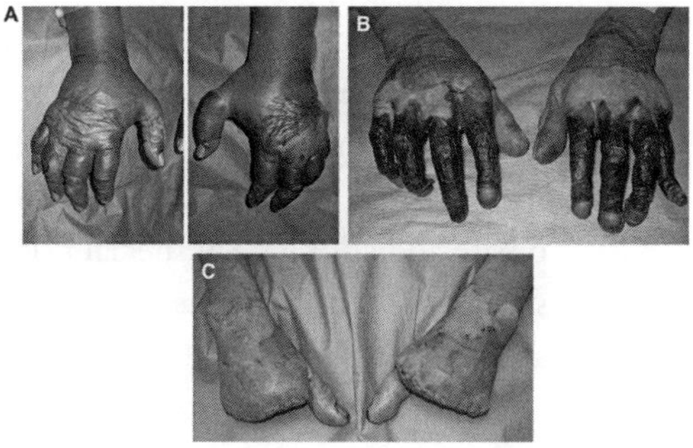

23. **Severe frostbite**
Deep (fourth-degree) frostbite in a man who arrived at the hospital twenty-four hours post-exposure. Despite treatment, all four fingers were lost on both hands – but he retained both thumbs.
Source: Mohr et al., 2009:487, © Elsevier. Reproduced under license, Elsevier.

When our core temperature drops to 35°C (95°F), movements become clumsy and we begin to have violent bouts of

TABLE 3. *Stages of hypothermia*

Stages of hypothermia, with symptoms and clinical signs. Paradoxical undressing occurs when people suffering from severe hypothermia become confused and remove their clothes; the reason may be due to a sudden dilatation of peripheral circulation causing a sensation of excessive heat on the skin surface. The lowest survived core temperature resulting from accidental hypothermia is 14°C (57°F), and the lowest core temperature from artificially induced hypothermia (e.g., during cardiac surgery) is 9°C (48°F). The longest recorded survival time with immersion hypothermia (in cold water) is sixty-six minutes. *Source:* Brown et al., 2012:1930–1936; Parsons, 2014:357.

Stage	Core temperature	Symptoms	Signs
1	35°C–32°C	shivering	increased metabolic rate
		clumsy movements	muscle stiffness
2	32°C–28°C	drowsiness	blood pressure falls
		shivering ceases	pupils dilated
3	28°C–24°C	paradoxical undressing	respiratory rate decreases
		loss of consciousness	pupils non-reactive
4	<24°C	unresponsive	cardiac arrhythmia (ventricular fibrillation)
		death	cardiac arrest

shivering – this stage is called mild hypothermia. Moderate hypothermia begins at 33°C (91°F) when our vision gets blurred, and we soon slip into unconsciousness. Shivering stops at a core temperature of 31°C (88°F). Below 30°C (86°F) is severe hypothermia, when the heart slows down and blood pressure drops, and death can occur at any time. Cardiac arrest is inevitable when the core temperature reaches 15°C (around 60°F).[30]

Without adequate clothing, exposure times leading to death from hypothermia are measured in hours. Depending on environmental conditions (and on other factors, such as a person's age and general health), the survival times for modern humans range from 1.5 to 12 hours. Accidental hypothermia generally happens outdoors when people are caught by a sudden change in weather, or if they get lost overnight while hiking in the wilderness. However, death from hypothermia can happen in cities and indoors at room temperatures between 20°C and 15°C (68°F and 59°F) – even in temperate climates such as that of Sydney. Aside from the elderly, people with alcoholism or opiate addictions are at special risk. The lower the ambient air temperature, the shorter the survival time. At −10°C (14°F, either in still air without wind or as an equivalent wind chill temperature), the time to death from hypothermia for healthy adults varies from three to six hours.[31]

In water, death happens more quickly because heat is lost more rapidly in liquids – water is twenty-four times more conductive than air. And with immersion hypothermia, clothing is useless. With a water temperature of 15°C (around 60°F), maximum survival time is up to five hours; however, at 5°C (around 40°F), the survival time is only two hours, and at near-freezing water temperatures (0°C, 32°F), typical survival time is around thirty minutes.

Not Drowning on the Titanic

24. ***Titanic*, 1912**
In 1912, the *Titanic*, the largest ocean liner in the world, struck an iceberg and sank in the North Atlantic on its maiden voyage to New York. There were too few lifeboats, but many passengers survived the sinking and stayed afloat with the help of life vests only to succumb rapidly to hypothermia in the water. This scene is from the 1958 film, *A Night to Remember*.
Source: Moviestore Collection Ltd / Alamy Stock Photo.

When the ocean liner *Titanic* sank in 1912 after colliding with an iceberg in the North Atlantic, many of the victims (nearly 1,500) probably survived the sinking only to succumb to hypothermia in the water – which was actually a little below freezing point. Most of those who failed to get into lifeboats were wearing life jackets so they could stay afloat indefinitely, and the "unsinkable" ship sank rather gently, taking more than two hours to go down. All the passengers and crew were well-dressed – some first-class passengers had fur cloaks and gowns. Most people from first class managed to get into lifeboats, but more than a hundred (mainly men) did stay aboard until the end. Regardless of class or dress, all their clothes were soon saturated. Once in the water they might as well have been naked – within an hour, their cries for help had faded away. Less than two hours after the world's largest liner went down, the rescue ship *Carpathia* arrived on the scene, but by then all the bodies floating in the water were ice cold.[32]

Frostbite and the Shrinking Penis

Hypothermia is the greatest danger, but exposure can lead to less lethal injuries – frostbite is the most familiar. Frostbite is not so life-threatening, but gangrene may lead to infection and blood-poisoning (septicemia), which can be fatal. Frostbite affects mainly the fingers, toes, nose, and ears – and sometimes the penis.

Although the well-known shrinkage of the penis with cold exposure serves as its main defense, penile frostbite has become more of a worry with the popularity of outdoor jogging. It can affect healthy men even in major cities, and it can happen quickly. In one case described in *The New England Journal of Medicine*, a New York physician was afflicted with penile frostbite while taking his usual evening jog after work early in December. The air temperature at the time was −8°C (18°F) with a severe wind chill factor. He was wearing what he thought was enough protection, given that he was generating extra body heat through physical exertion: polyester trousers and underpants together with a T-shirt, long-sleeved shirt, nylon jacket, and gloves. Luckily, as a doctor, he recognized the early symptoms and knew the right treatment: when he got back to his apartment, he was able to salvage the organ with gradual rewarming over fifteen minutes.[33]

Acclimatization and Its Limits

We can improve our tolerance of cold – but only up to a certain point. There are short-term adjustments called habituation and longer-term adaptations called acclimatization. For example, scientists working in Antarctica typically develop some degree of acclimatization over a period of months: they develop more resilience to cold pain and can manage with less clothing. However, these improvements are marginal, and research suggests there is little difference in the critical lower limits. Although there is no single limit, for modern humans who routinely wear clothes, the short-term safe limit without clothes is around −1°C (30°F). Beyond that point – or if our exposure is prolonged for more than an hour or so – we face the risks of frostbite and hypothermia.[34]

The main difference occurs among hunter-gatherers who are routinely naked from birth. Whereas the thermal "comfort zone" for us is 21°C to 24°C (70–75°F, with clothes), people who grow up from birth without clothes are better able to cope with cold exposure. Babies are more vulnerable than adults: they can start to develop hypothermia if left naked on their own at a temperature as high as 33°C (91°F). But nevertheless, a certain amount of safe cold exposure during infancy can lead to lifelong acclimatization. As occurs in other animals, there is probably a "critical period" during early infancy when our biological thermostat is set by environmental stimuli. In this way, early exposure to cold helped in developing the hardiness of groups such as the Fuegians in southern South America – whose capacity to tolerate cold weather so astonished Darwin.

Getting into Shape for the Cold

Due to natural selection, there are long-term genetic changes affecting body shape that develop among people in different environments. These differences in body shape and limb proportions are seen in many animal species. A stockier build will lower the surface area and result in reduced heat losses. We can visualize this effect if we compare two ideal bodies of the same volume, but with different shapes. A perfect sphere has the minimum surface area, whereas a long thin cylinder – same volume – has a larger surface area.

For this reason, indigenous peoples in Alaska have a stocky physique, so too did Neanderthals. In warmer places, such as tropical Africa, a slender build is better because it allows the body to lose heat more easily. Among modern human groups, these physical adaptations to climate (along with metabolic and

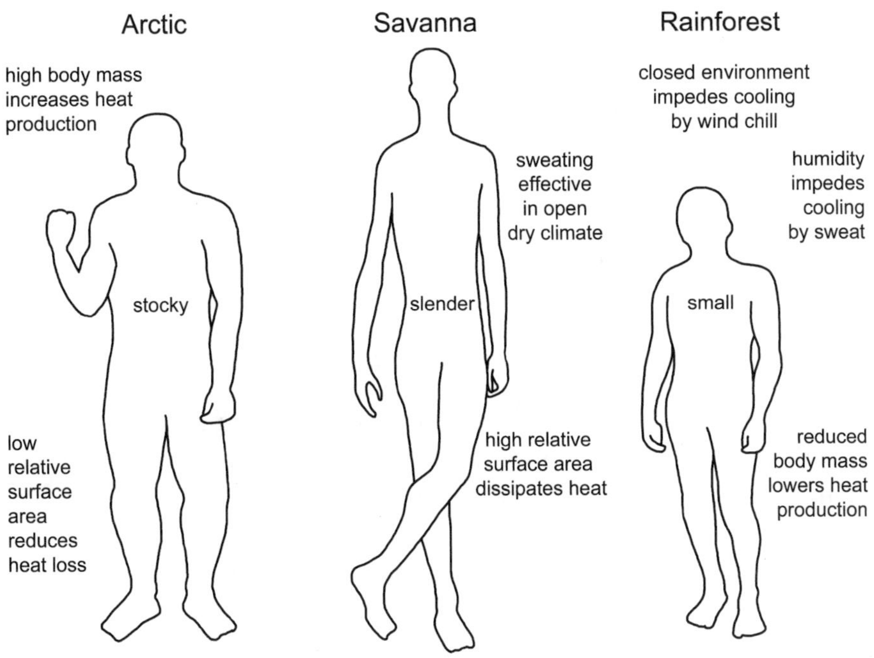

25. **Body shape and climate**
Human groups vary in body shape and limb proportions, reflecting adaptation to thermal stresses. Shape influences the relative surface area, which affects the net heat gain or loss. Body size (mass) can also be relevant thermally due to the amount of metabolic heat production. Pygmy groups, for example, may have evolved a smaller body size as a strategy to reduce total heat production in enclosed tropical environments where evaporative cooling from the skin surface is compromised by humidity and dense vegetation cover.
Source: Redrawn from Ruff, 1993:54. Reproduced under license, John Wiley and Sons.

other physiological adaptations) result in significant differences in susceptibility to hypothermia and frostbite. For instance, in the Korean War during the winter of 1950–1951, the US Army found that frostbite injuries were nearly five times more common among African American troops.[35]

This principle applies to arms and legs (and heads) as well as the torso: people from cold climates have shorter arms and legs, and rounder heads. It applies to other appendages too, such as the penis: among men adapted to warm climates, the penis tends to be longer (though probably not by quite so much, as some might claim). Clothing has an effect too: physical variation with climate is not so obvious where clothes have been worn for many generations.[36]

The adaptive benefit of shape is accompanied by other adjustments, such as having a more rapid rise in metabolic rate on cold exposure and a lower threshold for shivering. For these reasons, people differ quite a lot in their risk of frostbite. Compared to whites, those whose ancestors came from north-eastern Asia (including indigenous Americans) are not as prone to cold injuries whereas people with darker skin (whose ancestors hail from the tropics) are more susceptible to frostbite.

Clothes Can Make Us Feel Colder

The lifelong benefit of early cold exposure has an implication for clothing too: if we are routinely clothed from birth, we surrender a certain amount of cold tolerance. In other words, clothing has the paradoxical effect of making us more sensitive to cold. Once we are accustomed to wearing clothes, we become habituated thermally to the absence of cold, and so we want to wear more clothes to keep warm.

The Unusual Hypothermia of Australian Aborigines

Lacking clothes from birth, Aborigines in pre-colonial Australia could tolerate a surprising amount of cold. Even in the desert areas of central Australia, the weather can get cool: at night, the temperature can sometimes drop to a few degrees below zero. Yet, in their traditional lifestyle, Aborigines in central Australia could sleep comfortably without any clothes. When they were ready to go to sleep, they would construct little windbreaks and lie down behind them, and huddle around small campfires. Studies carried out by scientists measured their metabolic rates and skin temperatures during the night, comparing the Aborigines' reactions to those of the scientists who tried to sleep in the same manner (though with the benefit of clothes). They found some major differences – and they also reported how the whites were bothered by cold even in their clothes, sleeping only fitfully. In contrast, the locals slept soundly and woke up looking quite fresh in the morning.

The recordings of metabolic rate and skin temperature in the Aborigines revealed some unexpected patterns – quite different from the whites. In fact, the Aboriginal pattern is not like any other human group. First, the skin temperature on their limbs dropped to levels that would cause considerable pain for the rest of us. More surprising though – and most unusual – was the metabolic rate. Our main reaction to cold is to increase our metabolic rate – by as much as twice the normal rate in very cold conditions. But with the Aborigines, their metabolic rate actually fell during the night, and their core temperature dropped by a few degrees, which is quite the opposite to the hyperthermic response of other populations. In effect, the Aborigines allowed themselves to become mildly hypothermic.[37]

Having a hypothermic response to cold might appear to be a dangerous strategy: if the air temperature were to fall a little further, they could slip into deep hypothermia. Rather than feeling fresh in the morning when they woke up, they might not wake up at all. The likely explanation for this apparently dicey reaction is that it has one big benefit: they do not need to increase their food intake to sustain a higher metabolic rate – they can keep to their usual diet. In fact, their caloric requirements are actually lower in the cold. As for the danger, it can work safely if they are quite sure that nocturnal temperatures will not drop any lower. And this was indeed the case in their traditional societies: Aborigines had a very intimate knowledge of their natural environment – even without thermometers or meteorological records. They knew exactly how cold the weather could get. Their adaptation was unusual but efficient, made possible by the relatively mild climate of Australia and by their close connection with the environment – and by their routine lack of clothes.

THREE

HOW CLOTHES WORK TO KEEP US WARM

Whenever the air temperature is below 35°C (95°F), the surface of our skin will be warmer than the surrounding air, and our body will lose heat to the environment. Clothing works by holding little pockets and layers of air close to the body. The trapped air is warmed by body heat, which has the effect of lowering the thermal difference (or gradient) between the body and the environment. The result is that heat is lost more slowly. Without clothes, cool air next to the skin warms up quickly and moves away to be replaced by more cool air. The process is called convection, and convection has the effect of carrying away the body's warmth.

Clothing interferes in this process, creating a warm microclimate around the body. Heat is still lost to the outside environment, but more gradually. With sufficient clothes, we can reach a state of equilibrium where the net loss of heat from the surface of the clothes is matched by metabolic heat produced within the body. Natural fur works in much the same way.

The material of clothing does not make us warm. In fact, quite the opposite happens. As a solid object, the actual material will carry our heat away more rapidly – which is why clothes feel cold when we first put them on (and why blankets feel cold when we get into bed). It takes a few moments for the air contained by the fabric to warm up.

Other factors come into play in the real world, as always, and we will look at some of them in a moment. The most important point to appreciate is that anything that removes the trapped air will reduce the insulating effect. The most obvious cause of lost air is movement of air, which happens either from wind penetration or from body motion. But the other danger for clothing is moisture.

MOISTURE AND SWEATING

Along with wind, moisture is a sworn enemy of clothing. Moisture displaces the air, replacing it with a liquid medium that has more thermal conductance. Aside from environmental moisture on the outside, our body sweat is a constant internal source of moisture. Not only does clothing work best in dry environments but it also works best when we sweat less. The problem of sweat brings us to another challenge with clothing: physical activity. Clothing is compromised by motion, for a couple of reasons. Body movement disrupts the still air, and so it increases convective heat loss. It also produces moisture because any physical exertion causes more sweating.

Sweating, however, presents a special problem for clothes – a problem that is never really resolved. The moisture problem created by sweat increases with physical activity, but it never goes away completely, even at rest. For clothes to retain their thermal function, the moisture must be removed. The need to let moisture escape leads to a conflict: we want our clothes to enclose the body (to trap air), but we also want clothes to stay open in some way so that our sweat can evaporate.

We want it both ways, as usual. One solution is to have clothes that are easy to remove, as conditions require, but the most effective garments are harder to remove. The other complicating factor with sweating is environmental humidity. Sweat evaporates most easily when the surrounding air is dry, but in humid conditions, sweat tends to stick to our skin. So, the sweat problem will get worse when the climate is more humid. Fortunately, during the Pleistocene, the climate was not just colder but drier, which made wearing clothes more viable.

ANIMAL SKINS AND TEXTILES

Humidity becomes more of an issue when we look at what happened after the end of the ice age. Global warming was associated with a rise in relative humidity, which led to a new technology: clothes made from woven fabric. Later, we shall see why this textile revolution may have been relevant in the transition to agriculture.

During the ice ages, clothes were made primarily – perhaps entirely – from animal skins and furs. The problem with moisture and sweating was not so noticeable in those drier climates. To begin with, the moisture problem was reduced by having garments that were fairly open and easy to remove.

However, loose garments were less ideal as conditions got colder, when the garments had to enclose the body more fully. Even then however, as the climate got colder, it got drier too, so people could manage with tailored skin garments during the LGM. The dry climates meant that sweat could evaporate and moisture did not accumulate very much in the clothes.

THE VIRTUES OF FABRIC

Textiles came into their own when the weather became hot and humid. Fabric has a remarkable property: its woven structure allows moisture to escape. Textiles are an ideal solution to an insoluble problem: enclosing the body but at the same time allowing the body to stay open and to breathe. It may be true that the actual material of clothing matters less than the trapping of air, but with textiles the material does make a difference – or rather, the woven structure of the material makes an enormous difference.[1]

With regard to material, natural fibers have another wonderful property. At a microscopic level, the fibers have lots of little air pockets. So, as well as trapping air within the woven structure of the fabric, a certain amount of air is contained within the fibers themselves. The hair fibers of animal hides and furs have this property as well: some of the insulation is provided by air trapped inside the fibers. But when we wear an animal skin, we also have to carry the dead skin of the animal, which is less permeable. However, if we use the fibers alone to weave a fabric, we can dispense with the skin. And because the fibers themselves contain trapped air, they can still provide good insulation despite the porous structure of the fabric. With textiles, in addition to using animal fibers, we can also make use of fibers from plants (such as cotton), which likewise contain these microscopic pockets of air. So as a bonus, in terms of the natural resources that people could exploit, this meant that with textiles they were not restricted to hunting animals in order to obtain the materials for their clothes: they could make use of plants too.

Natural versus Synthetic Fibers

The advantage with textiles is not so great with synthetic fibers such as polyester; synthetic fibers have a simpler microscopic structure. Natural fibers are naturally superior because not only do they retain more air but they can absorb moisture within their fiber structure. Up to a limit, as with brief bouts of physical exertion, some of the sweat can get absorbed into the fibers and then evaporate later: this is called the wicking effect. However, synthetic fibers are less absorbent, and since they rely more on the macroscopic woven structure to trap air, synthetic fibers must be woven more tightly for warmth – all of which makes them sweatier. The advent of air conditioning – which lowers humidity – has made synthetics more viable in recent decades.[2]

Measuring the Thermal Value of Clothing

We can get a rough idea about how effective clothing is by measuring its thickness, which tells us how much air is trapped – approximately. Thicker clothes are generally warmer. Clothing scientists have devised more precise ways to measure the thermal value: the most well-known is a formula called the "clo" unit. The clo system was worked out with woven tailored garments, using a person sitting still on a chair in a room at an air temperature around 22°C, with relative humidity below 50 percent and minimal air movement (0.1 m/s).

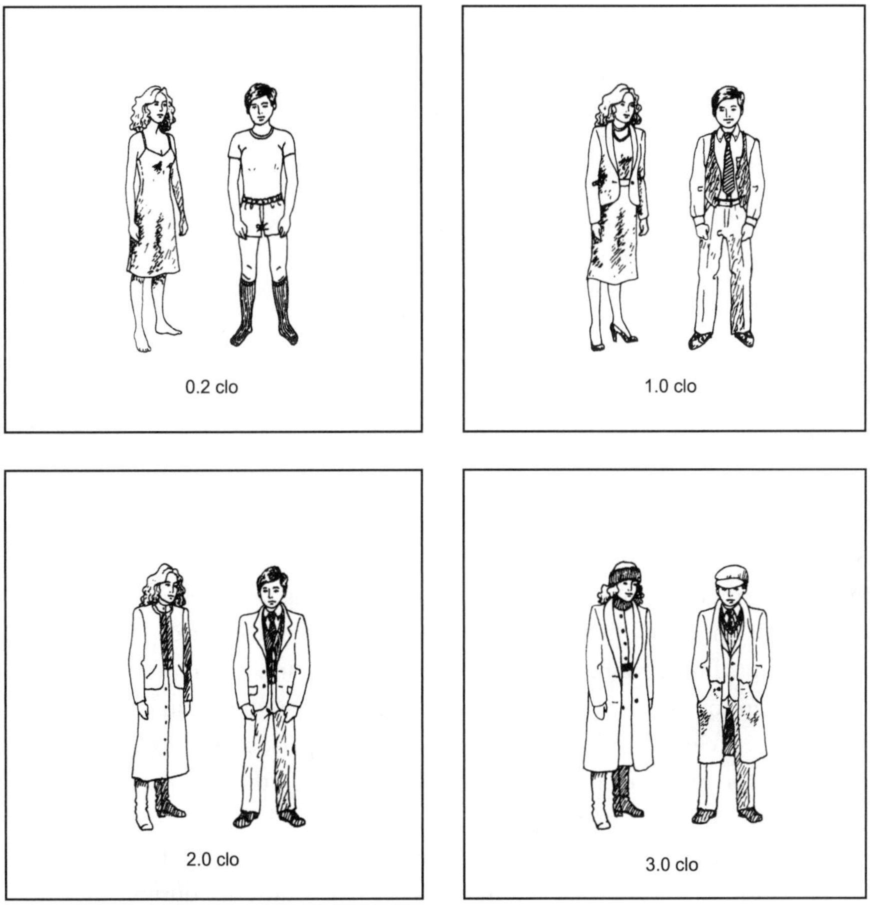

26. **Clo values and clothing layers**
The level of thermal insulation provided by clothes can be measured with "*clo*" values, based on laboratory studies with modern-day, woven, tailored garments. 1 clo corresponds to the amount of clothing needed for a person to feel comfortable (and to be in thermal equilibrium with their surroundings) in an indoor setting at 22°C, with low-moderate relative humidity and minimal air movement (that is, no wind chill). In an outdoor setting, clo values correspond loosely to the number of layers worn: adding an extra layer adds another 1 clo. A garment assemblage suitable for survival in Arctic conditions typically provides around 4 clo protection, with four layers.
Source: Bradshaw, 2006:17. Reproduced by permission of John Wiley and Sons.

TABLE 4. *Clo values of garments*

The total clo value of a clothing ensemble can be estimated by adding the clo values for individual garments; these clo values are for modern, woven garments. *Source:* Bradshaw, 2006:15.

Men		Women (where different)	
Garment	clo	Garment	clo
underwear – briefs	0.05	underwear – girdle	0.04
T-shirt	0.09	underwear – bra and panties	0.05
shirt, light, short sleeves	0.14	half slip	0.13
shirt, light, long sleeves	0.22	full slip	0.19
shirt, heavy, short sleeves	0.25	long underwear, upper	0.10
shirt, heavy, long sleeves	0.29	long underwear, lower	0.10
vest, light	0.15	blouse, light, long sleeves	0.20
vest, heavy	0.29	blouse, heavy, long sleeves	0.29
trousers, light	0.26	dress, light	0.22
trousers, heavy	0.32	dress, heavy	0.70
sweater, light	0.20	skirt, light	0.10
sweater, heavy	0.37	skirt, heavy	0.22
jacket, light	0.22	slacks, light	0.10
jacket, heavy	0.49	slacks, heavy	0.44
socks, ankle length, thin	0.03	sweater, light, sleeveless	0.17
socks, ankle length, thick	0.04	sweater, heavy, long sleeves	0.37
socks, knee high	0.10	jacket, light	0.17
sandals	0.02	jacket, heavy	0.37
shoes	0.04	stockings	0.01
boots	0.08	panty hose	0.01
hat and overcoat	2.00		

In terms of thermal comfort, typical summer clothing provides around 0.5 clo, winter clothing around 2.0 clo, work clothes around 0.7 clo, and outdoor clothes in polar environments around 4.0 clo. As an indication of the temperatures we can tolerate in terms of clo values and exposure times, an ensemble that provides 2.3 clo of protection would allow a person to feel comfortable at −10°C for up to an hour or so, while at −15°C, the exposure time with 2.3 clo is around forty-five minutes.[3]

In general, each clo unit equates to a single layer of covering. For example, a set of garments that would let humans survive outdoors during an Arctic winter has four layers, providing around 4 clo of insulation. In the real world, the number of layers corresponds roughly to the total thickness of the garment assemblage.[4]

There are limitations with these measures. First, most are based on modern woven fabrics – not the animal skins that were used by Paleolithic people in the ice ages (and by many recent hunter-gatherers, such as the Australian Aborigines). Another problem is the need to take air movement into account:

besides wind chill, any physical activity creates some movement of air, which leads to a loss of insulation. Body motion also results in air moving within the garments – the "bellows effect." For a person walking along briskly, the insulation can be reduced by up to 50 percent. Much depends on two things: the number of layers and whether the garments are loose or, instead, the layers are fitted closely around the body.

27. **Traditional Alaskan layered-clothing ensembles** More than 4 clo of insulation can be achieved by fitted, multilayered garments made from animal skins. This group from the Aleutian Islands, Alaska, were photographed in 1904 wearing traditional garments at the Louisiana Purchase Exhibition, St Louis, MO.

Source: Photo: Charles Carpenter, Field Museum Library, © Getty Images, # 550760427. Reproduced under license, Getty Images.

These two things – layers and fitting – are what will mostly determine the thermal value of clothes as insulation from cold weather. In the next chapter, we will see how these two aspects allow us to define two different kinds of clothing. Then, in the following chapters, we shall look at why this makes a world of difference when we come to look at the origin of clothing, particularly in relation to the evidence from archaeology and the role of climate change.

TWO TYPES OF CLOTHING

Two types of clothing can be defined: simple and complex. The difference comes down to a couple of things: extra layers and fitting. With either of these things comes a big difference in thermal value, but the difference goes further. When we look at the origin of clothing, there are really two origins. First, was simple clothing, which goes back a long way. In fact, it was probably invented many times – and dropped many times when no longer needed (as happened in Tasmania). Complex clothing was invented more recently and had many more consequences. For one, it was more enduring – indeed the advent of complex clothing has made clothing permanent.

Simple Clothing

Simple clothing is just a single layer and always loose. The material does not matter: it can be a cape made from the skin of a kangaroo or a caribou, or an antelope skin (called kaross) worn by the San people in southern Africa, or a modern garment made by a factory machine from synthetic fibers. It can involve sewing too, though less commonly. One example would be the possum-fur cloaks used by Aborigines: these were sewn together from many possum skins.

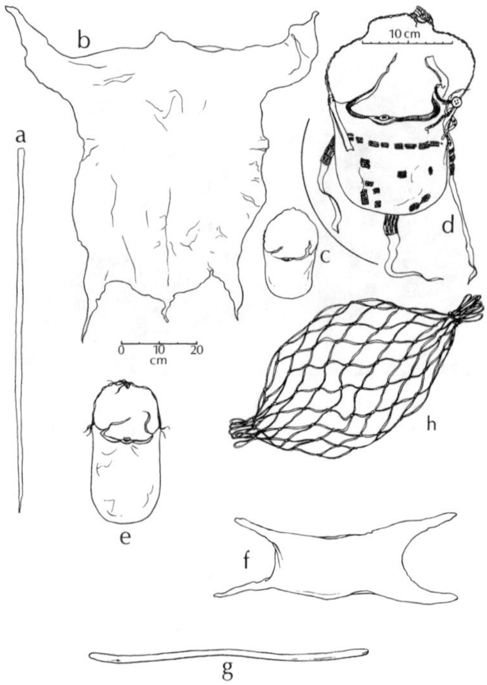

28. **San items, including the kaross**
The kaross was multipurpose, serving as a rug, blanket, and carrying device as well as a garment. Shown here is a collection of San gathering and carrying equipment: (a) digging stick, (b) kaross, (c) small bag, (d) small bag (detail), (e) man's bag, (f) baby carrier, (g) carrying yoke, (h) woven net.
Source: Richard B. Lee, The !Kung San, Cambridge University Press, 1979:125. Reproduced by permission of Cambridge University Press.

Nevertheless, these heavy cloaks had only a single layer and were loosely draped around the body. Although they were sewn, they were still simple.

In any classification, there will always be some annoying cases that do not fit nicely into a pigeon hole. What about if we wear two loose cloaks together, one on top of the other? A double layer of loose cloaks is complex because there are two layers, even though each garment is loose. But in practice, this rarely happens for practical reasons: it is hard to keep two loose garments in place. The inside layer, at least, usually needs to be fitted, in which case the ensemble will qualify as complex on both grounds: it is multilayered and fitted.

This raises another point: it is not always the garment itself but how it is worn that will determine whether it is simple or complex. A loose garment could be simple or complex at different times, depending on whether it is supplemented with another garment. Only with a fitted garment, such as a pair of trousers, will it always be complex, since it is fitted. Even as a single layer, a fitted garment will always be complex.

In terms of thermal properties, simple clothing is limited in two ways. First, the amount of protection is limited by the single layer. Although some thick furs can be quite warm, in general, the thermal value of simple clothing amounts to around 1–2 clo. The other limitation is wind chill. Because they are more open, simple clothes are less effective with wind. Even a thick fur can become almost useless once wind becomes a factor. For instance, a thick fox fur might provide up to 6 clo of insulation, but this applies only without any wind (clo values are determined in still-air conditions); a loose cloak made of warm fox fur will lose most of its thermal value once the wind picks up.[5]

Complex Clothing

Complex clothing is fitted, and it can be multilayered. Fitting refers to being fitted closely to the shape of the body, which can include the arms and legs as

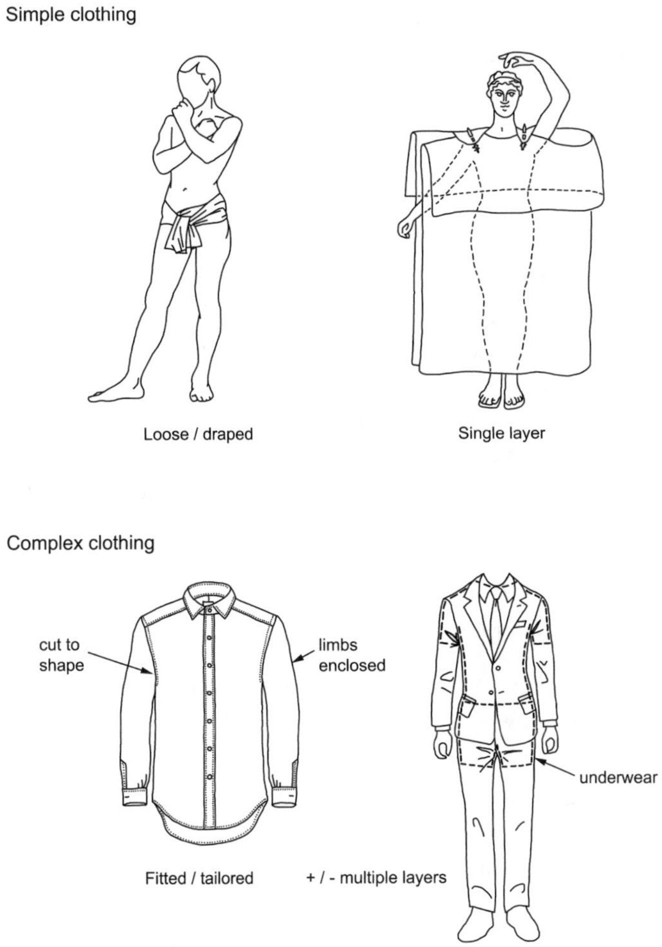

29. **Simple and complex clothing**
Simple and complex clothing. Simple clothing is draped and has only a single layer. Complex clothing is fitted (cut to shape), covering the torso and often enclosing the limbs as separate cylinders. Complex clothing can also have multiple layers.

well as the torso. A couple of things give complex clothing its great benefits: it covers more of the skin surface area more closely, and it resists penetration by wind. Even with a single layer, fitting makes a garment warmer and more effective as protection from the wind. It also means that moving around in cold weather is less of a problem since the trapped air is not so easily lost as a result of body motion.

The other advantage of complex clothing relates to layers. As shown in this chapter, adding extra layers will multiply the insulation value. Each layer adds around 1 clo. With three or four layers, we can achieve 3–4 clo and survive in very cold environments. Climates around the world are divided into clothing zones based on the number of layers required: for instance, an Arctic winter (with average monthly temperature between $-10^{\circ}C$ and $-20^{\circ}C$ [$14^{\circ}F$ and $-4^{\circ}F$] is designated as a four-layer clothing zone.[6]

If we want multiple layers, the garments ideally need to be fitted. So, these two aspects of complex clothes – layers and fitting – usually go together.

SEWING AND TAILORING

Complex clothes require sewing to join the limb segments and to ensure that a garment can enclose the body. So, people tend to say that fitted garments are tailored, meaning sewn. Yet, as with those Aboriginal cloaks made from possum furs, sewing can occur with simple clothes too.

Complex clothes are synonymous with tailoring, which implies sewing as well as fitting. Yet, sewing is not limited to complex clothes, so it is best not to speak about tailoring but whether clothes are fitted. The word tailoring has a double meaning that can cause confusion, and so it is best avoided.

COMPLEX EFFECTS OF COMPLEX CLOTHES

Complex clothing has had many repercussions – unlike simple clothes. Psychological and social aspects entered the picture, especially after the ice age, when clothes really came into fashion. Modesty emerged at some point too, meaning people had to keep wearing clothes when the weather improved. Even on the thermal side, the sheer effectiveness of complex clothes will reduce our naked tolerance of cold. When we wear this kind of clothing routinely, our bodies adapt to a warm and more uniform microenvironment. In effect, we become acclimatized to clothes, and as a result, we cannot cope so well with cold in the natural environment. Aside from any social or psychological need for clothes, we develop a greater physical need to keep on wearing clothes – we feel colder without clothes. Yet, once we possess complex clothing, we can conquer the whole world, including the polar zones – we gain access to every climate zone on the planet.

As seen with the indigenous garments of Australian Aborigines, simple clothes have no such effects. The functions are pragmatic, and people can drop their clothes when not needed for warmth. Such clothes serve no social purposes – society can function normally without clothing. Aborigines made good use of the naked body for social purposes: on formal occasions they got dressed up in paints and ornaments, and sometimes they would cut their skin to make elaborate markings (cicatrices). The most striking thing, from our modern point of view, is how they managed without any sense of shame about their naked bodies – their genitals were often on permanent public display.

Complex clothing began when humans needed more protection from cold (especially from wind chill) and better cover for their limbs. The need for

TABLE 5. *Features distinguishing simple and complex clothes*

Property	Simple clothes	Complex clothes
Structure		
fitted	no	yes
number of layers	1	1+
Thermal physiology		
wind chill protection	limited	excellent
still-air protection (generally)	1–2 clo	2–5 clo
Technology (Paleolithic)		
scraping implements	yes	yes
piercing implements (generally)	no	yes
cutting implements (generally)	no	yes
Repercussions		
impairs cold tolerance	no	yes
acquires decorative role	no	yes
acquires social functions	no	yes
promotes modesty/shame	no	yes
becomes habitual	no	yes

complex clothes never arose in Australia, even during the last ice age, because the climate never got that cold, though it did get rather close in Tasmania.

Once complex clothing comes into existence it tends to hang around – and it tends to become a part of us, for a number of reasons. First, we become more sensitive to cold as our thermoregulatory system adjusts to the artificial climate around the body. Second, any personal desires to decorate our bodies or any social needs for display get shifted onto clothes. Third, another reason to continue with clothes arises when we get so accustomed to being covered that we feel exposed or incomplete without being covered. In other words, we feel ashamed of nakedness. Modesty probably begins as a purely psychological process at the outset, when we become alienated from nakedness and the cover becomes incorporated into our being. The final step occurs when shame somehow becomes necessary for society – and society becomes civilized.

FOUR

THE TECHNOLOGY OF PALEOLITHIC CLOTHES

The invention of simple clothing was not a single event. During the course of hominin evolution, our ancestors would have adopted simple clothes many times whenever they found themselves exposed to cold as the climate changed during the Pleistocene. With simple clothes they could survive in cool environments up to a certain point, and they could often manage without clothes in summer or drop clothes completely when the climate warmed up again. However, they could only remain permanently in colder environments if they had complex clothes and, once equipped with complex clothing, they could stay in those places for as long as they wished. And then, at some stage, clothes became fashionable.

We can trace this process in the archaeological record by seeing how the early development of clothing was related to climate change. We can also see how the need for clothes became uncoupled from climate after complex clothing came into existence. To do this, we need to realize that although clothing is largely invisible in prehistory, it has left some visible traces. These traces are mainly technological: the tools that were used to manufacture clothes.[1]

SCRAPERS AND SIMPLE CLOTHES

To make clothes from animal skins, the basic tools needed are scrapers. A skin can be separated from a carcass with various implements, but cleaning the

TABLE 6. *Archaeological evidence for Paleolithic clothes*

Sources of archaeological evidence for Paleolithic clothes.

Technologies	Scraping, cutting, and piercing implements (e.g., scrapers, blade-based tools, awls, and needles)
Raw materials	Faunal / plant exploitation (e.g., faunal targeting) Animal body part distributions (suggesting skin removal)
Inferred presence	Known physiological limits to human cold tolerance Reconstructed thermal conditions / minimal clothing levels
Anatomical	Cold adaptations (e.g., Neanderthal body shape) Other (e.g., toe morphology – use of shoes)

inside surface is best done with proper scraping tools. Natural shells were used by hunter-gatherers where available, and people in coastal areas often used marine shells as hide-scrapers. But the most common scraper tools found by archaeologists were made from stones. The more clothes were worn, the more worthwhile it was for people to invest in making these scraper tools.

For simple clothing, scrapers were usually the only specific type of tool utilized. As we shall discover in the next chapter, there is plenty of archaeological evidence for scrapers in the Pleistocene. Indeed, one of the major technological trends before the last ice age was the advent and spread of Paleolithic industries based on scrapers. These scraper toolkits are good evidence for the invention and use of simple clothing. In a moment we shall look at how the distribution of these industries coincided with the changing climates – based on the physical need for simple clothes.

COMPLEX CLOTHING TECHNOLOGIES

To make complex clothing, scrapers were still needed, but some extra tools were also useful because people needed to do two extra things with the skins. First, the skins had to be cut into certain shapes, such as rectangles and triangles. Second, the cut pieces had to be joined together. These two activities – precision-cutting and hole-piercing – are the two extra steps required to make fitted garments, such as shirts with sleeves and trousers with separate legs. Using Paleolithic technology, the hides could still be cut with stone scrapers, but it was best to have tools with a long sharp edge. Stone tools with long sharp edges look different to scrapers; we call them blades.

Blade Tools

Toolkits with blades can be a sign of complex clothing, and these blade industries became more common as humans were exposed to colder climates. The distribution of blade toolkits in relation to changing climates represents good

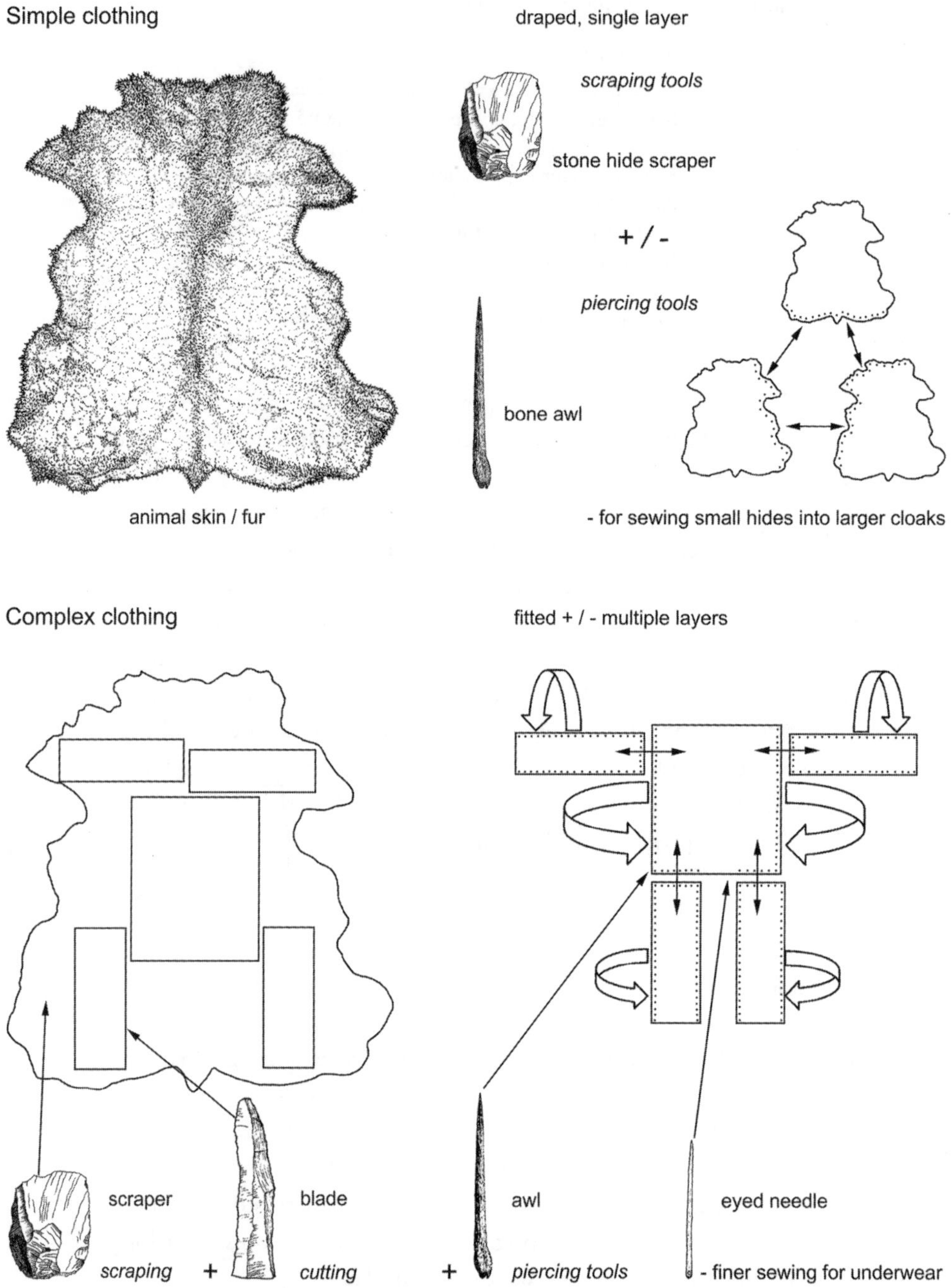

30. **Paleolithic technology of simple and complex clothing**
Technological aspects of simple and complex clothing in the Paleolithic. With simple clothes, the main technology is a scraper tool, with the addition of a piercing tool if multiple skins are sewn together to make a cloak. Complex clothes require scraper tools and, in addition, cutting implements (such as blades) and piercing implements (awls and needles). Eyed needles are particularly useful for making multilayered garment assemblages, facilitating the finer sewing required to make undergarments.

evidence for the thermal invention of complex clothing, and it shows how complex clothing enabled humans to spread into the coldest environments.

Piercing Tools

The second type of tool needed for complex clothing is a piercing tool, so that the hide segments can be sewn together. Scraper tools can sometimes be used for this purpose as well, if they have a pointed corner, but more typical are pointed hide-piercing tools called awls. Awls were often made from long animal bones that could be shaved and shaped into awls more easily than stones. Finer bone awls are called needles, and those with holes drilled at one end are the classic eyed needles. With the archaeology, one indication that clothing played a role in promoting these technological innovations is that both of these technologies (blades and awls) came together in the coldest environments of the last ice age.

FUNCTIONAL DIFFERENCES BETWEEN SCRAPERS AND BLADES

Archaeologists traditionally define different kinds of tools mainly on the basis of their shape (and to a lesser degree, on the different techniques that were used in their manufacture). We are naturally inclined to assume that these different shapes correspond to different functions. For instance, a hammer has a different shape to a screwdriver, and these tools have different functions. One of the basic differences in Paleolithic tools is the difference between scrapers and blades. We assume a functional difference: scrapers were used for scraping and blades for cutting. In relation to Paleolithic clothing, we can make a simplistic distinction between scrapers and blades: scrapers were used to scrape hides and blades to cut hides. This corresponds to the difference between simple and complex clothing: simple clothing requires only scrapers whereas complex clothing benefits from having blades as well as scrapers.

Tool Shape and Function

Things are a little more complicated in the real world. The relationship between shape and function is far from clear-cut: scrapers can be used for cutting and blades for scraping. We are probably all guilty of blurring this boundary too: we might sometimes use a screwdriver as a hammer (but come to think of it, some of us are not very good with a hammer either). Blades can be defined primarily on the basis of shape: a blade is more than twice as long as it is wide, for instance. This corresponds loosely with function, but only loosely. By virtue of its shape, a blade maximizes the length of the cutting edge. In fact some archaeologists explain the advent of blades in terms of efficiency: a blade maximizes the amount of cutting edge extracted from a piece of stone – it is a more efficient use of the stone. This is true, of course, but the need for efficiency still relates to the desire to produce a cutting edge. In general, microscopic use-wear studies of Paleolithic tools confirm that the functional distinction between scrapers and blades is really rather loose. However, if we accept that tool shape is only loosely indicative of function, the overall distinction actually holds up fairly well.[2]

Multipurpose Tools

There are more complications though, as usual. In real life most tools would have been used for more than one purpose. And in terms of the origin, the first reason to invent a particular kind of tool – if we can put it that simplistically – may not be the main reason why it was used later. Indeed its main functions may have varied over time and in different places. Neither can we assume that the final form of a tool – the one found by archaeologists when they excavate a site – necessarily reflects the original intention of its maker. The tool may have been reworked into different shapes during the course of its useful life, and it may have been reworked at different times by different people. The final product – be it a classical scraper or a blade, for instance – might in fact have undergone a number of transformations in shape and been used at different times for different purposes. Even assuming that a particular tool's final shape reflects its maker's original intention, the actual shape may be rather ambiguous. A stone point, for instance, might also function as a scraper if it has a more triangular shape – and it may in reality have served both as a hide-scraper and a hide-piercer. In terms of shape, it may be difficult – and misguided – to make a distinction between a point and a scraper. So to talk about scrapers and blades in a simplistic fashion as single-function tools based on their shape is rather fallacious, and it is certainly open to criticism – a criticism that is quite valid, technically.[3]

Manufacturing Techniques

An alternative approach with Paleolithic tools is not to classify them on the basis of their final shape but on the techniques used in their manufacture. This is a specialized area of research, but as an example, we can consider one of the main techniques used by Neanderthals in the manufacturing of their stone tools. The technique is called Levallois – and it was used also by *Homo sapiens* in some places. The Levallois technique involves first preparing the stone core by striking off flakes around its edges, then striking a blow across the core to extract a tool that has preformed sharp edges. The end result is a tool that is especially useful for scraping, with a maximum length of sharp scraping edge.

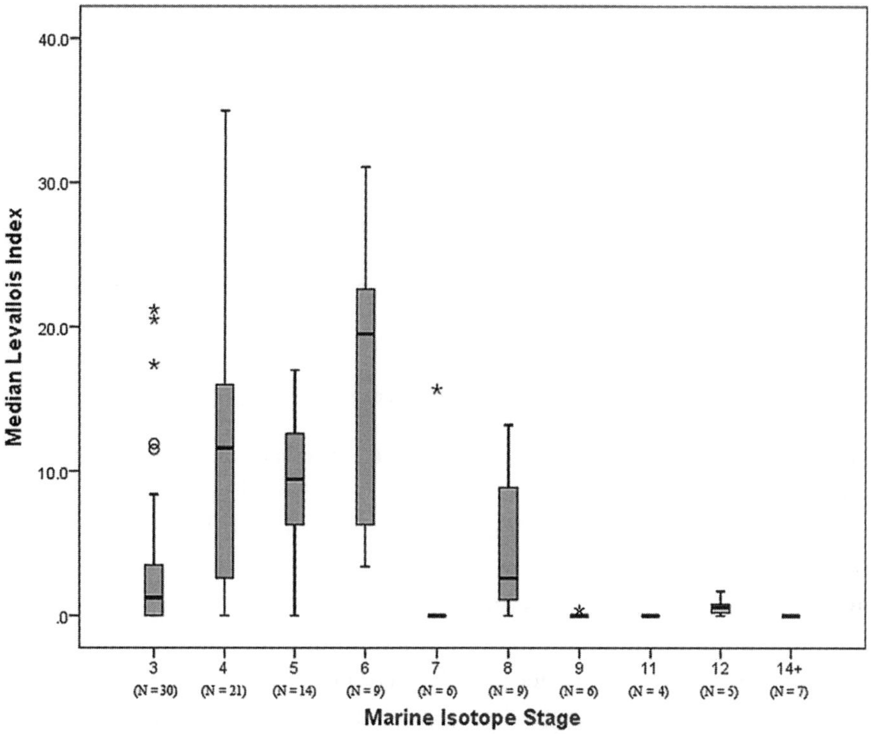

31. **Levallois tool-making technique and glacial episodes**
Levallois Index by Marine Isotope Stage (MIS). Lower and upper edges of boxes represent the 25th and 75th percentiles; the bold horizontal lines inside the boxes indicate the statistical median; asterisks indicate outliers; and circles indicate extreme cases. Note the climate pattern: higher Levallois Index in the even-numbered MIS stages, corresponding to colder (glacial) episodes.
Source: Redrawn from Monnier and Missal, 2014:73. © Elsevier. Reproduced under license.

The classic scraper tools used by Neanderthals were generally made in this manner, and it represents a more sophisticated technology than its predecessors. Later, we shall look at the climate trends in stone tools during the Pleistocene, but it is worthwhile mentioning here the research into how the Levallois technology varied in relation to the cold episodes. As shown in the graph, the Levallois technique – as a stone-knapping method that maximizes the useful scraping edge – fluctuates in concert with climate, reaching peaks during the glacial phases.[4]

Many Materials

Another complication with Paleolithic tools relates to the kinds of materials that the tools were used on. Use-wear studies show that most of the tools, blades and scrapers, were used not just to work on animal hides but on other materials as well. Butchering meat and woodworking were common functions in many cases, and often the same tool can show traces of being used on more than one kind of material. And it is not always easy to distinguish the functions or the materials; traces of hide-working, for instance, are notoriously hard to detect on older tools. Given the diversity in function and the loose connections with tool shape, some archaeologists argue that the differences in tool shape should not be used to infer functional differences. Nevertheless, functional diversity notwithstanding, there is good evidence from use-wear studies to support an overall distinction between scrapers and blades in relation to the manufacture of clothing.

SCRAPERS, BLADES, AND CLIMATE CHANGE

Support for this functional difference between scrapers and blades comes from use-wear studies at a European ice age site near the village of Pavlov, in the Czech Republic (latitude 50°N). The site was occupied by *Homo sapiens* between 29,000 and 23,000 years ago, leading into the LGM. Archaeologists looked at the use-wear patterns on scraper and blade tools and they found that hide-working was the most common function for both scrapers and blades – no real surprise there. But when they looked more closely at the traces on the working edges, they discovered a striking difference between scrapers and blades.

With scrapers, the traces on the edges of the tools were produced by a transverse motion on the hides – meaning that the scrapers were used with a sideways scraping motion. With the blade tools, they found the opposite pattern: the blades had a longitudinal wear pattern. That is, the working edges of the blades showed a lengthwise wear pattern – the blades had clearly been used for cutting rather than scraping the hides. So at this site in the last ice age where both scrapers and blades were used on animal hides, there was a difference in tool function: scrapers were indeed used to scrape animal hides whereas the blades were used to cut the hides.[5]

Another place where we see these trends is at Qesem Cave in Israel (32°N), which has some of the earliest scraper and blade industries in the world. Humans first occupied this cave during the very warm MIS11 interglacial around 400,000 years ago. The scraper industry begins toward the end of MIS11 and spans the MIS10 glacial, from around 370,000 to 330,000 years ago. The blade industry spans the following MIS8 glacial, from 300,000 to 240,000 years ago. So at this one remarkable site where early scraper and blade industries are found, the scrapers precede the blades, and both of these tool innovations correspond closely to climate change – namely, cold episodes.[6]

Use-wear analysis of the Qesem Cave tools also revealed the same functional difference between the scrapers and blades seen at Pavlov: the scrapers were used mainly for scraping and the blades for cutting.[7]

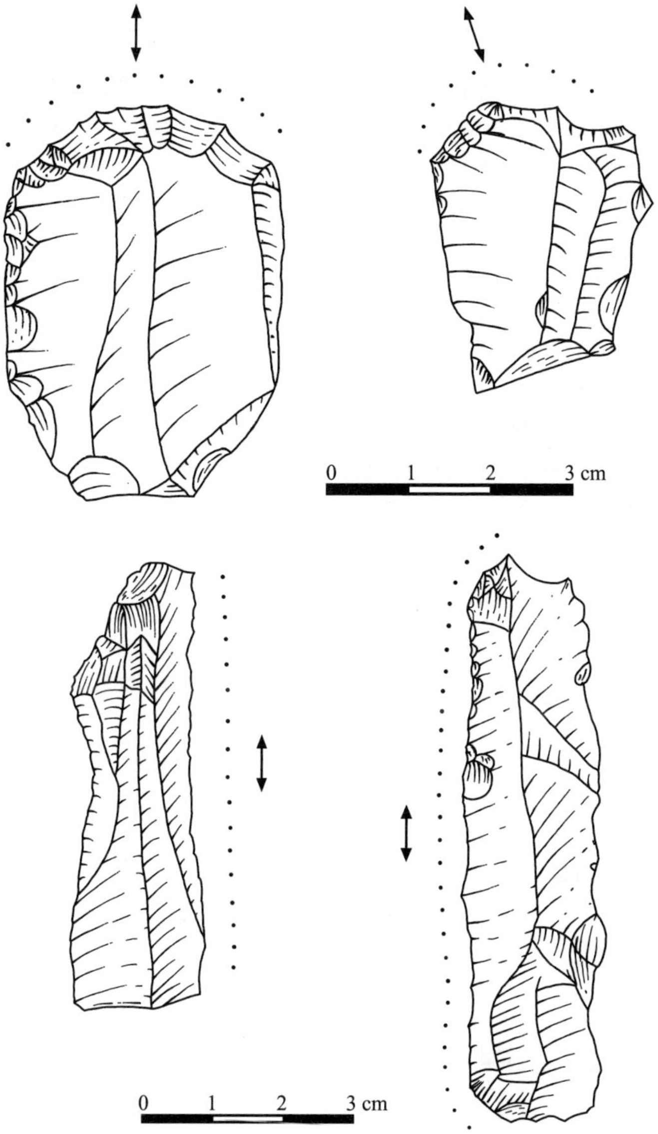

32. **Different use-wear patterns on scrapers and blades**
Scrapers and blade tools can have differing functions in the manufacture of clothing. Use-wear findings from the Pavlov I site in the Czech Republic, dated between 28,000 and 25,000 years ago, indicate that the scrapers (top) were used with a transverse (scraping) motion on animal hides whereas blades (bottom) were used with a longitudinal (cutting) motion.
Source: Šajnerová-Dušková, 2007:35, 36. Reproduced by permission of Archaeopress, and courtesy of Andrea Dušková and Jiří Svoboda.

THE TECHNOLOGICAL VISIBILITY OF PREHISTORIC CLOTHES

These Paleolithic technologies allow us to see the invisible clothing that was made by hominins in the Pleistocene. And insofar as they may serve as proxies for clothing, the tools allow us to test the proposition that clothing was developed as a means of keeping warm. We can see how simple clothing first came into existence (and sometimes went away) and how it was developed into complex clothing when environmental conditions got more challenging. And we can discern both aspects of complex clothing – the fitting of garments and the extra layers. Multiple layers demanded more careful cutting and sewing, especially for the underwear, which led to the invention of the eyed needle.

Awls in Australia

Australia illustrates some of the issues nicely. Its temperate climate meant that complex clothing was never developed, so we do not find classic blade industries – and nor do we find eyed needles – during the Pleistocene. However, in cooler areas of the continent simple clothing was required at times – more so as the LGM approached. And as we shall see later, scraper industries were developed in the most southerly region – Tasmania – during the LGM. The other technology that

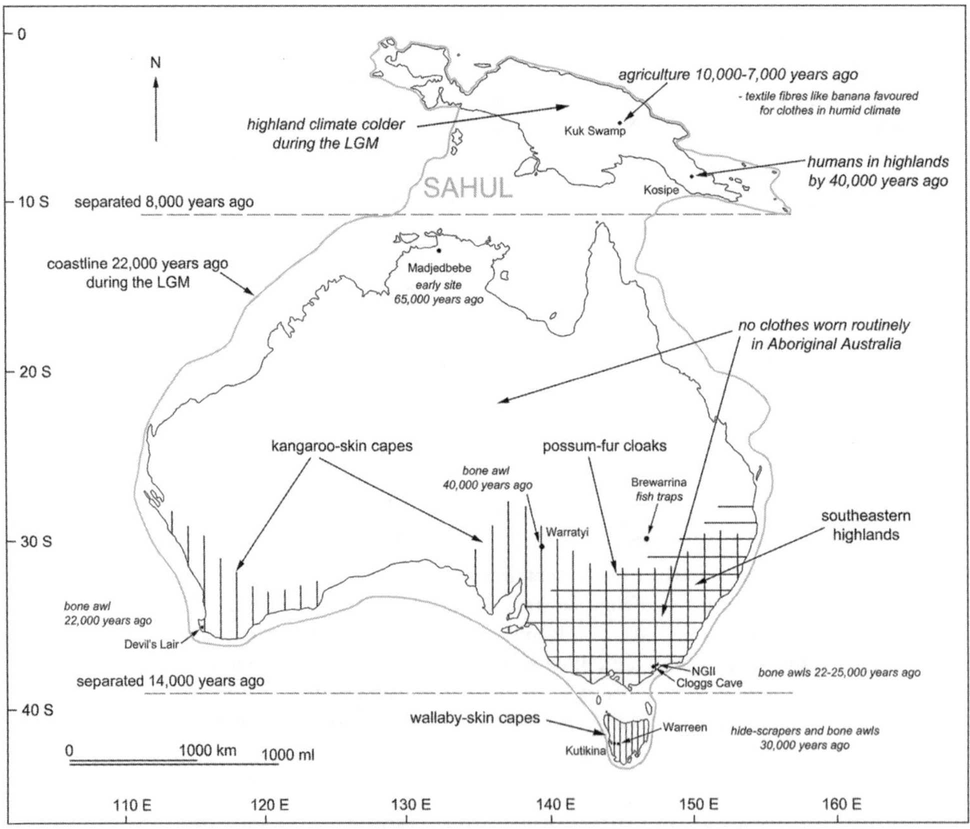

33. **Map of Australian region**

Australia, Tasmania, and New Guinea were joined together as one continent – called Sahul – during the last ice age, due to lowered sea levels. Shown here are key archaeological sites relevant to the early development of clothing technologies, and the ethnographic distribution of the major forms of clothing used in Aboriginal Australia: kangaroo-skin cloaks, possum-fur cloaks, and in Tasmania, wallaby-skin capes.

appears in Australia is the bone awl, which was used by people to sew smaller animal skins into larger cloaks – like possum-fur cloaks.

One of the earliest bone awls was found at Cloggs Cave in the southeast, dated to 22,000 years – the time of the LGM. Cloggs Cave has scrapers too, and the nearby site of NGII has a number of bone points, dated to around 25,000 years ago; use-wear patterns on the points are consistent with their function as awls for piercing animal skins. Across the continent in the southwest, a bone point was found in a level dated to the LGM (22,000 years ago) at the Devil's Lair cave site. Although no use-wear analysis was done on this artifact, it is very similar to bone points used by Aborigines in recent times to pierce holes in animal skins. Another bone artifact at Devil's Lair is a small triangular bone point that may have functioned as an awl, dated to between 32,000 and 25,000 years ago. The earliest bone point found in Australia – said

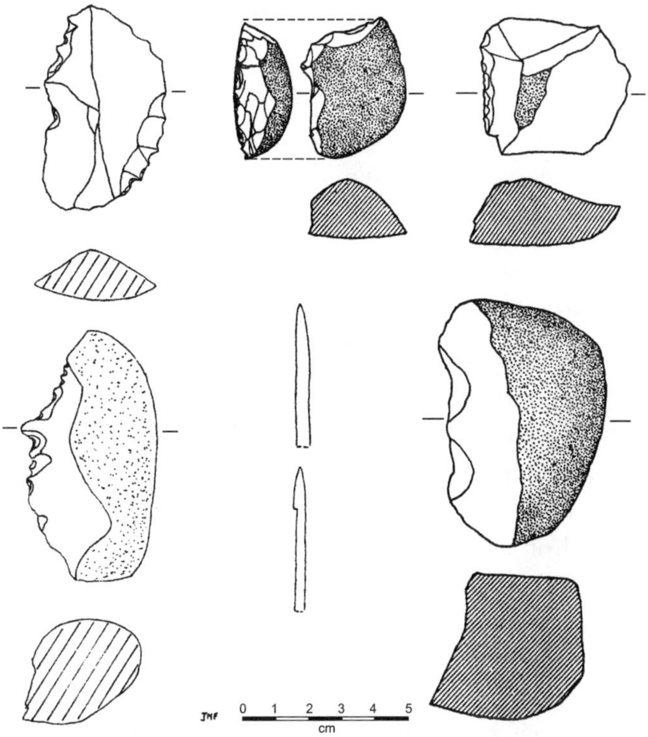

34. **22,000-year-old scrapers and bone awl at Cloggs Cave, Australia**
Stone tools and a bone point (lower center) from Cloggs Cave, southeastern Australia, dated to around 22,000 years ago – the time of the LGM. The site was excavated in the early 1970s by archaeologist Josephine Flood, who thinks these tools were used mainly for skin-working and that the bone point functioned as an awl for sewing animal skins together to make cloaks.
Source: Illustration by Josephine Flood (Flood, 1974:183). Reproduced by permission of John Wiley and Sons, and courtesy of Josephine Flood.

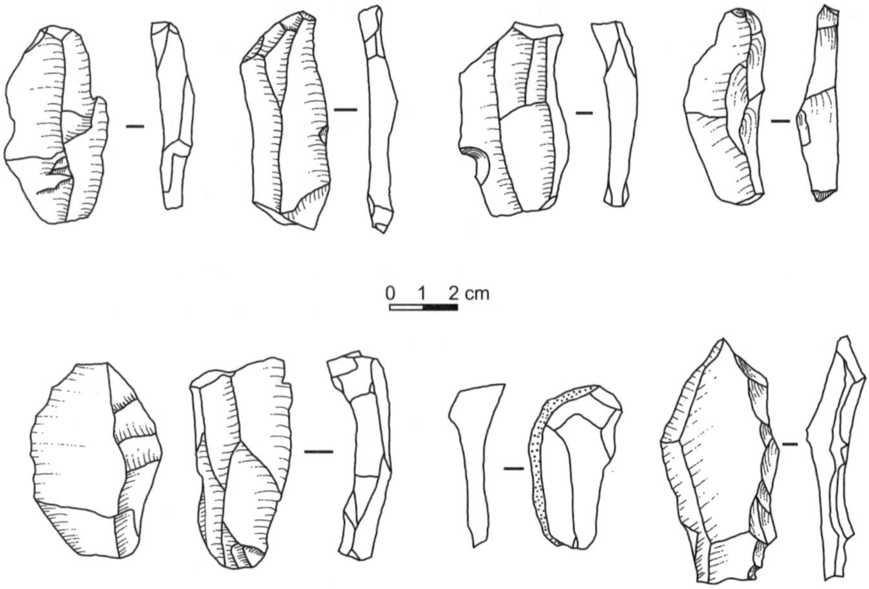

35. **40,000-year-old blades in northern China**
Blade tools appeared in China around 40,000 years ago at the Shuidonggou (SDG1) site in northern China.
Source: Peng, Wang, and Gao, 2014:16. © Elsevier. Reproduced by permission of Elsevier.

to look like an awl – was recovered from the Warratyi rockshelter in the southern interior, dated to between 40,000 and 38,000 years ago.[8]

Blades, Awls, and Needles in China

China also illustrates some of the main points about the archaeology of Paleolithic clothing and how the technologies were related to climate. We find the earliest blade industries in China around 40,000 years ago, at the site of Shuidonggou (SDG1, 38°N) in northwest China. This was a fairly cold period and, in all likelihood, the first *Homo sapiens* to reach northern China had complex clothes. We then find the earliest bone tools in China around 35,000 years ago at the site of Ma'anshan Cave (latitude 28°N) in central eastern China. Use-wear study of these bone points has identified them as awls for piercing animal skins. Then, as conditions became colder toward the LGM, we find the first eyed needles in China. One eyed needle was found at Shuidonggou dated to around 30,000 years ago, and a number of finely-made eyed needles have been found at the Xiaogushan cave site (40°N) dated to between 30,000 and 20,000 years ago; while at the

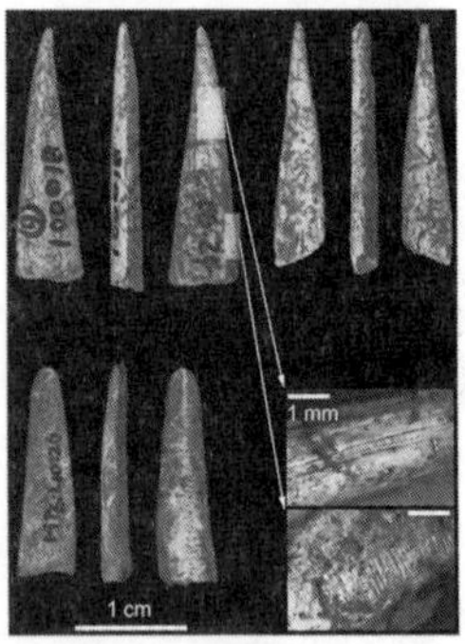

36. **35,000-year-old bone awls in China**
35,000-year-old bone awls found at Ma'anshan Cave, Guizhou Province, in central eastern China. Microscopic study shows evidence of polishing near the tips of the awls and scraping, as shown here (lower right), consistent with repeated grinding to maintain their sharpness for piercing animal skins.
Source: Zhang et al., 2016:63, © Elsevier. Reproduced under license, Elsevier.

site of Shizitan (36°N) in Shanxi Province, an eyed needle is dated to 26,000 years ago.[9]

EYED NEEDLES AND UNDERWEAR

The classic tool for complex clothing is the eyed needle. As expected, these fragile implements first made their appearance during the coldest times. Among the very first to appear anywhere in the world are found at the Russian site of Kostenki 15 (latitude 51°N) around 35,000 years ago – although the ones found at Denisova Cave (also 51°N) in southern Siberia could be a little earlier. The world's oldest may be at Mezmaiskaya Cave (44°N) in southern Russia, where a single eyed needle has been found in a layer dated to between 40,000 and 36,000 years ago.[10]

Eyed needles made their appearance later in Western Europe, where the winter temperatures were milder, beginning from around 30,000 years ago. They became more common toward the LGM – especially in the Solutrean industry, which spans the LGM. The timing of the Solutrean around 21,000 years ago corresponds to the coldest point of the LGM, so one of its hallmarks – eyed needles – likely reflects a heightened need for complex clothes. Moreover, climate reconstructions point toward a pronounced drop in winter minimum temperatures in Western Europe at precisely that time. However, it must be emphasized that the delayed appearance of eyed needles – around 10,000 years later than on the exposed plains further east – does not mean that humans were somehow managing to survive without fitted garments when they first entered Western Europe around 40,000 years ago. Making fitted, sewn clothing does not required eyed needles at all – it only requires pointed tools like awls. And bone awls are present from around 40,000 years ago, in the Aurignacian industry that accompanied the entry of *Homo sapiens* into Western Europe.[11]

Eyed needles are the signature tools of tailoring, but they may actually signify something more specific than complex clothes: eyed needles suggest a greater focus on intricate sewing. Finer handiwork would have been most in demand to make the inside garments of multilayered outfits, so the advent of eyed needles may indicate not just fitted garments but the need for people to wear more than one layer of fitted garments. In other words, rather than signifying tailoring, the first eyed needles may mark the invention of underwear.

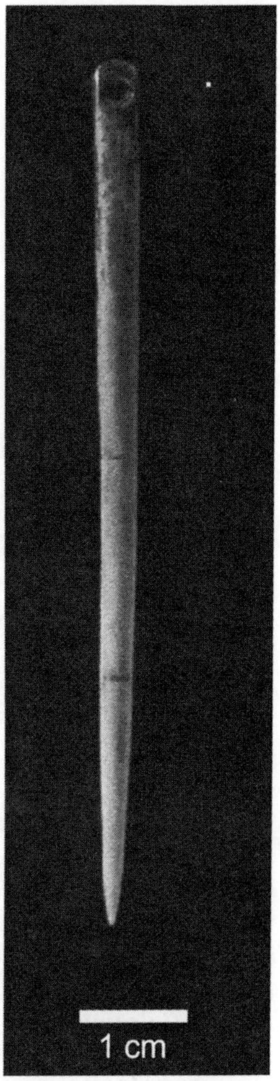

37. **30,000-year-old eyed needles in China**
Eyed needles are found in northern China during cold millennia leading into the LGM. One of the oldest eyed needles occurs at the Shizitan site, Shanxi Province (26,000 years ago), and another at the Xiaogushan cave site, which dates to between 30,000 and 20,000 years ago. Shown here is the eyed needle from Xiaogushan.

Source: Zhang et al., Journal of Human Evolution 59, 2010:517. © Elsevier. Reproduced by permission of Elsevier.

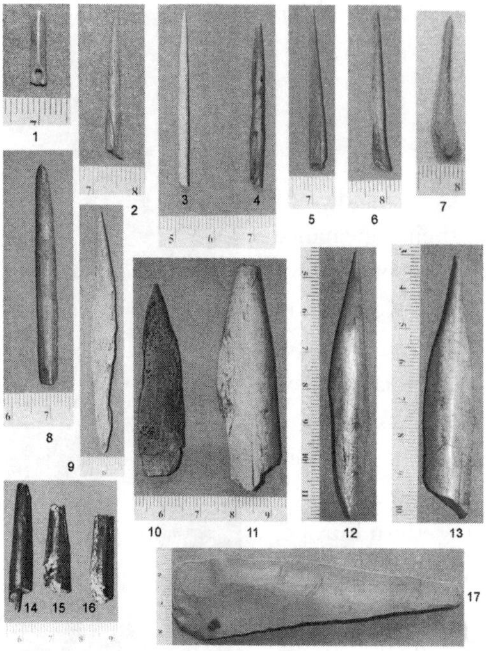

38. **World's oldest eyed needle in Russia 40,000 years ago**
The world's oldest eyed needle is between 40,000 and 36,000 years old, found at Mezmaiskaya Cave in southern Russia. The eyed needle fragment (numbered 1 here) is accompanied by other needles and bone awls in the cave in layers dated to between 40,000 and 28,000 years ago.

Source: Golovanova, Doronichev, and Cleghorn, Antiquity 84, 2010:308. Reproduced by permission of Cambridge University Press.

SKELETAL PARTS AND ANIMAL SKINS

Animal bones found at archaeological sites sometimes harbor another sign of Paleolithic clothing. Not only did people often target furry animal species – such as wallabies in ice age Tasmania – at some sites, archaeologists find that certain parts of the animal skeletons are not as common as they should be. The feet and tail bones, which are numerically common in the skeletons, are uncommon at the sites or completely missing. The likely reason is that people were not just butchering the carcasses for meat: they were carefully removing the skins from the animals. In removing the skins, they would often leave the tails and paws attached to the skins – to make them easier to carry, or to tie them around the body.

This pattern of separated skeletal elements is seen in colder parts of the world during the Pleistocene. For example, in Germany during the MIS9 interglacial 300,000 years ago, hominins were hunting mainly horses. At the site of Schöningen, where lots of horse carcasses were butchered, hoof bones are much less common than expected, and tail bones are almost absent. The stone tools at Schöningen are mainly flakes, but some scrapers were also found. And use-wear traces on the scrapers show that the tools were used on hides as well as wood. Archaeologists also found deep cut marks on the horse leg bones, which could be due to skinning. The same kind of cut marks are seen also on many of the animal bones – including horses, sheep, hyenas, and felines – at one South African site dated to between 65,000 and 60,000 years ago (during the cold MIS4 glacial). At that time in southern Africa, we also find tool industries with blades and bone awls, as well as scrapers. Meanwhile in ice age Europe, the bones of wolves and arctic foxes at many Russian and Ukrainian sites show this same odd pattern of separated elements: skeletons lacking paws or, sometimes, paw bones found separately as complete paws. At Kostenki 1, the partial skeletons of wolves and arctic foxes are found in Layer III, dated to between 38,000 and 34,000 years ago. Even cave lions were hunted for their pelts. At one cave in Spain, archaeologists found a collection of paw bones with the telltale cut marks showing how the pelt had been carefully removed from the carcass of the lion. And in Tasmania during the LGM when the Aborigines focused on hunting wallabies (and where we also find scrapers and bone awls), the wallaby skeletons likewise have a paucity of paw, foot, and tail bones, suggesting that people were carefully removing the skins.[12]

FIVE

CHANGING CLIMATES AND EARLY CLOTHES

We can now look at what archaeology tells us about how these clothing technologies varied with changing climates. We can look, too, at where hominin fossils are found, which tells us about when and where our ancestors first spread outside of the tropics. In this way we can get some idea of the weather conditions they experienced and whether they needed to wear any clothes for warmth. And if tools such as scrapers and blades are indeed connected with clothing, then we should be able to detect a climate pattern in these Paleolithic technologies.

Hominins began to spread outside of Africa by two million years ago. Before leaving Africa, though, there are places on the continent where simple clothes might have been needed at times, even before the Pleistocene. In southern Africa, winter temperatures and wind chill levels can approach the threshold at which early hominins might have needed some portable protection. This is likewise in northern Africa and perhaps in the highlands of Ethiopia too. But when hominins started to spread beyond Africa, they began to encounter new environments. *Homo erectus* had spread east to tropical Java by 1.6 million years ago – these are the famous Java Man fossils. To get all the way to Indonesia, they probably migrated through India and Pakistan – stone tools have been found in northern Pakistan (latitude 33°N) dated to around 1.9 million years ago. Still, the long trek to Southeast Asia may not have taken them very far from the tropics – especially if they stayed close to the coasts. Yet even at this early stage of the Pleistocene, some of our ancestors began to venture further north.

In southwestern Asia, by 1.8 million years ago, hominins had arrived on the doorstep of Europe at a place in Georgia called Dmanisi (latitude 41°N). In China they reached as far as 40°N – the latitude of Beijing – by around 1.7 million years ago. In both cases, local climates at the time were interglacial and warmer than now. At Dmanisi, for example, the climate was much warmer: mean annual temperatures were 3°C higher, and mean winter temperatures were nearly 5°C higher than today. The stone tools found at these sites are traditionally classed as Lower Paleolithic – meaning the tools were mainly pebbles, choppers, and flakes. However, one of the northern Chinese sites has some scrapers, which may date to as early as 1.4 million years ago.[1]

THE PULSING SPREAD OF HOMININS INTO HIGHER LATITUDES

Throughout most of the Pleistocene, our ancestors expanded into middle latitudes during the warm times only to withdraw during the colder episodes. We now have dozens of hominin sites scattered across mid-latitude Eurasia, but it appears that none date definitely to the coldest phases of the ice ages – at least not until Neanderthals made Europe their home. A case in point is one Spanish site, Barranco León, which is among the earliest in Western Europe, dated to 1.4 million years ago. When the climate turned cool, hominins abandoned the site, but they returned there for a second visit during the next warm phase. On both occasions, the local temperatures were warmer than today, and the stone tools found at the site are Lower Paleolithic.[2]

A possible exception to the warm pattern is a site in Norfolk – currently Britain's oldest hominin site. The previous oldest site was in Suffolk, which hominins visited during an interglacial around 700,000 years ago when the climate was warmer than it is now. What makes the Norfolk site unusual, however, is that it was occupied when the climate may have been cooler, toward the end of a warm interglacial. Although summer temperatures at the time were similar to those of today or perhaps a little warmer, the climate data suggest that winter temperatures might have been a little lower.[3]

SCRAPERS AND COLDER CLIMATES

As the Pleistocene progressed, we begin to find more scraper tools at sites in middle latitudes as hominins learned to cope with cooler conditions. Northern China is a good example, where *Homo erectus* (Peking Man) lived in a cave near Beijing during a series of glacial cycles from around 800,000 years ago. The toolkit found with Peking Man at the Zhoukoudian cave site has scrapers as well as stone awls, suggesting that these hominins may have manufactured simple clothes. The use of fire by Peking Man is also documented from around 800,000 years ago, and archaeological evidence for the construction of hearths is present from around 500,000 years ago. The early phase of occupation at Zhoukoudian from 800,000 years ago spans not only two interglacials but also the intervening glacial – although that particular ice age (MIS18) was "relatively mild."[4]

Meanwhile, in Europe scrapers became a "more persistent part of the lithic record" from 500,000 years ago. Some archaeologists relate the trend toward more prolific production of scraper tools at European sites to an increased use of clothing in the colder conditions. Hominins with scraper tools remained at the site of Schöningen in Germany at the end of the MIS9 interglacial 300,000 years ago, when winter temperatures fell to −4°C.[5]

The scrapers imply that simple clothing was used on a fairly regular basis by these hominins, at least during the winters. From that time onward, the global climate veered toward more severe and prolonged ice ages. Hominins in Europe evolved into Neanderthals who became better adapted – physically and technologically – to living in cool environments. Neanderthals developed specialized toolkits (called Mousterian) that have lots of well-made scrapers. These tools were multipurpose, serving a range of functions, such as cutting

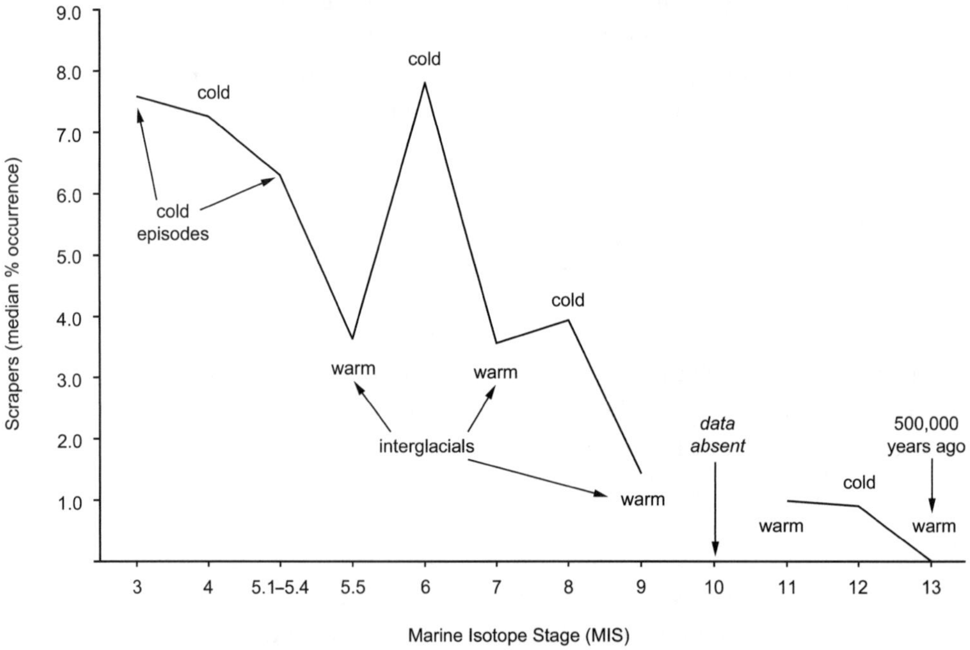

39. **Frequency of scrapers in relation to climate**

The frequency of scraper tools at sites in Western Europe fluctuates in relation to the climate phases. Data are absent for MIS10 due to lack of archaeological sites; note that MIS3 and MIS5.1–5.4 are not warm interglacials; MIS3 includes cold episodes.

Source: McNabb and Fluck, Current Anthropology 2006:732. © University of Chicago Press. Reproduced under license, University of Chicago Press.

meat and wood as well as scraping hides, and microscopic studies of their edges confirm the scrapers were used for all of these functions to varying degrees. Certain types of scrapers (such as end scrapers) were used mainly on animal hides. The frequency of these scraper industries in Western Europe varied in concert with the cold episodes, beginning before Neanderthals came on the scene.[6]

The frequency of scrapers in toolkits increased during the glacial phases and declined during the interglacials. As well as this temporal correlation with glacial cycles, there is a geographical correspondence with colder climates. Starting from the end of an unusually long interglacial (MIS11) around 400,000 years ago that lasted for 50,000 years, similar Mousterian-like toolkits with formal scrapers were developed by hominins in cooler regions – at the southern and northern ends of Africa, and in the Levant. These temperate locations can get quite cold in winter even now, and they got colder during the glacial episodes. On the other hand, toolkits full of scrapers are conspicuously absent or delayed in the tropics: while some steep-edged tools of various kinds could have been used to scrape hides, toolkits with significant proportions of formal scrapers do not appear on the Indian subcontinent until the last ice age, and they are largely lacking in Southeast Asia.[7]

In other words, when we look at the big trends, these scraper industries are essentially a cold-climate phenomenon – and this reflects a functional connection with the more regular use of simple clothing.

So with simple clothing, there were multiple and recurring origins. These origins coincide with the fluctuating climates and with the presence of hominins in cooler environments. With regard to technology, the key sign is the presence of toolkits with high proportions of stone tools that served as hide-scrapers. These toolkits became commonplace in cooler environments from around 300,000 years ago – especially with Neanderthals – but scrapers were popping up in some places much earlier than this; the earliest scraper tools may well have been in northern China more than a million years ago.

New discoveries are happening all the time, and we should not be too surprised to find scrapers anywhere that hominins were living in middle latitudes, anywhere from northern China right across to Western Europe. In some parts of Africa, winter temperatures were low enough at times during the Early Pleistocene to encourage the occasional use of simple clothing. Even parts of tropical Africa can get quite cool due to elevation, notably in the highlands of Ethiopia and Kenya. Despite occupying a low latitude in the tropics, winter temperatures today can drop to below 10°C (50°F) in Nairobi (elevation 5,000 feet); whilst on the central plateau of Ethiopia (elevation 7,000 feet), the temperature can fall to 5°C (40°F) in winter. Later we shall see how this same cooling effect of elevation occurs in another tropical location: the highlands of Papua New Guinea.[8]

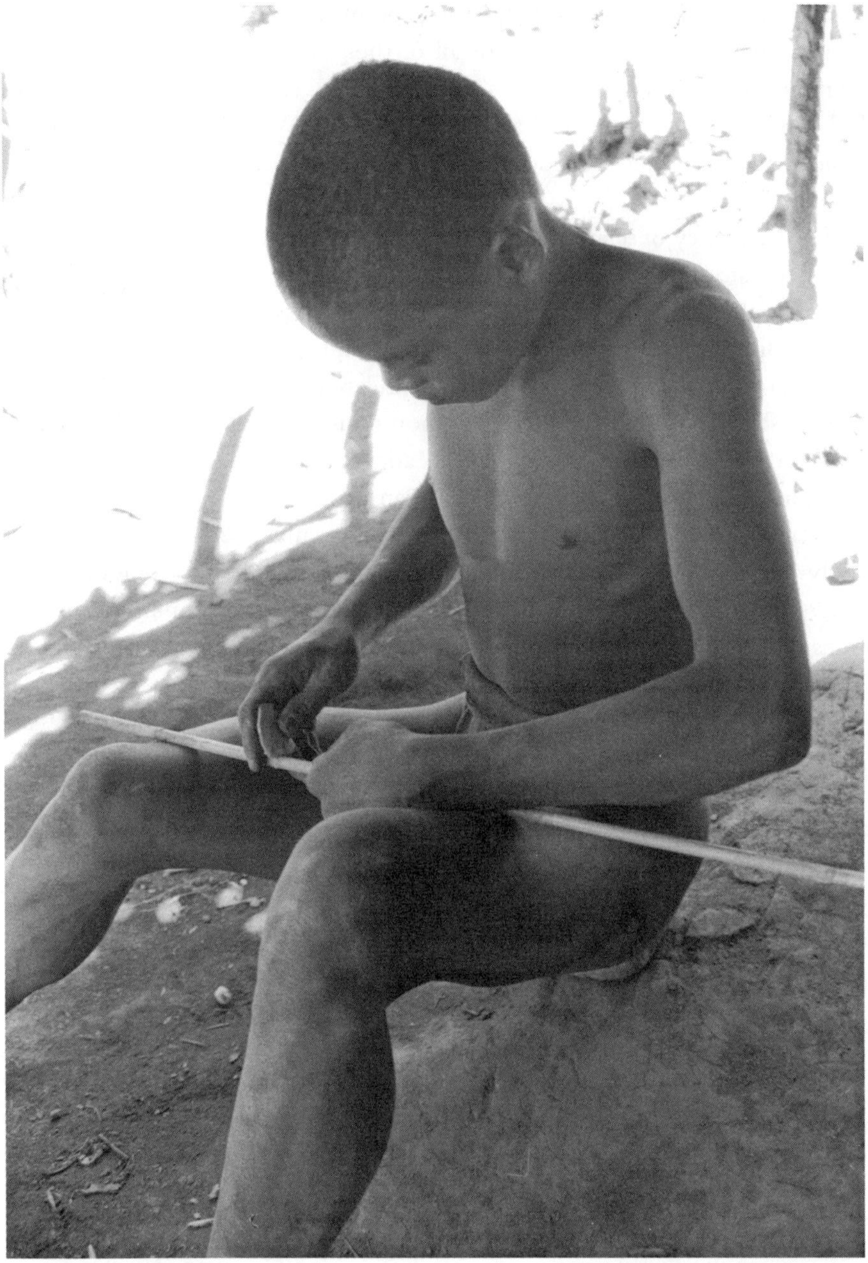

40. **Flake tools in Southeast Asia**

While formal scraper (and blade) tool types were developed in colder regions during the last few glacial cycles, in warmer regions such as Southeast Asia, people continued with basically the same simple technologies (such as flake tools), and often with little or no retouch. In this 1985 photo, a young Aeta man uses a flake tool to manufacture an arrow. The Aeta people are essentially foragers (though very much affected by the spread of agricultural practices) living in the Sierra Madre mountain range, northeast Luzon, in The Philippines.

Source: Photo by Johan Kamminga, © Johan Kamminga. Reproduced by permission of Johan Kamminga.

WERE EARLIER HOMININS MORE HAIRY?

The other thing to factor in here is the possibility that these earlier hominins carried a more convincing cover of body fur. We saw in Chapter Two that we lack firm evidence about when hominins became biologically naked. There are some indications that it happened before the beginning of the Pleistocene – perhaps before three million years ago – but all the evidence is indirect.

The only certainty is that nakedness was a fact of life by the time our own species came on the scene by around 300,000 years ago. We generally envisage Neanderthals and *Homo erectus* as having quite a lot more body hair than us, but that is mere supposition. Yet even if they were almost as hairy as chimpanzees, it would have made only a small difference in ice age environments when winter temperatures dropped more than five or ten degrees below 0°C (32°F).

SIMPLE CLOTHING AND EARLY HOMININS

We also lack any indication that complex clothing was invented before our own species appeared. The archaeological signatures of complex clothing are blade tools and awls (or needles). With one intriguing exception, this combination of technologies has not been found with other hominins, although there are some sites with early blades that crop up during the last few glacial cycles. In the northern hemisphere, early hominins appear to have contracted southwards during the ice ages (and vice versa), leaving the very cold environments close to the ice sheets unoccupied – despite the fact that these environments were often quite well-stocked with food resources. There were many cold-adapted animal species, such as reindeer and woolly mammoths, as well as more plant foods than in present-day tundras. By implication, clothing was restricted to simple clothing – complex clothing would have allowed hominins to thrive in those conditions. And indeed we find an absence of the requisite technologies: we find plenty of scrapers, but few blades and no needles. The one exception occurs with Neanderthals toward the coldest stage of the last ice age, just before they went extinct. We shall return to this hotly debated subject later.

COMPLEX CLOTHING AND THE SPREAD OF MODERN HUMANS

When members of our species began to spread out of Africa, they were limited to warmer regions for quite a long time. They had reached southern China by 80,000 years ago and entered Australia by 65,000 years ago, but they did not get very far north until around 45,000 years ago. In Europe we could blame Neanderthals for discouraging our dispersal into their homeland, and maybe the little-known Denisovans presented a similar disincentive in northern

China. Yet our genetic code harbors evidence for interbreeding with both these populations, so relationships with our neighbors were not necessarily antagonistic.[9]

An obvious reason for our reluctance to enter those northern environments was the winter cold. When our ancestors finally did venture into those regions from around 45,000 years ago, they had toolkits with lots of blades and hide-piercing implements such as awls and – a little later – eyed needles. By 45,000 years ago. they had reached the site of Ust'-Ishim (57°N) in Siberia – probably during a slightly milder climate phase (called Greenland Interstadial 12). By 32,000 years ago, they had spread into the far northeast of Siberia where eyed needles are found at the site of Yana (70°N) – a time when average winter temperatures were around −50°C. People even stayed in northern Siberia during the LGM, when the conditions were colder still. And in Europe there is evidence that people were wearing better shoes by then.[10]

The dispersal of modern humans into northern zones of the planet during colder climate phases depended on people possessing adequate portable insulation – in the form of fitted, multilayered clothing ensembles (complex

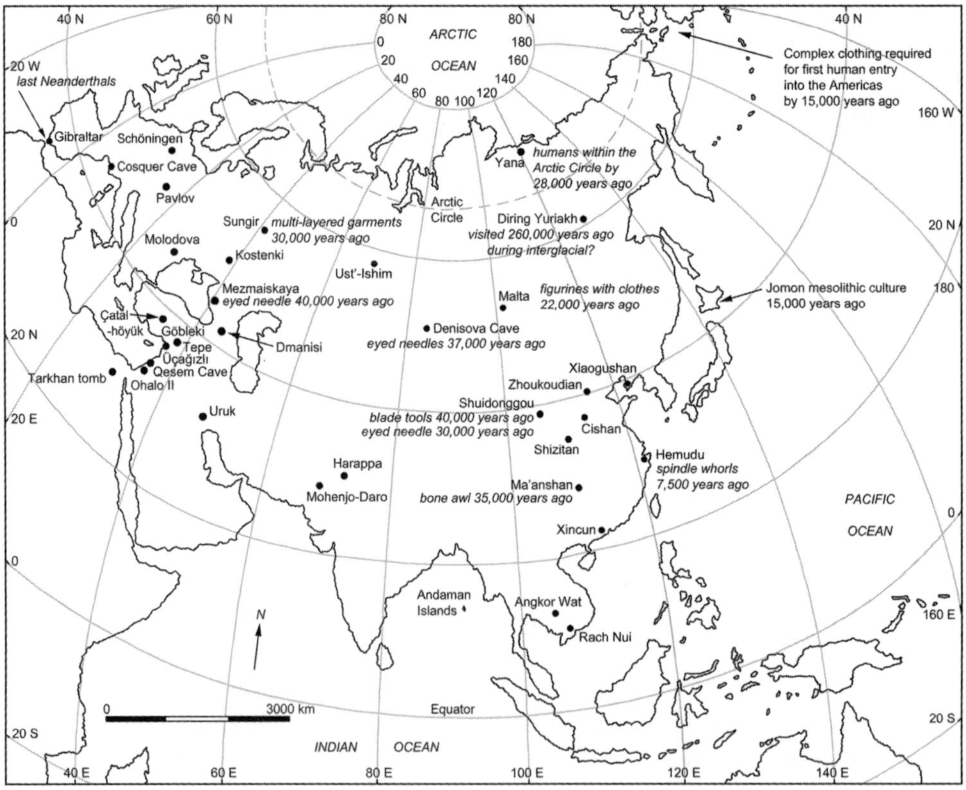

41. **Map of Eurasia**
Paleolithic clothing developments in Eurasia, with the locations of significant archaeological sites.

clothes). We can be sure of this because of what we know from the physiological data about cold tolerance in modern humans: the survival times without adequate thermal protection are measured in hours. However, there were other serious demands on humans in those environments, many of which relate to getting food.

EATING MORE TO KEEP WARM

People who live in cold environments need to eat more food than people in warm climates: to maintain higher metabolic rates to keep warm, our daily caloric requirements can rise more than 50 percent. To make matters worse during the Paleolithic, food resources in the northern environments were not always easy to extract, and the global decline in temperature and precipitation led to reduced plant food resources in many places. Hunting large mammals was one challenge, but people often needed to expand their resource base to include smaller species such as foxes and more elusive prey such as birds and fish. This involved the invention of more complex food-getting technologies – such as snares, traps, stone-tipped projectile spears, and so on. As with complex clothing, these technologies required multiple steps in their construction, and it is not clear whether earlier hominins, such as *Homo erectus* in northern China, possessed the cognitive capabilities to manufacture such complex technologies. Without complex food-getting technologies, humans would have struggled to meet their high caloric requirements in places such as the exposed land bridge that extended from northeast Asia to North America, known as Beringia. Archaeological evidence shows that the people who inhabited northeast Siberia and Beringia – and whose descendants subsequently migrated down the western shoreline of North America to become the first humans to enter the Americas – possessed complex food-getting technologies as well as complex clothes. In Alaska, at one of the earliest archaeological sites dated to 14,000 years ago, an eyed needle confirms the use of complex clothes. In addition to eyed needles, however, their survival arsenal included highly retouched stone points with stems – which would have been hafted onto wooden shafts as spearpoints – and toolkits with microblades, which probably served as barbs on projectiles. In other words, in order to occupy places like Beringia during the LGM, humans required complex technologies in general – not just complex clothes.[11]

OUT OF AFRICA WITH COMPLEX CLOTHES

Earlier evidence for complex clothing comes from the cooler parts of Africa – from South Africa mainly. And that evidence comes at a time when the global climate was getting colder – during a very cold phase (MIS4) that lasted from

75,000 to 60,000 years ago, when conditions in middle latitudes were almost as cold as the LGM. At that time, we find stone tool industries with lots of blades, and coincidentally, these toolkits also have what may be the world's earliest needles (non-eyed), made from animal bones.[12]

The current scenario suggests that some members of our species first ventured outside of Africa during the previous warm interglacial, which peaked around 125,000 years ago and was, at times, warmer than the present. They then spread into subtropical zones, arriving in southern China by 80,000 years ago. We lack any convincing evidence that they had complex clothing at that time. After the interglacial expansion, their geographical range probably contracted as the global climate cooled 75,000 years ago; the mere fact that they failed to gain a firm foothold in higher latitudes during their first foray into middle latitudes would seem to suggest they lacked complex clothing. However, it was during this next cooling phase that we find the first compelling signs of complex clothing. These appear in the cooler parts of Africa from 75,000 years ago – toolkits with scrapers, blades, and awls. Then, our species expanded its range again during the warm phase after 60,000 years ago. The toolkits containing blades disappear from southern Africa with the return of warm weather, but it seems that some of our ancestors in Africa – and in northern Africa as well – had learned how to make complex clothing by then. Presumably this was due to the intense cold around 75,000 years ago. So when the climate began to cool again around 45,000 years ago, *Homo sapiens* managed to migrate all the way into Europe and northern China – equipped with the right technologies to make complex clothing.[13]

SIX

DECORATED CLOTHES AND PALEOLITHIC ART

Archaeologists have long been perplexed by how signs of art and decoration become more frequent during the last ice age. These artistic developments also tend to show up alongside the technological signs of clothing – the blade toolkits and bone awls. To add to the mystery, decorative artifacts such as beads show a similar trend with climate – and this may be because these decorative items were often connected with clothes.[1]

LAGGING BEHIND EUROPE

In Australia, evidence for artistic capacities is present from the beginning, but the Australian evidence also reveals a problem. Although the capacities were present all along – Aborigines were using ochre pigments from the outset, presumably to decorate themselves with body painting – there is not much archaeological evidence for decoration and artwork compared to ice age Europe. There are some early decorative beads, for example, but these are few and far between. So while the capacities were obviously there, they do not show up so well in the archaeological record.[2]

Africa presents a similar challenge: some of the main signs of artistic talent and symbolic thinking – decorative items such as beads – are lacking until rather late in the picture (and they are not found widely until very late). We see the same problem with blade toolkits. It is not until around 75,000 years ago that we find blade toolkits, in southern Africa during the very cold MIS4 episode. Then these blade toolkits (called the Howiesons Poort industry) mysteriously disappear from the archaeological record 60,000 years ago, when warmer climates returned to the region. As with the blade toolkits, when we look at the bigger picture, the decorative items – and artworks to a lesser extent – are strangely delayed and restricted.[3]

DECORATION AND NAKEDNESS

Decorative and artistic talents were present all along, but these capacities were expressed mainly on the naked body. We can see this with ochre pigments used for body painting, for instance. However, when the naked body becomes covered up by clothes and less available to decorate, these artistic activities are displaced elsewhere – onto the clothes mainly. The shift away from decorating the naked skin does not happen so much with simple clothes. In that case, the garments are loose and still leave some of the skin exposed – and they are generally not worn continuously. For important ceremonial activities where decoration is indispensable, people with simple clothes can dispense with garments and still decorate their naked skin.

Simple clothing does not tend to displace body decoration onto clothes. In Tierra del Fuego, for example, the Selk'nam (or Ona) people wore guanaco cloaks as protection from the cold and wind chill. When they wanted to get dressed for ceremonial occasions, they would strip naked and paint their bodies. In other words, rather than these simple clothes being used for decoration, the garments were actually an impediment to decoration. Such clothes do not acquire decorative functions – nor lead to any sense of modesty. Even when wearing these loose cloaks draped from their shoulders, their genitals were often left on display. And to get dressed, the Selk'nam people would remove their clothes. For other important social functions such as settling disputes between the men, they removed their garments and wrestled in the nude (which, apparently, was a quite successful way of resolving disputes). With complex clothing on the other hand, the garments are harder to remove. And in a Paleolithic context, during the Pleistocene, the reason for people wearing complex clothes in the

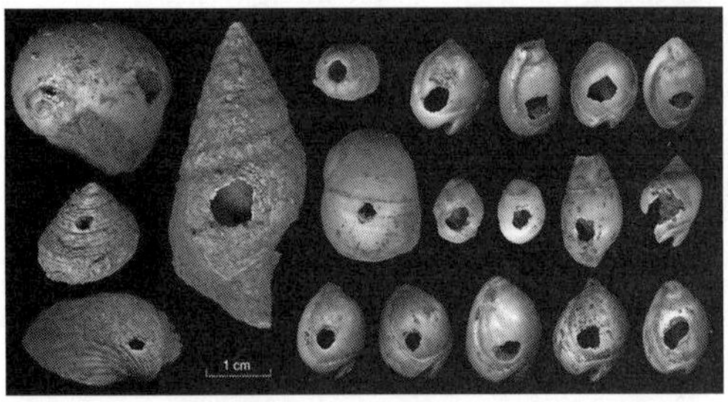

42. **Pierced shell ornaments in the Upper Paleolithic, Turkey**
Artificially perforated shell ornaments from Üçağızlı Cave I, an early Upper Paleolithic site on the southern coast of Turkey. The range of ornaments shown here spans more than 10,000 years, from 41,000 to 29,000 years ago, when the climate was becoming colder in late MIS3. Many of the shells have microscopic signs of use-polish in the perforations due to contact with cordage, pointing to their use as ornaments; some have asymmetrical cord-wear suggesting that they were hung in one position for long periods or fastened, perhaps to garments.

Source: Stiner, Kuhn and Güleç, 2013:387. © Elsevier. Reproduced under license, Elsevier.

first place was because the weather was bitterly cold – so getting dressed by painting the naked skin was no longer a viable option. Instead, people in colder regions during the last ice age got dressed by decorating their clothes.[4]

For a host of reasons, people are less likely to use the skin canvas for decoration when they have complex clothing. For one, it is often too cold – that is why they developed complex clothes in the first place. And not only is complex clothing harder to remove, but it also reduces cold tolerance and tends to create modesty. Only when complex clothing came into existence did people feel naked without it. And then there is this decorative function: once decoration is transferred onto clothing, clothing tends to become a social requisite.

Clothing and the Visibility of Decoration

Decoration of a fully clothed body has an interesting repercussion: it tends to become archaeologically visible. In contrast, painting the naked body is less visible archaeologically. We may find evidence that ochre was used (and we might suppose it was used as pigment in body paint), but there is no direct trace of the decoration. We might also find small stone tools or sharp shells that could have been used to make scars on the skin, but the evidence will usually be ambiguous. On the other hand, beads and pendants (often sewn onto the garments) can show up in the archaeological record as confirmation of decoration.

Most of the earliest beads are found in cooler regions during the last ice age, corresponding to places where complex clothing was required. As we would expect, if these items are linked to clothing, most of the evidence of decoration coincides with other evidence for complex clothing – such as bone awls

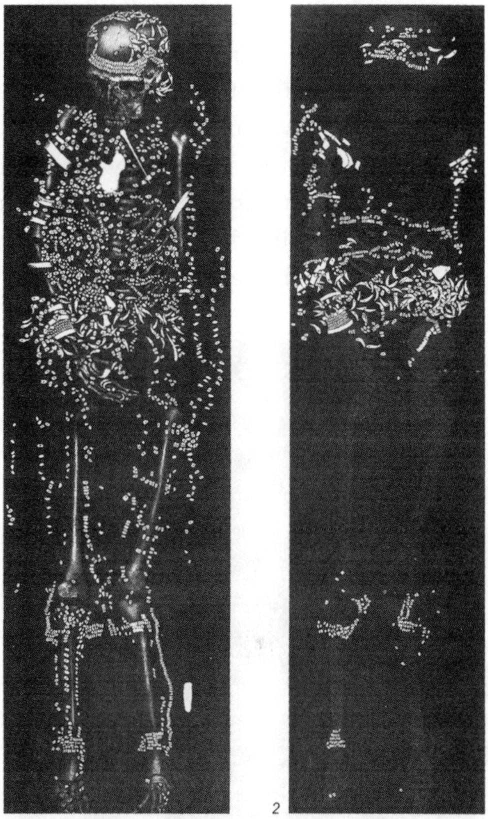

43. **Sungir burial showing underwear 30,000 years ago, Russia**
Archaeological evidence for multilayered clothing around 30,000 years ago, at the burial site of Sungir, 200 km (125 miles) east of Moscow. Three skeletons were covered with thousands of beads made from the tusks of mammoths. Shown here is one of the two skeletons in Grave 2, an adolescent boy aged around thirteen years. On the left is the distribution of beads and other adornments on top of the skeleton and at right, underneath. The arrangement of beads shows that they were sewn onto fitted garments, enclosing the limbs, and it also indicates the presence of two layers – the world's first evidence for underwear.
Source: Plate 18, Bader, 1998. Reproduced by permission of Nauchny Mir (Scientific World), Moscow.

and blade tools – and it first appears in the cooler environments. Early decorative beads appear in southern and northern Africa (and in the nearby Levant), and in Europe and northern China.[5]

Dramatic confirmation of decorated clothes occurs at the Russian site of Sungir, where thousands of beads were found on human burials that date to the latter part of MIS3. Sungir is located 200 km (125 miles) east of Moscow, where a man and two children were buried between around 35,000 and 30,000 years ago. The clothes have long since perished, but the skeletons are covered with thousands of perforated beads made of the tusk ivory from mammoths. The beads are neatly preserved in patterns that show how they were sewn onto tailored garments, such as shirts and trousers. And on each of the skeletons there are two layers of beads. So these people wore underwear – hardly surprising given how cold it was at the time. Sungir is remarkable not just because the ancient garments are rendered visible: this is the first archaeological proof of underwear.[6]

So instead of archaeological evidence that decorative talents began to develop among *Homo sapiens* after a long delay, what we really have is the delayed archaeological visibility of talents that were present from the outset. The increased visibility is related to the delayed and regionally restricted use of complex clothing; hence, the enigmatic pattern in the archaeological record. So the decorative function of clothing is rather relevant after all – not to the origin of clothing but the origin of art.

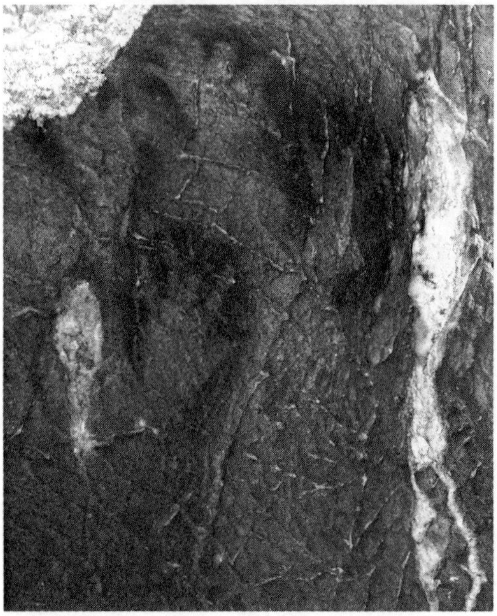

44. **27,000-year-old hand stencils in Cosquer Cave, France**

Hand stencils with shortened fingers – often called Gargas hands – are found in caves in ice age Europe. These stencils are in Cosquer Cave, France, and were made around 27,000 years ago. Archaeologists debate the cause of the shortened fingers: most favor cultural causes such as symbolism and signaling, but the patterns – with thumbs not involved – are also typical of hands affected by severe frostbite.

Source: Photo: Jean Clottes, © Jean Clottes. Reproduced by permission of Jean Clottes.

From Skin Surface to Cave Wall

Routine covering of the body surface with complex clothing will tend to displace these decorative and artistic talents not only onto clothes but further outside, into the external environment. The natural canvas for painting is the naked skin, but when this is no longer so easily accessible, then painting can shift onto other surfaces – such as cave walls.

This may be why there was an explosion of cave art in places such as France and

Spain during the coldest phases of the last ice age. The cave art signifies not some new artistic capacity that emerges in Europe but a greater emphasis on external artistic expression, favored by the loss of the naked skin canvas. Australian Aborigines would often paint their bodies to make themselves look like the animals they were hunting: there is really no difference between these painted "animals" and the painted animals seen on the walls of French caves, such as Chauvet and Lascaux. The shifting of artistic talent due to complex clothing shows up in other ways as well, such as in portable artworks like the beautiful little carved figurines – so-called Venus figurines – that appear in ice age Eurasia.[7]

As mentioned in Chapter Two, a few of these figurines actually show clothes – the earliest depictions of clothed humans – and some rock carvings depict what seem to be clothed human figures. We find other signs of ice age clothing too, such as perforated discs (sometimes decorated) that may have served as buttons. One of the rock engravings shows a human figure with a line of small circles stretching down the front that looks like a buttoned coat.

HAND STENCILS AS SIGNALS OF SOMETHING

Aside from animals such as horses and mammoths, some of the commonest artistic images from the ice age are human hands. Besides these stencils, images of humans are rather rare. A few of the hands are paintings or imprints, but the majority are outline stencils of hands made by blowing pigments around peoples' hands held up against the cave walls. Left hands far outnumber right hands, indicating that most stencils were made by right-handed individuals of their left hands – although some awkward locations suggest a second person probably helped. There are hundreds of these hand stencils in the caves of France and

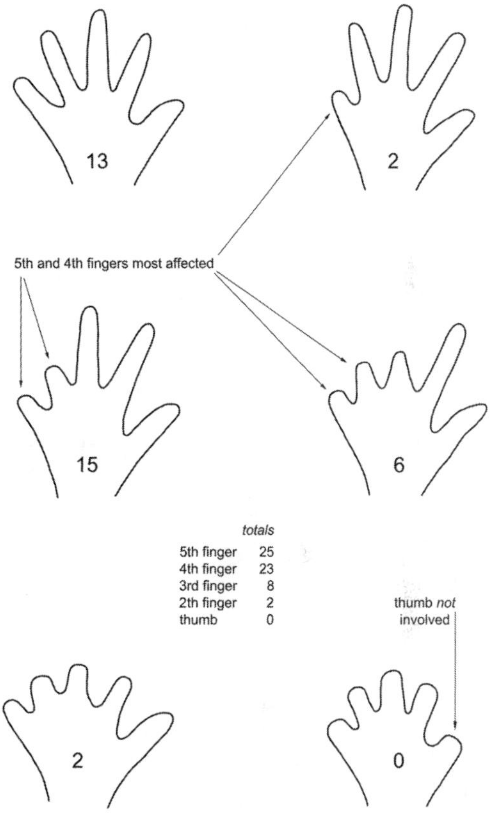

45. **Patterns of missing fingers in ice age hand stencils**
Hand stencils with shortened fingers at Cosquer Cave, France, dated to around 27,000 years ago. Numbers show the frequency of different patterns; thirteen of the hands are unaffected, and none have all five fingers involved. The pattern of missing digit segments is typical of tissue damage caused by frostbite, with the little and ring fingers most vulnerable and the thumb less susceptible.
Source: Redrawn from Clottes and Courtin, 1994:77. Original drawings by Jean Courtin, reproduced by kind permission of Jean Clottes.

Spain, and the oldest (in northern Spain) was created at least 37,000 years ago.[8]

At a few of these sites, however, the hands are quite abnormal: they have shortened fingers. Sometimes a finger appears as a mere stump, almost absent. One of the most famous sites with these abnormal hand stencils is Cosquer Cave in France. Cosquer Cave was discovered in 1985, and it is only accessible through an underwater entrance. The abnormal hand stencils are often called Gargas hands, after the Gargas Cave site in France where they were first found. Argument has surrounded these strange hand stencils for more than a century. French archaeologists tend to dismiss pragmatic causes of the stunted fingers, like frostbite. Instead, they are inclined to think that the causes are cultural: the finger patterns represent a kind of sign language, or perhaps people were practicing ritual mutilation.[9]

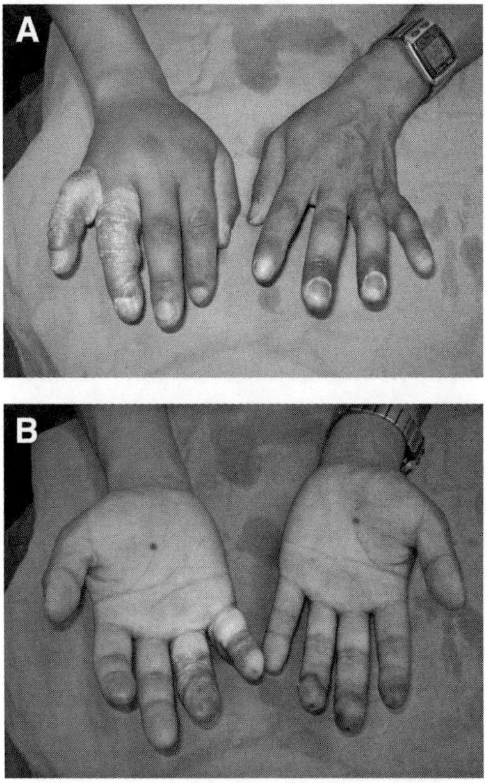

46. **Frostbite in the fingers of a Sherpa**
Frostbite in a twenty-three-year-old Sherpa man. When reaching the summit of Kanchenjunga, the world's third tallest mountain (8,586m [28,000 feet]), he removed his gloves to take photos. Note that the fifth and fourth fingers are most affected while his thumbs are not involved. With prompt hospital treatment in Kathmandu, he made a good recovery without any tissue loss, though he suffered persistent numbness in the fifth and fourth fingertips of his right hand.

Source: Subedi et al., 2010:128, © Elsevier. Reproduced under license, Elsevier.

Yet we can be quite sure that these fingers were shortened by frostbite, not bent or mutilated deliberately as part of some ancient symbolic practice or cult. The main reason is the pattern we see in the shortened fingers: it corresponds exactly to what we would expect from frostbite, and not what we should see with any cultural practices. We can also dismiss other pathological causes of shortened fingers, such as leprosy.[10]

Our fingers are not equally susceptible to frostbite. We saw earlier that one biological adaption to climate is body shape: a stocky shape is best in the cold. The reason is the ratio of surface area to volume: a slender shape has greater surface area, and so it loses heat more quickly. The thermal effect of shape applies to the limbs as well as the torso, and it applies to digits as well – toes and fingers. For this reason, slender digits are more prone to frostbite.

Consequences of finger frostbite can include amputation – either through auto-amputation (due to gangrene) or surgical amputation to remove infected digits or painful stumps. Our fingers are not shaped the same, and so some are more prone to loss from frostbite: the fifth (little) finger is most susceptible, followed usually by the fourth and third (middle). The thumb is least prone due to its stubby shape. We find the same pattern with toes: the fifth toe is most vulnerable to frostbite whereas the big toe is less often afflicted. An excellent example is the 5,300-year-old "Iceman"(also known as Ötze), discovered in the Italian Alps in 1991. He wore good shoes made of leather and stuffed with grass for added insulation, yet X-rays of his feet revealed signs of frostbite in his left fifth toe.[11]

Hands affected by severe frostbite will show a similar pattern of shortened fingers: the little finger most commonly shortened and the thumb rarely involved. And this is precisely what we see in these hand stencils: the frequencies of shortened fingers match the predicted pattern of frostbite. In all the hundreds of stencils, only a single thumb is shortened. The slender fifth finger is most commonly affected, and the thumb is spared. [12]

On the other hand, for any sign language – indeed any kind of symbolic practice – the thumb should be involved. In fact, if the fingers are being folded, the thumb can be folded completely out of view on its own – unlike the fingers. So it would be unusual (and rather too coincidental) if people in the ice age were engaging in some sort of linguistic or ritual practice without using their thumbs – unless perhaps they were mimicking the effects of frostbite. Either way, what we are seeing are signs of frostbite, not a sign language.

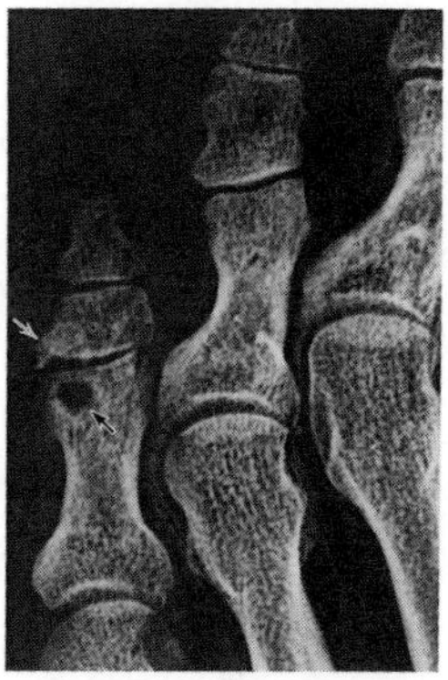

47. **Frostbite in the Iceman's left fifth toe**
X-rays revealed that, despite wearing shoes stuffed with hay for extra insulation, Otzi's left foot showed signs of frostbite (arrow). The area affected by frostbite involved the most vulnerable of his toes: the fifth.
Source: Murphy, W. A., zur Nedden, D., Gostner, P., Knapp, R., Recheis, W., & Seidler, H., The Iceman: discovery and imaging. Radiology 2003, 226: 614–629, p. 623. © Radiological Society of North America. Reproduced by permission of the Radiological Society of North America.

The other reason to blame frostbite is that we find thousands of hand stencils in other parts of the world, and not just from the ice age. In warmer parts of the world, the hand stencils are nearly always complete, even during the ice age – in Indonesia, for example. Some of the Indonesian stencils do have altered fingers as a kind of symbolic practice, but in this case the fingers are narrowed to appear slender – rather than shortened.[13]

In Australia the vast majority of hand stencils are complete with all fingers although there are a few hand stencils with shortened or missing fingers. Aborigines did sometimes bend their fingers as a kind of "sign language," but the patterns in Australia are quite different to the European stencils. Sometimes a foggy outline is visible where the fingers have been folded because the bent digit is raised from the rock surface, leading to "underspray" – and this fogging is less apparent with the European stencils. And as expected with any sign language, in the Australian stencils with missing digits, the thumb is often missing too.[14]

48. **Slender fingers in hand stencils, Indonesia** Hand stencils in the tropics sometimes depict abnormal shapes, but not the shortened fingers seen with the Gargas hands. In Southeast Asia, hand stencils occur from 40,000 years ago (and into the Holocene). And some have artificially narrowed fingers, as seen with the stencil on the right here, at Leang Sassang on the island of Sulawesi, Indonesia. *Source:* Oktaviana et al, 2016, *Rock Art Research* 33:34. Photo: David Bulbeck. Reproduced by permission of Robert G. Bednarik and David Bulbeck.

With the European hand stencils, the question arises as to why frostbite should be a problem if people had complex clothing – which presumably would include gloves. There are a couple of reasons why frostbite was still a big risk in these environments. One is that gloves are more practical and effective when made from woven textiles rather than from animal skins or leather – and Paleolithic clothes were not made from woven fibers. Another reason is the physiology of clothing. Gloves have separate cylinders that cover the fingers, but these provide only modest insulation because of the limited amount of trapped air. And once this air is heated to body temperature, a glove can have the paradoxical effect of reducing insulation since it effectively increases the surface area. The problem does not arise for large cylinders such as the limbs and torso, where the difference in surface area is relatively less and the amount of trapped air is much greater. For this reason, mittens are more effective than gloves, but they compromise dexterity. Many activities will require mittens or gloves to be removed, however briefly – exposing the fingers to frostbite. Experiments show just how quickly this can happen: at an air temperature of −15°C (5°F) and a wind speed of 40 km/hr (25 mph), most people will develop symptoms of frostbite within thirty minutes. And while frostbite is rarely lethal, we depend heavily on our hands and fingers. Ever since our early hominin ancestors adopted an upright posture, freeing our hands to manipulate objects and make stone tools, any damage to the fingers – or loss of fingertips, let alone whole fingers – would have compromised survival prospects. During the Pleistocene, people needed their fingers to make the tools to hunt animals and also to make the clothes that protected them from hypothermia – so frostbite affecting the fingers would have been a serious handicap.[15]

SEVEN

NEANDERTHALS AND TASMANIANS

The roles of climate and clothing in promoting technological innovation during the latter part of the Pleistocene can be illustrated by comparing what happened in two widely separated parts of the world. First, we shall look at Europe and, in particular, how Neanderthals coped – and in the end, did not cope – with climate change. Then, we shall move right around to the other side of the world, to a remote place at the southern edge of the Australian continent. In Tasmania, we find some unexpected technological developments in a region that has traditionally been considered the most backward corner of the world.

NEANDERTHALS ON THE VERGE

The limitations of clothing in ice age climates could be relevant to one of archaeology's great debates: why did the Neanderthals go extinct? The possible role of clothing and climate change in their demise has only recently been considered, and it serves to illustrate the value of making a distinction between simple and complex clothing.[1]

Before we bravely broach this topic, the first question to ask is whether Neanderthals wore any clothes at all.

Did Neanderthals Wear Clothes?

We can only guess whether Neanderthals were much hairier than *Homo sapiens*, but in any case, their skeletons suggest that they were better adapted physically to life in cold conditions. Although nothing is known about possible physiological adaptations, such as higher metabolic rates or changes in blood circulation to various parts of their anatomy to reduce the risk of frostbite, their skeletons alone suggest that they would have fared better than us. Neanderthal body shape was quite stocky, and their limb proportions were typical of cold-adapted populations. And their high muscle mass would have afforded some extra protection too.[2]

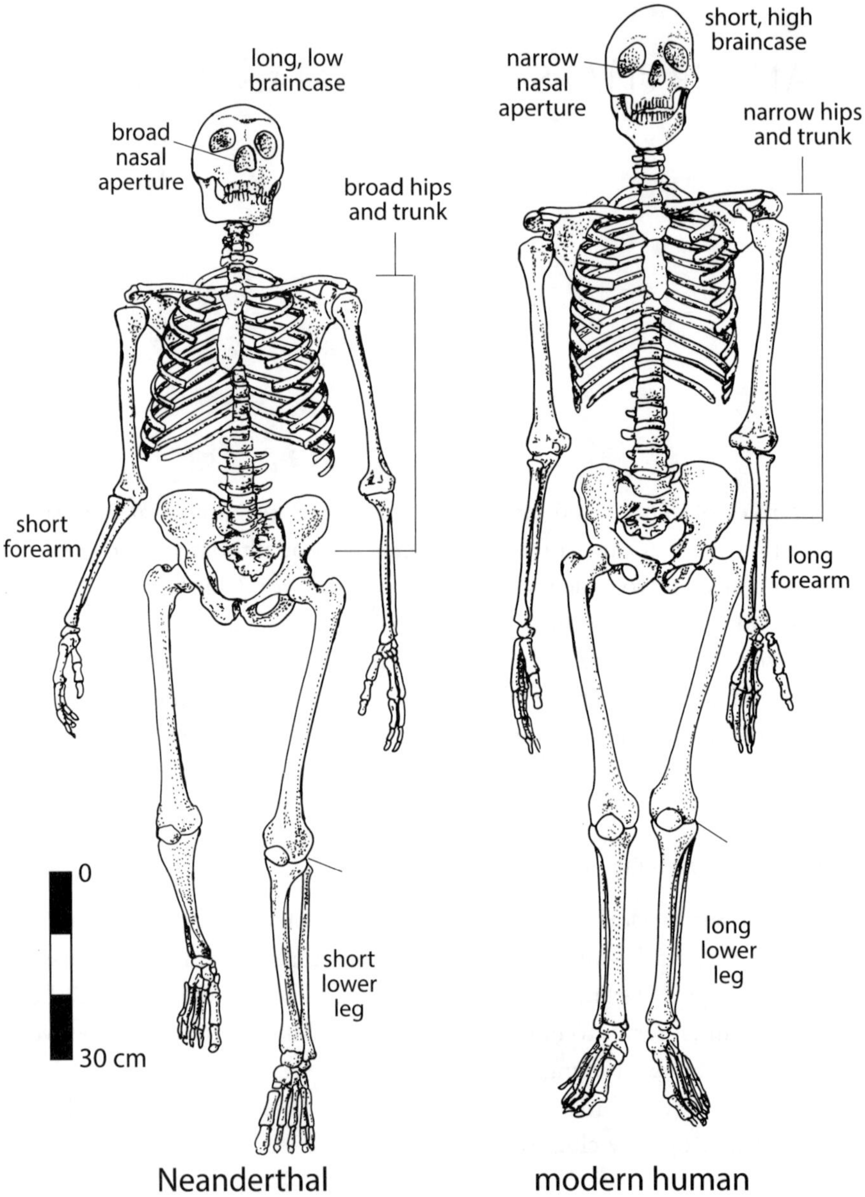

49. **Neanderthal and modern human skeletons**
Comparison of Neanderthal and modern human skeletons. The stocky body-build and shorter limb segments of Neanderthals reflect adaptation to cold climates, reducing their need for clothing.
Source: Klein, 2009:448. Drawing by Kathryn Cruz-Uribe. Reproduced by permission of University of Chicago Press, Kathryn Cruz-Uribe and Richard Klein.

With regard to clothes, archaeology tells us two things. The first is that while Neanderthals thrived in Europe during a series of ice ages, it would seem that they could not cope with extremely cold weather. The pattern of their living sites shows how they were restricted to milder climates: they avoided the northern zones, and their geographical range shrank southward during the colder phases.[3]

The second clue about Neanderthal clothing is technology: their classic toolkits were full of scrapers, with few blades and no bone tools. It is fair to say Neanderthals specialized in scraper technology, and use-wear studies show how these tools were often used on animal hides. These two things – their failure to penetrate colder environments and their scraper toolkits – point to them having clothes, but only of the simple kind.[4]

Neanderthals and Simple Clothing

Climate reconstructions indicate that simple clothing – which typically provides around 1–2 clo of insulation – would have been needed by Neanderthals during the winters, even if they possessed some physical adaptations to cold. Their stocky body-build may have made only a slight difference – some studies suggest that it would have improved their level of cold tolerance by only a few degrees Celsius.[5]

The northern limit of the Neanderthal world corresponds to winter temperatures where complex clothing would have been required, even with a cold-adapted physique. In regions where the average winter wind chill levels fell much below −10°C (15°F), fitted garments and multiple layers would have been mandatory for any hominins to survive the likely extremes.[6]

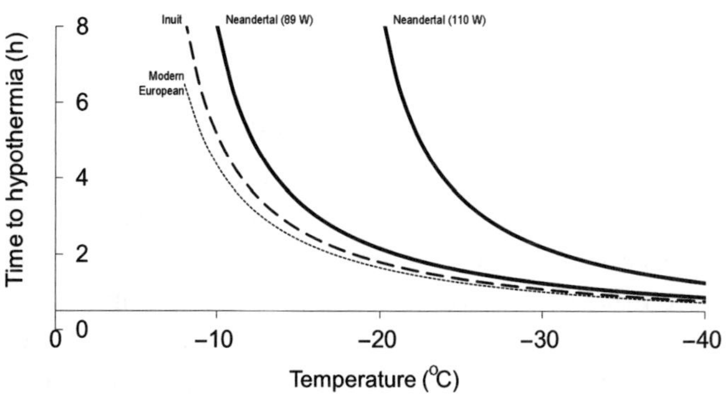

50. **Limitations of Neanderthal cold tolerance**
Time to hypothermia for Neanderthals with simple clothing (providing around 2 clo of insulation). Due to superior physical cold adaptations, Neanderthals had an advantage over modern humans, shown here using two estimates of body heat production (low and high basal metabolic rates, Europeans and Inuit). The Neanderthal advantage diminishes as the ambient temperature falls below -20°C, where survival times without complex clothes are similarly short for Neanderthals and modern humans.

Source: Churchill, 2014: 147. Reproduced with permission of John Wiley and Sons, and courtesy of Steven Churchill.

A lack of complex clothing is suggested also by the Neanderthal physique. Their stocky build implies that they still experienced a considerable degree of cold stress – which would be the case if they relied on simple clothes.[7]

Why did Neanderthals not invent complex clothing? The answer might lie in their better ability to cope physically with moderate cold. Their superior physical adaptations meant they could get by with simple draped garments. As long as they were happy to stay within their comfort zone – and to move north and south with the pulsing ice age cycles – then they had no need to bother with all the toil of tailoring complex clothes. Manufacturing fitted garments with sleeves and legs is a much more tedious and time-consuming task than simply preparing a hide to wear as a loose cloak. The failure of Neanderthals to invent complex clothes does not mean they were stupid or lazy: they were simply well-adapted to their local environments – and they had plenty of room to move around as the weather changed. Indeed, they had a whole continent to themselves.

Climate Change and Neanderthal Extinction

But the weather changed, and it changed dramatically. From 50,000 years ago, not only did the world get cold again, but the climate also became very unstable, and there were a succession of unusually swift and massive swings between mild and very cold conditions.

What is most unusual is that these swings were so sudden. As mentioned earlier, some of the swings happened more rapidly than we can detect with the current climate proxies. A few of the climate swings (called Heinrich events) occurred not on a millennial scale but on a centennial scale. In fact, some climatologists say that the initial cooling during these episodes could have occurred over a decade, or even less. Heinrich events were precipitated when huge numbers of icebergs broke away from the expanded northern ice cap. As all of the icebergs drifted south and slowly melted in the already cold waters of the North Atlantic, they caused a sudden chilling right across Europe.

Heinrich events were not the only climate swings: climate scientists can now count at least five full-scale swings in the European climate between 50,000 and 40,000 years ago. To make matters worse, the temperatures dropped more in winter than in summer, to judge from data at a site near Barcelona. One of the Heinrich events (H5) happened around 46,000 years ago, and another (H4) was very abrupt and struck Europe 40,000 years ago – which is when Neanderthals finally went extinct.[8]

Besides cold temperatures, the other stress for Neanderthals was wind chill: these climate swings were associated with stronger winds. Various wind proxies (such as dust records) indicate higher average wind velocities in the northern hemisphere during the latter part of MIS3. In the southern hemisphere, a detailed dust record shows that the strongest average winds of the past 200,000 years are found between 45,000 and 40,000 years ago. Wind chill was especially marked in the northern hemisphere, when Heinrich events were accompanied by intensified northwesterly winds that brought icy temperatures down from the Arctic zone.[9]

These climate spikes would have been lethal for any hominins in Europe without complex clothing.

Running Out of Room

How did Neanderthals react? They probably did what they usually did and retreated to warmer climates in the south – although this time they had to move faster and further. Their populations became thinner on the ground as they departed their northern territories – which is exactly the pattern we would see with hypothermia: groups of healthy individuals could just disappear overnight. But their southward retreat ran into a couple of barriers this time.

In the southeast, they ran into *Homo sapiens*. During previous oscillations in climate, as Neanderthals moved south into the Middle East during the colder phases, our ancestors had politely moved further south in response to the colder conditions, making room there for Neanderthals. But this time our ancestors did not move south: if anything, they were starting to spread northwards. The new response to climate change was down to the fact that our ancestors had already invented complex clothing, which we can surmise from their toolkits, which had plenty of blade tools and bone awls. So not only were our ancestors better prepared for the sudden onset of cold weather, but they also were perhaps less prepared to make way for Neanderthals.[10]

In the southwest, Neanderthals came up against another barrier: Gibraltar. The last sites occupied by Neanderthals are found in the caves of Gibraltar, in the southwest corner of their world. It is almost as though they ran out of room or fell off the edge of their world. Did they fall, or were they pushed?

There is a tendency to discount a direct role of cold in the demise of Neanderthals. Instead, we are inclined to blame competition from incoming *Homo sapiens*. Perhaps this scenario appeals to our sense of superiority. Yet throughout much of Western Europe, there is no convincing archaeological evidence for any sustained contact between retreating Neanderthals and incoming *Homo sapiens*. At sites where the two species followed each other, there is often a gap of maybe one or two millennia. Unfortunately, this critical period when Neanderthals disappeared is close to the limit of radiocarbon dating, and a lack of fine resolution applies also with the climate data – it is hard to match sites precisely with the climate swings.

The available data suggest our ancestors moved in after Neanderthals had vacated the premises. An absence of direct competition is consistent with what we know about previous interactions between the species: there was not aggressive competition or violence, but rather they were good neighbors. Genetic studies confirm that there was interbreeding (which started before *Homo sapiens* colonized Europe), and we also have anatomical evidence for interbreeding from a child burial in Portugal. The skeleton is no older than 25,000 years – long after Neanderthals had disappeared – but while it belongs to *Homo sapiens*, there are some hybrid anatomical features pointing to Neanderthal ancestry.[11]

The conventional scenario of Neanderthals being pushed over the edge by invading *Homo sapiens* neglects the likely role of clothing – and neglects also the limitations of Neanderthals' simple, loose garments. It probably reflects a little arrogance on our part too, and both these factors could have been involved: cold stress and competition from incoming *Homo sapiens*. In the conventional account, however, it is unclear how blade and bone tools gave our ancestors any great advantage over Neanderthals as hunter-gatherers. Yet the technological connection with complex clothing gave *Homo sapiens* a big advantage in terms of survival. Tailored, multilayered garments also allowed them to spend more time out in the open, increasing their mobility in the cold and expanding their territorial ranges compared to Neanderthals. And once our ancestors managed to enter Europe and Central Asia, they could spread further into the frigid north – further than Neanderthals had ever been able to venture during the height of an ice age.

Modern at the Last Minute

Another clue about the role of clothing in the demise of Neanderthals is a recent revelation about our cousins. Archaeologists have discovered that Neanderthals did in fact develop a blade and bone tool industry. This industry appeared in France by around 45,000 years ago, and it is called the Châtelperronian industry. For many years, archaeologists presumed these technologies were a product of incoming *Homo sapiens* – although no fossils of either species had been found at the sites. Then, to everyone's surprise, skeletal remains of Neanderthals were found with the blade and bone tools at a couple of sites, which seems to prove that these blades and bone tools (including bone awls) were actually made by Neanderthals.[12]

Arguments continue to rage about why Neanderthals began to make these new tools. Some archaeologists doubt that Neanderthals invented them on their own: they say the tools were acquired or copied from *Homo sapiens*. The jury is still out on this question. However, some bone tools that were evidently used on hides have now been found at a couple of Neanderthal sites that are dated to between 51,000 and 42,000 years ago – before any *Homo sapiens* entered Western Europe. So it looks like Neanderthals started to use bone tools to make better clothes on their own, before our ancestors arrived in the region.[13]

51. **Neanderthals caught in a blizzard**

Between 50,000 and 40,000 years ago, Neanderthals in Europe were confronted by sudden, severe cold snaps. Around the same time, they adopted new tools (such as blades and bone awls) that would have helped them to manufacture complex garments. In this painting, the individual on the left is shown wearing tailored trousers – artistic license perhaps, but it could be quite realistic.

Source: Charles R. Knight, Snowbound (1911). Collection of Staten Island Museum. Reproduced courtesy of Staten Island Museum, New York City.

Another thing that causes so much heated argument is not only that the new industry has blades and bone awls, it contains ornaments like perforated beads – signs of decorative art. So there is a lot at stake: the Châtelperronian industry implies that Neanderthals had the same artistic talents that we tend to regard as a prerogative of *Homo sapiens*.

Physical Inferiority and Technological Superiority

The discovery of blade and bone tools at a few late Neanderthal sites means that in the context of severe cold stress, some Neanderthals did begin to make complex clothes. There is really no reason why they should not have done so. Indeed, they began to make complex clothes for the very same reasons we did – only in our case, we did it sooner because we were more susceptible to cold. Our ancestors started to develop this sophisticated technology earlier in the cooler southern and northern zones of Africa. By the time of the big sudden swings in climate, our ancestors were already familiar and proficient with making complex clothes. In effect, *Homo sapiens* were preadapted: with fitted garments, they had a superior clothing technology that was more effective and flexible. They could add extra layers and so easily increase the level of insulation when required. Archaeologists have found this blade technology extending along the southeast fringe of Europe between 50,000 and 40,000 years ago, throughout the area that extends from Israel through Lebanon and Syria into Turkey. Similar blade industries occur all the way across southern Eurasia, from southeast Russia into the Balkans, further across into Central Asia and southern Siberia, and ultimately even into northern China. Although skeletal remains of modern humans are generally lacking at most of these sites, it appears that scraper industries associated mainly with Neanderthals were replaced by blade industries that were probably produced by *Homo sapiens*.[14]

In the case of Neanderthals, this technological advance was delayed because they did not need it until around 45,000–40,000 years ago. And perhaps another thing that conspired against Neanderthals at the time was the extreme instability of the climate. The brief cold spikes were certainly very severe, but each was soon followed by a sudden return to warm conditions. From 50,000 to 40,000 years ago, there were no fewer than five of these rapid warming episodes, each taking no more than 200 years, and each witnessing a massive rise in mean temperature – between 8°C and 15°C (15°F and 30°F).[15]

The repeated return of warm conditions may have discouraged a sustained acquisition of complex clothing among Neanderthal populations. No sooner were Neanderthals trying to adapt to freezing cold than the weather got warm again. Either way, it was a case of too little, too late.

Complex Clothing and Neanderthals

The other intriguing aspect of the Neanderthal experiment with complex clothing is how it seems to be associated with decorated artifacts. At some sites, ornaments found in the underlying Neanderthal levels may have been shifted down from higher levels, so the ornaments might have been made by later modern humans. However, this mixing of artifacts from younger to older layers is less likely to be the case at other sites where the ornaments are found with Neanderthal remains. So it looks like Neanderthals were starting to transfer adornment of their bodies onto their clothes, which is really no surprise: they had been using colored ochre for a long time, presumably for body decoration.[16]

When Neanderthals started to wear complex clothes, they enclosed their bodies more fully with fitted garments, and these garments then inherited this decorative function. Complex garments made the decoration more visible in the archaeological record – as sewn beads and pendants, for instance. And for the same reason (a displacement of art from the skin surface to external surfaces), we begin to see some cave art with Neanderthals toward the end: archaeologists have found engravings on walls in one of the Gibraltar caves.[17]

Even if Neanderthals acquired these new tools and ornaments from incoming *Homo sapiens*, it still begs the question of why they suddenly found it so useful to make these particular implements at that time. Even if the technology was borrowed and the decorative items really belonged to modern humans, there is little doubt that some of the blade tools were manufactured by Neanderthals. Why did they bother? And if the decorative artifacts are indeed theirs, why did they suddenly develop a talent for decoration? In reality, they had this capacity all along but, as happened with our own species, their decorative talents became more visible in the archaeological record with the advent of complex clothing – which coincided with climate change.

TASMANIANS ON THE VERGE

On the other side of the world, soon after Neanderthals went extinct in Europe, some Aborigines in Australia walked across an exposed land bridge to Tasmania around 35,000 years ago – and so became the most southerly human population in the world at the time. The climate then was not as cold as it was in Europe, but it was still getting too cold for people to manage without any clothes. As the Australian archaeologist Richard Cosgrove says, what happened in Tasmania bears some remarkable similarities to what happened with Neanderthals and their technologies in Europe – and he is not the only one to point out the parallels. These similarities in behavior and technological innovation at two extreme ends of the human world demand an explanation – they seem too striking to be a coincidence.[18]

Ice Age Developments in the South

As the climate got colder, the Tasmanians began to visit highland caves in the rugged southwest during the winters. Their behavior at the time is quite a mystery, even a paradox: as the climate got colder, they gravitated toward a colder (higher) latitude and to a colder (higher) altitude – and they did this in the coldest season. Why would they do such an odd thing? The answer lies in the fact that the highlands have many deep valleys and natural caves that offered refuge from the wind. So despite cooler air temperatures in the highlands, the effective temperatures there were actually a little warmer because the valleys and caves were protected from wind chill.[19]

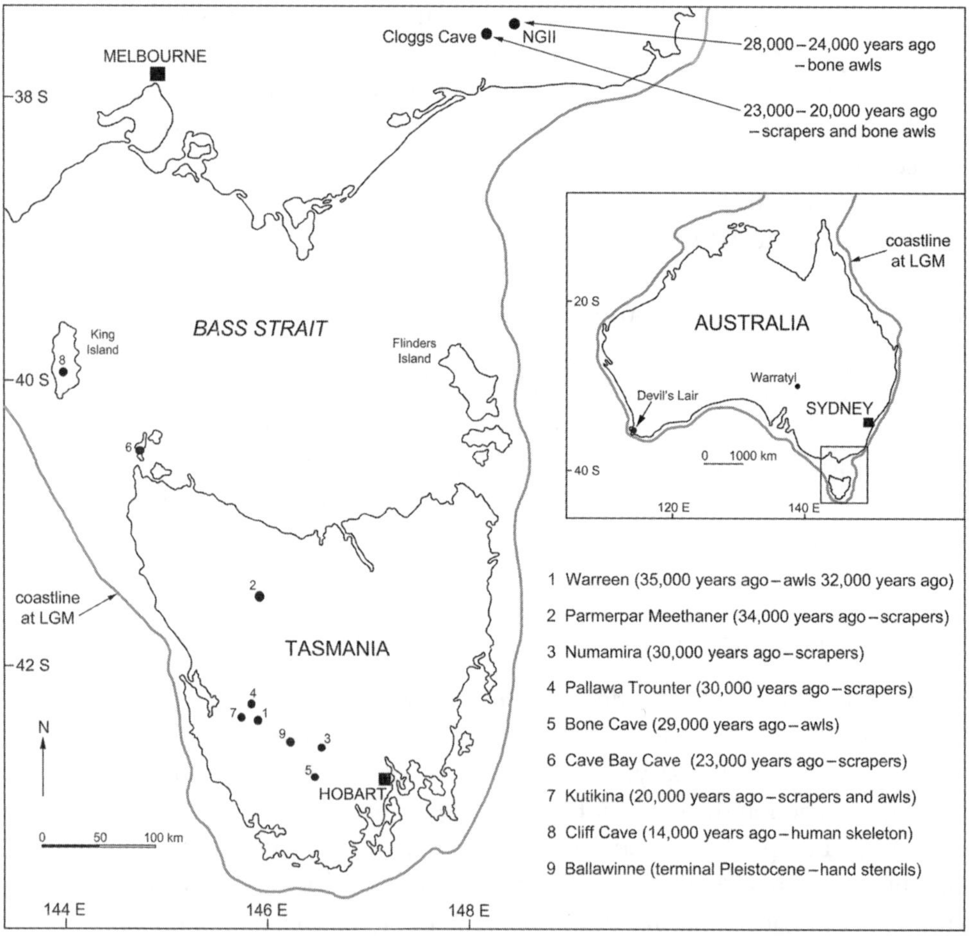

52. **Map of Tasmanian region**
Tasmania and the adjacent southern mainland of Australia, showing the extended coastline during the LGM when sea levels were lower and Tasmania was joined to the mainland. Locations of key archaeological sites are shown with approximate dates for early technologies that may relate to the development of clothing.

More surprising, in those caves archaeologists have found heaps of carefully crafted stone scraper tools. Like Neanderthals – but unlike Aborigines elsewhere – the Tasmanians specialized in making hide-scrapers. They specialized also in hunting furry animals – namely wallabies. Yet their technology differed in one key way from the typical Neanderthal toolkit: the Tasmanians also manufactured bone tools. These bone points were likely used as spearpoints to hunt the wallabies and also as sewing awls to pierce holes in the wallaby skins. A use-wear study has shown that the points have polish at the tips indicating how they were used as awls as well as spears, and the scrapers too were used for various purposes, including hide-working.[20]

53. **Valleys and caves in southwest Tasmania**
Valleys and caves in the rugged southwest of Tasmania offered shelter from wind chill during the last ice age. In many of the caves, archaeologists have found huge numbers of stone hide-scraper tools and also awls made from wallaby bones, suggesting ice age Tasmanians were making more substantial clothes. Shown is a view of the Gordon River from atop the Gordon Dam, looking west-southwest.
Source: Photo by the author, © Ian Gilligan.

So it looks like the Tasmanians were sewing the small wallaby hides together to make bigger and better clothes. But whereas bone awls were connected with complex clothes in the colder climates of Europe, in Tasmania these awls do not signify complex clothing. There was a different need for the awls in Tasmania: whereas in Europe humans could hunt lots of large furry animals, the largest animal species available to the Tasmanians was the little wallaby – too small to make a decent cloak.

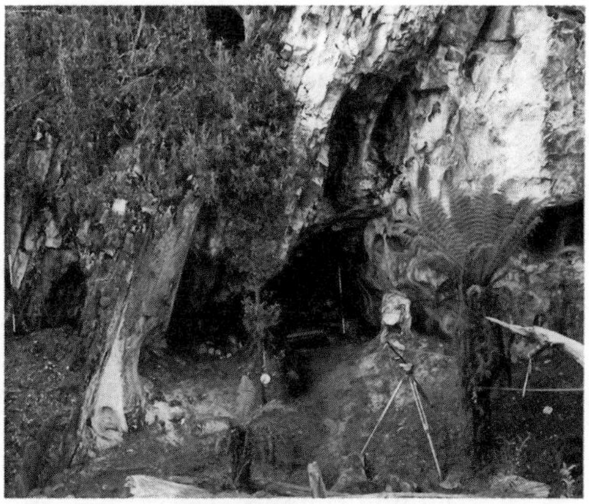

54. **Numamira Cave entrance, Tasmania**
Entrance to Nunamira Cave, southwest Tasmania, showing the excavation in 1988 led by archaeologist Richard Cosgrove. Nunamira is one of many caves in the region with stone scraper tools. At Nunamira Cave, the scrapers date from around 30,000 years ago during the last ice age.
Source: Photo by Richard Cosgrove, © Richard Cosgrove. Reproduced by permission of Richard Cosgrove.

Simple Clothing with Bone Needles

While Neanderthals were beginning to use bone awls to make complex clothes, the Tasmanians invented this new technology to make simple cloaks. In both cases, this need for sewing arose as the climate got colder. And just as we start to see decoration and artwork among Neanderthals, we begin to find some cave art in Tasmania – hand stencils as it

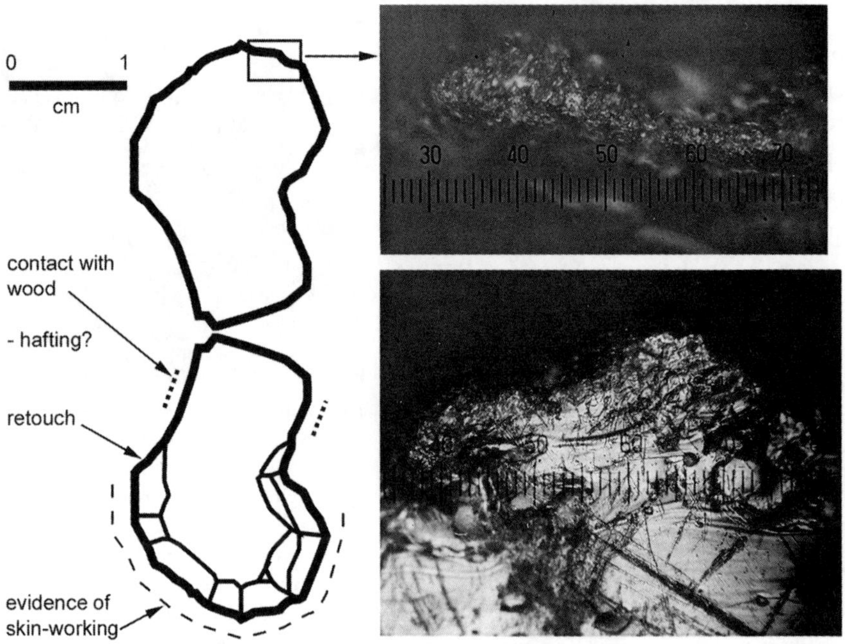

55. **Use-wear showing hide-working traces on Tasmanian tool**
Kutikina Artefact FCF81 A3SW 10, a Darwin Glass bipolar flake, showing retouch and use-wear (dashed line), and zones of use-polish that suggests contact with wood, possibly from hafting (dotted line). The rectangle indicates the location of use-wear micrographs to the right. The upper image (end-view) shows marked edge-rounding and abrasive smoothing indicative of skin-working. The lower image (plan-view) shows the used edge with striations and edge-rounding.
Source: Images and drawing: Richard Fullagar, © Richard Fullagar. Reproduced by permission of Richard Fullagar.

happens (but without any missing fingertips). As Cosgrove points out though, despite all of these new developments in ice age Tasmania, there are no blade tools.[21]

Clothing makes this easy to explain. In Europe, the bone tools are found together with blades because both technologies were connected with complex clothing (among *Homo sapiens* and with some Neanderthals toward the end). In Tasmania, however, the bone tools were needed only for simple clothes – hence, no need for blades.

Revealing the Role of Clothing

Neanderthals and Tasmanians illustrate how the technology of clothing can shed light on the technological innovations we see in the archaeological record – and why these occur with climate change. Both Neanderthals and Tasmanians specialized in scraper technology in cold climates, and they both invented bone tools as the climate got colder. Whereas Tasmanians needed these needles to make cloaks from small animal skins, Neanderthals had access to large animal hides but they needed bone tools and blades to tailor complex clothes. So with Neanderthals, the sewing tools occurred with blades.

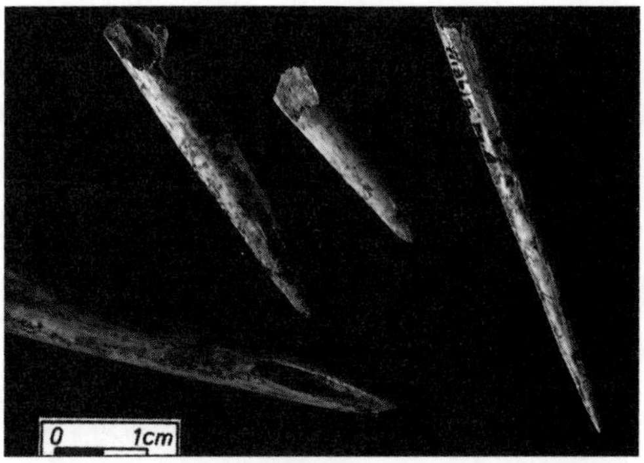

56. **Bone awls from Warreen Cave, Tasmania** Points made on wallaby bones excavated at Warreen Cave, southwest Tasmania, dating from around 32,000 years ago during the last ice age. Use-wear studies on similar bone points at another cave show traces consistent with hide-piercing and polish. This finding suggests the points functioned as awls to pierce holes in wallaby skins and to make large cloaks as protection from the cold and wind chill.

Source: Photo by Richard Cosgrove, © Richard Cosgrove. Reproduced by permission of Richard Cosgrove.

Another parallel between Neanderthals and Tasmanian Aborigines is how they both managed to cope with cold climates by wearing less clothing than their neighbors. In the case of Neanderthals, the evidence suggests they wore simpler garments than their *Homo sapiens* neighbors who had tailored and layered garments. At the time when Europeans landed in Australia, the Tasmanians too were wearing less protection than their Aboriginal neighbors on the southern mainland, where Aborigines availed themselves of large kangaroo skins and heavy possum-fur cloaks when required. Yet despite the colder (and windier) weather further south in Tasmania, the Tasmanians were generally naked, and they only sometimes wore a small wallaby skin around their shoulders. In both cases, the reason may relate to people in cold climates developing better biological adaptations to cold. Neanderthals for instance had a stockier body-build, and the same may be true for Tasmanians, although the skeletal evidence is scanty. Nonetheless, the available skeletal evidence for Tasmanian Aborigines suggests a stockier build than Aborigines on the mainland. And as applies with Neanderthals, their long ancestry in a cooler climate – and a prolonged period of isolation that would have promoted genetic changes in their population under selection pressure for cold adaptations – probably led to enhanced metabolic and other physiological adjustments. As a result, just like Neanderthals, the Tasmanians' physical need for clothes was likely to be less than that of their neighbors on the mainland.[22]

As colder weather closed in upon them, both Neanderthals and Tasmanians were on the verge of taking the extra step to making complex clothes. A slow response on the part of Neanderthals was down to their natural resilience, but then they were caught off guard by severe cold shocks in the climate – and their ultimate demise might have been hastened by the arrival of *Homo sapiens*. Our ancestors, with their tropical bodies, had a greater need for the added protection afforded by complex clothes, and so they were technologically prepared for the worst weather. On the other hand, after they developed better clothes in the LGM, Tasmanians were confronted by the opposite challenge faced by Neanderthals: global warming. After the ice age, the Tasmanians could drop their clothes altogether and stop making bone tools – because in the milder climates of the southern hemisphere, even during the ice age, they had never needed complex clothes.[23]

EIGHT

THE VALUE OF MAKING CLOTHES VISIBLE

Paleolithic clothing is far from invisible. Once we recognize its thermal origins and make the technological connection with tools such as scrapers, blades and needles, its origins and development can be rendered quite visible. And when we make the distinction between simple and complex clothing, we can disentangle the archaeological patterns and see why these patterns were associated with past climate change.

Before moving on to see what happened after the ice age, this chapter summarizes what can be said about the origin of clothing.

SCRAPERS AND THE ORIGIN OF SIMPLE CLOTHING

Simple clothing had its origins early in the Pleistocene and was used at different times by a number of hominin species, even before Neanderthals. Simple garments such as capes would probably have been used, for instance, by *Homo erectus* (Peking Man) in northern China 800,000 years ago. In terms of technology, the earliest draped animal skins would have been prepared with flake tools, and this rudimentary kind of clothing probably goes back more than a million years. When these garments were used on a more regular basis, we see an increasing presence of scraper tools. The main trend emerges following a prolonged and very warm interglacial (MIS11) around 400,000 years ago. From that time onwards, we find toolkits with well-made scrapers, especially in cooler regions and more so during the glacial periods. These toolkits became common in northern middle latitudes, notably with the Mousterian toolkits of Neanderthals. We do not see these scraper toolkits in warmer regions such as Southeast Asia and Australia – with the interesting exception of Tasmania.

Simple clothing would have been discarded when not required for warmth. Simple clothing did not lead to modesty, and nor did it lead to other motives for wearing clothes. Since the naked body was not so completely covered, the human desire to decorate our visible surface was not transferred from the skin surface onto the surface of clothing. For this reason, simple clothing was not linked so reliably with decorative artifacts such as perforated beads and pendants. Nor was simple clothing associated routinely with bone tools –with the notable exception of, again, Tasmania.

BLADES AND THE ORIGIN OF COMPLEX CLOTHING

Blades and bone awls were the Paleolithic tools most useful for making complex clothes. Blades helped with cutting the hides into precise geometric shapes, so they could be fitted properly onto the body, and bone tools such as awls and needles helped with sewing the pieces carefully together. When we look at the archaeological record, we find that toolkits with lots of blades start to appear in cooler parts of the world following that long interglacial 400,000 years ago. The very first blades are found earlier in Africa around 500,000 years ago (possibly during the MIS14 glacial) in the highlands of western Kenya.[1]

Toolkits with more blades show up in in the Middle East from 300,000 years ago during the MIS8 glacial. Blade toolkits later spread into Europe with *Homo sapiens* and into northern China and Siberia during the coldest part of the last glacial cycle from 40,000 years ago.

Bone tools were first used by hominins in South Africa more than a million years ago, apparently to dig into roots or termite mounds. However, the systematic production of bone implements in toolkits occurs much later, among *Homo sapiens* in South Africa. These awls and spearpoints appear in archaeological deposits after the last interglacial from around 100,000 years ago, and bone awls become more common during the MIS4 cold episode around 75,000 years ago.[2]

The South African toolkits with bone awls also have blade tools, and it is these toolkits with both blades and bone awls that provide the best early archaeological evidence for complex clothing. It is true that some stone tools with pointed ends could have functioned as awls to pierce hides, although these would have been fairly clumsy tools for accurately piercing lots of holes in the smaller hide pieces required to make sleeves and leggings in complex garments – let alone the finer sewing needed for making undergarments. If we allow for this possibility (stone points used as awls), then the convergence of awls and blades would be less well-defined: it could extend back into the last few ice ages from 300,000 years ago. If, however, we restrict the routine production of complex clothing to the confluence of blade tools with bone awls, then its origins are better constrained to a time early in the last ice age, beginning from 120,000 years ago.

BODY LICE AND THE ORIGIN OF CLOTHING

A new line of evidence about the origin of clothing is the genetic analysis of body lice – or as they are often called, clothing lice. These little insects occupy an unusual ecological niche: they live mainly on clothes and they jump onto humans to feed on our blood. Body lice have sometimes been preserved in textiles at archaeological sites; one of the oldest is a woolen fabric with lice from 3,500 years ago, found at a Bronze Age salt mine in Austria.[3]

Aside from causing skin irritation, body lice can carry microorganisms that cause serious diseases, such as epidemic typhus, trench fever and louse-borne relapsing fever. Historically, these diseases have been associated with overcrowding, poor sanitation, and trench warfare. While becoming less prevalent since the advent of antibiotics and effective louse control measures, these diseases continue to affect homeless people and have recently resurged in refugee camps.[4]

Since clothing lice depend largely on the presence of clothes, the time when clothing lice split from head lice might serve as a way of discovering the date for the origin of clothing. It is not clear, though, whether the genetic study of body lice refers specifically to complex clothing – lice can survive on blankets and rugs that frequently come into contact with human skin. They can also survive on simple clothes when these loose garments are worn on a regular basis – which probably happened many times over the last million years. So the split of clothing and head lice should relate, at least, to the continuous use of blankets or simple garments, and perhaps complex clothes. Either way, the lice studies can give us another angle on the subject of clothing origins. A research team in Florida led by

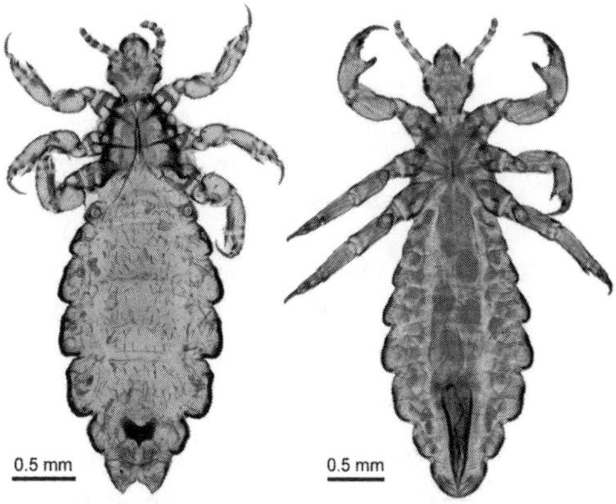

57. **Head and body louse**
Body (or clothing) lice live in clothes and bedding, and they move onto human skin to feed on blood. They evolved from head lice, probably when humans began to wear clothes regularly. For this reason, genetic analyses of clothing lice may provide a means of estimating when humans adopted complex clothes. Head and clothing lice are generally considered to belong to one species, differing only marginally in form, that exploit different habitats. Shown here is a head louse *Pediculus humanus capitas* (left) and a body (clothing) louse *Pediculus humanus humanus* (right).

Source: Bonilla et al., 2013, *PLoS Pathogens* 9, e1003724:2. Reproduced under Creative Commons (CC-BY) license, courtesy of the Public Library of Science.

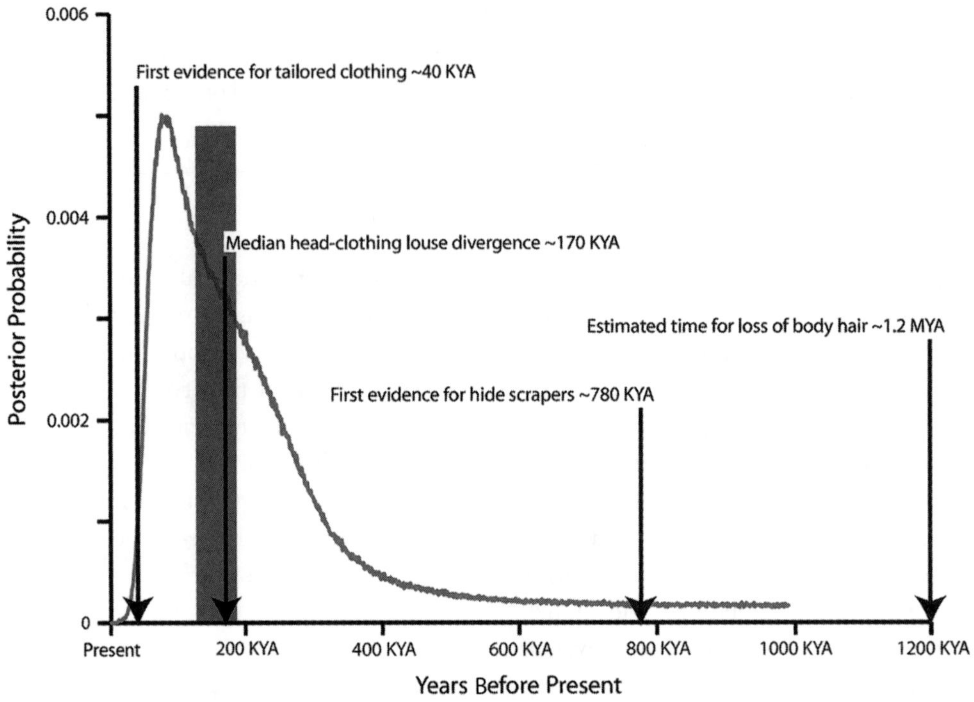

58. **Lice research and clothing origins**
Genetic research on the divergence between body (clothing) lice and head lice can be used to estimate a date for the origin of clothing. David Reed's team reported a likely date between 80,000 and 170,000 years ago.
Source: Toups et. al., Molecular Biology and Evolution 2011:31. Reproduced courtesy of Oxford University Press under CC-YB license, and David. L. Reed.

entomologist David L. Reed has found that clothing lice most likely evolved by around 80,000 years ago, and maybe as early as 170,000 years ago.[5]

Taking all of the available evidence together, our best guess is that complex clothing originated among *Homo sapiens* in Africa early in the last ice age. The location can be either northern or southern Africa, or both. If we entertain the earlier date of 170,000 years ago for the origin of clothing lice, this could suggest an earlier origin of clothing in the previous ice age (190,000–130,000 years ago). In that case, we might have to assume that at least one group of *Homo sapiens* continued to wear clothes on a regular basis during the last interglacial – perhaps unlikely, remembering it was generally warmer then than now – or that lice survived on blankets and rugs (perhaps more feasible). The differing dates from Reed's team are statistical values: 80,000 years ago is the mode (the most common value) while 170,000 years ago is the median value (the middle value in the probability distribution). Fortunately, another genetic analysis of clothing lice was carried out by a different research team in Germany. The German team arrived at a time for the origin of clothing lice early in the last ice age, consistent with archaeological evidence for complex clothing: their date is about 100,000 years ago.[6]

CLIMATE AND TECHNOLOGY

The connections between climate change and technological change in the Paleolithic provide yet more evidence that we first invented clothes due to our vulnerability to cold as naked hominins. To put it bluntly, the connections are too coincidental – and the evidence from body lice fits in nicely too. The need to invent (and improve) clothing gives us logical reasons for the technological changes – reasons that are conspicuously lacking in all the conventional attempts in archaeology to explain these innovations in terms of changing food strategies, for instance, or more efficient tool-making techniques, greater cognitive capacities, or even perhaps an inherent evolutionary trend toward more modern behavior. There may be some truth in some of these ideas, but none of them can account easily for the coincidence with climate change or explain the specific advantages of particular tools.[7]

Neanderthals and Tasmanians are two examples that highlight the issues. We can explain not only the emergence of scraper, blade, and bone tool industries but also the absence or delayed appearance of these technologies in warmer parts of the world – notably in Southeast Asia and Australia. When some of these technologies finally did make an appearance in warmer regions, it was only later as populations with derivative technologies (like microblades) spread around the globe, mainly during the postglacial epoch (the Holocene). Tasmania alone remained completely isolated from these late diffusions of technologies and populations. And neither should we forget the Hobbit on the tropical island of Flores, Indonesia. The tools of the Hobbit were basically simple cobbles and flakes, and it looks like these tools stayed unchanged for a million years.[8]

CLOTHING AND TECHNOLOGY

Clothing is the missing link between climate change and technological change in the Paleolithic. Some of the main Paleolithic transitions relate to developments in clothing that were linked to climate change during the Pleistocene.[9]

The conventional categories are the Lower, Middle, and Upper Paleolithic. The corresponding technologies are the original pebble, chopper and flake tools, then scraper toolkits, and finally blade-based industries. In terms of clothing, the Lower Paleolithic corresponds to routine nakedness, the Middle Paleolithic to the routine use of simple clothing, and the Upper Paleolithic to complex clothing.[10]

TABLE 7. *Stone Ages and clothing*

Simplistic view of clothing developments in relation to the conventional European Paleolithic and postglacial stages. In Africa, the Lower, Middle, and Upper Paleolithic are termed the Early, Middle, and Late Stone Age, respectively.

Neolithic	textiles
Mesolithic	mix
Upper Paleolithic	complex
Middle Paleolithic	simple
Lower Paleolithic	none

The original aim here was not to explain these patterns in Paleolithic technology, nor to account for the connections with climate change. It just so happens that in finding evidence for the origins of clothing, we find that these connections are rather obvious. Too many things come together for the patterns to be coincidental – and the reasons why they come together are rather too logical. The crucial distinction to make is between simple and complex clothing. Making this distinction allows us to make the connections with scraper and blade technologies and to see why bone tools became more useful. So the thermal origin of clothing can explain more than just the origin of clothing: it shows how the development of clothing may be more important in prehistory than anyone has realized.

Much the same happens with the next step: the Neolithic and the advent of agriculture.

PART III

GLOBAL WARMING AND AGRICULTURE

NINE

TIME FOR NEW CLOTHES

When the climate changed at the end of the last ice age, a couple of new things happened. One was that people began to settle down to live in permanent villages. Archaeologists call this sedentism, and sedentism is one of the great unexplained events in human prehistory. The other new thing was the advent of agriculture. Together these two new developments led to civilization: the first civilizations arose where people were living in towns with an agricultural economy.

We can link both of these new trends to clothing. And with agriculture, the link is quite tangible. We tend to overlook another new thing that was happening: all the people who made these momentous changes were wearing clothes.

Unlike earlier times, at the start of the present warm epoch around 12,000 years ago, people in some places were no longer prepared to be naked – a situation that had never happened before in the entire history of our species. In these societies, clothing had finally come into fashion, meaning there was a new need for people to stay covered regardless of climate. And in terms of basic resources, it meant that as well as obtaining food and water, people had to find materials to make clothes. Not that the climate was irrelevant – far from it. The global climate entered a new phase at the end of the Pleistocene: the weather became warmer, wetter and more humid, and this meant that wearing clothes became more of a problem.

NOT SUCH A GREAT IDEA

We will look at the problem with clothes in a moment. In the meantime, we can remind ourselves that the origin of agriculture has become more of a problem than people used to think. While agriculture might look to us now like a great way of getting food, anthropologists have come to realize that it probably would have made little sense to any self-respecting hunter-gatherer. Yet it was hunter-gatherers who first started with agriculture, not us.

Early agriculture was full of drawbacks, and it was not as though no one knew how to go about growing plants (or herding animals) until some genius came up with the idea – or more precisely, a lot of bright people in different places happened to come up with the same idea at around the same time. Hunter-gatherers were always well aware of how they could sow seeds in the soil, water the seeds, and wait around for the seeds to grow into mature plants, or how to tame young animals and keep them alive. And they probably did so at times, even in Australia. Their ignorance of agriculture is an urban myth. Indeed, hunter-gatherers knew much more about managing wild plants and animals than most of us ever will. In their traditional lifestyle, they chose not to bother with agriculture – and for good reasons. What made some of them change their minds?

It is time to plant some seeds of doubt. And time to see how clothes can answer that question. Although clothes rarely rate a mention, there was a great technological change that happened with clothes after the ice age. People changed their clothes – literally. They changed from wearing animal skins and furs to wearing woven fabrics made with textile fibers. And that may be what changed their minds.

GLOBAL WARMING AND THE TEXTILE REVOLUTION

We saw earlier that moisture is one of the enemies of clothing. If wind acts like a thermal assassin, moisture is more like a secret saboteur. The threat from moisture is a double threat, in fact: a threat from the outside – the environment – and a threat from the inside: from the human body. The moisture problem applies with moisture in the environment – rain and humidity – and moisture on the inside, from our sweat. Once clothes are soaked with moisture, any thermal benefit is lost, and they become heavy and too uncomfortable to wear. Wet clothes are a liability, especially in windy weather. Garments that are soaked with moisture stick to our skin and actually make us feel too cold, because the water absorbs body heat rapidly and creates extra cooling as it evaporates. Even in hot weather, the chilling effect of wet clothing on our skin is unpleasant. Wet clothes are worse than no clothes.[1]

The two sources of moisture – from the environment and from the body – can combine to sabotage our ability to wear clothes. If the relative humidity is high (absolute humidity is not so relevant), our perspiration cannot evaporate so easily. The sweat collects on our skin and in our clothes. And if the air temperature is higher, we sweat more profusely. So having a combination of higher environmental temperatures and humidity will make clothing less practical.[2]

That is exactly what happened with the global climate at the end of the last ice age. The global climate got warmer, and it also got wetter and more humid. Moisture from all of the melting ice drained into the oceans (adding to a rise in sea levels) and, with the higher temperatures, there was more evaporation from the oceans into the atmosphere. The warmth and wetness of the weather was a real nuisance if people wanted to keep on wearing clothes. In contrast, ice age climates were drier, so wearing clothes was more practical in the Pleistocene.[3]

The weather at the beginning of the present warm period (the Holocene) was stressful in terms of clothing for a couple of reasons. One was the suddenness of the switch from glacial to interglacial conditions: it happened with amazing speed, probably over a timescale as brief as fifty years – that is, within the individual lifespans of people living at the time. Adding to the drama, the global climate at the beginning of the Holocene became even warmer and wetter than it is today. Between 11,000 and 8,000 years ago, temperatures rose as high as 5°C (around 10°F) above present levels in some areas, while humidity and rainfall also increased to levels higher than today. In Africa, this warm and wet climate phase is called the African Humid Period. During the early Holocene, the Sahara was a green and lush landscape, and the water level of the Nile River reached a peak around 9,500 years ago. In other words, the weather around much of the world suddenly went from being cold and dry to being warm and wet – even warmer and wetter than it is at present.[4]

Global warming presented a problem for people who wore clothes. They found that their clothes were more uncomfortable. The best solution was to stop wearing clothes, which is exactly what earlier hominins had done with simple clothes in previous interglacials (and what the Tasmanians decided to do).

There was a difference though at the end of the last ice age: some people were wearing complex clothes. Whereas simple loose clothing does not present such a problem with humidity and perspiration, the full enclosure created by complex clothing prevents moisture from escaping very easily. For those people who wanted to keep on wearing clothes, one option was to change back to simple garments. But dropping clothes altogether was no longer an option, for a couple of reasons – including modesty.

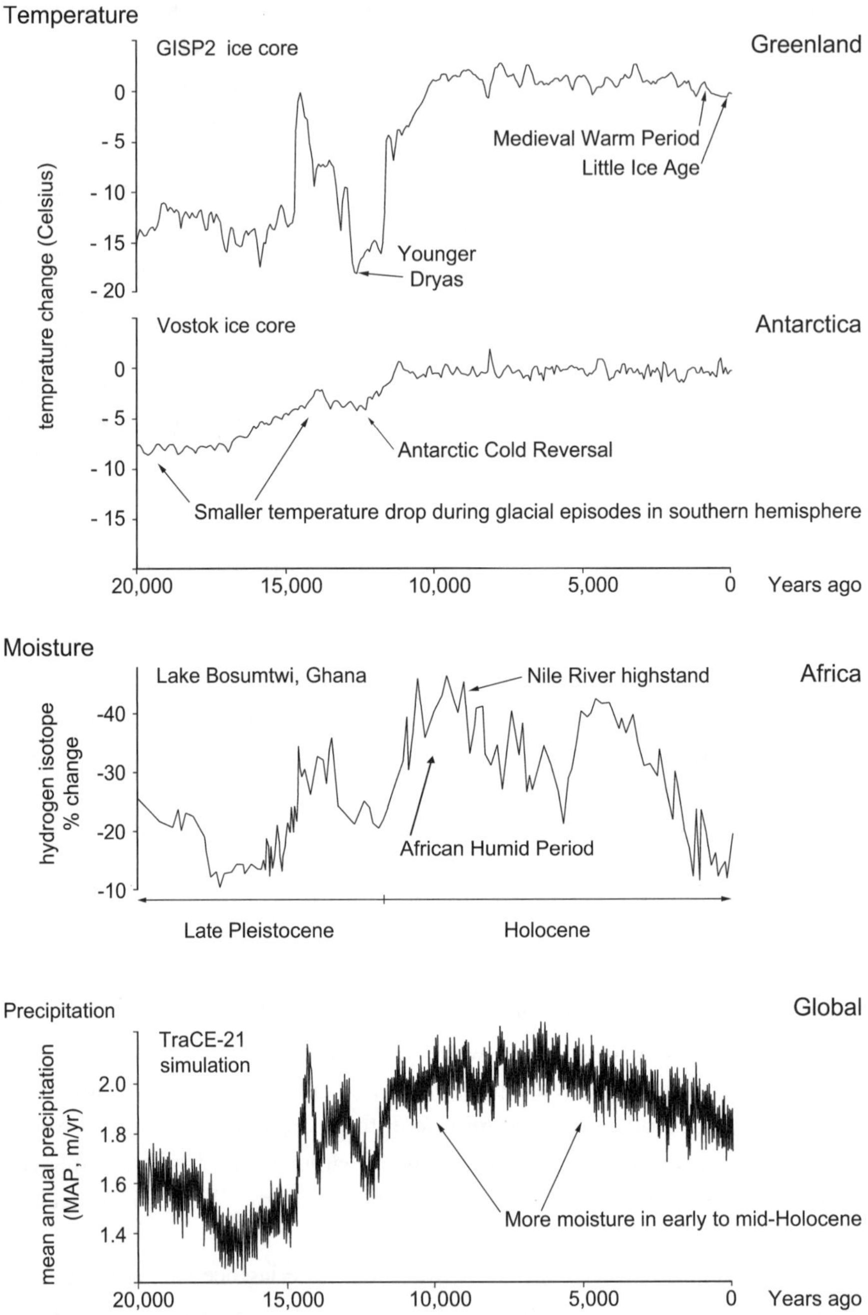

59. **Moisture trends in climate over the past 20,000 years**

Temperature and moisture trends over the past 20,000 years. Global warming at the end of the last ice age was rapid and accompanied by a massive increase in moisture levels. The warming trend occurred from 15,000 years ago, interrupted by a sudden return to cold conditions – termed the Younger Dryas in the northern hemisphere and, in the southern hemisphere, the (slightly earlier) Antarctic Cold Reversal. Moisture levels peaked during the early Holocene. In Africa, this rise in moisture levels is called the African Humid Period. Compared to the present global climate regime, temperature and moisture levels were higher in the early Holocene.

Source: Shanahan et al., 2015:141.

From Shivering to Shame

After wearing complex clothes for millennia – from at least 40,000 years ago in the middle latitudes of Eurasia – it would seem that casual exposure of the naked body was no longer socially acceptable. We may wonder why this was the case (and indeed we should), but we can be reasonably sure that nakedness had become an issue. Decoration was connected with clothing by that stage too, but this alone would not have prevented people going back to simple garments, or even decorating the naked body.

Modesty had presumably come into the picture. In places where complex clothing was worn routinely, it would appear that covering the body – at least the genitals – was now compulsory.

We have evidence for modesty by 10,000 years ago. At an amazing site in Turkey called Göbekli Tepe, archaeologists have uncovered a huge megalithic complex that looks almost like Stonehenge, and on some of the massive stone pillars there are carved pictures that show people wearing loincloths. These garments were made from fox pelts: we can make out the hind legs and the long bushy tails. Evidence of modest clothing is seen also on a small limestone figurine found at the 11,000-year-old site of Gilgal 1, on the West Bank in the

60. **Fox loincloth in Turkey hints at modesty**
Modesty had probably emerged as a motive for wearing clothes in some parts of the world by the beginning of the Holocene. Archaeological evidence for modesty is found on this stone pillar unearthed at the megalithic site of Göbekli Tepe in Turkey, dating to 11,000 years ago. The image carved on the pillar shows a person wearing a loincloth – in this case, a fox pelt with the long tail attached.
Source: Photo Vincent J. Musi, © National Geographic. Reproduced under license to National Geographic Creative, and with permission of Vincent J. Musi.

Levant, a very early agricultural settlement where barley and rye were cultivated. The female figurine at Gilgal I has a girdle covering her pudenda.[5]

Simple clothes were a viable option, but with the proviso that sexual organs were covered in public – with loincloths for instance. Loose garments can function adequately as cover when nakedness is not allowed routinely in public, like we see with the draped capes and togas in Ancient Greece and Rome, and with traditional gowns in Arab and Islamic societies. In warmer climates these loose garments have the advantage of letting sweat escape easily – and a little wind chill will actually help with cooling.

Provided that any rules of modesty were met, people after the ice age could retain complex clothes or revert to simple garments. Or they could use both together, with complex garments as underwear and draped garments on the outside. Either way, the problem of moisture in the postglacial world favored a great innovation, a fundamental change in material: from animal skins to woven fabrics.

From Furs to Fibers

Fabric solves the moisture problem. As described earlier, the woven structure of the material not only traps air, but at the same time it lets moisture escape and evaporate through the material. Unlike animal hides and furs, woven fabrics are highly porous.[6]

Climate change at the end of the last ice age led to a revolution in clothing: the textile revolution. Textiles put the cloth into clothing. The cause was global warming, which magnified the moisture problem for two reasons. First, warmer temperatures caused more sweating. Second, higher levels of humidity made it harder for sweat to evaporate. For people who wanted to keep on wearing clothes, textiles were the way to go.[7]

Besides physiology, another factor was ecology. Hunters were often faced with declining herds of large furry animals in the warmer environments. As well as the weather getting too warm for these animals, their habitats changed too. Many animal species retreated from middle latitudes, and some species went extinct. Woolly mammoths are an example: these massive mammals began to struggle in the warm weather. The last few survivors survived in the frigid environments of northern Siberia until nearly 4,000 years ago, the same time Ancient Egyptians wearing linen loincloths were piling up huge stone blocks to build the pyramids.[8]

THE ANTIQUITY OF TEXTILE TECHNOLOGY

As with Paleolithic clothes, we have very little direct evidence for the first fabrics. Luckily, we do have a few precious textile fragments from early in the postglacial period. Most of the evidence though is indirect. Sometimes we find

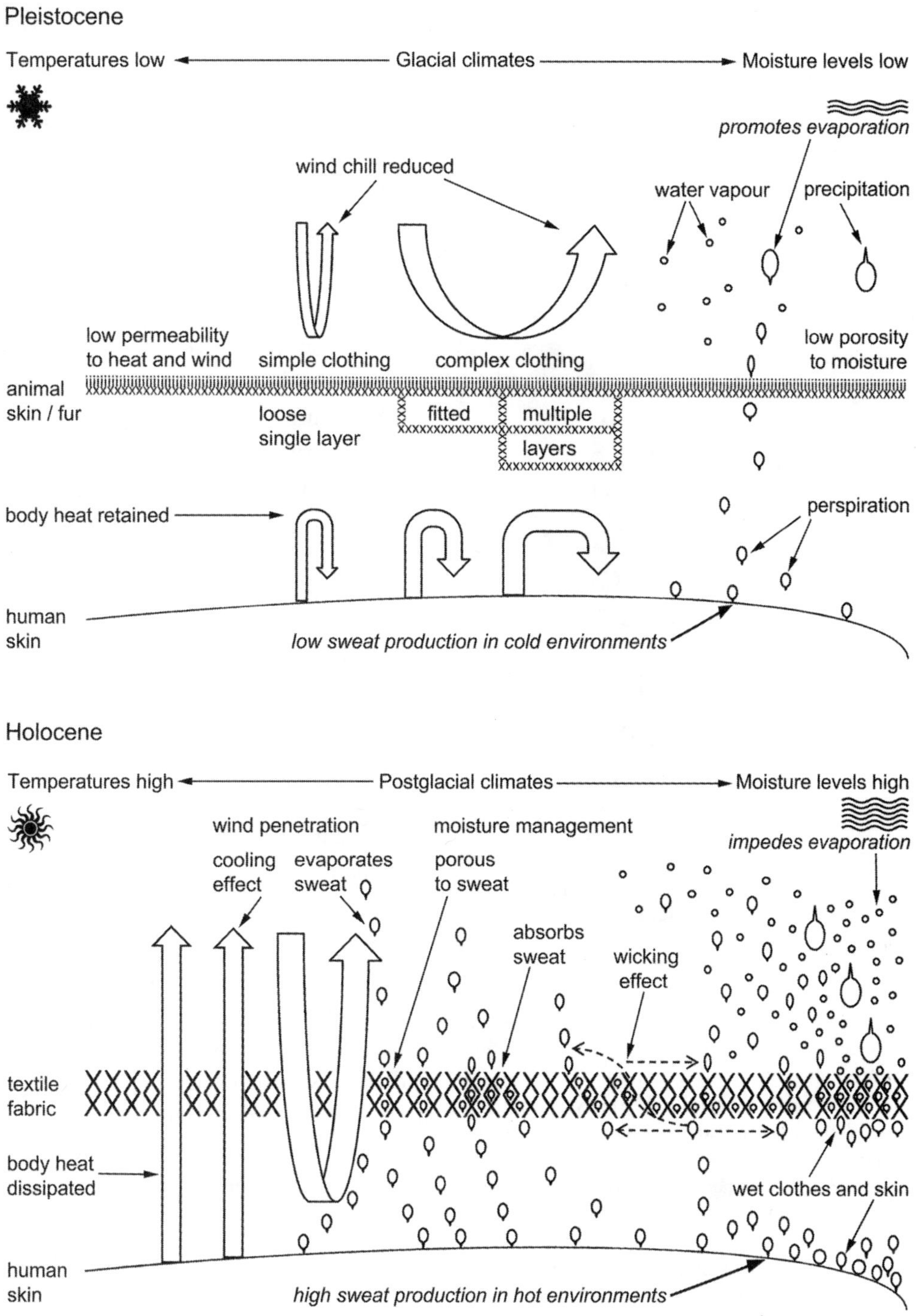

61. **Textiles and moisture management**

Textile moisture management. Compared to animal skins (top) used for clothes in drier ice age climates, woven textiles (bottom) were preferred in warm, moist postglacial environments. The porous fabric structure of fabric is permeable to heat and moisture, allowing body heat and sweat to dissipate. Wind penetration can be advantageous, enhancing evaporative cooling; also, the woven structure can absorb and wick perspiration away from the skin surface. Environmental moisture (humidity and precipitation) exacerbates the problem of removing perspiration from the skin surface. These factors – increased body heat and sweating, and greater levels of environmental moisture – put a premium on the permeability of woven fabric. The porosity of fabric allowed clothes to be worn comfortably in the postglacial world.

TABLE 8. *Factors favoring textiles after the ice age*

Ecological	decline in large hide-bearing animals
Climate change	temperature
	humidity
Physiological	sweating
Structural	thermal flexibility

62. **The Iceman**
Discovered in 1991 in the Italian Alps, the 5,300-year-old Iceman (known also as Ötzi) dates from a time after agriculture had already spread into the region from the Near East, by around 8,000 years ago. Yet Ötzi's clothing comprised a combination of elements from domesticated and wild resources. Shown here is a reconstruction – minus his coats – at the South Tyrol Museum of Archaeology in Bolzano, Italy.
Source: Reconstruction by Kennis, © South Tyrol Museum of Archaeology – www.iceman.it. Reproduced by permission of the South Tyrol Museum of Archaeology.

signs of weaving technology – like spindle whorls that were used to spin the fibers into yarn to make cloth. We also find that people were exploiting – and sometimes domesticating – plants and animals to produce fibers to weave cloth. This raises an intriguing aspect of the textile revolution that we shall pursue in the following chapters: the textile revolution coincided with the agricultural revolution.

Ice Age Textiles

Animal skins were the main material used for making clothes during the Paleolithic, but people were also making some textile artifacts during the last ice age. What is not known is whether woven materials were used to make garments, as well as to manufacture items such as ropes, mats, and baskets. However, any woven garments probably played only a minor role in everyday attire during the last ice age. We know that people were using tools such as scrapers and blades to prepare hides (as well as awls and needles to sew the hides), but there is no evidence for textile clothing.

Given the cold and dry climates that prevailed at the time, animal skins were a better option than cloth – especially in view of the need to resist wind chill. While the porosity of textiles makes them more permeable to sweat, this also means that wind can penetrate more easily. Even today, people often prefer to wear leathers and furs instead of fabrics in cold regions (especially as outer garments). A good example is the clothing of the Iceman: although woolen textiles were available in Europe 5,000 years ago, his Alpine attire comprised a couple of leather coats, underwear made from sheep and goat skins, and also a warm hat from the fur of a wild brown bear.[9]

63. **The Iceman's clothes**
Ötzi's clothing included (clockwise from upper left): hay-stuffed shoes with laces from cattle hide, a heavy outer coat of sheepskin, lighter coat of sheep and goatskin, goatskin leggings, a fur hat from a brown bear, grass matting, and a sheepskin loincloth.
Source: Image © South Tyrol Museum of Archaeology, Bolzano. Reproduced by permission of Niall O'Sullivan and the South Tyrol Museum of Archaeology.

Early evidence for the use of fibers is found 36,000 years ago at Dzudzuana Cave in the Republic of Georgia, western Asia. Some of these fibers were twisted into yarns and dyed, but no actual fragments of woven fabric were recovered at the site. Most of the fibers are said to be wild flax – the same plant species later cultivated to make linen fabric – and also there were some wool-like fibers from a wild goat species. Even Neanderthals probably made strings and cords from plants, judging by some twisted plant fibers recovered on stone tools at one French site that dates to 72,000 years ago.[10]

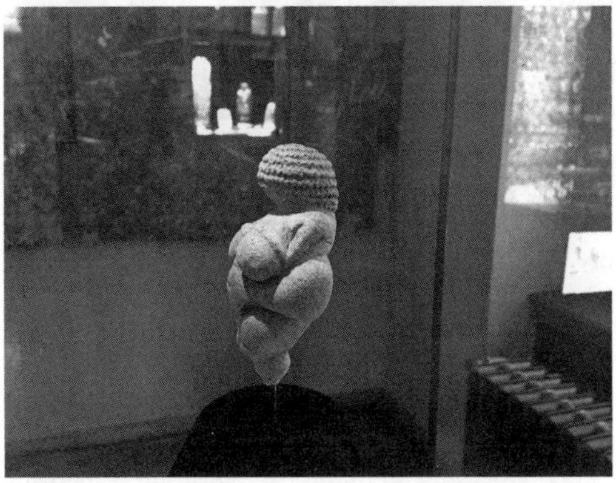

64. **Venus of Willendorf with woven cap**
The Venus of Willendorf, an ice age figurine found in Austria dated to between 28,000 and 25,000 years ago. She wears what appears to be a woven cap, suggesting textile technology was sometimes used to make items of clothing in the last ice age. Displayed at the Naturhistorisches Museum (Natural History Museum), Vienna.
Source: Photo by the author. © Ian Gilligan.

The earliest evidence for woven artifacts is found around 28,000 years ago at sites in Western Europe and Russia during the height of the last ice age. Clear impressions of weaving are preserved on pieces of fired clay, but the artifacts are more likely bags, nets, or mats rather than clothes. Some of the bone tools found at ice age sites – awls and needles – could have been used for weaving as well as sewing.[11]

Tantalizing hints of woven fabrics appear on the so-called Venus figurines found in ice age Europe. The Willendorf figurine from Austria, for example, has what appears to be a woven cap on her head. One of the oldest figurines was excavated recently at Hohle Fels Cave in southwestern Germany, and it is at least 35,000 years old. She has numerous lines incised across her breasts, arms, and torso, which are said to be "suggestive of clothing or a wrap of some kind."[12]

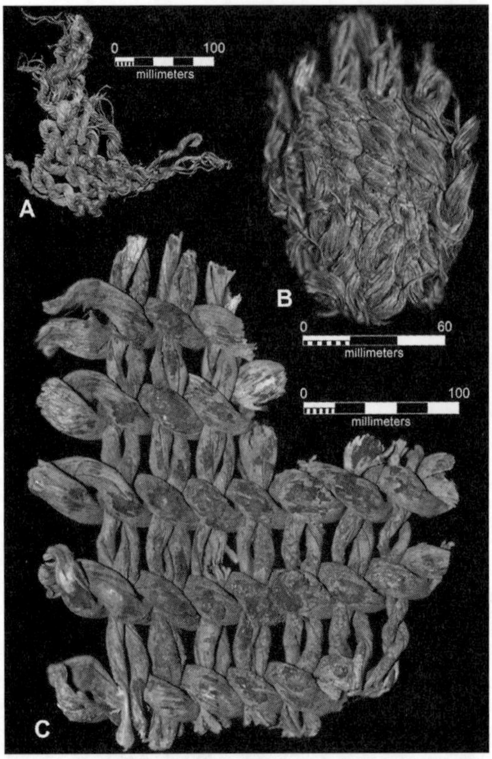

65. **11,000-year-old textiles in Peru**
The world's oldest fragment of a textile that may have served as clothing is 11,000 years old, preserved in the dry highland environment of Guitarrero Cave, Peru (elevation 2,580 m [9,350 feet]). Among the textile specimens shown here, the fragment labeled A may be intrusive, and hence younger. Fragment B is radiocarbon-dated to 11,000 years ago, and probably derives from a bag or clothing. Fragment C is dated to 12,000 years ago, and is probably matting or perhaps basketry.
Source: Jolie et al., 2011:290, © University of Chicago Press. Reproduced with permission of the University of Chicago Press, and courtesy of James Adovasio.

More compelling evidence for textile garments comes from what look like woven caps or beanies on the heads of some ice age figurines, like the one at Willendorf. Another sign of weaving is visible on the beautiful Venus of Lespugue in France (25,000 years ago). She wears a skirt that politely covers her posterior, consisting of twisted cords suspended from a belt that looks like it was made from plant fibers.[13]

The First Fabrics

Only at the beginning of the postglacial era do we find actual pieces of fabric. The world record for the oldest is 11,000 years ago, held by cloth fragments found in Guitarrero Cave, Peru. Archaeologists could not identify any of the fiber sources, but the plants might include maguey (sometimes called sisal hemp), extracted from a cactus-like plant later cultivated for its fiber. Along with cotton, maguey was woven for everyday clothes by the Incas in Peru and by the Mayans and Aztecs in Mexico.[14]

The next oldest fabrics are found in the Middle East. These come from Nahal Hemar Cave in Israel and from a site called Çayönü in Turkey, where flax (linen) cloth is dated to around 9,000 years ago. One of the most spectacular finds is another 9,000-year-old piece of linen cloth discovered in 2013 at Çatalhöyük (also in Turkey), a village complex regarded as the world's oldest town.[15]

Elsewhere, textiles woven from wild sedge grass – probably used as nets and mats rather than as clothes – are preserved in the Russian Far East at Chertovy Vorota Cave, northeast of Vladivostok. These textiles are radiocarbon-dated to around 9,000 years ago. In North America, archaeologists have found a 10,400-year-old sandal at Fort Rock Cave in Oregon, made from twined sagebrush cordage. Another remarkable site for textiles is the Windover peat pond in Florida that dates to between 8,000 and 7,000 years ago. At Windover, finely woven fabrics were made from the fronds of palm trees and were likely used for clothes. The oldest preserved textiles in Europe are some rope fragments recovered from La Draga, a water-logged lakeside site in Spain, dated to around 7,000 years ago.[16]

66. **9,000-year-old linen fabric in Turkey**
9,000-year-old piece of linen cloth, unearthed at the early town site of Çatalhöyük, Turkey. The fine weaving of flax fibers attests to advanced textile technologies at the time (despite the absence of spindle whorls), and suggests that cultivation of flax was well established.

Source: Photo Scott Haddow, © Scott Haddow. Reproduced by permission of Scott Haddow and courtesy of Ian Hodder.

In China, the earliest woven textile is a floor mat made from reed stems dated to 7,000 years ago, at a Neolithic site south of Shanghai. Hemp that might have been used for textiles has also been recovered from a site near the Yangtze River dated to a little earlier, between 9,000 and 8,000 years ago.[17]

So the technology of weaving was not new – weaving goes back a long way. What was new was a more widespread use of woven material for clothes. This shift to using textiles for clothes means that climate change at the end of the ice age led to people wanting to extract new kinds of resources from the environment. If they wanted to wear clothes made from cloth, then this put a premium on the extraction – or production through agriculture – of fibers to make fabrics. Also relevant to agriculture, the shift to using textiles meant that people could make clothes from plants as well as from animals.

TEN

A HALF-BAKED REVOLUTION

Before we take a look at how the textile revolution may relate to the agricultural revolution, we should discuss a recent revolution in the archaeology of agricultural origins. There have been some surprising discoveries in Papua New Guinea and in the United States, for example, and even Australia is involved. As a result, the whole concept of agriculture has been revised, and almost deconstructed.

Ironically, this revolution means that archaeologists are no longer so happy with the idea of an agricultural revolution. They now realise things were less clear-cut, and messier.

There were not just a few agricultural centers that sprung up after the end of the ice age in Southwest Asia, northern China, Peru, and Mexico: these are the classic centers from where agriculture then spread out to much of the world. There were also many other parts of the world where people began to change how they were relating to natural resources (and to the natural environment in general), but these regions did not always see a complete transition to agriculture. People often experimented and dabbled in different ways of manipulating or managing resources that did not necessarily lead to cultivation and domestication – and they may have been doing this for longer than we used to think. Yet this recent revolution in how archaeologists look at agriculture is really not so radical.

A REVOLUTION THAT CHANGES NOTHING

Despite all of the revision and the new discoveries, in one way nothing has changed. And as a result we are none the wiser about why things started to change after the ice age. What has not changed – what is still not questioned – is our most basic assumption about agriculture.

The assumption is that agriculture is about food. So entrenched is this assumption that a popular synonym for agriculture is food production. And in a similar vein, textile fibers such as wool are called secondary products. It is not as though we have a theory that agriculture started because of issues relating to food. If it was a theory, then we might be more aware of its hypothetical status and more able to doubt it. But since it lies so deep within our view of things, at the very center of our perception, we do not perceive it as an assumption.

A gastronomic obsession also means that we look mainly for evidence about food, which can result in a bias in collecting and reporting data. There is no conspiracy – merely a failure to look beyond food. And to be fair, there really has been no compelling reason to look beyond food, nothing else to look for. Until now.

What is Wrong with Agriculture?

The short answer to the above question is: quite a lot. There is a lot that is wrong – or rather, mistaken – in how agriculture is defined narrowly as food production. And there is a lot wrong with agriculture itself – that is, agriculture as a way to get food.

The most basic question is why it took so long for agriculture to start. We are used to the idea that agriculture could only happen once the climate improved after the end of the last ice age. Or less plausibly, that it had to await some long accumulation of learning or some slow process of social evolution before agriculture could be viable. Either way, we must account for the delay – which is not easy.

People like us, fully modern humans in the biological sense, have been around for at least 300,000 years. Even if we widen the concept of agriculture to embrace looser kinds of resource management among hunter-gatherers, we struggle to find any sign of it before the end of the last ice age, a mere 11,700 years ago. Similarly, if we invoke environmental opportunities or constraints, we tend to forget that the last 300,000 years span not just the last ice age and the previous couple of ice ages. There were also a couple of warm interglacials that generally ran for around 10,000 years (between 130,000 and 120,000 years ago, for instance) – much the same as our present interglacial. Even during the glacial periods, we cannot assume there were never any chances for people to start agriculture of some kind. And it is even harder to imagine no good opportunities to start agriculture existed during the last interglacial. But nothing happened.

Then there is the coincidence with climate change at the end of the last ice age. Most attempts to explain the origin of agriculture acknowledge this coincidence and suggest some kind of connection, directly or indirectly. Yet there was a similar change in global climate at the end of the previous ice age. What was so different about the end of the last ice age? And we are inclined to think that earlier hominins were too stupid – otherwise they would have started agriculture. On the other hand, if we could perhaps permit the possibility of a mental capacity for agriculture among our more recent ancestors, then we are dealing with a much longer span of time and more glacial/interglacial cycles.

The problem of the long delay is addressed by employing one of our most useful scientific strategies: ignoring it. Few debates about the origin of agriculture bother to mention the delay at all. Yet even when we deal with the delay in this time-honoured fashion, another big problem is not so easy to ignore.[1]

The Stupendous Stupidity of Agriculture

Most theories about agriculture have to assume that for some reason, our old reliable hunter-gatherer adaptations became inadequate in some way. Or that agriculture could offer some advantages, or solve some kind of problem. But we have yet to clearly identify those advantages or show why agriculture was better. On the other hand, what we have learned about the flexibility and security of hunter-gatherer adaptations – and the mere fact that these adaptations served our ancestors quite adequately during all those upheavals in global climate during the Pleistocene – belies any attempt to explain agriculture as a better option.[2]

Australian Aborigines, for instance, were exceedingly well-informed about all of the food and water resources available to them in their environments, even in desert areas. They never worried much about how or where to find their next meal:

> That is why you can never come across or hear of an Aboriginal dying of thirst or starvation. He is well informed about where and how to procure water and food.[3]

We are inclined to underestimate (and to undervalue) the benefits of hunting and gathering. And especially in its early stages, agriculture meant greater risk than foraging if people were silly enough to rely on it for their survival. And we are inclined, also, to forget that agriculture required a lot more work. In terms of the net food return for the amount of effort expended, early agriculture was demonstrably inferior to foraging: it meant doing more work to obtain a sufficient amount of food.[4]

A Healthy Choice – Not

And it gets worse. To their surprise, archaeologists have found that the transition to agriculture did not lead to any improvements in human health. Quite the opposite in many cases: malnutrition was not uncommon in the settlements, and famine was never far away.[5]

Nor does population growth prove that it was better; there might have been another reason for the population explosion, as we shall see later. The ultimate success of agriculture occurred despite its drawbacks, and some of the early attempts did not succeed. Yet people did seem to get locked into agriculture once it started – perhaps against their better judgement. One of the effects of farming is that it makes hunting and gathering less productive: it reduces the amount and the variety of wild food resources in the vicinity. We now realize that many hunter-gatherer communities were very reluctant to adopt agriculture, and they often tried to resist its spread for as long as they could. Agriculture certainly can feed a lot more people in the long run, but only after it becomes established and if people are prepared to work harder for future rewards – which has little appeal to hunter-gatherers.[6]

From a hunter-gatherer perspective, agriculture really does not add up: it is not worth all of the effort, nor the risks. The security of modern agriculture results from many improvements in recent millennia. We should not make the mistake of projecting backwards its benefits and stability in the world today to help explain its prehistoric origins. We are also inclined to forget that the food supply provided from agriculture was less varied and – from a hunter-gatherer point of view – often less palatable than their traditional diets. Considered solely in terms of food and from the perspective of people at the time, it is hard to see why agriculture ever got started at all.

Strange Harvest

There are more problems. Even when agriculture got established, people often continued to rely on foraging to meet most of their dietary requirements. In some places, the bulk of their dietary intake was still supplied by hunting wild animals and collecting wild plant foods long after they started with agriculture. Now this does not make much sense given all the effort they were putting into agriculture. What on earth was going on?

And it gets worse, much worse. Even when we look at the most orthodox cases of early agriculture in places such as in Southwest Asia where our marvelous cereals like wheat and barley were first cultivated, or in China where rice was domesticated, the story takes a few surprising turns. Not only did people often rely more on wild food resources at the time, the crops themselves are not that sensible as food choices.

Our modern varieties of wheat and rice result from millennia of selective cultivation and domestication, but the wild varieties were less attractive as comestibles. They yielded much less than modern strains in the way of seeds, and the seeds had to be processed laboriously before they could sustain a population, or even a family. Recent hunter-gatherers typically regard such plants as not worthwhile, and the seeds are not considered particularly palatable. Hunter-gatherers would generally resort to these foods more in times of scarcity (which was not often), as a fallback option. Even in the early days of agriculture when cereals were domesticated, these crops seem to have been of "minimal importance" in the human diet – they often comprised only 10–15 percent of plant foods consumed.[7]

And we are inclined to forget that all of our great cereal crops – including corn, or maize – were originally just grasses. We humans do not naturally depend upon grass for food. But some other species do.

The Contradiction of Animal Domestication

This raises the issue of animals. We have been talking here about agriculture as cultivation of plants, but the other aspect of agriculture involves animals. The domestication of farm animals tends to get overshadowed nowadays by a focus on the cultivation of plants, which is unfortunate because the situation with animals is quite revealing in terms of exposing flaws in our conventional ideas.

There are a couple of basic issues with the animals, and perhaps we can start with the most basic. There is a fundamental difference between hunting and herding – then domesticating – animals. Hunting means killing the animal whereas domestication means keeping the animal alive. Now this is a big difference (not just for the animal), especially when we remember that keeping an animal alive usually means feeding and protecting it. With the exception of animals such as dogs and pigs that domesticated themselves in settlements – we shall look at these later – domestication typically involves quite a lot of work on our part to keep the animal alive. And if it really is meat alone that we want, then we will have to kill the poor beast anyway. From a hunter's point of view, why not just kill it?

Keeping an animal alive by feeding and protecting it suggests that the animal is more useful to us as a living resource than as a carcass. Why might that be? Many people have gotten themselves into all kinds of tangled arguments to explain why hunter-gatherers began to realize how they could get a reliable supply of meat by domesticating animals. And this all assumes that people were worried about the reliability of their food supply, which hardly gels with what we know about hunter-gatherers: they were confident and quite relaxed about obtaining food, even in marginal environments. If a particular favored species went into decline – through over-exploitation by humans, or due to environmental change – hunter-gatherers were not fazed. When they were faced with a food shortage, for which we have no compelling evidence in the early days of agriculture, the traditional hunter-gatherer response was to find an alternative resource, or move on (or both). Hunter-gatherers had a basic trust in nature and a well-founded faith in their extensive knowledge of natural resources.

A concern with reliability is a projection of our own disconnection from nature: we have lost that trust and lost the intimate knowledge of natural resources that gave hunter-gatherers their confidence. The supposed need to secure a more reliable supply of meat reflects our anxieties, not theirs. Effectively, what we are saying is that by going through all the bother of keeping the animals alive and breeding them for generations, people could eventually get what they had previously got by killing wild animals on the spot. Is it any wonder that hunter-gatherers fail to see much sense in this? And the animals need to be fed. Many of the early farm animals feed on... grasses.

Keeping animals alive in order to kill them later might seem like a good idea to us, but it makes no sense to hunter-gatherers – at least not to naked hunter-gatherers. On the other hand, some species do provide another resource – a renewable resource – that is supplied (and resupplied) for as long as the animals are kept alive. So it represents a better reason to keep them alive – but only for people who wear clothes.

Renewable Resources Are the Answer

The renewable resource is wool. Coincidentally – and we do seem to be finding a few coincidences – quite a few of the first farm animals grew fibers. In Southwest Asia, these were the first animal species to be deliberately domesticated: sheep and goats. In the Americas, the only major domestic animals were llamas and alpacas. Fibers are a renewable product of a living animal. Unlike meat, fibers such as wool represent a reason to keep the animals alive. Rather than serving just as walking larders, sheep and llamas were walking wardrobes.

In archaeology, wool is widely considered a secondary product of sheep (and llamas). To support this view it is commonly said – correctly – that in the case of sheep, wild sheep do not have a permanent fleece. The fleece developed after sheep had already been domesticated for a few thousand years. Of course this alone may suggest selective breeding for wool, but lack of a permanent fleece does not mean that wild sheep did not have wool. In fact wild sheep did produce lots of wool, and they did not need any people to shear them. Wild sheep shed their thick coat of wool every year in the spring – just

67. **Primitve Soay sheep shedding wool**
Soay sheep are descended from a feral population on Soay Island, Scotland, and retain some features of primitive sheep, including an annual molt. Like the mouflon, these sheep lack a permanent fleece but produce a dense coat of wool during winter that can be collected from the ground or plucked from tame animals – as was the case when wild sheep were first herded and domesticated.
Source: Photo: Cindy Hopkins / Alamy Stock Photo, image # C4WNRW. Reproduced under license, Alamy.

like many other species that molt after winter and just like the surviving primitive breeds of sheep. The wool falls off their backs of its own accord, or the sheep might rub against a shrub or a fence to get rid of the wool as the weather starts to get warm. So wild sheep did produce wool – and they continued to produce more wool on a regular annual basis as long as they stayed alive.[8]

This is not to say that sheep and goats were not killed for meat, or llamas and alpacas were never eaten – although alpacas were usually kept exclusively for their wool. To the Incas, killing an alpaca was almost a crime. They even hunted another species – the vicuña (ancestor of the alpaca) – for its very fine wool, which can be harvested only every few years. The vicuña was too troublesome to tame so the Incas would go out and hunt them. After carefully collecting the wool, instead of killing them for meat, the Incas would release the animals back into the wild, so they could hunt them again in a couple of years for more wool.

THEORIES OF AGRICULTURE

We face many challenges in trying to explain the origins of agriculture. The consensus view among archaeologists is that currently there is no consensus. Some leading archaeologists admit that all of our existing theories are clearly unsatisfactory, and we really have no idea why agriculture began in the first place.[9]

Who Needs a Theory?

As a symptom of the mounting malaise, some say that the quest for a general theory is misguided and doomed to failure. Instead, they say we should be searching for particular causes that might explain the transition in certain places. We should accept that different causes could have operated in different parts of the world at different times. This pessimistic attitude to general theories relates, also, to doubts about the definition of agriculture and whether we should draw a clear distinction (or dichotomy) between agriculture and foraging. Yet there are dissenting voices too, people who point out how this denial of a meaningful divide may conveniently sidestep the problem. In 2009, a symposium was held in Mexico, organized by a couple of prominent researchers who summarized the state of play:

> At the end of our time together, we did not determine why agriculture originated. We did not even agree on whether its causes were global or local...
>
> Today, an eerie synchronicity in the timing of the first domesticates around the end of the Pleistocene is emerging...[10]

Whatever our biases, we must explain a few basic things: the long delay, the "eerie synchronicity" between the first agricultural experiments around the world, and the coincidence with climate change. And there are some rather awkward facts to challenge our assumptions about the supposed advantages of agriculture. We must address these questions as well: why was there often an ongoing reliance on foraging for food? Why the often strange choice of species to domesticate initially? And last but not least, why should agriculture ever begin at all – given the costs and risks and the typically negative view of agriculture among hunter-gatherers?

To quote Peter Bellwood, one of the leading researchers on early agriculture, "In fact, we do not really know why farming began anywhere in the world...."[11]

Population Pressure as a Lost Cause

Two theories deserve an honorable mention, not because they are valid but because they draw attention to the issues. The first has been around for many years in various guises and it still refuses to go away – much as many archaeologists probably wish that it would. The second is more recent, and it highlights the evidence that tends to get overlooked.

The first theory is population pressure. A need to feed more people was long seen as a likely reason for agriculture: increased production of food could solve the problem of wanting to feed more people. Alas, archaeologists discovered that evidence to support this common notion is lacking – which came as quite a shock. Population growth did occur in some cases, but it generally happened only after agriculture had already commenced. Those pioneering communities that first began to experiment with agriculture were often no larger than their hunter-gatherer counterparts – and nor were they facing any food shortages, as far as we can tell.[12]

Nonetheless the leading proponent of this population theory – Mark Cohen, Professor of Anthropology at the State University of New York – makes some very good points. He says we really do need to find some common cause – a general theory – to explain why agriculture began:

> My perspective was then and is now that such widespread common events require relatively simple common core events and causes. To argue otherwise defies the odds of coincidence...[13]

Cohen makes a few more points. He insists that we do have evidence for population growth in early farming contexts. Specifically, there was an increase in human fertility despite the poorer health and the likely higher mortality rates – and it was the higher fertility that resulted in population growth. He cites a reduction in breastfeeding as a factor, which would reduce birth-spacing – we shall return to this topic later. Cohen also makes a few other valid points. He criticizes the common supposition that agriculture was better because it produced a food surplus, allowing the storage of food (such as grain) as a risk-reduction strategy. As Cohen says, food storage carries its own risks – which we tend to forget – such as destruction by rot and vermin. More important, storing food suggests that people favored future food over immediate consumption – which flies in the face of logic and contradicts the hunter-gatherer ethos of immediate sharing, rather than accumulating wealth for the future. In any case, storing a surplus is a less secure strategy compared with the security and flexibility of mobile hunting and gathering.[14]

Cohen offers no solution to this "paradox" of food security as a myth of early agriculture: it seems that people started to work harder – much harder – to produce a food surplus that was less secure than hunting and gathering. Cohen says simply that we must face the inconsistences in the evidence, and in our assumptions.

Feasting amid Famine

Another theory is the feasting hypothesis, proposed by Brian Hayden (Emeritus Professor of Archaeology at Simon Fraser University in Canada). Hayden argues that agriculture was not about staple foods so much as luxury products. He says this happened because societies were getting more complex. Luxury products functioned as valued goods in societies with social hierarchies where status and prestige had displaced the egalitarian principles of simple hunter-gatherers. These luxury products were often not used routinely but were reserved for special occasions, such as feasts.[15]

Alas, as with population pressure, most of our evidence for social complexity follows rather than precedes early agriculture. Nonetheless, what is so worthwhile about Hayden's theory is how he draws attention to some of the anomalies. He points out that agriculture often involved producing not only food but textile fibers for woven fabrics – which he regards as luxury items. And with food, Hayden highlights the awkward fact that many of the first plant domesticates were not staples – peppers, for instance, which occur early in South America. Likewise, some of the first animal domesticates were not always consumed as staple foods – pigs and cattle, for instance, were often reserved for special occasions. In the case of Southeast Asian tribal societies, Hayden points out that meat from domesticated animals (cattle, buffalo, pigs, ducks, and chickens) was often not consumed at all other than for feasting and sacrifices. Hayden's main contribution though is how he targets the common assumption that cultivating cereal crops was a great idea.[16]

68. **Hayden's feasting theory of agriculture**
In Sulawesi, Indonesia, Torajan farmers consume surplus rice and domesticated pigs mainly on special "feasting" occasions, not on a regular daily basis. The special occasion in this instance is a funeral.
Source: Photo by Brian Hayden, © Brian Hayden. Reproduced by permission of Brian Hayden.

As Hayden points out, the wild ancestors of our major cereals (wheat, rice, and corn) were poor food options compared to other wild foods – which is why they rarely made it onto the menu for hunter-gatherers. A classic example is rice, which only became a food staple for people in Asia after agriculture had already commenced. Wild rice was always more suited as feed for animals (chicken and pigs in the case of China), but even after rice was domesticated – when it began to yield more return in terms of feeding humans – it was not always a favorite food:

> Given its low productivity, wild rice must have been ranked very low on the scale of optimal caloric returns...
>
> Certainly hunting, fishing and gathering wild plants continued to be extremely important aspects of these subsistence economies for thousands of years... It remains unclear what role rice may have played in overall subsistence, even after initial domestication.[17]

Cohen and Hayden both agree on the need for a general theory: the coincidences between the different regions demand some kind of general explanation. But these two theories – population pressure (Cohen) and social complexity (Hayden) – are not supported well by the available evidence. In both cases, their proposed causes tend to follow on after the advent of agriculture. Nevertheless, their critiques of conventional ideas about agriculture are valuable and essentially valid.

Yet these theories still assume the priority of food – food for human consumption. This is where we need a more profound critique. Only if we realize that people at the time were seeking more resources than food will we ever be able to account for the patterns and coincidences (and the anomalies). Before considering the evidence for textile resources and how this may help resolve things, we need to look at a couple of other ingredients that were involved. The first is another new trend that began to emerge toward the end of the last ice age, a trend which often played its own role in the transition to agriculture: sedentism.

SEDENTISM AND AGRICULTURE

Before we look at textiles as a reason for agriculture, another big change happened in how people were living their lives, a change which often (though not always) played a role in the origin of agriculture. Rather than moving around from place to place, people in some areas began to live in permanent settlements.

The first archaeological signs of village life appear before we see any agriculture. One early site is a campsite called Ohalo II in Israel, where we also find early textile fibers and possibly some early signs of plant cultivation (with wheat and barley). The textile fibers were twisted into lengthy strands that might have been used to make ropes, baskets, or fishing nets – a forerunner of woven cloth. Regardless of whether the Israeli site represents an early (and given its transience, a failed) attempt at agriculture, it does seem to signify a shift toward a more sedentary human existence at a remarkably early time: around 23,000 years ago – the height of the last ice age.[18]

The Attractions of Village Life

Although the causes of sedentism remain obscure – we shall return to this question later – archaeologists are quite sure that it happened separately from agriculture. Many of the early village communities did not embark upon agriculture at all. Instead, they continued to rely completely for their food on hunting and gathering (and in coastal areas, fishing). The combination of a hunter-gatherer economy with a sedentary village lifestyle is called the Mesolithic – which means Middle Stone Age, midway between the Paleolithic (Old Stone Age) and Neolithic (New Stone Age). The name came about originally because when archaeologists first discovered it in the nineteenth century, they assumed that the Mesolithic was a stepping stone to agriculture. Now we know that it was a separate trend, an alternative lifestyle based on the independent trend towards sedentism.

While sedentism was independent from agriculture, it did sometimes lead to agriculture – inadvertently. One reason is that when people started to settle down to live in one location, it altered the surrounding ecosystem. Some plant species were favored in the vicinity – grasses for instance – but more important, the villages attracted certain animal species. For these animals, the villages provided shelter from the elements and protection from predators and – perhaps the main attraction – lots of easy food in the form of garbage and also food in the form of other animals attracted to the settlements. Many of these uninvited visitors were not welcome: rats, ants, and spiders, for instance. But some of the species were not so troublesome, and they even made themselves rather useful to people. Over generations, these animal species came to depend more on humans, and biologically they were often altered physically through natural selection in the new environments. There was some artificial selection involved too, as people selected certain traits that made them more attractive or useful. So these species became domesticated.

In this way, sedentism on its own sometimes led to the domestication of certain plant and animal species. Domestic animals that made themselves at home in the human settlements are called commensals. The domestication of commensals was more of a passive process on the part of humans, as opposed to an active process whereby people may have intentionally targeted certain species. Sheep and goats, for instance, were actively hunted by humans, and then later they were herded, which implies a more deliberate process of domestication. In reality, active and passive processes were involved in most cases, in a positive feedback fashion. Insofar as we can usefully distinguish between these active and passive processes, the passive process that sometimes happened in sedentary communities represents an alternative pathway to agriculture.

Self-domesticating Species

Among our favorite pets, dogs and cats are prime examples of species that probably domesticated themselves in this passive manner. As people settled down in villages, dogs and cats were soon attracted to the settlements. These animals started out as wary scavengers, but in close proximity to humans they soon got friendlier – and people found them to be quite useful. They helped to recycle all of the rubbish that accumulated in and around the villages, and they kept vermin in check – cats are good at hunting rats (a less welcome commensal). And of course we found them to be good companions.[19]

Dogs were actually the first species to be domesticated. Wild dogs first began to approach humans in communities that were becoming more sedentary – before agriculture began. The date and location (or locations, plural) of dog domestication are still debated. Evidence from archaeology and genetics now suggests dogs were domesticated somewhere in Eurasia before the end of the last ice age. There have been some disputed claims for wolves evolving into dogs in eastern Siberia – Siberian huskies – as early as 33,000 years ago. Other claims based on skeletal remains that are said to be dogs rather than wolves have been reported from Russia, Belgium, and the Czech Republic between 35,000 and 30,000 years ago. At present, based on more conservative assessments of skeletal material and the genetic evidence, we have three favored locations: northern China, Southwest Asia, and Europe, with estimated dates ranging between 16,000 and 11,000 years ago. Whatever the location, it seems that dogs were domesticated before the end of the last ice age and perhaps before 20,000 years ago – and this happened among hunter-gatherers who were probably becoming less mobile, not among agriculturalists.[20]

Cats are an interesting case. House cats are shown in the art of Ancient Egypt from around 4,000 years ago, but their wild ancestors were presumably attracted to human settlements much earlier in Southwest Asia. Cats had spread to the Mediterranean island of Cyprus by 11,000 years ago, along with pigs and cultivated wheat and barley (although at that time, the cats were still physically wild). Domesticated cats spread as far as northern China by 5,000 years ago, appearing in agricultural sites where they made themselves useful as predators on all the rats that were attracted to crops such as rice. Studies of isotopes in the cat bones show that these Chinese cats were not only eating the rats but also the cereal crops, which at that stage in northern China was mainly millet. So this major Chinese crop was evidently feeding not only people but also farm animals – dogs, pigs, chicken, and cats.[21]

Domestic animals that started out as commensals include dogs, rats, pigs, fowl, and cats, along with house mice and the house sparrow. Some of them – notably chicken and pigs – soon became major foods for people in the settlements, and these animals were fed with the cereal crops. So the presence of the self-domesticating species was an added incentive for agriculture as food production. And as happened with grasses such as wheat, barley, and rye that sustained the sheep and goats (and later, cattle) in Southwest Asia, we are reminded that the main cereal crops in China were grown not just to feed people but also to feed their animals. This applies with rice too, which started out as just one of the so-called barnyard grasses that grew around early Chinese settlements in the Yangtze Basin from 10,000 years ago. Only later did rice become a staple food for humans. Chicken also eat rice as well as millet, and domesticated chicken appear in various parts of Asia from around 10,000 years ago.[22]

The Meaning of the Mesolithic

Sedentism was often linked to agriculture by this passive commensal process whereby certain animal species were attracted to human settlements. These animal species effectively domesticated themselves in the novel ecological niche. This same process probably promoted the cultivation of food crops to feed the animals on their favorite diets. However, this happened only in some places. We cannot say that sedentary life always (or even typically) encouraged people to adopt agriculture. Despite the commensal process, sedentism alone cannot be considered as a general cause of agriculture.

Most of the sedentary communities that emerged toward the end of the last ice age did not engage in agriculture to any great extent. These are the so-called Mesolithic societies. The Mesolithic lifestyle was a sedentary kind of existence in which people subsisted on wild food resources. They settled down in villages but carried on with hunting and gathering – and often fishing as well. Mesolithic communities were common in places where wild food resources were plentiful in the local environments. In these regions, people had no need to bother with agriculture – neither for food nor for clothes. We find Mesolithic communities spread throughout Europe, North and South America, and in Eastern and Southeast Asia. In some cases, their settlements grew into very large villages. The Mesolithic represents a viable alternative to agriculture; it was another option for people who preferred to settle down (for whatever reasons). After the last ice age, the Mesolithic lifestyle was more common than Neolithic agriculture in many parts of the world, continuing as a stable and successful adaptation in its own right for thousands of years. Mesolithic societies eventually disappeared as agriculture spread around the world – although some Mesolithic communities held out until quite recently in parts of Southeast Asia and South America. Because they have disappeared – and because our own civilized societies are founded on agriculture – we tend to forget about the Mesolithic.

The meaning of the Mesolithic is that it challenges our assumptions about the benefits of agriculture – even for those people who preferred to lead a sedentary lifestyle. Despite the outdated connotations of its name as a middle stage between the Paleolithic and the Neolithic, the Mesolithic was not a transition so much as a challenge to agriculture. When faced with pressure to adopt agriculture – which often involved pressure from invading agricultural populations – people leading this sedentary Mesolithic lifestyle nonetheless did sometimes find it fairly easy to adopt some agricultural elements. Unlike mobile hunter-gatherers, Mesolithic people did not always need to surrender their mobility to adopt agriculture – sometimes, for instance, they were already living in permanent or semipermanent settlements. Nevertheless, they generally resisted a full transition to agriculture for as long as they could. They were reluctant to become fully agricultural because they could see little benefit and many disadvantages. To sacrifice the reliability of their broad resource base in exchange for a restricted dependence on just a few species meant a reduction in their economic security (as well as a less varied diet). The reduced security was not adequately offset by a food surplus, for which they had no obvious use. Values were involved too: they valued the closer involvement with nature that went along with the hunter-gatherer economy, and they also valued the egalitarian principles of sharing and social equality that were undermined by an emphasis on surplus production and the acquisition of material wealth. And they could see that agriculture involved a lot more work.[23]

Resisting Agriculture in the Rainforest

Even in the world today, these same issues arise in South America and Southeast Asia where a few hunter-gatherer communities try vainly to preserve their traditional values and resist the adoption of agriculture. Their cause has been taken up by environmentalists, who fight a losing battle against the destruction of the rainforest habitats where these indigenous peoples have led a relatively easy existence until recent decades. In Southeast Asia, in the Malaysian province of Sarawak on the island of Borneo, there still exist some mobile and semisedentary hunter-gatherer groups living alongside neighbors that have adopted rice agriculture. These foragers used to wear simple clothes made from bark cloth, but now they wear fashionable jeans and T-shirts reflecting contact with missionaries and government agencies, and recent exposure to commercial advertising. Yet among these groups, the people realize that cultivating rice involves doing more work and having less connection with the natural forest environment. They recognize too that agriculture entails an unwelcome shift from an egalitarian social structure to one based on status, accumulated wealth and prestige – and on regular feasting with rice, as Hayden would point out.[24]

The transition to agriculture involved a host of transitions – not just economic but psychological and ethical – that are intrinsic to agriculture. There is also a textile transition in the realm of clothing to keep in mind, and as we shall see, there is a psychological side to sedentism too. Agriculture will never make sense unless it is considered in the wider context of all the other transitions. The rainforest dwellers of Borneo are more aware of these other aspects because they sit right on the cutting edge – the sickle blade. We are so far removed from the transition that we can no longer appreciate all that is involved (and lost) by adopting agriculture.

ELEVEN

AGRICULTURE AND TEXTILES IN EURASIA

Armed with these new doubts and possibilities, we can look afresh at the evidence for early agriculture in different parts of the world. We will do this in a systematic fashion, region by region. The account given here is unbalanced and biased – to balance a biased perception of agriculture as food production. And in the literature, there is a frequent failure – with the heroic exception of a few brave souls such as Brian Hayden – to even allude to the long delay before humans started agriculture, not to mention its dubious benefits when compared to hunting and gathering.

In moving from region to region, a number of doubts will stand out. First is the food issue, which has a few angles. Did early agriculture really contribute much to the human diet? Or did the people still rely mainly on wild resources for their daily bread? Another question is whether cultivated plant foods were fed to farm animals as well as to people. With the animals, we need to consider if they were commensal – whether they domesticated themselves in sedentary situations. The other issue relates to textiles: we should look at whether the animals provided food alone, or if they also offered materials for making clothes. The multipurpose role of domesticates applies with crops too: as well as feeding animals, some crops yielded fibers (see Appendix). So we need to look critically at each region, and ultimately, we need to wonder what was really going on.

THE MANY REGIONS OF EARLY AGRICULTURE

As mentioned earlier, archaeologists now realize that agriculture began in many parts of the world. And we now tend to include places where new species were domesticated, regardless of whether these places may have been affected by the spread of agriculture from other regions. For example, the Indus Valley is traditionally considered a secondary center – influenced by the spread of earlier farming developments in Southwest Asia and China. Still, a number of important species were first domesticated there, including a new species of cattle and cotton. If we include regions where new species were domesticated regardless of whether they were independent, the total number of centers is around fifteen. This includes Japan, where one variety of millet (barnyard millet) was first domesticated – although the transition to agriculture in Japan was very likely related to earlier developments on the Asian mainland. Centers of domestication are not necessarily centers of agriculture.[1]

One newly-discovered region is in eastern North America, where sunflowers and possibly tobacco were first grown. The eastern woodlands region in the United States is now considered to be an independent agricultural center, although agriculture started earlier in Mexico. In assessing the

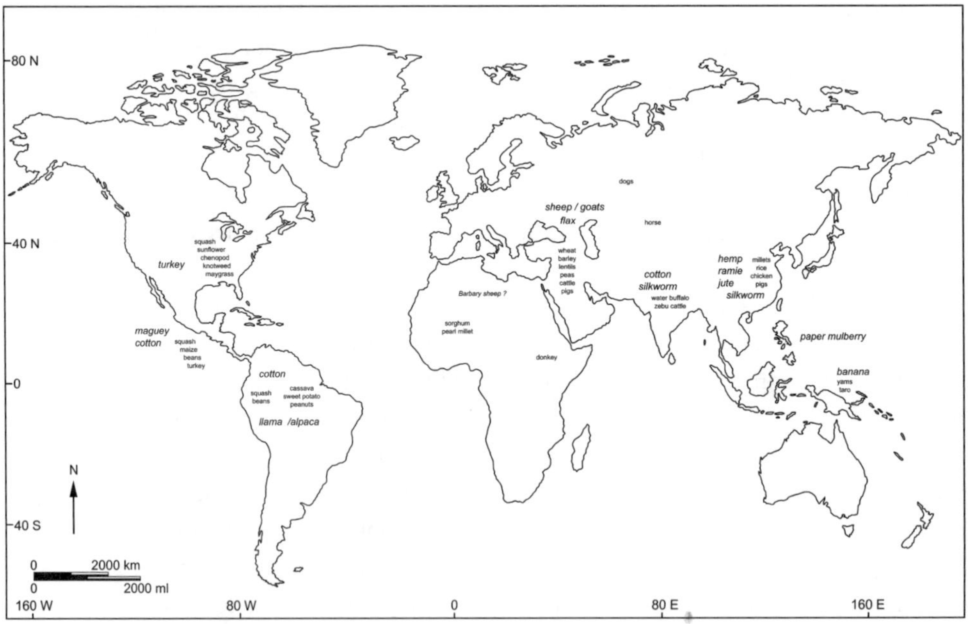

69. **World map showing fiber products in agricultural centers**
Areas of early agriculture and some of the major plant and animal species domesticated, showing fiber resources (in italics) and food resources. Among the latter are food crops that served as animal feed, while some of the animal (and plant) species were commensals attracted to human settlements. Paper mulberry is included as it was cultivated to produce bark cloth, although bark cloth is a felted rather than a woven material.

status of all these candidates for early agriculture, archaeologists are inclined nowadays to downplay the role of diffusion and instead emphasize the unique contributions made by many regions. Yet it is the earliest cases that still grab our attention, and it is true that most of the world's major food crops and farm animals derive from the few classic regions where agriculture first began.

We shall begin with Southwest Asia – the region that stretches from Iran across to Turkey and down to Israel – which still has the honor of the earliest well-documented agriculture. Then there is China – especially the Yellow River valley in the north and the Yangtze Valley where rice was first cultivated – and also two regions in the Americas: one in Mexico and the other in northwest South America, covering mainly Peru. We can then look at the latest entrant on the list, Papua New Guinea. We can look also at recent claims that the concept of agriculture should be extended to encompass some of the traditional practices of hunter-gatherers – such as the Australian Aborigines.

SHEEP, GOATS, AND GRASS IN SOUTHWEST ASIA

Although dogs were domesticated as commensals in early settlements perhaps stretching back into the late Pleistocene, the first farm animals appeared at the end of the ice age, and these were sheep and goats. Archaeologists used to think that cereal crops like wheat were domesticated before sheep and goats, but it now looks like the plants and animals were domesticated together around 11,500 years ago. The simultaneous domestication of these animals and crops matches very closely the massive climate changes that occurred at the end of the last ice age 11,700 years ago – the beginning of our Holocene epoch.[2]

To begin with sheep and goats, the assumption is that meat was the sole resource involved – and that wool was a secondary product that became relevant only later with the development of a permanent fleece in sheep. Yet whereas obtaining meat means killing the animals, there was clearly a new emphasis on keeping these animals alive. On its own, this effort to husband living animals implies that people had more to gain from the living animals, which suggests an interest in the renewable resource of their natural fiber. Yet it is widely held that wool could not have been the resource that led to their domestication. Two reasons are cited: wild sheep have no wool, and early domestic sheep and goats were exploited mainly for meat. The first is simply false, and the second is debatable.

Woolly Thinking

Regarding the wool of wild sheep, we saw earlier that wild sheep do produce plenty of wool, which they shed annually after winter. Surviving primitive

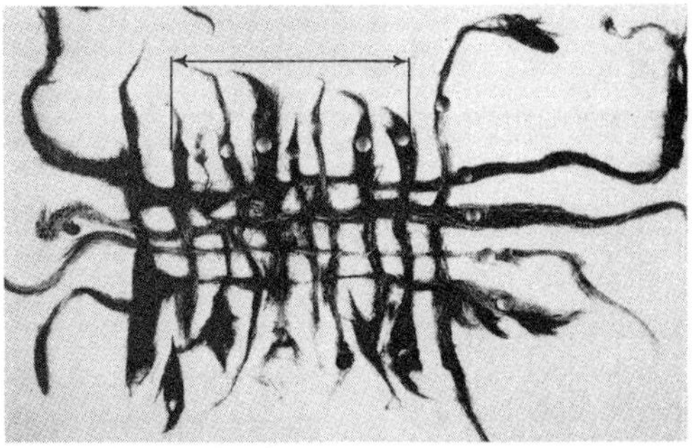

70. **Fabric woven from mouflon wool**
A piece of loose fabric woven by hand from twisted strands of fibers formed naturally in the coat of a mouflon wild sheep. The indicated length in the photo is 23 cm (9 inches). The fibers tend to become twisted into a yarn of their own accord during the molt, and the length of fibers varies from a few centimeters to more than 100 cm (40 inches).

Source: Photo by Michael Ryder, in Ryder, Antiquity 38, 1964; Plate LVIb. Reproduced by permission of Cambridge University Press.

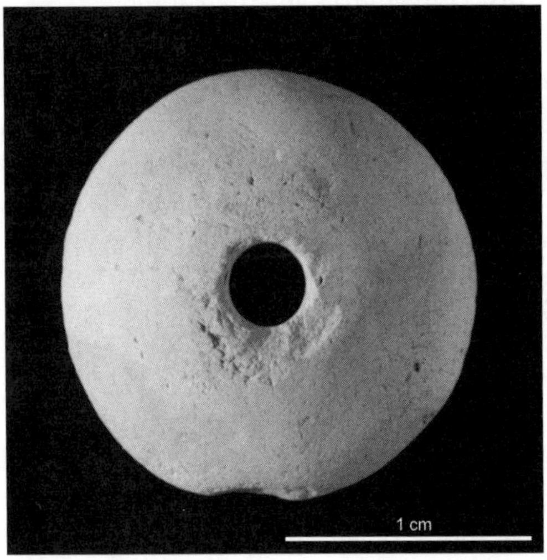

71. **6,000-year-old spindle whorl in Iraq**
Ceramic spindle whorl from the city of Uruk in the Mesopotamian civilization of Sumer, around 6,000 years ago. Sumerian clothing was made from sheep and goat hides (often with the fleece attached) and also from woven fibers, mainly flax (linen) and wool – both products of early agriculture in the region. This spindle whorl was excavated in 1960–1961 during the Joint Expedition to Nippur, Baghdad School of the American Schools of Oriental Research, and The Oriental Institute of the University of Chicago.

Source: Metropolitan Museum of Art (accession # 62.70.87). Image reproduced under Creative Commons (CC0–1.0) license, courtesy of the Metropolitan Museum of Art, New York.

breeds of sheep (such as the mouflon and Soay) produce copious wool that can be collected or plucked from tame animals – and easily woven into cloth. Genetic studies point to the wild mouflon as the ancestor of all modern sheep breeds.[3]

Goats do not produce wool as such, but their hair is like fine wool, and some varieties (such as angora and cashmere) are excellent for weaving into fabrics. As with wild sheep, the fiber of wild goats is shed naturally in the annual molt, although mohair from angora goats is nowadays usually harvested by shearing, often twice a year.

The development of a permanent fleece in domestic sheep occurred by 6,000 years ago, which coincides with finding many more spindle whorls and loom weights in the archaeological record. At some sites, an increase in spindle whorls from around 8,000 years ago is associated with changes in the slaughter patterns of the flocks that may indicate a permanent fleece as early as 8,000 years ago. The slaughter pattern has a larger proportion of older sheep: the adults were kept alive for six years or more – presumably because they had a permanent fleece that was harvested annually. From this point onward, archaeologists recognize the importance of wool in the local economies. The emergence of a market-driven textile industry from around 6,000 years ago marked a major socioeconomic change that culminated in the rise of civilization; this phase has been called a secondary products revolution.[4]

A few archaeologists are now wondering whether we can ignore the molting of wool in wild sheep (and the wool-like hair in goats) as a renewable resource that encouraged people to herd them in the first place. They also question how the slaughter patterns are interpreted to infer the priority of meat (and to exclude any role for wool). There is no doubt that sheep and goats were killed for meat: it is a question of whether this was all that was happening in the beginning.

The slaughter patterns confirm that young adult animals were killed, consistent with meat as a product. Yet it is also clear that older adults (especially females) were kept alive too. Conventionally, this is said to reflect the need for herd maintenance, which is true enough – but this also permits a potential role for fiber exploitation. A good example occurs at a settlement in central Turkey where sheep, still wild in terms of their skeletal characteristics, were kept alive in stables between 11,000 and 10,000 years ago. The data from dental counts suggest that around 40 percent were kept alive for more than two years, and more than 10 percent survived in captivity until they were between six and ten years old. The pattern of killing most of the young animals is said to show how herd management was "geared principally or exclusively to meat production," and yet plenty of sheep did escape slaughter as lambs; moreover, the culling of juvenile male sheep is not so evident at most sites in the region.[5]

The other problem with these slaughter patterns is how they are compared with modern-day herds that are geared to produce a massive wool surplus in the context of market economies. A big wool surplus is not so relevant to early farmers. Wool derived from a few sheep with annual molting would have been quite enough to meet local community needs. We should also keep in mind that woolen garments are reasonably durable: they do not need to be replaced every year. For these reasons, some archaeologists now concede that in the crucial early stages of domestication, a causal role for wool "cannot be ruled out completely."[6]

Fodder for Thought

Southwest Asia was also where some of our major crops were first cultivated. Wheat is the most significant for feeding people in the modern world, but the earliest crops in this region comprised a collection of cereals (wheat, barley, and rye) together with legumes (such as lentils and chickpea). As Hayden points out, the wild ancestors of cereals such as wheat were poor choices as staple foods for humans. Rye, for instance, is used more widely to feed animals, and rye might have been cultivated as early as 13,000 years ago along the Euphrates River in Syria – which would make rye the first crop.[7]

Barley is also grown widely as a fodder crop for animals, but it could have been used to brew beer too, of course. And if that was the case, then maybe it could explain the weird choices: people were brewing beer and getting inebriated.[8]

A more sober possibility is that this suite of crops served the same purpose then that it serves in the world today: as a perfect diet for most of our farm animals. The need to feed animals would also explain why people wanted a food surplus: sheep and goats are quite greedy when it comes to grass. The ideal diet for modern breeds of sheep (like the Merino) is around 60 percent cereal grass and 40 percent legumes. Grazing animals such as sheep and cattle consume not only the grass but also the seeds (grain), and grain is used commonly to fatten these animals prior to slaughter. So the greater seed yield associated with the domestication of cereals does not necessarily reflect a focus on feeding people with cereal crops.[9]

The simultaneous domestication of these grazing animals and their natural food might begin to make sense if we stop supposing that hunter-gatherers decided to depend on these crops for their own food. In this scenario, the impetus for a food surplus – and for people to work harder to make a surplus – arose when people wanted to feed sheep and goats as well as feeding themselves. We tend to forget that domesticating these animals required first taming them by finding ways to feed them. And to keep them close to the settlements on a year-round basis, people could store surplus grain and straw as fodder to see the animals through the winter months. Otherwise, the animals were likely to wander away in search of greener pastures. Once this process was underway, it would favor a shift in the human diet to include processing cereal seeds, if only for reasons of efficiency.

Farmers, crop scientists, and historians are well aware that much of the world's agricultural activity throughout history has been devoted to producing food for animals and fibers for textiles. In Australia for instance, prior to the advent of synthetic fibers such as nylon, the national economy depended mainly on wool production – and on crops such as wheat to feed the sheep. Australia rode on the sheep's back – and that common saying was true right up until the mining boom of the 1970s. Producing food for the people was a minor part of the Australian agricultural system: in fact, feeding the human population was almost an afterthought. And that situation was hardly unique to Australia.

72. **Agriculture in colonial Australia revolved around wool**
Agriculture in colonial Australia was focused on wool production and the cultivation of crops (especially wheat) to sustain the sheep population. The Australian economy remained heavily dependent on revenue from wool production until the mining boom of the 1970s.
Source: Tom Roberts, *The Golden Fleece*, 1894, oil on canvas, Art Gallery of New South Wales, accession # 648. Photo: Jenni Carter, © Art Gallery of New South Wales. Reproduced under license, Art Gallery of New South Wales.

Archaeologists can now get some insight into whether early agriculture involved feeding farm animals as well as humans: they can measure isotopes in bones to look at prehistoric diets – the diets of animals as well as humans. At one of the early agricultural sites in Turkey where wheat and legumes were cultivated, and sheep and goats were probably domesticated, archaeologists found a couple of surprises when they measured the isotopes in the bones. They found that meat from the animals comprised only around 10–15 percent of human meat intake: most of peoples' meat supply still came from hunting wild animals – which would seem to contradict the idea that sheep and goats were herded primarily as a meat resource. To further confound the researchers, they found that the animals were sharing in the crops, especially the legumes. In other words, these domesticated animals were supplying little meat for people, and yet people were cultivating plants to feed them.[10]

A Wild Wheat Harvest

If people were feeding sheep and goats with cereal grasses and legumes, then this might resolve one of the big anomalies with early agriculture in Southwest Asia. The problem was made clear by a famous experiment carried out by an American crop scientist in the 1960s, Jack Harlan. His little study was one of those great experiments in the history of science: it was simple, and yet it exposed a fundamental flaw in our thinking.

Harlan's simple experiment involved going to where wild wheat still grows naturally in Turkey. He wanted to see how much seed he could gather from the wild plants using his bare hands, and also by using a flint sickle blade like the ones used by Neolithic farmers. To his amazement, he found that he could easily collect enough grain with his own bare hands to feed many people in a very short time. In just one hour, he collected nearly a kilogram of grain. At that rate he calculated that a family could collect enough grain within a few weeks to feed themselves for a whole year. This raises a simple question – a question that remains unanswered: if it is really so easy to get plenty of grain from natural stands of wild wheat, why would anyone start cultivating? Instead of planting and tending seeds, they could just come back next year and collect plenty of wild seeds again.[11]

Harlan's experiment has been replicated in Israel with barley as well as wheat, and also with legumes. In the case of legumes, the researchers discovered the opposite problem: in terms of seed productivity, wild legumes are much less productive than wheat – and yet legumes were cultivated in the early days of agriculture. Why would people bother to cultivate legumes as well as wheat? Did they suddenly develop a taste for pea soup or a craving for lentils? To add to the mystery, with peas it was the least productive variety (in terms of seeds) that people first chose to domesticate, yet this variety of pea happens to be the one preferred as animal forage. Further doubts arise with legumes due to seed dormancy: only 10 percent germinate in the first year. Each plant that does germinate yields an average of 10 seeds, so a farmer who carefully planted and tended 100 seeds would harvest a total of only 100 seeds the following year. That is the same number of seeds she planted in the first place. So there is little incentive to cultivate wild legumes with the aim to feed people with peas or lentils, even if they did want soup. To make matters worse, the yield with lentils is not just low but quite erratic from year to year, which undermines the notion of food security as a motive. Yet we know that people did start to cultivate legumes along with cereals in the early days of agriculture.[12]

The need to feed sheep and goats with cereal grasses can explain both the motive to produce a surplus beyond any human requirement and also the motive to cultivate legumes – animals consume virtually the whole plant, so seeds are less relevant. To think that agriculture began as a strategy to create a more secure food supply for people with grass seeds does not add up (and it never will add up) when we look at it from the perspective of hunter-gatherers. And in Southwest Asia, there is another early crop that will always challenge our cherished assumptions about why agriculture began.

Flax as a Forgotten Founding Crop

Flax gets overshadowed by cereals, but it was one of the founding crops of agriculture in Southwest Asia, along with cereals and legumes. Flax seeds are harvested for vegetable oil (linseed) while its fibrous stems are processed to weave one of the world's major fabrics – linen. People were exploiting flax for its fiber long before the Neolithic. As we saw earlier, archaeologists found twisted wild flax fibers that may have been woven into baskets and nets (and perhaps clothes) at a 36,000-year-old Paleolithic site in Georgia. Cultivation of flax likely dates from around 11,000 years ago, with linseed found in northern Syria at one early agricultural site. However, the physical changes in the seeds, which archaeologists use to define the domesticated variety, do not appear until around 9,000 years ago. Yet we do have some preserved linen fabrics at a couple of sites in the region between 10,000 and 9,000 years ago, so flax was presumably cultivated for its fiber prior to 9,000 years ago.[13]

Flax fibers are quite long and are reasonably easy to spin by hand, and spinning flax fibers to make longer lengths of yarn for linen cloth would have been done by hand in the beginning. Tools to help with spinning (such as spindles) were employed in due course, and these were probably made from wood. Unfortunately, we have no archaeological evidence for spinning until the advent of heavy spindle whorls made from baked clay and ceramic pottery. These made spinning more efficient and they became common at Neolithic sites throughout Southwest Asia from around 7,000 years ago.

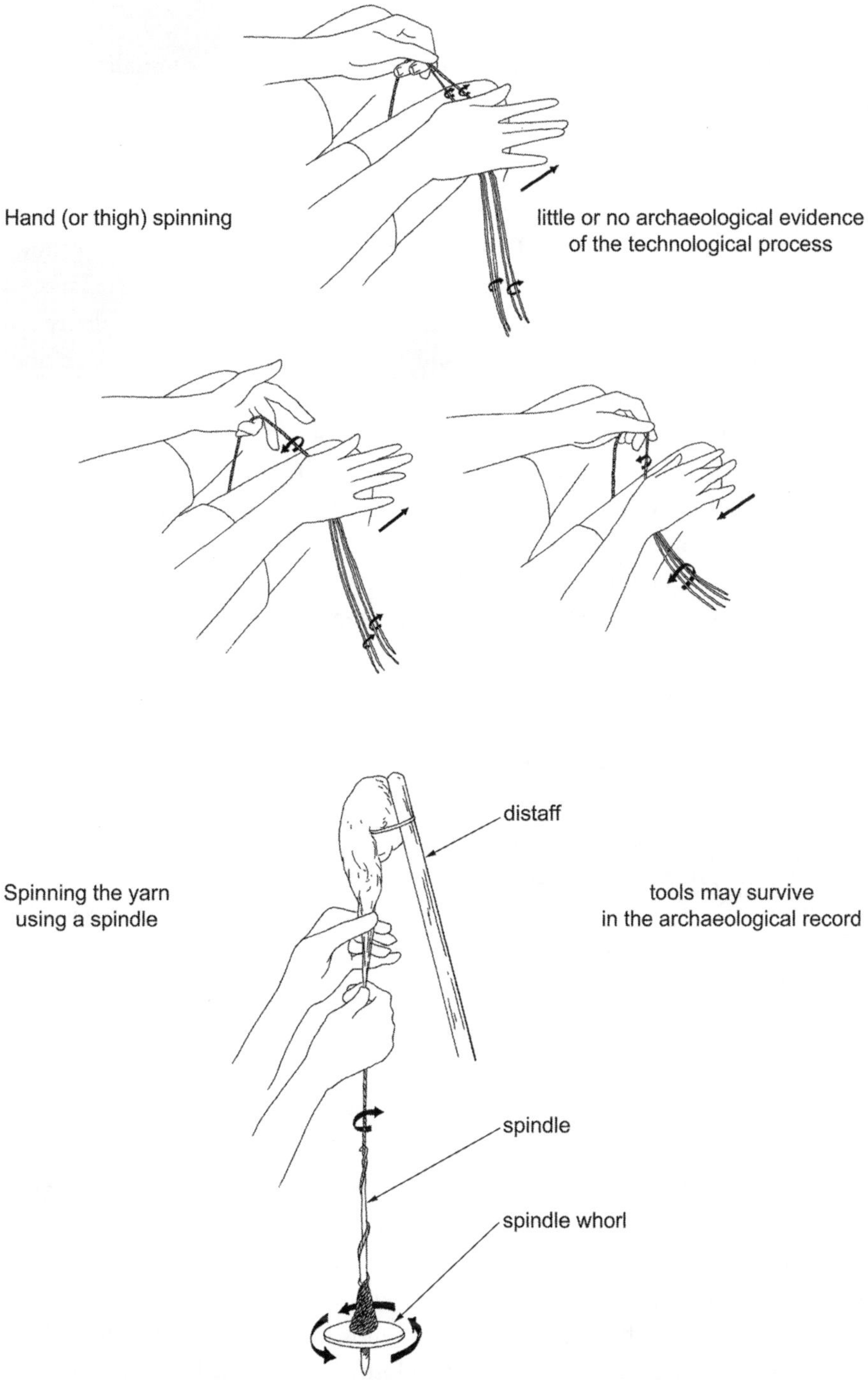

73. **Spinning fibers by hand and with a spindle**
Hand-spinning (top) allows fibers to be spun into yarns without using technology that might be preserved in the archaeological record. The spindle was a later innovation that made the process more efficient, and the spindle whorl – often made from stone or pottery – can leave tangible evidence of fiber-spinning in the archaeological record.
Source: Tiedemann and Jakes, 2006:295–296. Reproduced by permission of John Wiley & Sons, Inc.

Invisible Textiles and Invisible Tools

One problem we face with early textiles is not just the poor visibility of the textiles but poor visibility of the tools used to make them. Until people began to use heavy spindle whorls (and loom weights), textile-making tools such as spindles (and looms for weaving) would have been made from perishable materials, primarily wood. In effect, we actually have less archaeological evidence for textile clothing in the Neolithic than for much older clothing made from animal skins in the Paleolithic. As shown in previous chapters, although no clothes have survived from the ice ages, there are plenty of resilient stone tools such as scrapers and blades that were used to clean and cut hides to make clothes. In the last ice age, we also have bone awls used for sewing and from nearly 40,000 years ago, toward the coldest phase, eyed needles. But with the shift from hides to woven fabrics after the ice age, there is a shift to using wooden tools. So we have a paradox: early textile technologies are often not as visible as older technologies where the main tools were made from stones and bones. The oldest preserved wooden spindles have been found in a couple of desert caves in Israel, dated to around 6,000 years ago.[14]

So for this crucial period when agriculture began and textile clothes replaced animal skins, we depend mainly on finding fragments of woven cloth – which are few and far between. Yet these fragments do exist and that is the important thing. And as time goes by, archaeologists will find more. For example, we now have evidence for the weaving of linen fabric from well before when we see any spindle whorls in the archaeological record. There are sophisticated linen textiles preserved from around 9,500 years ago at a site in Syria, without spindle whorls. The linen cloth was presumably made from flax fibers spun by hand, or with wooden spindles and perhaps with whorls made from perishable materials such as wood or non-baked clay.[15]

Textiles Can Disentangle the Text

To summarize, in Southwest Asia there was an early transition to agriculture that coincided with climate change at the end of the last ice age. People began to domesticate plants and animals, but many problems arise if we try to make sense of this solely as a way to feed people. We should not assume it was superior to foraging. In fact, early farmers around the world often carried on with hunting and gathering as a way to get most of their food for thousands of years. These early farmers were wearing clothes, so they had to find resources for clothes as well as food. And agriculture coincided with a major change in clothing technology: the change from wearing animal skins to fabrics. The change of clothes was related to climate change too: woven cloth was a better material for clothes in the warm and more humid weather.

The first animal species domesticated in the region – sheep and goats – offered people useful fibers in the form of wool. These fiber resources were available on a renewable basis while a portion of the herd was kept alive. Unlike meat, wool was a reason to keep these animals alive rather than killing them – wool provided a rationale for herding rather than hunting. To keep the animals alive, people fed them with grasses such as wheat, barley, and rye and with legumes such as lentils and peas. The new need for forage and fodder for animals favored surplus production, promoting cultivation of the plants. In addition, one of the first crops – flax – yielded fibers that were woven into linen cloth.

From the outset, most of the domesticated resources (plants and animals) were recruited to supplement the human diet. Cattle were added as a meat resource and were fed with the same crops as sheep and goats; milk was another renewable resource offered by cattle and goats. As with Paleolithic tools such as scrapers and blades, most innovations will soon become multi-purpose, regardless of the main reason for their initial appearance. And the initial function may be overshadowed by the additional functions, and these may subsequently become more important than the first function in maintaining the innovation and driving further developments. In the case of agriculture, we can suppose that producing food for human consumption would have been incorporated into agricultural practices from very early in the process, even if producing fibers for textiles was what prompted people to first start herding animals – or with the cereal crops, to cultivate grasses to feed the animals.

In relation to the archaeological evidence, this means that neither the timing nor the quantity of food produced for human consumption is necessarily a reliable indicator of peoples' priorities in the beginning. With sheep and goats, most young animals could be killed for meat even though wool was the original motive to herd them. The delayed herding of cattle, however, has always hinted at meat not being the main motive. And with cereals, we can assume that people would include cereal grains in their diet, while the animals were grazed on the grasses. The bulk of seeds may have been consumed by people, especially with wheat – although the majority of early cereal crops (barley, oats, and rye) were probably grown primarily as animal feed.

The other factor was sedentism, which attracted a range of animal species as commensals – dogs, mice, pigs, and birds. Pigs proved to be especially popular as a food resource, and they also helped in processing all of the rubbish. Cats were attracted to the settlements too, and they helped to reduce the impact of rodents (and birds) on the field crops and stored food – which included fodder for the farm animals.

So there was a lot more going on than just producing food for human consumption. And, as a reason for why these things began, making food for humans was not necessarily the main reason. Fibers for textile clothing are implicated from the outset. And unlike producing unnecessary food for people, the new need for textiles represents a more sensible incentive for hunter-gatherers to embark upon the new venture of agriculture.

SETTLING DOWN IN CHINATOWN

Agriculture started in China around the same time as in Southwest Asia, in the northern region along the Yellow River basin. Much to everyone's surprise the main crop there was not rice but another grass, millet. Archaeologists have found evidence for the grinding of millet seeds by hunter-gatherers stretching back to the LGM around 23,000 years ago. Evidence for clothing is also found at these sites in the form of eyed needles between 26,000 and 23,000 years ago. Signs of millet domestication first appear at the end of the last ice age around 11,000 years ago, at a site near Beijing.[16]

The First Chinese Villages

Chinese agriculture was linked closely to a sedentary lifestyle. The first villages are found in northern and southern China (in the Yellow and Yangtze River basins) between 10,000 and 9,000 years ago. Rice was cultivated from 9,000 years ago in the south, but the seeds of this grass did not contribute much to the human diet until 6,000 years ago. Along with dogs, Chinese villages attracted two commensal species that soon became major food resources for people: chicken and pigs. Domesticated dogs (consumed as food) are dated to 10,000 years ago, and chicken may have been domesticated in northern China by then; domesticated pigs appeared in northern and southern China by 8,000 years ago. Yet as with rice, none of the major domesticates – plants or animals – became food staples for people until later, between 7,000 and 5,000 years ago.[17]

Food crops were fed to farm animals as well as people. Millet in particular was very popular as feed for the animals. In fact, isotope studies of bones from animals and humans show that cultivated millet often contributed more to the diets of the animals than the people. Two kinds of millet were cultivated in the early days of Chinese agriculture: broomcorn and foxtail millet; foxtail millet is grown mainly to feed people while broomcorn millet is grown primarily as animal feed – especially for fowl. Both varieties of millet – along with wild rice – probably began as weeds around the first villages. Rice was also a major food for the pigs. So like in Southwest Asia, early agriculture in China involved an integrated feeding system that provisioned not only people but also animals in the settlements.[18]

Textile Weaving

The transition to a settled life in China was accompanied by the development of a textile industry, with or without agriculture. At the end of the last ice age 11,700 years ago, people were still sewing skins from wild animals. Some of the sites in northern China were specialized "sewing camps" where people manufactured "sophisticated, fitted clothing" with eyed needles made from long animal bones; skeletal remains of the animals at these sites include a lot of furry species, mainly hares.[19]

Between 8,000 and 7,000 years ago, we find more archaeological evidence for textile industries. During this time the awls and needles at village sites were supplemented by spindle whorls – for instance at the early Neolithic site of Hemudu from 7,500 years ago, located 100 km (60 miles) south of Shanghai. Hemudu has also yielded bone shuttles that were probably used to weave fishing nets, and similar shuttles have been found at the Cishan site in northern China around 8,000 years ago, where millet was cultivated from 9,000 years ago. Climates in northern China remained fairly dry until around 9,000 years ago, which may have delayed a transition to textile clothes in the north. However, underlining the archaeological invisibility of prehistoric textiles, early textiles would have been woven by hand, and even quite complex Chinese looms that appeared later were manufactured from highly perishable (primarily wooden or bamboo) materials.[20]

Unfortunately, no fabrics have survived from this period in China, and

74. **7,000-year-old spindle whorl at Hemudu, eastern China**

Two pottery spindle whorls unearthed at the Hemudu (early Neolithic) site in 1977. The whorl on the left is 3.0 cm in diameter and on the right, 6.4 cm. These decorated spindle whorls attest to a sophisticated textile industry in China during the initial transition to an agricultural economy. At that time – between 7,500 and 5,500 years ago – hemp was likely cultivated for making woven garments, and the cultivation of rice was beginning to displace wild food resources derived from foraging as a major contributor to the human diet.

Source: Hemudu Site Museum, Zhejiang Province, Photo code 315414. Reproduced by permission of Hemudu Site Museum.

75. **Wooden loom from the Hemudu culture, China**

Wooden loom parts were recovered from the early Neolithic site of Hemudu, dated from 7,500 years ago in eastern China. This miniature diorama at The Field Museum, by Aaron Delehanty, shows a backstrap loom based on the archaeological finds. The loom parts are displayed at the Hemudu Site Museum, Zhejiang province.

Source: Photo by Karen Bean, © The Field Museum, Digital ID GN92118_021d. Reproduced by permission of The Field Museum, Chicago.

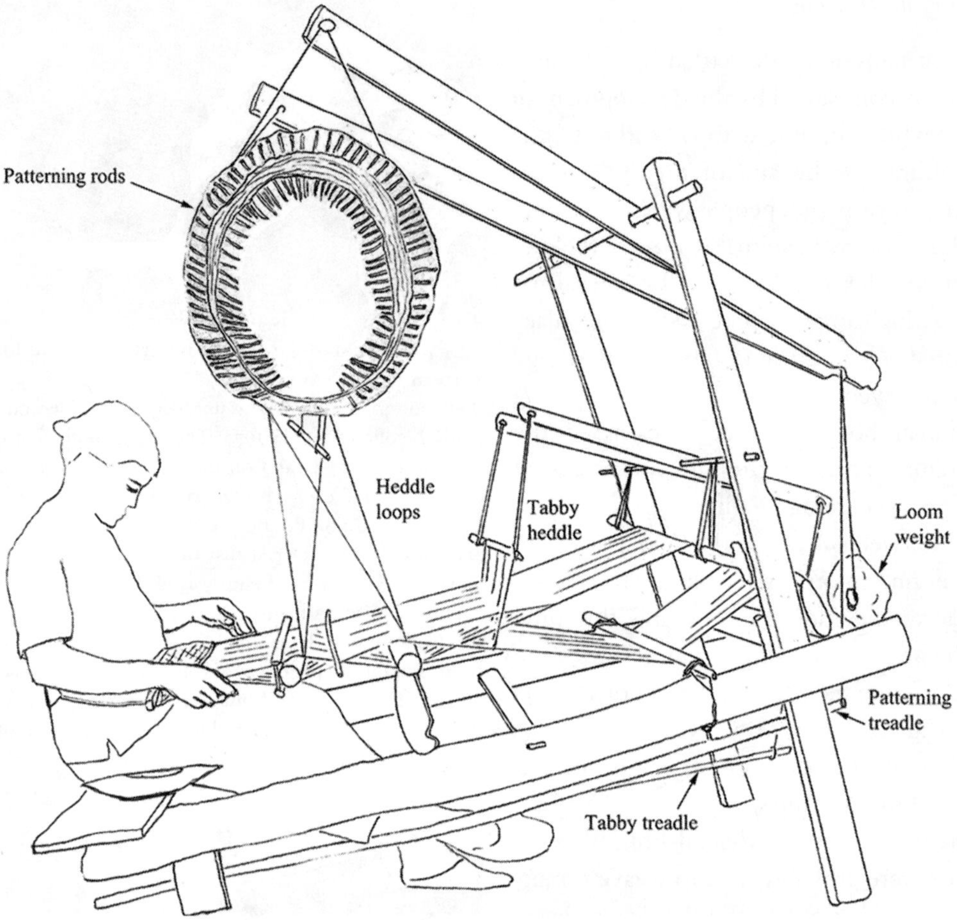

76. **Complex Chinese loom for weaving patterned fabrics**
A complex wooden loom may leave little trace in the archaeological record. Only the heavy loom weight (usually made from stone) is likely to survive, giving little clue as to the technological sophistication. Shown here is a traditional Maonan loom from Guangxi province, China, that employs a "programed" textile pattern, saved in the form of bamboo rods embedded in cords around a rotating bamboo drum.
Source: Drawing by Eric Boudot, in Buckley & Boudot, 2017:2. Reproduced from *Royal Society Open Science* under Creative Commons (CC-BY) license, with the kind permission of Christopher Buckley and Eric Boudot.

we can only guess what kinds of fibers were woven; probably wild plant species in the beginning. There were no wool-producing animals until 7,000 years ago when local sheep – the Mongolian breeds – were domesticated in the north. The oldest sheep remains are found in Inner Mongolia, and judging from the isotopes in their bones, these sheep were fed on cultivated millet. Foreign sheep from Southwest Asia – together with goats that grew cashmere wool and wheat as a fodder crop – also found their way into China, traveling with nomadic pastoralist tribes through Kazakhstan from 7,000 years ago.[21]

Hemp and Other Fibers

Aside from silk, early Chinese fabrics were woven with plant fibers. Candidates for the plant fibers used to weave cloth between 10,000 and 7,000 years ago are hemp, ramie, wisteria, and jute. These are all well-known from ancient Chinese texts as fibers for clothing (and for ropes and fishing nets), but their early cultivation is not documented in the archaeological record. Like flax (and also the fibers from nettles) these are called bast fibers, denoting the long fibers extracted from the stems. Wild plants that yield bast fibers can be cultivated without developing any physical changes in the seeds that would qualify them as domesticated. To further obscure their role in Chinese agriculture, it is not very easy to distinguish between different kinds of bast fibers, even with a microscope.[22]

Hemp was likely the main fiber used in everyday clothes, especially in northern areas, while ramie and wisteria were common in central and southern regions. Bark cloth (a felted rather than woven fabric) was used in southern areas, where the oldest stone bark cloth beater dates to around 8,000 years ago. The oldest archaeological remains of hemp in China – the oldest in the world – were recovered from a water-logged site in the Yangtze River basin. The site belongs to one of the first Chinese Neolithic cultures that started between 9,000 and 8,000 years ago. For perhaps a few millennia, hemp was cultivated as a wild plant, and it was finally domesticated in northern China by 7,000 years ago. Ramie seeds, and a rope fragment made from ramie, are documented at Hemudu 6,000 years ago. A textile fragment woven with fibers from the wisteria vine is dated to between 6,000 and 5,000 years ago, at a site near Shanghai. All these bast fibers – hemp, ramie, jute, and wisteria – were largely replaced as a material in Chinese clothes by the spread of cotton from India during the last millennium.[23]

Silk and Silkworms

Silk was first woven into cloth later than hemp. Silk weaving may have begun on the lower reaches of the Yellow River in the north, although the oldest confirmed domesticated silkworms are found further south and date to around 5,000 years ago, at a site not far from Shanghai. Earlier evidence for the presence of silk has been recovered from Neolithic tombs in Henan province, central China, dating to 8,500 years ago.[24]

Traditionally, silk was always a luxury fabric whereas hemp was worn widely until cotton began to spread from India into China 2,000 years ago. The production of silk was more complicated since it required a simultaneous domestication of two species, one animal and the other plant: the silkworm and the mulberry tree. A combined domestication process may look unusual or tedious, yet it is really the same as what happened with sheep and goats. In domesticating the animals for fiber, people cultivated the animals' favorite foods – mulberry leaves for silkworms and grasses such as wheat in the case of sheep.

Cotton and Agriculture in India

The Indian subcontinent is an example of a secondary center. Agriculture in the region only started after sheep and goats had already spread from Southwest Asia through western Pakistan 9,000 years ago, along with cattle and cereal crops. Some new species were first domesticated on the subcontinent, such as the zebu (humped cattle) and one type of water buffalo, as well as new plant crops such as the local millets. Fiber crops included flax and hemp – both introduced from outside, the latter from China.

Silk was present on the subcontinent from around 4,500 years ago and was always assumed to have spread from China, but it now appears different species of silkworm were domesticated separately on the Indian subcontinent. Another significant fiber resource to be first cultivated in this region was a new species of cotton.[25]

The Indian variety of cotton – known as tree cotton – is no longer popular because its fibres are shorter and coarser than the other varieties. Nowadays, most of the world's commercial cotton (around 90%) is based on the Mexican variety. However, the Indian strain was grown locally for textiles for a long time. The mineralized remains of cotton thread have been found in Pakistan, dated to around 8,000 years ago – although it may not have been domesticated. Nevertheless, the Neolithic nature of the site suggests that whether or not it was domesticated, the Indian variety of cotton was cultivated at that early time.[26]

77. **Cotton in India**
Cotton was domesticated in at least three regions: Peru, Mexico, and on the Indian subcontinent. The Mexican variety now dominates agricultural production around the world. Shown here is a tribal farmer in the Shiv Krishi Utthan Sanstha cooperative, Nimad region, Khargone, India.
Source: Joerg Boethling / Alamy Stock Photo.

Textiles played a prominent role in the local development of civilization in the Indus Valley, which straddles Pakistan and India. The Harappan civilization was centered on the city of Harappa 5,000 years ago and then, from 4,500 years ago, Mohenjo-daro. Textile fibers included the local variety of cotton as well as flax, wool, and hemp. Spindle whorls occur more commonly at archaeological sites on the subcontinent from 6,000 years ago, indicating a shift to large-scale fabric production.[27]

TWELVE

AGRICULTURE AND TEXTILES IN THE AMERICAS

Moving now to the Americas, there were two early agricultural transitions – in Mexico and Peru – and both led to the rise of civilizations. Agriculture began at the end of the last ice age, although the shift to agriculture in the New World was more gradual than in Southwest Asia and China. As was the case elsewhere, much of the human diet was still supplied by hunting and gathering. Aside from domesticated dogs – which had followed the first human immigrants from Siberia – early domesticated animals were limited to wool-bearing camelids, llamas, and alpacas (in Peru and Bolivia). Mexico and Peru both witnessed the cultivation of fiber crops for textiles at an early stage with two different varieties of cotton, domesticated independently in the two regions, and another fiber crop in Mexico: maguey.[1]

MAIZE AND MAGUEY IN MEXICO

To begin with Mexico, archaeologists are mystified by the limited evidence for America's main food crop: maize (corn); it now seems maize did not play a leading role in the Mesoamerican transition to agriculture. Given that it is now one of the world's major food crops, the absence of maize in early Mexican agriculture is quite amazing. The first food crops in Mexico include a few varieties of edible gourds (squash and pumpkins) around 10,000 years ago. Maize begins to appear 9,000 years ago, and the common bean follows later, around 3,000 years ago. Even by 5,000 years ago, maize was only partially domesticated.[2]

Feeding People and Animals

Civilization in the region began with the Olmecs 3,000 years ago followed by the Mayans, then the Aztecs. These state societies developed after a relatively late transition to a sedentary lifestyle – late compared to Southwest Asia and China. Pottery and the loom weaving of textiles begin to appear between 4,000 and 3,000 years ago and the settlements attracted wild fowl, with two species domesticated as commensals: the turkey and Muscovy duck. People consumed dogs and rabbits as well as fowl, and these animals were typically fed with maize. Wild animals (especially deer) continued as major meat resources, but dogs were more popular on the menu from 5,000 years ago. Dog skins were sometimes used in garments too, and one unusual dog breed developed around 2,000 years ago was the Mexican hairless dog (called the Xolo). Rabbits were also kept and fed on maize from around 2,000 years ago, probably for fur as well as meat. Some bird species – notably tropical parrots such as the brightly colored scarlet macaw – were bred for their feathers, fed on maize, and even exported to the North American southwest.[3]

Near modern Mexico City is the ancient city of Teotihuacan, built nearly 2,000 years ago. Some of the wild animals and birds that figured prominently as cultural icons were kept in captivity, although not domesticated. Isotope studies from the skeletal remains of jaguars, pumas, and eagles excavated by archaeologists inside the Sun and Moon Pyramids reveal these wild animals were fed with maize and probably (in the case of the felines) with maize-fed rabbits – and also with the hearts of maize-fed human captives.[4]

Maguey and Mesoamerican Clothing

Textiles in Mexico were woven mainly with fibers extracted from cactus-like plants called maguey, which belongs to the agave family. More than a hundred varieties were used in Mexico, and these served many purposes besides supplying fiber for clothes. Before the spread of maize, people in western Mexico relied heavily on agaves for food, and the plants were used also as fodder. Agaves are adapted to dry conditions, storing water in their succulent leaves as a sap that can be drunk fresh as a sweet liquid. The juice is fermented into alcoholic beverages known as pulque, which can be distilled as tequila and mescal; the psychedelic mescaline comes from a similar Mexican cactus.

Maguey fiber is sometimes called sisal hemp, but sisal actually refers to a tougher fiber from one variety used mainly for ropes and matting. The softer varieties are ideal for clothes and were probably woven throughout

Mesoamerica from an early stage. Only some species were domesticated – including a few used for fiber and a couple for alcohol – but many more were cultivated, without changing much from their wild forms. Thanks to the dry climate, maguey fibers and cordage are preserved at archaeological sites from around 9,000 years ago. The oldest occurs at a site in Honduras where maguey is present throughout a long series of occupation phases spanning from 10,000 to 1,500 years ago; the earliest maguey fibers there are radiocarbon-dated to 9,000 years ago.[5]

78. **Maguey farm, Mexico**
From early in the Holocene, textile fibers from a variety of cactus-like agaves were used to make everyday clothes in Mexico. The main fiber plants were various varieties of maguey, which was cultivated extensively before the mid-Holocene. Other varieties were exploited mainly for food and also for their sap, a drink that can be processed for alcoholic beverages. Subsequently overshadowed by cotton as the main textile fiber in Mexico, domesticated varieties of agave are now grown mainly for tough sisal fibers and to make alcohol, especially tequila. Shown here is a plantation of blue agaves (*Agave tequilana*) in the hills of Oaxaca, Mexico. *Source:* flowerphotos / Alamy Stock Photo.

Maguey was cultivated in the settlements from 4,000 years ago and, judging from the number of spindle whorls, textile production increased in the first civilizations. Maguey was often grown along with maize in terraced irrigation systems in the highlands, and cotton became popular too. The spindle whorls come in two sizes: larger ones for maguey and smaller ones for spinning the finer cotton fibers. Cloth played an important economic role in these complex societies and functioned as a kind of currency, with surplus cloth paid by villagers as tax to the state. Cotton was more valuable than maguey – like the situation in China where silk was more valuable than hemp.[6]

Compared to Peru, the ready availability of maguey might have delayed the widespread cultivation of cotton. The earliest cotton in Mesoamerica dates to 5,000 years ago, and by then the cotton plants were already domesticated.[7]

DOUBLE TROUBLE IN SOUTH AMERICA

In comparing food and fiber as causes of agriculture, of all the regions around the world that can serve as a test, this is the best. In South America the transition from hunting and gathering involved both plants and animals. What makes South America pivotal is that in both instances, the transition to agriculture involved textile fibers.

Cotton was one of the first South American crops along with peanuts, beans and squash – but not corn. In northern Peru, cotton was cultivated by 8,000 years ago and cotton yarn has been preserved in archaeological deposits from around 7,000 years ago; cotton textiles dyed with indigo blue are dated to around 6,000 years ago. We saw earlier that the world's oldest textile fabrics – woven with wild plant fibers 11,000 years ago – are found in Peru. Not only was cotton one of the founding crops, in Peru, cotton was often a focus of early agriculture and its cultivation was a driving force in the emergence of civilization. With cotton we can hardly doubt that its fiber was the main motive – cottonseed and the edible oil were not likely the products in question.[8]

Cotton in Peru

Early cultivation of crops in South America happened mainly along the coast in the northwest, in the region that stretches from Ecuador to Peru. Food crops were involved from 10,000 years ago and chili peppers were domesticated by 6,000 years ago. Maize entered the picture around 5,000 years ago – when it was consumed by dogs as well as people in the settlements. The first maize occurs 8,000 years ago at some sites, but it was not a significant aspect of the early agriculture; nor was maize a staple food in the early civilizations. Like the situation with rice in China, archaeologists are perplexed to see how this great cereal crop played such a minor role in the Peruvian transition to agriculture.[9]

But cotton is the big shock. Cotton often dominates the agriculture, while the main industry in the settlements was weaving textiles – to make fishing nets as well as fabrics for clothes. At sites that span the period leading up to the first civilizations, cotton was often the main crop. One well-studied site is Huaca Prieta on the northern coast of Peru, where cotton yarn is dated to around 7,000 years ago.[10]

Most stunning is the site of Caral, located 200 km (125 miles) north of the modern capital Lima. Caral is a ceremonial complex built in the desert not far from the coast, and archaeologists have unearthed an impressive irrigation system to support the crops. With a date of nearly 5,000 years ago, Caral is now claimed as the first city in the Americas – indeed it is one of the first cities in the world. Not only was cotton the main crop, but the whole city was sustained economically by cotton textiles. In fact, the agricultural base for this first American city was not food but textiles. The residents' food supply came mainly from marine resources, which were traded for textiles (including nets) with fishing communities on the coast.[11]

The discovery of Caral and how its economy revolved around cotton has created a furor among archaeologists. Caral seems to raise questions about agriculture arising as a way to feed people, and it raises doubts about the role of the food economy in the emergence of civilization. Some remarkable textiles have been preserved in the dry climate, including an almost complete dress woven with cotton. We see a similar picture at another early city in Peru, El Paraíso (built around 4,000 years ago). Again, cotton was the dominant crop.[12]

An expert on the Incas and their forebears is Professor Michael Moseley at the University of Florida, and he highlights this astonishing evidence about how agriculture was based on textiles rather than food. Caral is a challenge to conventional assumptions and, as he says, it is "demanding of explanation."[13]

79. **City of Caral, Peru**
In the Supe Valley near the coast of Peru is the city of Caral – at nearly 5,000 years old, one of the oldest cities in the world. Agriculture in the vicinity was dominated by cotton, with virtually no food crops. The people of Caral relied for their food on hunting and gathering and, especially, trading cotton for fish with nearby coastal populations – where cotton was used in fishing nets as well as clothes.
Source: age fotostock / Alamy Stock Photo.

Llamas and Wool in the Andes

The South American evidence is telling not just with plants but also with animals. While domestic animals did not feature prominently in American agriculture, there is one exception in the Andean highlands. In this high mountain region where the climate is cooled by altitude even in tropical zones, we find an independent transition to farming in the form of herding animals. The transition was unusual in a few ways: it was not connected with a sedentary lifestyle, nor did it involve cultivating any crops. Likely reasons relate to local ecology: cultivating permanent pasture to feed animals – or people – was not feasible at the elevations inhabited by native camelids (above 3,000 m). Instead the animals were kept on a mobile basis, with people moving along with the herds as the animals grazed on natural pastures. Two species – llama and alpaca – were domesticated from their wild parents, the guanaco and vicuña. These wild camelids were hunted (and possibly herded) from early after the ice age, when they replaced wild deer as the dominant animal remains found at archaeological sites. Skeletal changes that identify the domesticated species are visible by 6,000 years ago.[14]

Unlike the surreal situation with wild sheep where the presence of wool is often disputed (and discounted as a reason for domestication), there is no disputing the presence – and the value – of wool in the wild camelids, both guanaco and vicuña.[15]

Wool from the guanaco is like cashmere, and vicuña wool is the world's most valuable natural fiber. So we can safely assume that the first American animal domesticates could provide people with wool for textiles – because both of the wild progenitors obviously produce wool. During historical times, llamas have served more as multipurpose assets – as beasts of burden and to supply meat as well as wool – whereas alpacas were always kept mainly for

80. **Llama, Peru**
Llama at Machu Picchu, Peru. The two wild species of South American camelids – guanaco and vicuña – grow excellent wool, and both species were domesticated by humans in the Andean highlands before the mid-Holocene. Along with cultivation of cotton in coastal areas of Peru and Ecuador, the two domesticated animal species – llama and alpaca, respectively – represent an independent fiber-based transition to agriculture.
Source: Efrain Padro / Alamy Stock Photo.

fiber. Wool fibers – probably from the fleece of guanaco – have now been found at archaeological sites between 10,000 and 9,000 years ago. So even at that very early time when people were hunting wild camelids for meat, they were collecting the wool.[16]

The quality of woollen fiber has actually deteriorated since the Spanish invasion in the sixteenth century. At that catastrophic time the camelid population – along with the indigenous human population – was decimated by up to 90 percent. Modern-day wool varieties in Peru result from poorly controled breeding and hybridization since then. Archaeologist Jane Wheeler has examined the fibers on llama and alpaca mummies in southern Peru that were buried around 1,000 years ago. Her findings show that the wool in preconquest herds was superior to the wool of present-day domesticates (including alpacas). Not only was alpaca wool at that time better but so too was the llama wool, and she suggests that along with alpacas, llamas were bred mainly for their wool.[17]

As in Mesoamerica to the north, textiles played a big role in the rise of South American civilizations. Textiles sustained the first cities on the coast and the same is true in the Andes. Early highland settlements and regional states – culminating with the Incas – developed with the integration of coastal cotton and highland wool economies via expanding trade networks. Textile goods were the top commodity, sometimes woven with blends of cotton and woollen fibers. Long caravans of llamas carried their heavy loads through steep mountain passes, stopping at way stations where the textiles and other goods were traded. Archaeologists have found skeletal signs of pathology reflecting years of physical stress in the foot bones of the llamas. These complex Andean economies also produced a range of new food crops such as potato, and maize was adopted (eventually). Maize later became more important in the human diet and was fed to domestic animals as well, not only llamas but dogs and then guinea pigs. The latter is a little rodent that started out as a commensal species, attracted by all of the litter in the settlements; domesticated guinea pigs were fattened on maize and consumed for meat.[18]

Domesticating the Amazon

Trade across the Andes stretched not just to the western coast but to the east, where agriculture developed in the Amazon basin from around 7,000 years ago. We like to think that before Europeans arrived and spoiled things, the Amazon was a pristine wilderness inhabited by hunter-gatherers (naked or nearly naked). But recent archaeological finds have revealed that many indigenous populations were cultivating plants of various kinds from at least midway through the Holocene. They still relied heavily on wild plants and animals, and we now realize that many of these early agriculturalists (not just in the Amazon but elsewhere) engaged in low-level food production as a stable economic strategy. Some were semisedentary and horticultural, growing mixed domestic crops and wild plants in garden plots which they would abandon on a periodic basis. One of the main food crops first domesticated in the Amazon was manioc, of which there are a number of varieties like cassava.[19]

Cotton had spread into the Amazon basin from Peru and Ecuador, possibly via Colombia, and cotton is still grown by some remote tribal groups in Brazil. Clothing generally was minimal in these hot and humid climates – often nothing more than a woven waistband for women and a penis string for men.

Most of these South American societies were egalitarian, but some developed more hierarchical social structures, which American archaeologists refer to as chiefdoms. By 3,000 years ago, there were quite complex societies in parts of the Amazon – so-called mound builders. Most of the mounds started out as natural formations in the landscape, with people adding to the mounds as they built houses – and as refuse accumulated in the settlements. Excavations have unearthed elaborate pottery vessels and other ceramic artifacts including spindle whorls, testifying to a textile industry. Fabrics and items such as strings and ropes were woven from wild plants as well as cultivated cotton (and bark cloth as well); a few textile fragments have been recovered by archaeologists on the large island that lies in the mouth of the Amazon, Marajó Island.[20].

THANKSGIVING IN NORTH AMERICA

Before leaving the Americas, another independent center of agriculture has been discovered by archaeologists in recent decades, in the eastern woodlands region of North America. Beginning around 5,000 years ago, it was a relatively late starter, and at least three new plant species were domesticated – marshelder, chenopod, and sunflower. Seeds of other plants have been found at some of the earliest agricultural sites but without any physical signs of domestication, although these plants nonetheless may have been cultivated: these likely crops include erect knotweed, little barley, and maygrass. Squash was also among these domesticates, and it may have been the first plant to be domesticated in eastern North America. The presence of squash among the first North American domesticates might suggest that agriculture had spread northwards from Mexico, where squash was domesticated earlier, beginning around 10,000 years ago. However, evidence from genetic studies and archaeology points to an independent domestication of squash in eastern North America. All these crops were grown to feed people living in sedentary or semisedentary village societies – some were mound-building chiefdoms similar to those in the Amazon. As was the case in much of North America, the communities were Mesolithic rather than Neolithic or Paleolithic: neither settled farmers nor mobile hunter-gatherers, they were hunter-gatherers who settled down in villages and who sometimes started to cultivate crops. Neither

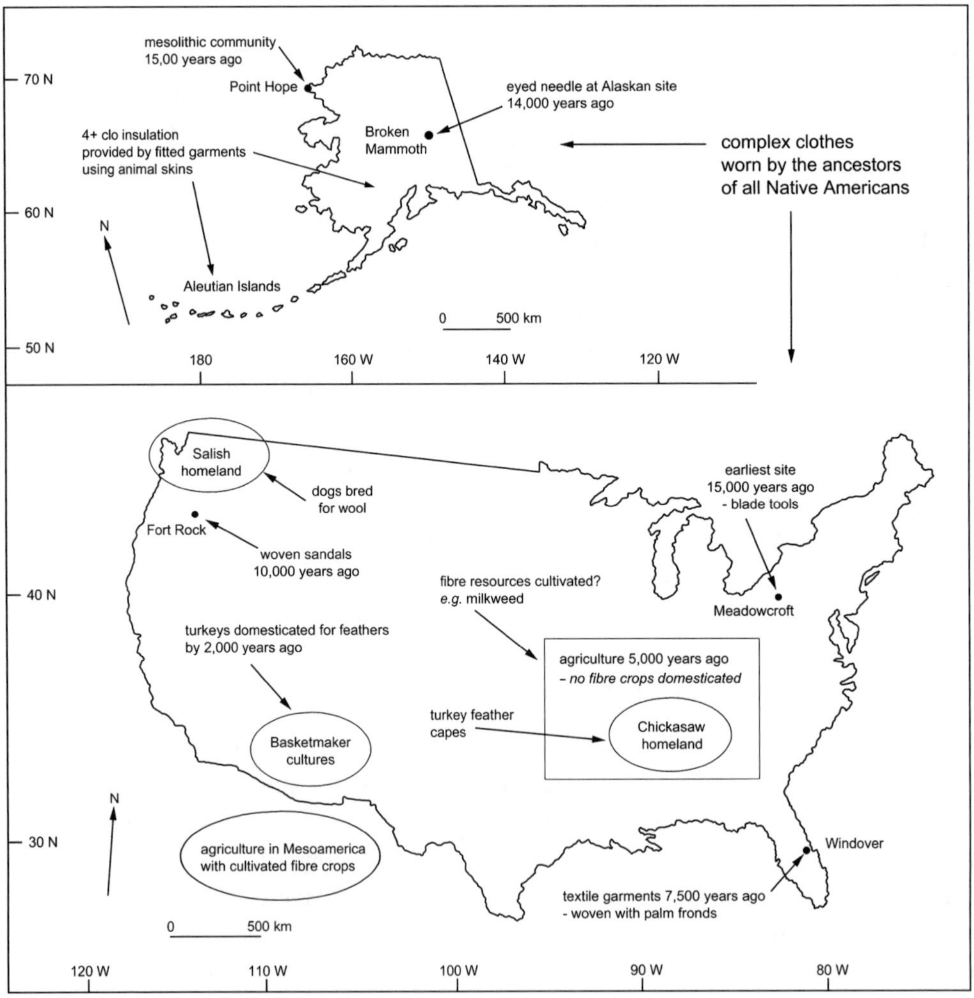

81. **Map of USA showing sites and the eastern agricultural center**
Major prehistoric and ethnographic clothing trends in the USA in relation to climate and early agriculture, with sites mentioned in the text.

were they naked: they wore clothes, including textile garments. Even when they had crops, they often relied mainly on wild foods, and their local environments were well-stocked with natural resources – for clothing as well as food. In those areas where agriculture was practiced more intensively, the local food crops were largely replaced by maize that had spread from Mexico by around 2,000 years ago.[21]

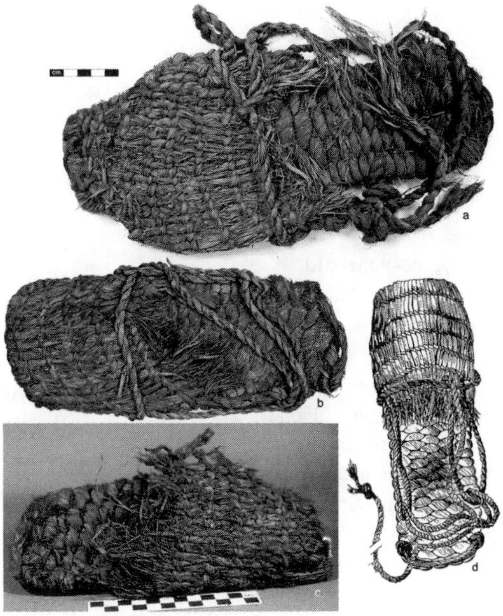

82. **10,000-year-old woven sandals from Oregon**

Early textiles in North America include cordage dated from 12,000 years ago. Sandals made from twined sagebrush are dated from 10,400 years ago at Fort Rock Cave in Oregon. Shown here are sandals from (a) Catlow Cave, (b) Fort Rock Cave, and (c) Elephant Mountain Cave; (d) type drawing (slightly reduced scale).

Source: Connolly, T. J., Barker, P., Fowler, C. S., Hattori, E. M., Jenkins, D. L., & Cannon, W. J. (2016). Getting beyond the point: textiles of the Terminal Pleistocene/Early Holocene in the northwestern Great Basin. *American Antiquity* 2016:496. © Society for American Archaeology. Reproduced with permission, Cambridge University Press.

As for textiles and clothes, weaving technologies were well-developed throughout North America. Archaeological remains of baskets, nets, ropes, and perhaps fabrics for garments are reported from sites dating back to around 12,000 years ago. At one of the earliest sites, Meadowcroft near Pittsburgh, a piece of cut bark that is probably from a basket fragment is dated to at least 15,000 years ago. In recent historical times, clothes were made from animal hides as well as textiles, and tools such as awls, scrapers, and needles are found at agricultural sites. Traditional fabrics included blankets woven from plant and animal fibers, and feathers too. Common plant fibers were yucca, nettles, milkweed, the local variety of hemp (dogbane, often called Indian hemp) and fibers from various tree barks and roots, while animal fibers came from wild mountain goats, moose, rabbits, and even woolly dogs. Among the Mesolithic Salish peoples who lived in the northwest around Seattle and Vancouver, a local variety of dog was bred with a dense woolly coat. The wool was woven into elaborately decorated blankets that functioned also as cloaks in winter. In some of the surviving examples at the Smithsonian Institution, the woolen fabric from dogs is held together by cedar bark cordage, sometimes supplemented with down and feathers. Along the Atlantic and Gulf coasts, people made fabrics from the fibers of Spanish Moss, a flowering plant that grows over trees in humid climates. As mentioned earlier, one of the earliest North American textile finds is an 11,000-year-old sandal made from twined plant fibers, found at a

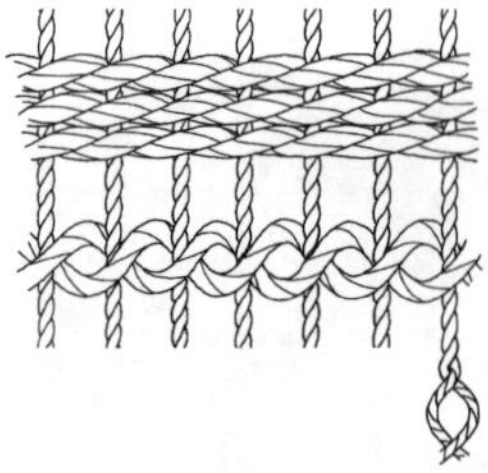

83. **7,500-year-old textile at Windover bog, Florida**
7,500-year-old textiles are preserved at the Windover Bog site in Florida, including artifacts such as bags, blankets, and garments woven from various wild plant resources, including palm fronds. Some items comprised loom-woven cloths, and the assemblage demonstrates a range of complex weaving patterns.
Source: Adovasio et al., 2001:24. Reproduced with permission of SAGE Publications, and courtesy of James Adovasio.

cave in Oregon. Also mentioned earlier, a remarkable site for textiles is the Windover peat pond in Florida, which dates to around 7,500 years ago. On some of the skeletons in the Florida pond, archaeologists found fragments of finely woven fabrics that they think were probably worn as everyday clothes; the fibers in that case were extracted from the fronds of palm trees.[22]

So the transition to agriculture in eastern North America occurred in the context of sedentary, or semisedentary, peoples who were wearing technologically sophisticated clothes, including textiles woven from a host of wild fiber resources.[23]

Agriculture without Fibers?

Taken at face value, this transition to agriculture appears to refute the notion that textiles led to agriculture. It would seem that no fiber crop was domesticated, and neither were there any wool-producing domestic animals. But the evidence from North America presents another problem: it seems to refute all of the other theories as well. According to leading researcher Bruce D. Smith at the Smithsonian, the evidence seems to refute both social complexity (Hayden's feasting model) and population pressure (Cohen's argument). The North American evidence also fails to implicate major environmental stresses such as global climate change as possible causes for people to start cultivating these plants for food. With regard to the environment, the most that can be argued is that there was a mid-Holocene stabilization of the riverine floodplain systems that favored some of the plants involved and that created attractive resource zones for human settlements. These environmental changes might provide some kind of local explanation – Smith is skeptical of general theories about the origin of agriculture, and he prefers instead to construct local models.[24]

Yet this can lead to a limited and rather retrospective approach. Local environmental situations probably served more as a precondition rather than as a cause. After all, humans would have encountered favorable conditions and similar opportunities at many times and places during the past 300,000 years, without developing agriculture. Even in North America, regions such as California offered some excellent opportunities, but the people there did not start any agriculture.[25]

Smith mentions the presence of textiles (mainly basketry and cordage), but as he says, there is a big bias because these perishable materials are less likely than hard seeds to survive from so long ago, and this applies particularly with fragile clothing fabrics. Smith also points out that we tend to forget about another plant because it was not used for food, namely the bottle gourd (a variety of squash): this "utilitarian" domesticate reached eastern North America by 7,000 years ago where it served mainly as a container, and it is "frequently" present at the early agricultural sites. And Smith also points out that in the early days of agriculture in eastern North America, food from cultivated plants seems to have made only a small contribution to the human diet.[26]

Cultivated if Not Domesticated

Although we have only four or five plant species that were domesticated, others may have been cultivated but kept their wild forms. These wild plants could have been involved in the agricultural process, cultivated along with domesticated plants. Also, the sunflower was used for other purposes besides food. Sunflowers provided medicines and dyes (purple and yellow, for body paints and textiles), and sunflower seed oil was used ceremonially to "anoint" their heads; the stalks of sunflowers were used as a construction material and possibly for textiles.[27]

As we have seen, textiles and woven fabrics have survived at quite a few early sites in North America. One important site is the Newt Kash shelter in Kentucky, where a vast array of textiles has been recovered including fabrics, mats, strings, and ropes, along with domesticated plants. This site dates from a little over 4,000 years ago, which places it at a fairly early stage of agriculture in eastern North America. Crops cultivated at Newt Kash include sunflower, sumpweed, chenopod (goosefoot), maygrass, giant ragweed, bottle gourd (inedible squash), fleshy (edible) squash, maize, and tobacco.

Among the wild plants used for the textiles at Newt Kash were Indian hemp and milkweed, traditionally woven into cordage and cloth. Milkweed is a dual fiber source: the fine fibers from its seed are similar to cotton and can be spun into yarn to make cloth for garments, while tougher fibers from the stem can be used for making strings, ropes, and baskets. In eastern North America, fibers such as milkweed and Indian hemp were often thigh-spun without spindle whorls, which may account for a paucity of spindle whorls at archaeological sites.[28]

So we may have one or two fiber plants in the early agriculture that were not formally domesticated. At least one – milkweed – was collected as a wild plant around some of the settlements, and may have been cultivated. The same is probably true for Indian hemp and maguey-like yucca fibers and various nettles. Textile fibers were used not so much for clothing as for cordage and string, and as thread for sewing. In these climates where the winters get cold, people favored warm animal skins, which were worn loosely – and often

84. **Native American woman weaving milkweed fibers**
Milkweed fibers were used widely by Native Americans to weave cloth and other textiles. While not domesticated, wild milkweed may have been cultivated along with food crops in the agricultural center of Eastern North America (ENA), which developed nearly 5,000 years ago. Shown here is a Native American woman weaving milkweed at Plimoth Plantation, Plymouth, MA.
Source: Photo by Shannon Hayes, Sap Bush Hollow Farm, West Fulton, NY. © Shannon Hayes. Reproduced by permission of Shannon Hayes.

minimally – in summer. Scraper tools are often found at the early agricultural sites, along with bone awls (made from deer and turkey bones), suggesting that preparation of animal skins was commonplace.

A couple of things to keep in mind are that this agricultural transition in eastern North America did not happen among mobile hunter-gatherers who were naked: it happened among people who were wearing clothes and who were settling down in villages. As we saw earlier, all the indigenous American populations are descended from ancestors who had complex clothing. Without such warm garments, they could not have reached the New World from northeast Asia at the end of the last ice age. And even as hunter-gatherers, in many places they were moving toward a sedentary lifestyle.

We saw earlier how a sedentary existence can favor agriculture by attracting certain animal species (like chicken and pigs), animals that then become domesticated of their own accord in the villages. A similar thing can happen with plants: the ones involved in eastern North America probably started out as weeds that grew around settlements. With the exception of the sunflower, nowadays most of the indigenous crop plants are regarded more as weeds than as crops (and they were all superseded by maize as a food crop). Even the sunflower may have started out as a humble weed in clearings around settlements. At some point, after collecting the seeds from wild plants in their surroundings, people probably began to actively plant the seeds and make more use of the sunflower as a food resource, leading to the plant's domestication. The question is whether this would have happened had the plants not already become established around the settlements as weeds, through a passive, commensal process akin to how many animal species were attracted to human settlements.

Turkeys to the Rescue

As well as milkweed as a possible fiber crop, there is one other species to mention – not plant but animal. During historical times, the sunflower has been used mainly as food not for humans but for farm animals. The small seeds of the sunflower are a favorite feed for domestic fowl – sunflower is almost the quintessential chicken feed. As it happens, one of the main meat sources for the early farmers in North America was a native fowl – the wild turkey. These wild fowl were attracted to all the grasses that were cultivated in the clearings around the settlements – as happened with chicken and millet (and wild rice) in China. The big birds were valued not just as food but also for their feathers: turkey feathers are a feature of traditional American costume. And bird feathers offer good insulation in the cold – Native North Americans sometimes made elegant winter cloaks from turkey feathers.[29]

Which brings us to one last surprise. We saw how turkeys were domesticated in Mexico, where they were fed with maize. Yet archaeologists recently discovered that the wild turkey was domesticated in North America as well. Turkeys were domesticated by 2,000 years ago, and this was a separate event from the Mexican domestication. These North American domestic turkeys are found in the southwest, but genetic analyses suggest they were domesticated earlier and maybe they spread into the southwest from eastern North America.

A key finding comes from a site in Utah where it turns out that turkey was not a major item in the menu. Archaeologists were surprised to find that the domestic fowl was not a food staple. Instead they suspect it was kept and fed – with maize – for its feathers. Traditionally, turkey feathers in the region were woven into brightly colored feather blankets and into garments as well, with the fanciest feathers reserved for ceremonial dress. And in the Eastern Woodlands, women wove warm cloaks with turkey feathers.[30]

85. **Chickasaw turkey feather cloak**
Turkey feather cloak: Contemporary recreation of a traditional Chickasaw turkey feather cloak, made by Chickasaw elder Robert Perry and displayed at the Chickasaw Cultural Center, Sulphur, OK.

Source: Photograph by Matthew Bradbury, © Matthew Bradbury. Reproduced by permission of Matthew Bradley and Robert Perry.

So with the turkeys there is good reason for thanksgiving: the only indigenous animal domesticate in North American agriculture was probably domesticated for its feathers, not for food.

THIRTEEN

AGRICULTURE FROM AFRICA TO AUSTRALIA

Before we look at recent discoveries in Papua New Guinea – the most surprising new pristine center – we can briefly review developments on the African continent, even though these were probably not pristine centers of early agriculture. Some were agricultural centers in the sense that new species of plants or animals were first domesticated, but they are not pristine because the early agriculture was affected or contaminated by external influences, either by direct contact with other agricultural centers or the spread of domesticated species. Earlier we looked briefly at the Indian subcontinent as a classic example of a secondary agricultural center where new species were domesticated. Since we cannot say that hunter-gatherers in these regions developed agriculture entirely of their own accord, these secondary regions are not ideal for testing theories about the origin of agriculture. Still, they can illustrate some points. We should also keep in mind that these other centers might also have begun to develop agriculture on their own, even if they not been affected by external influences. In the case of the Indian subcontinent, for instance, we might wonder whether agriculture would perhaps have begun anyway by the mid-Holocene, had the region not been inundated by the earlier spread of agricultural elements from both sides – the west and the east. Alas, we will never know. In fact, in Africa, there is one tantalizing sign that agriculture could have started among local people of its own accord, only to be nipped in the bud by the rapid expansion of farming from Southwest Asia.

CENTERS OF DOMESTICATION IN AFRICA

86. **Barbary sheep**
In Africa during the early Holocene, there was an independent agricultural experiment. In Libya and Algeria, people began to herd the local Barbary sheep. These docile creatures have lost the wool coat on their backs, perhaps as an adaptation to life in a hot environment. The herding experiment 9,000 years ago (when the sheep may have had more wool) was short-lived, as domesticated sheep spread into northern Africa from the Levant. These Barbary sheep are at Toronto Zoo.
Source: Sergei Torockov / Alamy Stock Photo.

From 6,000 years ago, a range of new plant species were domesticated on the African continent. Local crops such as sorghum and pearl millet were preceded by the spread of sheep, goats, and cattle (together with cereals and flax) from Southwest Asia around 7,000 years ago. Sorghum appears to be the earliest of the local plant species to be cultivated, a crop used primarily as a food for grazing the animal domesticates. So while Africa was certainly a major center of plant domestication, it was not really an independent center of agriculture. However, we may have one intriguing sign of an earlier – and quite independent – attempt at farming.[1]

In northern Africa it appears that the local species of wild sheep – the Barbary sheep – was herded by hunter-gatherers in Libya and Algeria between 9,000 and 8,000 years ago. Not only does it look like these docile wild sheep were kept in pens but, to judge by the content of their dung, they were fed and foddered with grasses collected by people to feed the sheep.[2]

Herding of the Barbary sheep represents an entirely independent African transition to agriculture among local foragers. Barbary sheep have reduced wool (as an adaptation to the warmer climate), but nonetheless, this early herding experiment involved people taming and protecting animals as living assets by feeding them with grass. However, the Barbary sheep was soon abandoned in favor of foreign sheep with a substantial wool coat.

A more successful local animal domesticate was the donkey, bred from the wild ass by around 6,000 years ago in the eastern "horn" area of the continent (Ethiopia and Somalia). From the outset, donkeys were probably utilized not so much for meat but to transport people and agricultural goods along trade networks that were developing across northern and central Africa.[3]

Linen in Ancient Egypt

Beginning 5,000 years ago, we witness the first African civilization. Ancient Egypt arose out of farming settlements around the Fayum Oasis in the lower

87. **5,000-year-old linen garment in Ancient Egypt**
The world's oldest fitted textile garment is the so-called Tarkhan Dress. This 5,300-year-old linen tunic was excavated in 1913 from an Egyptian tomb at Tarkhan, 50 km (30 miles) south of Cairo, but only recently radiocarbon-dated. The garment has pleated sleeves and bodice, but the hem is missing, so its length is uncertain.
Source: Petrie Museum of Egyptian Archaeology, UC28614B1. Reproduced courtesy of Maria Ragan, Anna Garnett and the Petrie Museum of Egyptian Archaeology, UCL.

Nile, beginning from 7,000 years ago. Sheep from Southwest Asia were the main domestic animal in the Fayum, and the crops included flax, grown for its textile fiber. A remarkable discovery is a complete linen shirt found at the tomb site of Tarkhan, just north of Cairo. The exquisitely-woven shirt has recently been dated to a little over 5,000 years ago – making it the world's oldest surviving garment.[4]

Production of linen cloth was a big industry in Ancient Egypt, and factory-style vertical looms appeared 3,000 years ago during the New Kingdom. Although technologically sophisticated, these linen fabrics were often worn as loosely draped garments – corresponding to simple rather than complex clothing. Simple garments were more appropriate as cool attire in the hot climate, and loose garments were generally preferred throughout Africa.[5]

Following the Sheep

The spread of agriculture across Africa was led by domesticated animals rather than plants. As farming spread, the local foragers were displaced or assimilated into mobile and semisedentary pastoralist economies that relied on gaining access to grazing land. To varying degrees, the increasing human dependence on domesticated animals was combined with the cultivation of crops. Although cattle later became prominent, the initial agricultural expansion involved mainly sheep.

Sheep first arrived in eastern Africa between 6,000 and 5,000 years ago and reached South Africa by 2,000 years ago (together with cattle), marking the beginning of agriculture at the southern end of the continent. Although some local people retained their traditional lack of clothing, many agricultural groups had animal skins (often cattle hides) as well as wool, supplemented by cotton from India during the last millennium. Wool fiber was also provided by the African camel – the one-humped variety (or dromedary) that was domesticated in Arabia between 4,000 and 3,000 years ago. The dromedary was used for milk as well as for meat and wool, and also as a mode of transport. In western Africa a woolen fabric has survived from around 2,000 years ago, and while its identity is uncertain, the fiber is more likely derived from the dromedary than from sheep.[6]

As was the case elsewhere, the cultivated plants often served as feed and fodder for the animal herds. Wild foods also contributed to the human diet; people rarely relied exclusively on crops until recent historical times. Among the new local crops, cowpea was a fodder crop while another cultivated plant was the local Ethiopian variety of banana, called the enset. The Ethiopian enset is a large tropical plant grown not only for food but for the long fibers in its stem that are used to make textiles and ropes; its massive leaves also serve as wrapping and roofing material. In its wild form, the enset was often regarded as a poor food option: the edible corms have been described as "unpalatable" even when cooked, whereas the fibers were always useful.[7]

WILD BANANAS IN PAPUA NEW GUINEA

We come now to the last of the pristine centers. Of all the locations where hunter-gatherers started with agriculture of their own accord, Papua New Guinea is the biggest surprise. It was discovered when a team of archaeologists led by Jack Golson and Tim Denham from the Australian National University found evidence of early farming in the tropical highlands. In their excavations at the swamp site called Kuk, they uncovered raised earth mounds and stake holes that show how people were practicing a kind of garden-based horticulture, starting from 10,000 years ago. By 7,000 years ago, the locals were constructing irrigation ditches. The plants involved were yams and taro – yielding starch-rich tubers and corms – and bananas. While all three plants were cultivated, the first two may not have been domesticated, but the banana was definitely domesticated – Papua New Guinea is where bananas were first domesticated.[8]

Archaeologists used to believe that agriculture had spread from Asia into Papua New Guinea, with pigs and dogs as part of the foreign package. Like dogs, pigs are not indigenous to Melanesia, and they must have arrived from Southeast Asia at some point, already domesticated (or perhaps feral). All three cultivated plants – yams, taro, and bananas – served as fodder for the pigs. But whatever the functions of those early crops in the highlands, it turns out that pigs were not present in the beginning: firm evidence for pigs is lacking before 3,000 years ago. On the other hand, wild yams were consumed by people from when they first ventured into the highlands by 40,000 years ago, and the processing of taro for food is known elsewhere in Melanesia from around 30,000 years ago.[9]

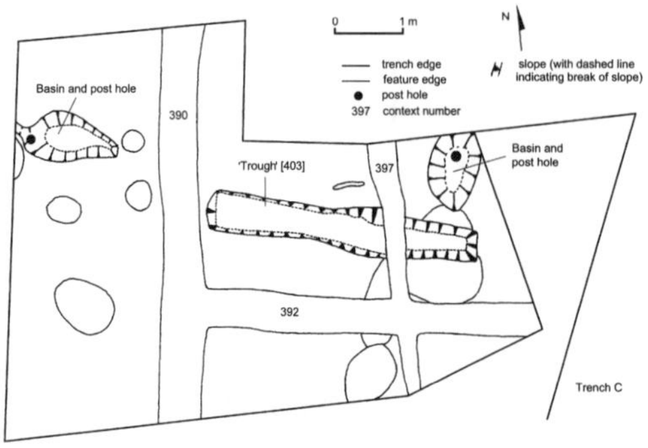

88. **Plan of Kuk agricultural site, Papua New Guinea**
Wetland agriculture began at Kuk Swamp in the highlands of Papua New Guinea 10,000 years ago, with archaeological evidence of drainage channels and post holes that may have supported the cultivation of wild banana. Abundant phytoliths confirm the cultivation of banana by 7,000 years ago, when the site has more regular drainage features, as shown here.
Source: Denham, Golson, and Hughes, 2004. Reading early agriculture at Kuk Swamp, Wahgi Valley, Papua New Guinea: the archaeological features (Phases 1–3). *Proceedings of the Prehistoric Society* 47:283. Field drawing by Golson in 1975, reproduced by permission of Cambridge University Press, and courtesy of Jack Golson.

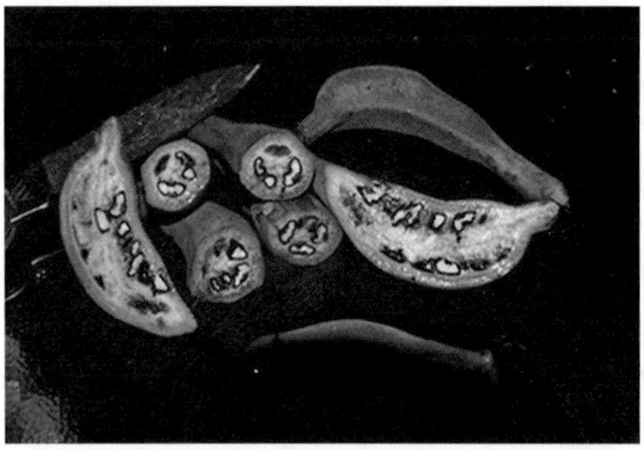

89. **Ancestral wild banana fruit with seeds**
Wild banana plants have small fruits that are full of hard seeds and contain relatively little pulp compared to most modern varieties (some of which are now completely seedless). Shown here is the fruit of *Musa balbisiana*, one of the wild ancestors of modern cultivated bananas; it is often considered inedible.
Source: Photo by Pat Heslop-Harrison, © Pat Heslop-Harrison. Reproduced under Creative Commons (CC-BY) license, and with permission of Pat Heslop-Harrison.

Bananas are a more slippery proposition. Yams and taro were quite edible as wild foods, but the wild precursor of the modern banana presents us with a problem. A big problem to be more precise. As we saw in the last chapter with the enset plant in Africa, the various varieties of banana – and there are many, such as plantains – are not as edible as the modern domesticated banana. In fact it looks like the wild ancestor of our beloved banana was practically inedible.

Yes, We Have No Bananas

Most varieties of domesticated bananas are seedless, and the large fruit is full of soft sweet pulp. But the smaller fruit of the wild banana is quite different: it is loaded with hard seeds and has little pulp, and eating the fruit would be almost like eating a bag of pebbles.[10]

So yes, we have no bananas – at least not very edible ones. Yet the stem of the wild banana plant provides a good fiber for ropes and textiles, and the banana plant has been exploited widely for its fiber in southern and eastern Asia. In the Philippines, for instance, one of the main varieties was grown mainly for the fiber, woven into a sheer fabric to make the traditional translucent garments.[11]

Another variety of banana is grown to produce a coarse fiber – abacá or Manila hemp, which is still used industrially to make ropes. And these examples are not exceptional: in many places where banana plants were cultivated, people often focused more on the fiber than the fruit. In China the banana fruit was never a staple food and cultivation was aimed at the "production of fibers from the leaves and stems"; banana may also have been domesticated independently in the Harappan civilization of the Indus Valley around 4,000 years ago, where its primary function as a source of fiber is said to be "plausible."[12]

Together with the poor food quality of the wild fruit, the usefulness of the fiber has led some leading researchers to suggest that the banana was first cultivated in Papua New Guinea not for food but for other reasons. One scientist who is unraveling the complex history of bananas is Jean Kennedy at the Australian National University. Kennedy highlights all of the other uses of the banana plant (including its medicinal uses). She points particularly to its common use for textiles, and she goes so far as to say that early cultivation of the banana probably had "little or nothing to do with edibility of the fruit."[13]

Another researcher who specializes in banana domestication is more emphatic:

> There is enough evidence to conclude that people originally used wild banana plants for purposes quite different from fruit consumption, such as for textile making...[14]

Textile Clothing in Melanesia

So in Papua New Guinea, a fiber crop was cultivated during the transition to agriculture, raising the question of whether people were using banana fiber as a textile for clothes – and whether this may have been a motive for its cultivation. Unfortunately, we have no direct evidence about what people might have been wearing in the highlands around 10,000 years ago. Yet we do have a couple of clues. One clue is the kind of clothing worn recently in traditional communities in the highlands; the other clue is the climate.

Traditional clothing in the highlands was quite scanty by Western standards, but even prior to any historical contact with Europeans (and allowing for the influence of missionaries who often preceded the arrival of anthropologists), it looks like people were wearing at least some kind of cover for reasons of modesty – unlike the situation in nearby Australia. A penis sheath or gourd (often rather large) was common among the men – though in a few areas, men did not always cover their genitals. Skirts made from hand-spun plant fibers were worn by the women, and often by men as well. Colorful bird feathers featured as decoration on ceremonial occasions. Cloth was woven by hand from various plant fibers including sisal hemp (which had originated in Mexico) and in all likelihood, banana fiber. Strangely, the use of banana fiber is not so well documented in the highlands in recent times – maybe it was replaced by the sisal hemp. Much the same thing happened with the food crops. Taro and yams were ditched in favor of sweet potato, which arrived from the Americas a few centuries ago, along with maguey – sisal hemp.

Traditional skirts made from woven banana fiber or from strips of banana leaves are still well known in other parts of Papua New Guinea, notably in the Trobriand Islands and in coastal areas around the modern-day capital, Port Moresby. Elsewhere in Melanesia, garments made from banana fiber and leaves are found in Vanuatu, while in the Solomon Islands on festive occasions the men wore decorated loincloths woven on backstrap looms from shredded banana leaves. In the highlands, weaving technology was advanced and fibers from some fifty plant species were used traditionally to make string, nets, and cordage. Sisal hemp was woven to make the brightly colored bags (called bilums) that served also as small cloaks in cool weather, and sometimes larger cloaks were made from bark cloth. In itself, the sheer presence of modesty – covering the genitals – suggests that clothing in the region is of some antiquity.[15]

Getting Cold in the Tropics

The other clue is climate. Despite a geographical location in the tropics, the altitude of the highlands means that temperatures can be surprisingly low. The fall in temperature with altitude is called the environmental lapse rate, and it averages 0.6°C for every 100 meters, or 3.5°F every 1,000 feet. In the middle of the eastern highlands at Goroka (latitude 6°S, elevation 1,600 m), the monthly minimum temperature is a rather cool 12–14°C.

90. **The moist climate of highland valleys in Papua New Guinea**
The highland climate of Papua New Guinea is cooler than its equatorial latitude would suggest – and it was colder when humans were present during the LGM. The climate is humid too, favoring the use of textiles for garments. This region is one of the world's earliest agricultural centers, where banana was domesticated between 10,000 and 7,000 years ago. Shown here is the Chauve Valley, in the central highlands.
Source: Photo by J. Peter White, © J. Peter White. Reproduced by permission of J. Peter White.

The highland climate is relevant in two ways: moisture and temperature. With regard to moisture, while there is some seasonal variation – precipitation is a little higher from December to March – there is really no dry season as such: every season is wet, and it rains on the majority of days in every month of the year. Relative humidity remains high, averaging 60–90 percent throughout the year. These high moisture levels mean that woven textiles were the most suitable material for clothes, and this may have been true even during the LGM 22,000 years ago when the relative humidity was lower. Moreover, banana fiber is especially suited as a material for making clothes in tropical conditions: banana is one of the most moisture-absorbent of textile fibers. This exceptional ability to soak up moisture means that it can absorb body perspiration and so it is more comfortable to wear in humid environments – hence the popularity of banana fiber for weaving traditional garments in the Philippines.[16]

91. **Weaving banana fiber in The Philippines**
Banana plants provide fibers for weaving textiles, and some species are used mainly as fiber resources rather than as food. In the Philippines, abacá (*Musa textilis*) – also called Manila hemp – has been traditionally cultivated for its fiber. Shown here is loom weaving of banana fiber by a woman in Cebu province, the Philippines.

Source: Photo: John S Lander, © Getty Images, # 167611323. Reproduced under license, Getty Images.

Frost on the Equator

The archaeology is not so helpful here since any textiles or wooden tools used for weaving in Papua New Guinea have perished long ago in the moist climate. We used to think that the highlands were abandoned during the LGM, but we now know that people stayed on in some of the highland valleys (elevation 1,400 m) during the coldest phase.[17]

During the LGM, temperatures in the highlands may have dropped by as much as 10°C. A drop of that magnitude would equate to average low temperatures close to 0°C. Some climatologists doubt that the weather got so cold, but even if temperatures only fell by half that amount, we are looking at monthly average minimums below 10°C. And we should take into account the occasional extremes, which are masked by average figures. Even now the region can experience quite chilly conditions: in 2015 for example, the highlands were hit by a cold spell that caused widespread famine when most of the crops were lost due to frost. And this happened during an interglacial.[18]

So although we lack archaeological evidence for clothes when agriculture began in the highlands, there is good reason to believe that people had already adopted clothes. Moreover, the moist climate always favored textiles from the outset, and a key crop involved in the transition to agriculture – the wild banana – was a source of fiber for textiles. Food crops – yams and taro – were cultivated alongside banana, probably from the outset. This should come as no surprise: once people begin to engage in agriculture, for whatever reason, food resources are likely to be incorporated. In Papua New Guinea however – as in many places where agriculture began – a fiber-yielding resource was involved from the beginning.

THE FORAGER'S NEW CLOTHES IN AUSTRALIA

We need to look at one more region as a test for any theory about the origins of agriculture. Papua New Guinea may be a challenge, but neighboring Australia is really a bigger test. In fact it is one of the best illustrations of why agriculture and textile clothes are connected: both were absent. The absence of agriculture on this continent is an anomaly, which is why Australia often tends to get forgotten (or conveniently overlooked) in the debate about agriculture: it is hard to explain. Yet any hypothesis about the transition from hunting and gathering to agriculture must account for why it did not happen in Australia.[19]

Unless it did. There have been two recent challenges to the notion of no agriculture in Australia. One claims there was actually some agriculture in Australia. The other argues that hunting and gathering is really a kind of low-grade agriculture. So the apparent absence in Australia is the result of a conceptual flaw, a false dichotomy. The two issues are related: if we loosen the concept of agriculture sufficiently, then foraging can be seen as a kind of agriculture. In that case, it becomes quite easy to find examples of agriculture in some areas of Australia. We shall return to this loose concept of agriculture in a moment. First, we shall ask whether there was any agriculture in the strict sense.

A Halfhearted Experiment with Agriculture

It now appears that there was. After discovering agriculture in Papua New Guinea, Australian archaeologist Tim Denham and his colleagues looked at the situation in northern Australia, which was connected to Papua New Guinea until 8,000 years ago. They found that all three of the plants cultivated in the highlands – yams, taro, and banana – were present in northern Australia. One of these – the domesticated yam – was adopted by Aborigines.

The likely scenario is that yams spread southward before Australia was separated by rising sea levels. It looks like taro was never cultivated, and the banana remained wild in Australia. The wild banana was regarded as a minor food resource (like taro), and its fiber was of no great interest. The yam though was definitely exploited if not grown by Aborigines, at least for a while. Yams were also adopted by some Aboriginal groups on the western coast of the continent from Dutch castaways in the seventeenth century, but in that case, we are witnessing the acquisition of a food crop that was domesticated elsewhere.[20] This applies also to the dog (or dingo), their only domesticated animal.

Adoption of a crop already domesticated elsewhere was likely the case in northern Australia too: the yam had been domesticated earlier in Melanesia. So if there was an Aboriginal experiment with agriculture in northern Australia, it was not an indigenous transition but the result of outside influence. In any case it clearly had no enduring appeal: the Aborigines soon "abandoned" cultivation of yams, and they did so "for as yet unknown reasons."[21]

Farming without Being Farmers

The other examples in Australia are based on looser notions of agriculture. These include the "sowing" of wild millet in the Darling River basin (which entailed "broadcasting" seeds onto the ground followed by "harvesting," without necessarily any tending of the crop); the "accidental" propagation (by digging) of edible roots such as the daisy yam in southeastern Australia; and the construction of stone weirs and dams to trap fish and eels – "eel farming." Also, the Aborigines actively managed wild resources by setting fire to the landscape to promote growth of preferred plants and to attract animals – "firestick farming." Many fire-tolerant species thrived as a result of such intervention and came to depend on regular fire; in this sense we might say that the plants (and the animals that fed on them) were managed, or even loosely domesticated.[22]

But Aborigines were reluctant to get trapped into relying on agriculture or to surrender their mobility – though they did construct villages and become semisedentary in some areas like the Murray Valley. In the words of historian Bill Gammage, if we think of these traditional practices as a form of agriculture, we could say that Aborigines engaged in a kind of farming without allowing themselves to become farmers.[23]

92. **Brewarrina fish traps, eastern Australia**
Brewarrina fish traps, southern Australia, photographed around 1890. These complex structures may date to around 40,000 years ago or even earlier, attesting to sophisticated management of wild (non-domesticated) resources by Aboriginal people in Australia.

Source: Photo attributed to Henry King; Tyrrell Collection, Museum of Applied Arts and Sciences, # 96/79/1. Reproduced by permission of the Museum of Applied Arts and Sciences, Sydney, and Bradley Hardy, Brewarrina Aboriginal Cultural Museum.

Not so Happy as Hunter-Gatherers

There are a couple of dangers here. One is political, the other is a danger for science. The political danger is that depicting any indigenous peoples as hunter-gatherers may harm them because it carries unfashionable connotations. The sentiment is summed up nicely in the words of Aboriginal writer Bruce Pascoe:

> ...Aborigines did build houses, did cultivate and irrigate crops, did sew clothes and were not hapless wanderers across the soil, mere hunter-gatherers.[24]

To describe the Aboriginal lifestyle as "mere" hunting and gathering is not just unfashionable nowadays but almost derogatory – like showing them as naked. Despite efforts to preserve or re-create their former lifestyle, some key aspects of their traditional lifestyle are disowned by the urban descendants of pre-invasion Aborigines as a political liability. Like their habitual nakedness, reminders of their hunter-gatherer past are now a handicap, even an embarrassment. They did have sewn cloaks, so they were not naked. Worse, to deny them the status of agriculture is to conspire in the colonial dispossession of their land.

But we like to have it both ways, as usual: to be a hunter-gatherer is to be closer to nature, like with nakedness. Nowadays we all want to be natural – although not many of us want to be nudists. We can forget about nakedness, but with agriculture the trick is to have a continuum. If foraging is really a kind of farming, then this could salvage the secondhand dignity of Aborigines and it would mean that agriculture is natural too.

The Disappearing Difference

One can almost hear a collective sigh of relief, a sigh that is audible all the way from Washington to Canberra, from the Smithsonian to the Australian National University. Not only is there no dichotomy, but there is not much difference: we are all farmers, and we always were. So there is no transition to explain, which suits archaeology just fine: it means that there has been no failure of theory. We were quite mistaken to ever think that we needed one. Now we can just get on with the job of documenting this imaginary continuum by joining all of the dots with lots of data.

If only it were true. The continuum between foraging and farming is really a mental trick, but we want to believe it – and it solves the political problem. Foragers are really farmers in disguise (or farmers without domesticates). By inference, nakedness is likewise no different from being clothed – nakedness is simply being dressed without clothes. If we can drop all the outdated conceptual dichotomies, we can reveal the continuity that connects us all: we are one big happy family of well-dressed farmers. Or, to turn it around: maybe we are all hunter-gatherers in disguise. But there is an elephant in the room. In fact there is a whole herd of them, and these animals are definitely not domesticated.[25]

Something quite momentous happened at the end of the ice age, something that has played a momentous role in making our modern world. We really have no idea why it happened. We are not even sure what actually happened. We have not tamed the elephants. Yet if we are not careful, we may well succeed in explaining them away.

PART IV

FEEDING THE MULTITUDE

FOURTEEN

A REALLY REVOLUTIONARY REVOLUTION

The new evidence from Papua New Guinea and Australia has made archaeologists query all their assumptions about agriculture – the definition and the causes. We now realize that there were many different kinds of agriculture, ranging from the management of wild resources by hunter-gatherers to garden-style horticulture in Melanesia and the Amazon, and to classic mixed farming (with domesticated animals and cereal crops) in centers like Southwest Asia and China. Where do we draw the line between foraging and farming? Or perhaps there is no line, no transition, or revolution, but it is more of a continuum?

Domestication of species – plant or animal – does not always follow cultivation (or herding in the case of animals). Cultivation and herding are agricultural activities that may – and in fact must, in the early stages – involve wild species. In some cases (notably with root crops or vegeculture), there may be little or no domestication involved, which can make life hard for archaeologists because they cannot rely on signs of domestication to detect the early agriculture. We saw, for instance, how the Barbary sheep may have been herded in northern Africa after the ice age, without being domesticated. So we should not conflate these processes: cultivation (and herding), domestication, and agriculture.[1]

To add to the challenge of explaining the transition, there has recently been a retreat away from seeking universal or single-cause explanations for the origin of agriculture. The many varieties of early agriculture almost seem to undermine any such quest for a universal process. Some archaeologists suggest not only that we have been relying too much on domestication; they say we need to contextualize each of the situations where agriculture developed and adopt a more "contingent" interpretation of agriculture.[2]

These archaeologists like to prioritize local data about agriculture over general theories about its origins. However, others worry that we may be putting the cart before the horse. Facts are always embedded in theory (whether we realize it or not), and theory directs our search for data. With textiles, for example, a theoretical bias can blind us to data: in Peru most archaeologists are preoccupied with finding the first food crops, and they barely acknowledge all the cotton and wool. And while many archaeologists have now grown skeptical about the prospect of finding any universal explanation, others caution that we should still attempt to make "comparative syntheses" and try to tease out the common causal factors – and in fact we must do so if we are ever to understand the transition at a global level.[3]

The worldwide coincidence of agriculture in the environmental context of global warming at the end of the Pleistocene remains one of the elephants in the room – or perhaps it is a woolly mammoth? Even scientists who stress facts over theory can be inclined to avoid certain awkward facts. Not all facts are equal: some are special because they reveal flaws in our thinking. In earlier chapters when we looked at how clothing was linked to climate and technological change during the last ice age, we saw how Tasmania represents a valuable test case. And just as Tasmania can serve as a test for the Paleolithic, South America could be an ideal test for the Neolithic. And we can safely say that agriculture (as food production) fails the test in South America.

The failure to explain the origins of agriculture at a global level is now accommodated by science in a classic manner, by invoking a couple of face-saving strategies. One is to argue that we need locally specific and multivariate theories to explain all of the variation. Such multi-faceted theories have the subtle advantage of hiding any weaknesses: whenever we fail to find enough evidence for any one factor, we can always say that it must be due to some of the other factors instead. The process can continue indefinitely, ad infinitum, shifting our focus from one factor to another as the situation requires. Nothing is ever pinned down or easily refuted.

So the fact that the evidence from South America (cotton on the coast and wool in the highlands) refutes the food paradigm can be ignored. There must be other factors involving food, and we have yet to find them. We just have to keep on looking for the food – and ignoring the fibers.

The other useful strategy is to deny any fundamental difference, to posit a smooth continuum from foraging to farming – which can have the convenient effect of dealing with an unanswered question by denying the validity of the question. If there really is no difference, if it is just a matter of degree, then the fact that we cannot answer the question reflects the fact that our question is misguided, based on a misconception that something really new was happening.

BEYOND THE FOOD PARADIGM

The critique of agriculture has not gone far enough: it needs to go further, beyond food. From a scientific point of view, the food paradigm has been overcooked. Agriculture is not just food production, and it never was. In some places, such as Peru, it probably had very little to do with food in the beginning. The same is true for the causes: most theories presume the transition to agriculture was primarily about food. Yet the data about food clearly have major problems, even contradictions.

A good example is the work of Melinda Zeder (at the Smithsonian in Washington), one of the world's leading researchers on domestication. She compared the two main ideas about how agriculture developed, based on food. One idea says that agriculture developed when global warming created zones of plenty where people could settle down as farmers. The other theory says the opposite: climate change led to scarcity and uncertainty in food resources, and agriculture solved the problem. So either there was lots of food around (according to some) or not enough food (according to others). Zeder can cite plenty of evidence to support both of these competing theories, even though they make opposite predictions about food.[4]

After all this time, all those decades of research, if there really is that much doubt about the status of food, then surely it is now time to consider another possibility: agriculture was not necessarily about food, at least not in the beginning. Of course the idea that clothing was responsible seems radical and hard to swallow – but that is only to be expected with new ideas. So it should come as no surprise if, as a reason for agriculture, clothes are quite hard to digest compared to food.

FIFTEEN

COVERING BREASTS AND MAKING MORE BABIES

One reason why we think agriculture was all about food is one undebatable fact: regardless of why it started, agriculture created a food surplus that allowed the human population to increase, leading to the population explosion that continues to this day. The presence of a food surplus seems to prove that agriculture was primarily about food, and to justify the idea that agriculture was an evolutionary trend, an improvement in how people extracted sufficient sustenance from the natural environment.

Population size is the ultimate measure of evolutionary success. Insofar as agriculture facilitated a food surplus that could sustain more people than hunting and gathering (at least eventually), it can be construed as a natural consequence of evolution based on the universal quest for food. Yet we are wrong on both counts: food was not the cause, and the population explosion does not prove that agriculture was a better way to feed people.

EXPLODING THE MYTH OF THE POPULATION EXPLOSION

We all know that the population explosion is one of the greatest threats that humanity poses to the global environment. And the population explosion represents one of the biggest threats to the stability – and the future viability – of civilization. From archaeology we know that it began around 10,000 years ago, coinciding closely with the origin of agriculture. What we do not know is why it started in the first place, and neither do we really understand how it actually happened.

Although population growth was associated with agriculture in Neolithic societies, it may have happened in Mesolithic societies too, where people settled down in villages but carried on with hunting and gathering. So the connection with agriculture is not necessarily straightforward. And we saw too that population growth was not an original cause of agriculture; instead, it seems to have happened once agriculture was underway. Nevertheless, there is a strong connection with agriculture, and some theories about why the human population started to grow are based on its connection with agriculture. Predictably, they suggest it was because there was more food.

There is no doubt that human populations could never have expanded in this fashion unless there was plenty of food around. Moreover, the massive demographic explosion that occurred once agriculture was established could not have happened without a food surplus – from the cultivation of cereals in particular. Yet the availability of extra food does not account for the onset of population growth. There are a couple of problems with this kind of explanation. First, is the notion that food was not plentiful – that the number of surviving babies in forager societies was limited by a lack of food, which is not valid. In fact we have no convincing evidence for any food scarcity or stress preceding the adoption of agriculture. The other problem relates to the mechanism of how the human population started to grow in the beginning.

For a population to grow, there must be some change in the balance between the birthrate and the death rate. The various factors that can influence each of these variables are rather complex, but in essence, unless there is a reduced infant death rate, there must be a net increase in the number of babies produced. A reduction in death rate does not seem to have happened with early agriculture. On the contrary there is probably more evidence for a higher mortality rate, if anything. There was a decline in general health and a likely increase in mortality due to infectious diseases and epidemics in the settlements (and the occasional famine too) – and possibly also from increased violence and warfare. Most archaeologists believe the birthrate increased, igniting the population explosion. The crucial question is how (and why) the birthrate increased.

In hunter-gatherer societies, women seem to have no trouble producing babies. The total number of babies per woman depends on the spacing between births: the average is around five babies per woman, each separated by a space of four to five years. In early agricultural societies, the average number of babies produced per woman increased to seven – an increase of two babies per woman. Not a massive increase yet quite enough to cause a big increase in population. In order for that to happen, there must have been a reduction in the space between births.

The popular view is that reduced spacing between births was due to the availability of high-calorie cereal foods. Or maybe there was less physical stress on mothers with the shift to a sedentary lifestyle, since they no longer had to carry heavy babies around, and so as a result they became more fertile.[1]

Yet the one thing we do know for sure is that women stopped breastfeeding their infants for so long. And this earlier weaning of infants would have reduced the spacing between births.

Breastfeeding as Natural Contraception

In hunter-gatherer societies, most women in their reproductive years are either pregnant or breastfeeding (or both). That is, they are fully occupied in the business of having babies and with feeding them. Moreover, they typically breastfeed their offspring for up to four or five years, sometimes even longer. Yet in agricultural societies the space between births was reduced and women weaned their infants much earlier – at around two years of age, instead of age four or five (the norm in hunter-gatherer communities). Early weaning is quite a mystery and, rather than resulting from earlier pregnancies, it might be the reason why women got pregnant sooner. The reason is that breastfeeding – so long as it is intense and almost constant (as indeed it was among hunter-gatherers) – acts as an effective form of contraception.[2]

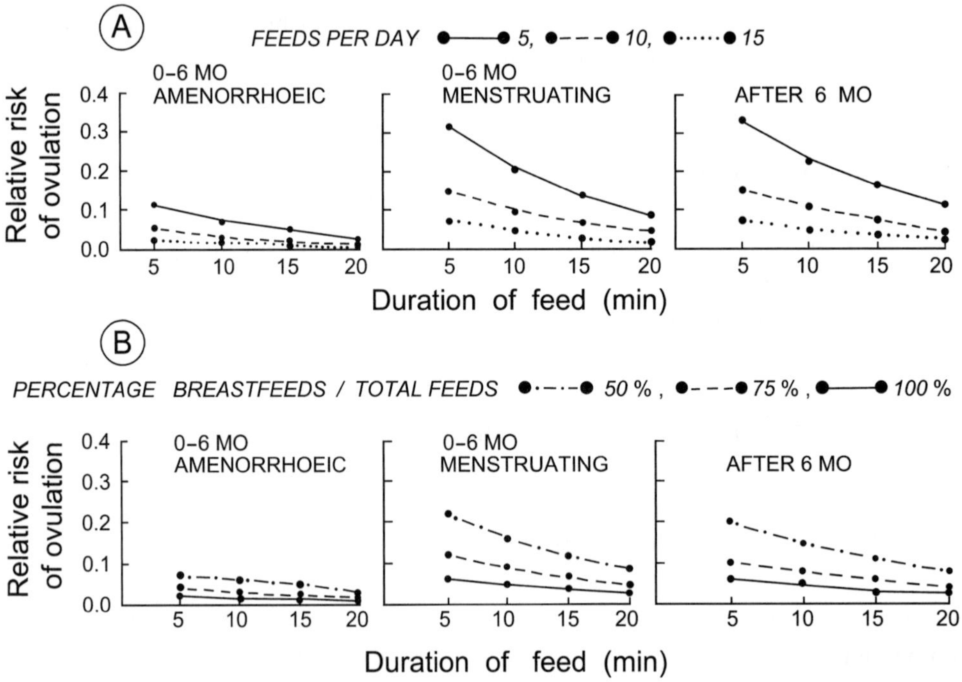

93. **Lactation and ovulation**

The contraceptive effect of breastfeeding depends on frequency and intensity of suckling. Shown here is the risk of ovulation in relation to frequency of breastfeeding (A, feeds per day) and intensity (B, measured as percentage of breastfeeds involving a full feed). Even beyond six months postpartum (the third graph in each line), intense and frequent breastfeeding provides a contraceptive effect comparable to oral contraceptives.

Source: Reprinted from Gray, 1990, *The Lancet*, 335, "Risk of ovulation during lactation," p.27, © 1990, with permission from Elsevier.

What makes early weaning plausible as the cause of population growth is that it can be independent of agriculture (and food), and it avoids all of the dubious assumptions in alternative explanations. If, for whatever reasons, women began to wean their infants early, this would automatically result in less space between births and more babies. It could happen in sedentary Mesolithic societies as well, where the food was still obtained by hunting and gathering. The other advantage is that this mechanism – called lactational amenorrhea – is consistent with all of the evidence we have from ethnography and archaeology.

From ethnography we know that hunter-gatherer women breastfed infants for much longer than has been the norm in agricultural societies throughout history. In Tasmania, for example, early French visitors in 1773 were astonished to see children as old as five or six being freely suckled:

> I was at first surprised at the size of the children I had seen take their breasts, but I have been much more so when instead of one I have seen three of them, quite old and of different stature, of whom the eldest was not less than five or six years of age, go one after the other to take their share of milk of these poor mothers. It is difficult to conceive how they can have had enough for such suckling. . .[3]

In archaeology too, we have good data for early weaning during the transition to agriculture. Isotope studies of skeletons show that infants were weaned a few years earlier in agricultural communities.[4]

With regard to food, a surplus may have helped mothers to wean earlier – but then we have to wonder why they would want to stop breastfeeding as soon as possible. We cannot assume that breastfeeding was a burden for them. In a similar vein, it is often argued that a food surplus allowed more infants to survive, but again we need to be careful: this might imply that food was scarce among hunter-gatherers (which we cannot assume). Either way, given what we know about the nursing behavior of mobile foragers and the contraceptive effect of lactation, any reduced birth-spacing would seem to require early weaning.

Modesty and Modern Women

If the population explosion was due to weaning infants early, the next question is why women would have allowed – or wanted – this to happen. Maybe it was the same reason as women are so reluctant to suckle their infants intensively (and publicly) in the world today: modesty. And it might go a little deeper: maybe it is not just breast exposure that was a problem. Many societies that require clothes for modesty do not require women to cover their breasts, and women can sometimes breastfeed young infants openly in public. The real problem with breastfeeding may relate more to its pleasurable and sensual

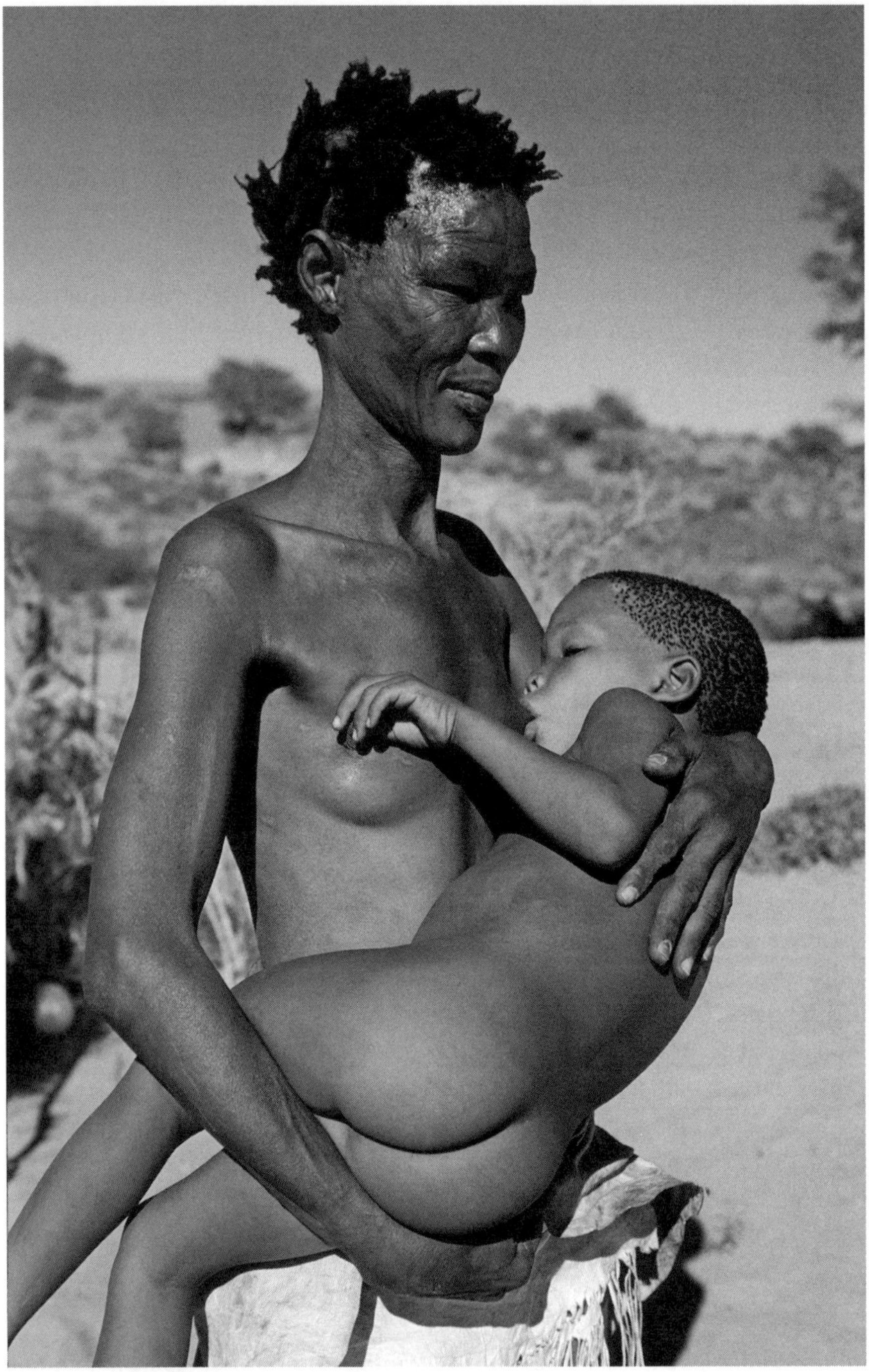

94. **San woman breastfeeding a child**
Among mobile hunter-gatherers, prolonged and intense breastfeeding of infants – typically up to age five or more years – acted as an effective contraceptive. As a result, birth-spacing was around five to six years, which maintained stable population levels. Early weaning – by age two years – emerged in early agricultural communities from around 10,000 years ago. This had the effect of reducing birth-spacing and ignited the population explosion. Shown here is a San woman breastfeeding her son, in the Kgalagadi Transfrontier Park (formerly the Kalahari Gemsbok National Park), South Africa.
Source: Photo by Robert J. Ross, © Getty Images, # 128115542. Reproduced under license, Getty Images, and courtesy of Robert J. Ross.

aspects, making it more problematic to feed older infants and children in this manner.[5]

We really have no reason to think otherwise. We can safely assume that things were no different: modesty and shame had entered the picture. In other words those Neolithic mothers were thoroughly modern women.

MORE MOUTHS TO FEED

Clothing turns upside down our conventional view of agriculture. The conventional view says that food was the sole primary product in the beginning, and later there was a so-called secondary products revolution. These secondary products were textiles (wool from sheep, goats, and llamas, and plant fibers from flax, cotton, and hemp), together with milk (mainly from cattle), traction (from water buffalo for instance) and transport (with horses, llamas and donkeys). However, we can now turn this upside down and say the real revolution in secondary products involved a shift to producing food for human consumption. There were many reasons for why this occurred: one was the sheer efficiency of combining food and fiber production and another was a decline in food returns from foraging around the agricultural centers.

Last but not least, an added focus on food reflected population growth – which resulted from early weaning. Although not a cause of agriculture in the first place, the growth in population promoted the use of agriculture to produce food. So we may say that population pressure was a cause of agriculture as food production – but not of agriculture itself. In reality, the shift to food production would have occurred almost simultaneously with fiber production in many cases, although it was delayed elsewhere. The secondary status of food refers not to the amount of food produced (or whether there was any delay) but to its lower priority as a cause for the transition.

Food versus Fiber

To summarize, producing food for people is unlikely to be the main reason why people first embarked on agriculture in the early Holocene. There are too many problems and contradictions involved in this conventional way of looking at the agricultural transition – as much as it may seem otherwise to us from where we stand now. On the other hand, producing fibers for textile clothing is an alternative explanation that – while it might not be so obvious to us now – represents a better reason to embark on agriculture in the moist climates of the early Holocene. During the historical era, agriculture has often been more about producing fibers for clothes than food for people, as we saw earlier. In different regions and at different times, there have been many shifts in the relative importance of food and fiber. Since the middle of the twentieth

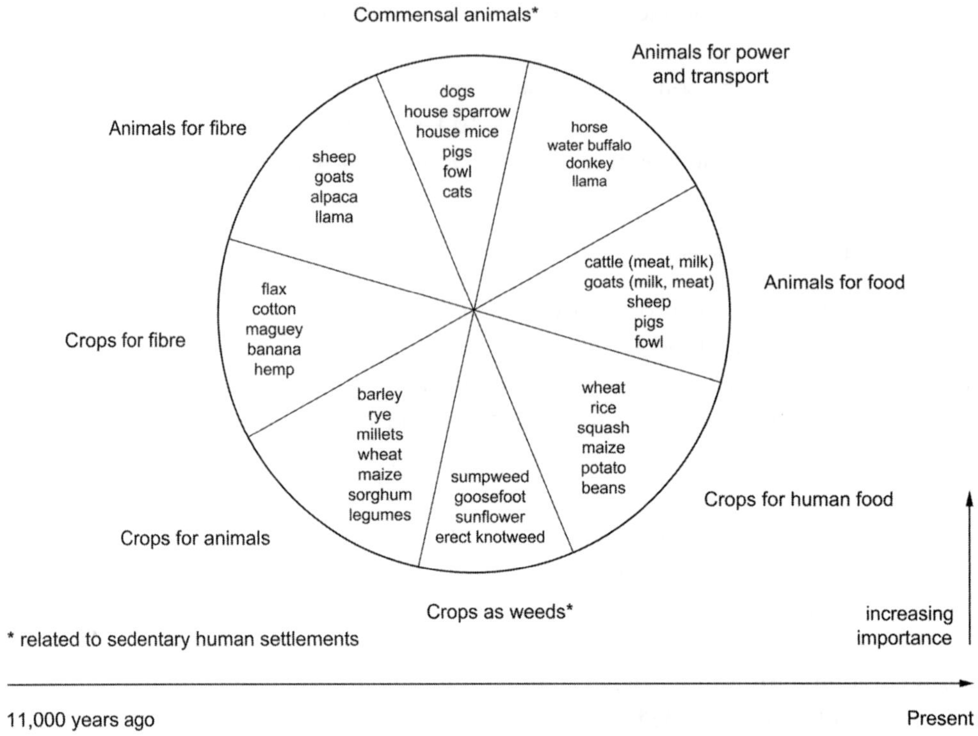

95. **Plant and animal domesticates supplied food and fiber**
Schematic view of the food, fibers, and sedentism in the transition to agriculture. The relative importance of producing food and fiber has varied throughout the historical era, and between different regions. Since the early Holocene, the growth in human population has fueled an increasing demand for meat and food crops while in more recent times, the rise of synthetic fibers has reduced demand for natural fibers, especially wool.

century, for instance, a steady rise in the use of synthetic fibers for garments has led to a decline in wool production, while the global demand for meat has escalated – especially for beef but also for chicken.

At a minimum, we can safely say that early agriculture was multipurpose, not solely about feeding people. However, there are two important caveats about food. First, people were likely to utilize agriculture to help feed themselves from the beginning, even as they continued to rely mainly on wild food resources. Second, early weaning promoted an early shift to food production, to provide weaning foods and to sustain the growing population.

In most areas, production of textile fibers was soon outstripped by food production as human population levels grew out of control. We can see this especially in eastern Asia, where rice farming began to dominate agriculture from the mid-Holocene. Agriculture (as food production) facilitated the demographic expansion of farming peoples, in a positive feedback fashion. Without a food surplus, people – especially infants – would have starved. In

TABLE 9. *Agricultural centers and major products*

Multiple purposes were served by most early agricultural products. Comestible products include crops that were fed to domesticated animals, in addition to humans.

Agricultural center	Early products useful for fiber, fodder, and other purposes	Early products useful primarily as staple human foods
Near East	Sheep, goats, dog (herding)**, einkorn wheat*, barley, rye, oats*, flax, legumes*	Emmer wheat*
Peru	Cotton, llama/alpaca, peppers	Beans, guinea pig**
China	Hemp, millet*, ramie, jute, soybeans*, rice*, silkworms, mulberry tree, bottle gourd	Rice*, pig**, fowl**, millet*, soybeans*
Mexico	Maguey, cotton, bottle gourd, tobacco (?), chilies	Squash, maize, avocado, Muscovy duck**
Papua New Guinea	Banana	Taro, yams

* Combined fodder/human food.
** Likely commensal.

that context, producing food for people often became the main impetus for agriculture. So to say that producing fibers for textiles was probably the main reason in the beginning does not deny the fact that producing food for humans was often the main focus of agricultural activity, virtually from day one. Though food may not have been the primary cause of agriculture on its own, the incorporation of food into farming had massive ramifications. With both clothes and food now provided by agriculture, people no longer depended on wild resources for their livelihood, and so they did not need to engage so closely with nature.

PART V

SEDENTISM AND DOMESTICATION

SIXTEEN

SOME LOOSE ENDS

As important as agriculture was in laying a foundation for civilization, it was only one of the remarkable changes that happened quite recently in human prehistory. The other momentous, new trend was sedentism. A settled lifestyle was related to agriculture but not exclusively, and it was especially important for the emergence of civilization. In this chapter we shall look at how sedentism may relate to clothing, and in the final chapter, we will try to tie these trends together.

THE MYSTERIOUS MOVE TO SETTLING DOWN

The trend for people to settle down in permanent villages – sedentism – was a major transition, one of the biggest changes in the whole of human prehistory. And on its own, it has had massive repercussions.

We used to think that sedentism was always connected to agriculture. Perhaps people decided to settle down in villages so that they could grow crops and raise animals. Or maybe it was the other way around: they first decided to settle down, and then they discovered how agriculture was possible. Or maybe it happened accidentally after they settled down. We know that this was true in some cases: certain species of animals were attracted to settlements and domesticated themselves (like chicken, dogs, and pigs, not to mention rats and cats). A similar process probably happened with some crops too, which started out as weeds around the settlements. Or maybe all of these different scenarios were played out, in different ways in different places.

The problem is that we have good evidence to support all of these alternative scenarios – and good evidence to refute each of them as a universal explanation. As with the food explanation for agriculture, what this tells us – or what it should tell us – is that sedentism was not related causally to agriculture. Sedentism was neither a cause nor a consequence of agriculture, at least not in any consistent manner. The only exceptions are the commensal domestication of some species, and these are special cases – we know that commensalism cannot explain all of the agricultural transitions. The situation is similar to what we found with population growth: although it was connected in various ways to agriculture, sedentism was really a separate trend.

Pots and Rats

Early archaeological evidence for sedentism is ambiguous at best. The classic sign is the presence of pottery – one of the original elements that defined the Neolithic. The assumption was that mobile hunter-gatherers could not carry such heavy and fragile objects around with them, and so pottery is a sign of a more sedentary lifestyle. A connection between sedentism and pottery is generally true, but there are some exceptions – mobile pastoralists sometimes had pottery too. The same is true for textiles: it was generally thought that weaving cloth required heavy looms and hence a sedentary lifestyle, but again many pastoral tribes do make sophisticated textile artifacts – with portable backstrap looms for instance. And their pottery is sometimes decorated with impressions of woven cloth.[1]

The oldest pottery in the world is found in eastern China where it dates to 20,000 years ago, around the time of the LGM. The archaeologists are not sure whether this site was occupied on a year-round sedentary basis. If so, it would mean that people began to settle down 10,000 years before they started agriculture.[2]

The other sign of sedentism is the presence of commensal animals – especially rats and house mice. The advantage of rodents – notably house mice – as archaeological signs of sedentism was highlighted by the Israeli biologist, Eitan Tchernov. Rodents are good indicators of sedentism because they can appear without any domesticated animals or crops – they are attracted to the refuse that accumulates around permanent settlements, with or without agriculture. As we saw earlier, archaeologists in Israel have found possible evidence of an early failed agricultural attempt at a 23,000-year-old campsite (Ohalo II). Aside from the brush huts and "proto-weeds," one sign that this was a sedentary camp is the presence of rat remains. By 15,000 years ago, house mice are found at various sites in the Levant.[3]

So we have some signs that people may have started to settle down in some places at the height of the last ice age – in Southwest Asia and in China. And in both cases it looks like sedentism preceded agriculture (maybe by as much as 10,000 years), underlining the likelihood that we are looking at an independent trend. At most we might say that sedentism often favored agriculture. And vice versa: agriculture favored sedentism. But we would be mistaken to think this was always so. In both cases we have some good counterexamples to prove us wrong. The first example is where people began agriculture without settling down: nomadic pastoralism. The second is where people settled down in villages without starting any agriculture: the Mesolithic.

Pastoralism as Mobile Agriculture

We have already seen a classic example of pastoralism: llamas and alpacas in South America. Herding these native camelids was an independent innovation among clothed hunter-gatherers after the end of the ice age, and the animals provided wool. With a few exceptions – for instance seminomadic Nuer people in Africa who adopted domestic cattle – pastoralists around the world wore clothes. In many cases pastoralism developed out of sedentary agriculture as it spread into marginal areas, where the animals could only be fed by moving between pastures. Besides cattle the main animals involved were sheep, goats, reindeer, and horses. These beasts provided a range of resources including milk, clothes, transport, and carrying loads. Meat was rarely the main product – and perhaps never the sole product.

Horses were the most significant animal domesticated by pastoralists, first tamed in western Eurasia (probably in the Kazakhstan region) around 5,500 years ago. Archaeological evidence shows that their domestication was linked to hide-working – for tents as well as clothes, and also to make leather straps, probably for harnessing. Their function as transport is supported by studies of tooth wear indicating the use of bits for riding, and milk was another product of early domesticated horses.[4]

Mobile agriculture also involved plants, and in some places this was the main kind of agriculture, with no permanent sedentism. We see this pattern in much of Amazonia and Melanesia, where the shifting garden-style of cultivation (horticulture) could include wild plants and weeds as well as domesticated crops – such as cotton in the case of the Amazon. Whether plants or animals were involved, or both, all these different kinds of mobile agriculture show that although agriculture did often coincide with sedentism, settling down in permanent villages was not always necessary for agriculture.

THE MESOLITHIC VILLAGE AS THE BEST OF BOTH WORLDS

Likewise, the Mesolithic lifestyle shows that agriculture and sedentism did not always go together. These village communities were widespread in many parts of the world after the last ice age and, although Mesolithic people settled down in villages, they still relied on wild resources for all of their basic needs – for both food and clothes. Their clothing was typically made from animal skins and furs, although they often did weave textiles from wild plants for items such as baskets, bags, ropes, and fishing nets, and sometimes for garments.

A well-known Mesolithic society is the Jomon culture in Japan. The first Japanese villagers produced some of the world's oldest pottery (around 15,000 years ago). Jomon people wore clothes made mainly from animal skins and from mulberry bark cloth, and they also made textiles from wild plants including ramie and hemp. Some of the plant species may have been cultivated at a later stage, including hemp by around 6,000 years ago. Cereal grasses such as rice and millet could have been cultivated later too, but these foods were never staples in the indigenous sedentary culture of Japan. Mesolithic communities like the Jomon were common in North America and Southeast Asia, and also in Europe prior to the spread of agriculture.[5]

The other aspect of the Mesolithic is that social structures often became less egalitarian and more hierarchical, or complex. Some archaeologists regard the emergence of social complexity as a more important change than agriculture or sedentism. For them, the main lesson to be learned from the Mesolithic is that complexity did not depend on the transition to agriculture: social complexity was not necessarily related to any fundamental change in the realm of food. Social complexity could arise even when people continued with hunting and gathering. So whether we look at sedentism or complexity, the message of the Mesolithic is that food was not a priority, or even relevant.[6]

The Mesolithic was a kind of halfway house. In some ways, it was the best of both worlds: people enjoyed the benefits of village life without becoming divorced from nature. Compared to living in agricultural settlements, they kept in close contact with nature by continuing with hunting and gathering. The Mesolithic is significant also for our theorizing about the origins of agriculture: the Mesolithic means that in itself, settling down did not cause agriculture. The Mesolithic underlines the lesson that we can learn from nomadic pastoralism: that while they often went together, agriculture and sedentism were independent trends.

NO THEORY OF SEDENTISM

An intriguing aspect of sedentism is that although it was independent of agriculture, it did parallel the origin of agriculture. Sedentism began very late in hominin evolution, long after our species emerged by around 300,000 years ago. There might be some early signs of people making a move toward sedentism from the time of the LGM around 20,000 years ago, before there was any sign of agriculture. But even that is still very late in the picture, and sedentism only becomes commonplace after the end of the last ice age around 12,000 years ago. And as with agriculture, this late appearance of a totally new lifestyle raises some awkward questions about its causes.

Archaeologists have always wondered why some people started to settle down. In the next paragraph, we can summarize all of the existing theories about the origin of sedentism.

There are none.

96. **Tasmanians at Oyster Cove**
In 1847, the few remaining Tasmanian Aborigines on Flinders Island were transported to a derelict settlement previously used to house convicts at Oyster Cove, near Hobart. This photograph was taken c.1858. On Flinders Island, Commandant Robinson officially succeeded in making them civilized (one of his favorite words), teaching them how to sew clothes and sow crops. Following this achievement he was appointed as Chief Protector of Aborigines in the Melbourne area; Robinson was always proud of how he turned the naked Tasmanians into well-dressed farmers.
Source: Popperfoto / © Getty Images, # 79657671. Reproduced under license, Getty Images.

That is a slight exaggeration, but not much. We have always assumed that settling down in one place offered many attractions, but as with agriculture, the great benefits came after the event and do not necessarily explain the origins. These attractions are "commonsense" ideas, but they are retrospective and do not necessarily survive close scrutiny. Settling down allowed people to construct big buildings and to collect lots of nice possessions, for instance. And surely, traipsing across the landscape must have gotten rather tiresome, and so on. These notions reflect our modern biases, but they are not what we hear when we listen to what hunter-gatherers have to say on the subject. Again, Australian Aborigines can provide us with a good example: they valued their mobility highly, and they hated to be tied down to one place, or detained within four walls, or burdened with material possessions. For them the mere thought was depressing, like a kind of death. And in fact they did suffer depression and death when kept in settlements, as happened with the Tasmanians on Flinders Island.[7]

And as with agriculture, any obvious benefits of settling down should have led to sedentism long ago – 300,000 years ago or even among some of our earlier ancestors a million years ago. Yet there are no signs of it. And then there is this dubious assumption – as with foraging – that the ancient lifestyle was unpleasant or difficult, or that mobility became an issue for some reason. If so, we really have no idea why.[8]

SEVENTEEN

ENCLOSURE AND FABRICATION

We have only one theory of agriculture – that it was about food, which happens to be wrong – and we have no theory of sedentism. All we really have is a notion that settling down was a good thing, which does not get us very far from a scientific point of view.

As mentioned in the first chapter, archaeologist Colin Renfrew (at Cambridge University) describes this mysterious late emergence of modern life as the "sapient paradox." Renfrew is mystified by the absence of key developments – notably agriculture and sedentism – before 20,000 years ago. Many people focus on the advent of language, but as he points out, the human capacity for language probably developed well before then, and this talent was possessed by mobile hunter-gatherers too – as Renfrew says, "language itself does not seem to have made much difference."[1]

Renfrew suspects the solution lies with the emergence of sedentism. Settling down facilitated a whole new range of engagements between humans and the material world. For Renfrew, sedentism was even more crucial than agriculture. And he advocates for a psychological approach to these fundamental transitions – in what he calls cognitive archaeology. We do need a more psychological approach, but the limitation with cognitive archaeology (as with cognitive psychology in general) is the very stress on the cognitive – that is, on thoughts at the expense of feelings. We need to move beyond cognition to encompass emotional perceptions and attachments – or perhaps more to the point, detachments. In any case, Renfrew sees sedentism as a pivotal change, but like everybody else, he has no idea why people wanted to settle down. Or if he does have a theory, he is keeping it to himself.

SEDENTISM AS ENCLOSURE

Sedentism mirrors the problem with agriculture: we need to explain why it did not happen sooner than it did. Why not 300,000 years ago, or even much sooner for that matter among some of our earlier ancestors? And why was it not a universal trend? The pattern is enigmatic and surprisingly similar to agriculture, and the emergence of sedentism often paralleled the emergence of agriculture. We now know that both of these trends were reversible (especially in the early stages) although we have more evidence for people shifting back from sedentism to a mobile existence than reverting from agriculture to foraging. Once agriculture got started, it was probably more of a trap.[2]

The sedentary trend started in the last ice age. In northern Eurasia, at sites such as Kostenki and Molodova on the exposed East European Plain, archaeologists have unearthed large circular structures made of mammoth bones. The circles of interlocked mammoth bones may have supported domed houses that were covered with animal hides; so the hides served as a form of shelter as well as clothes. Some of these structures were built in shallow hollows to make them almost semisubterranean, providing extra protection from wind chill, and with hearths in the middle. In a few places, the circles of bones occur in village-like clusters. One of these mammoth-bone houses at Kostenki 11 is dated to around 21,000 years ago, the peak of the LGM, when the mean winter temperatures were between −20°C and −30°C (−5°F and −20°F). Temperatures on the coldest winter nights would have been even lower than these average figures, and wind chill at times would have been extreme.

97. **Excavating a mammoth-bone dwelling, Kostenki, Russia**
Archaeologists excavating one of the mammoth-bone dwellings at the Kostenki site complex, on the banks of the Don River, southeast Russia. Recent excavations led by A. E. Dudin have dated some of these dwellings to the time of the LGM. The dwellings contain hearths and were likely covered with the hides of mammoths and other animal species. *Source:* Photo by John Hoffecker, © John Hoffecker. Reproduced by permission of John Hoffecker.

A move toward sedentism may have begun before the LGM, as people pushed into higher latitudes during the milder climate phases between 40,000 and 30,000 years ago. Perhaps this is when wild wolves first began to approach the small settlements and

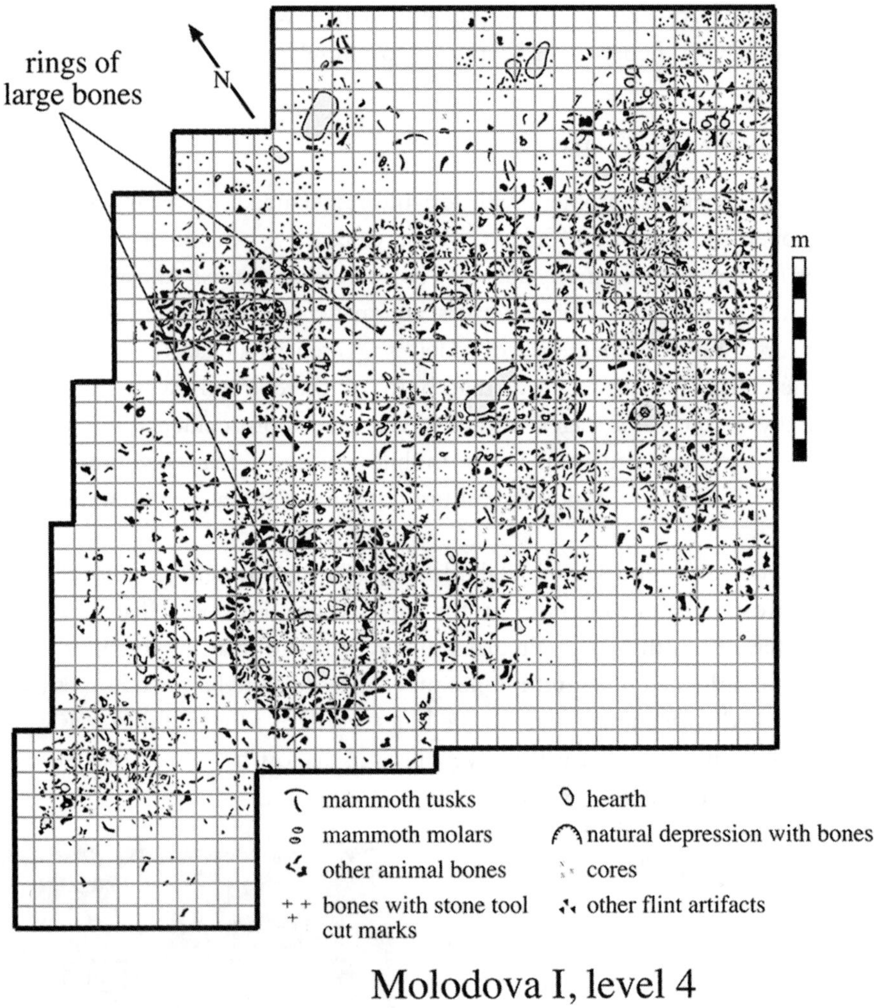

98. **Site plan of Molodova dwelling, Russia**
Site plan of Molodova 1, level 4, eastern Ukraine, around 45,000 years ago. The site has rings of mammoth bones that may be remnants of artificial structures covered with animal skins, built as protection from wind chill on the exposed plains.

Source: Klein, 2009:546. Reproduced by permission of University of Chicago Press, and courtesy of Richard Klein.

become more familiar with humans. Wolves would have been attracted by the smell of food and the warmth, and wolves probably started to follow people when they went outside on hunting expeditions and when people shifted their transient settlements with the changing seasons. So our first domesticated animal, the dog, probably became our first commensal domesticate at some time between 40,000 and 20,000 years ago – as indeed the genetic and archaeological evidence seems to suggest.

Around 20,000 years ago, we start to find the first archaeological sites that may have been occupied permanently, on a year-round basis (like Ohalo II in Israel),

99. **Reconstruction of ice age dwelling, Russia**
Hypothetical reconstruction of an ice age dwelling at Molodova, with mammoth hides covering the structure.
Source: Klein, 1973:70. Drawing by Richard Klein, © Richard Klein. Reproduced by permission of Richard Klein.

and we also find the world's first pottery, in China – a possible sign of a more sedentary lifestyle. Again there seems to be some connection with climate, and sedentism then became more widespread with global warming after the end of the ice age. There could even be signs of a more sedentary lifestyle emerging in parts of Australia – in the cooler southeast part of the continent, where Aborigines wore more clothes. For the first half of the Holocene, from 10,000 to 5,000 years ago, sedentism was actually more widespread globally than agriculture.[3]

The temporal parallel between these two separate trends – agriculture and sedentism – is an extraordinary coincidence. In fact it would be incredible if it were just a coincidence. Like the situation with all those agricultural developments that began in different parts of the world around the same time, it implies the presence of some common causal processes. And Renfrew may be on the right track when he says that we need to consider a role for psychology. Either way, it looks like sedentism and agriculture do share some underlying commonality – that they are two facets of some more subtle phenomenon or set of processes.

Needless to say (but necessary) sedentism, like agriculture, was connected with people who had clothing. The clothing involved was mainly complex: that is, clothes that routinely cover and effectively enclose the human body.

The psychological connection with clothing is that sedentism, like agriculture, acts as a kind of enclosure.

Settling down permanently in one location represents a retreat from active physical engagement with the environment: a withdrawal from the natural world. And simultaneously with the withdrawal from the wild, sedentism entails the creation, or fabrication, of an artificial world as an outward extension of our enclosure by clothes. It matters not that sedentary people might actually move over great distances – nowadays we sedentary peoples travel right around the world – but rather that we no longer feel at home in the open, and instead we seek to build a home base. Staying permanently in one spot is different from moving around within a home territory like hunter-gatherers, and it amounts to a qualitative difference. Not only does it signal a break from traditional mobility, sedentism reflects a new psychological preference and a radical departure for humanity; it is a part of our departure from nature.

Besides Renfrew, some other archaeologists are also beginning to think about this psychological aspect. We have the case of the Natufian in the Levant, where hunter-gatherers began to settle down at the end of the last ice age. Even much later, when people constructed massive enclosures such as the rectilinear structures at Angkor Wat in Cambodia around a thousand years ago, many of the enclosed structures seem to serve no pragmatic purpose: they represent enclosure for enclosure's sake, a psychological preference for walling off the human world from its surroundings. In this vein, Brian Boyd (at Columbia University in New York) suggests we should start to think of the early Natufian stone architecture as reflecting "changes in human perceptions and understandings of place."[4]

The Natufian experiment reflects an early attempt to construct a new place in nature – or rather a place set apart from nature. Sedentism signifies a retreat from nature and facilitates the fabrication of an enclosed world; moreover, it embodies a fundamental alteration in our relationship to the environment. Specifically, it reflects an extension into the environment of our enclosure by clothing. As such, sedentism is an externalized form of clothing.

What this means for archaeology is that we can account for the enigmatic pattern we see with the origin of sedentism. Similar to agriculture, the connection with clothing can address a key question: why was it delayed until so late in the picture? And another question: why was it so widespread and yet still not a universal trend? No other perspective on sedentism (or agriculture) can address these questions so readily. If we consider sedentism as enclosure, as a novel psychological development (or sentiment), then there is a logical (though more psychological) connection with clothing – and a link with climate change too. Once humans became fully enclosed by clothes, which only happened for the first time in the last ice age, then our attitude to the natural environment was altered. Yet this preference for enclosure was never total, or complete: it was always ambivalent – and it still is.

AGRICULTURE AS ENCLOSURE

Agriculture reflects this same preference for enclosure. With sedentism, the enclosure is environmental, an enclosure of the physical environment. With agriculture, the enclosure is ecological: an enclosure of the living environment. In both cases, a corollary of enclosure is an artificial separation between two worlds, a dividing of the world into two: a world that is inside, and a world that is outside. This separation of a familiar world controlled by humans from an unfamiliar, wild world is ultimately what we mean by domestication.

So there is a psychological dimension with agriculture, and this psychological factor is not just a passive reflection of the new sentiment, a mere epiphenomenon. Perhaps agriculture was not possible in the first place unless people wanted to disengage from the wild world of nature. Agriculture is an attempt to enclose that living segment of the wilderness upon which we still depend for resources, the outside world with which we must still do business. In this wider sense, the connection with clothing is more subtle, and it is not restricted to textiles.

If we widen the notion of agriculture to include ecological enclosure as a psychological effect of clothing, then the role of textiles can be seen as a catalyst rather than as a single universal cause. In the broadest sense, agriculture is a likely development among people who are enclosed psychologically by clothes and whose worldview reflects their enclosure. In relation to ethnography, this means that agriculture will have no great appeal to people who remain naked. With regard to the archaeology, it means that we should start to see some early signs of agriculture when people first became enclosed – during the Late Pleistocene and especially from the time of the LGM. The transition to textile clothing with global warming at the end of the ice age merely provided a more pragmatic impetus. As such, the thermal advantage of textiles in warmer and more humid weather represents a physiological factor that contributed to the origin of agriculture.

With textiles as a catalyst for agriculture, we can see how allowing for this factor can explain many of the anomalies with early agriculture. For instance, it can explain why certain animal species became more valuable as living creatures that could supply us with renewable resources. And with the crops, cultivating cereal grasses could feed domestic animals as well as people.[5]

Some leading archaeologists have begun to think in ways that lend themselves to this view of agriculture as ecological enclosure. Bruce D. Smith at the Smithsonian, for example, advocates for a wider notion of agriculture within the conceptual framework of niche construction theory. From this standpoint, we can think of agriculture as the human construction of an enclosed niche. Likewise, Tim Ingold, who has written much on the concept of domestication, draws a distinction between "open" and "closed" views of the world. Humans either "inhabit" or "occupy" these respective worlds – and the trend to occupy rather than inhabit the environment corresponds to the enclosed world of agriculture.[6]

The reality of this psychological dimension – and its likely significance for people who made the ecological transition to agriculture – can be seen in the contrasting attitudes between foragers and farmers. Earlier, we looked at the differing perceptions of agriculture between the few surviving hunter-gatherers in Borneo and their rice-growing neighbors. The rice-growers still depend on foraging for much of their food, and they cultivate rice more as a prestige crop. Yet not only do the foragers see agriculture as rather silly, requiring extra work for no real benefit, they are very conscious of the fact that agriculture entails an unwelcome separation from nature.[7]

So while archaeologists doubt that the difference between agriculture and foraging amounts to a dichotomy, a quantum change, it would seem that people who are involved in the transition may perceive it that way. The real dichotomy could be a psychological one. Foragers recognize agriculture as a qualitative change, a subjective separation from nature. The same applies with the mobile and sedentary lifestyles. Agriculture and sedentism both signify a human retreat from open engagement with the natural environment.[8]

DOMESTICATION AS WITHDRAWAL FROM THE WILD

This commonality is encapsulated in the concept of domestication. The term has a quite restricted meaning with regard to agriculture: it refers to physical changes in plants and animals that result from human control (or at least, their interaction with humans). We now realize that agriculture did not always lead to domestication in this restricted sense: some wild plants may have been cultivated, and some animals tamed and herded, without developing any of the physical changes that would qualify them as domesticated species. So we no longer define agriculture by the presence of domesticated species. Yet domestication also has a much broader meaning that relates to both sedentism and agriculture.

The word domestic derives from "domus," the Latin word for house or home. As with many words, the opposite meanings can be quite revealing too: the domestic is opposed to what is outside, unfamiliar, foreign, or untamed – wild and frightening, even dangerous. Like being stark naked on the exposed East European Plain during the LGM. There is a contrast between what is safe and unsafe, controlled and not controlled, or out of control – like the sexual drive that if not contained, can entice us to expose ourselves and lead to wild abandon – with all of its dire consequences. And a contrast between what is safely enclosed, as against what is open and exposed. So domestication has some profound meanings that denote the wider implications of this new human sentiment, and these meanings are connected also with notions of becoming civilized. A similar sentiment underlies sedentism as well as agriculture: the sentiment of becoming enclosed and separated from nature, or rather, becoming safely separated from a nature that no longer feels familiar, and which can no longer be trusted.

The archaeologist Ian Hodder explored this theme in his 1990 landmark book, *The Domestication of Europe*. Hodder emphasized the social dimension where the spread of Neolithic farming into Europe after the ice age was connected with greater social control of the individual – that is, domestication of the individual human being. Hodder identified various archaeological signs of formal boundaries between the domestic and the wild, ranging from agriculture to architectural features such as houses that demarcate the human from the natural world. The construction of permanent dwellings with heavy stone walls – made possible by sedentism – served to reinforce the separation. Architecture and sedentism enjoyed a two-way synergism: sedentism allowed for the construction of substantial dwellings, and a desire for such dwellings favored sedentism. For Hodder this new sentiment was expressed in the social and symbolic dimensions as well as in the material and economic realms. And likewise with his subsequent excavations at the early town of Çatalhöyük in Turkey, Hodder has identified an increasing symbolic opposition, or tension, between what is safely domestic and controlled, and what represents a danger to the need for cultural and personal control. In the enclosed rooms of the houses at Çatalhöyük, there are ritual symbols of wild animals on the walls: horns, teeth, claws, and beaks of animals and birds, and phallic symbols – a preoccupation with violence and sexuality. The same symbolic images are seen on the monuments at Göbekli Tepe, where there are wild animals with erect penises, and a headless human body with an erect penis. Moreover, Hodder found evidence to suggest that this new sentiment of enclosure and control actually preceded and was a causal factor in the subsequent developments, including agriculture and sedentism.[9]

100. **An early town in Turkey**
The 9,000-year-old town of Çatalhöyük in Turkey is the forerunner of the modern metropolis, where people lived within fully enclosed rooms and buildings. Archaeologist Ian Hodder describes how the iconic imagery seen in the town symbolizes a distinction between the human and natural worlds, between the wild and the domesticated – and he describes how the various archaeological elements suggest that domesticated people were becoming entangled within a fabricated web of their own making.
Source: blickwinkel / Alamy Stock Photo.

Enclosure facilitates the fabrication of a divide between the human world and a newly externalized nature – between the wild and the domestic, between the cold outside and the warmth of the hearth inside and, on the inside, an internal alienation from the wild nature that always lurks within. These are psychological ramifications that flow from enclosing the human body with clothing. Clothing allows us to connect the whole phenomenon more closely with climate change – both in the Late Pleistocene (when the body was effectively enclosed) and in the Early Holocene, when global warming led to woven cloth.

Cloth as Fabrication

The significance of textiles is not limited to their role as a catalyst for agriculture. Textiles signify fabrication: the weaving of fabric for clothes marks a transition to a more fabricated existence. During the Paleolithic era, our clothes came from the skins of wild animals, and so the material of enclosure was still entirely natural. Although those clothes (in complex form) separated people from nature, the material itself still connected them with nature. The use of textiles for clothing was different: a further separation, a replacement of the animal with the fabricated. The fibers were still natural and not yet synthetic, but nevertheless, the weaving of natural fibers into cloth meant that clothes were one step further removed from the natural world. Once created, woven fabric is intrinsically artificial and not so natural. Weaving (and wearing) woven cloth signifies a manipulation of the natural to create the manufactured, perhaps more so than any other prehistoric technology, even pottery (with which it often coincided). As a fabricated material, cloth has only recently been approached in significance by plastic, which derived in some measure from textile technologies. Psychologically as well as technologically, woven cloth was the prehistoric precursor for many of the later material transformations and fabrications of the modern world.

Our attachment to cloth marks an attachment to the material. And our attachment to cloth is simultaneously a detachment – from the wild and from nature. Cloth is almost synonymous with material, the definitive material of the modern world. We spend more time in contact with cloth than with any other kind of material – indeed, we are almost constantly in contact with cloth. Our engagement with cloth is a disengagement from the natural – which begins with the naked skin.

Textiles and Entanglement

With agriculture and sedentism, enclosure within a fabricated world leads to interdependence between humans and their fabrications, an increasingly intricate entanglement that, as Ian Hodder describes, involves a kind of entrapment within the artificial. Agriculture has been conceptualized as a sort of ecological niche construction; a process that once commenced, entangles animals, plants, and humans within an ever more complex web from which we cannot easily escape. But the process is not a passive one: the threads of entanglement play an active role, changing the way we behave and how we see our surroundings, and even how we relate to ourselves. Entanglement entails both transformation and entrapment.[10]

If we are enclosed by anything, we are enclosed by clothing. And if we are entangled with anything, we are entangled with textiles – even more so than with text. The word "text" is actually derived from textiles, not the other way around: writing is almost a kind of weaving. In so many ways, the modern world is entangled in fabric.

With the origin of agriculture, the role of textiles was crucial, but so too was the new preference for enclosing the human world ecologically by bringing

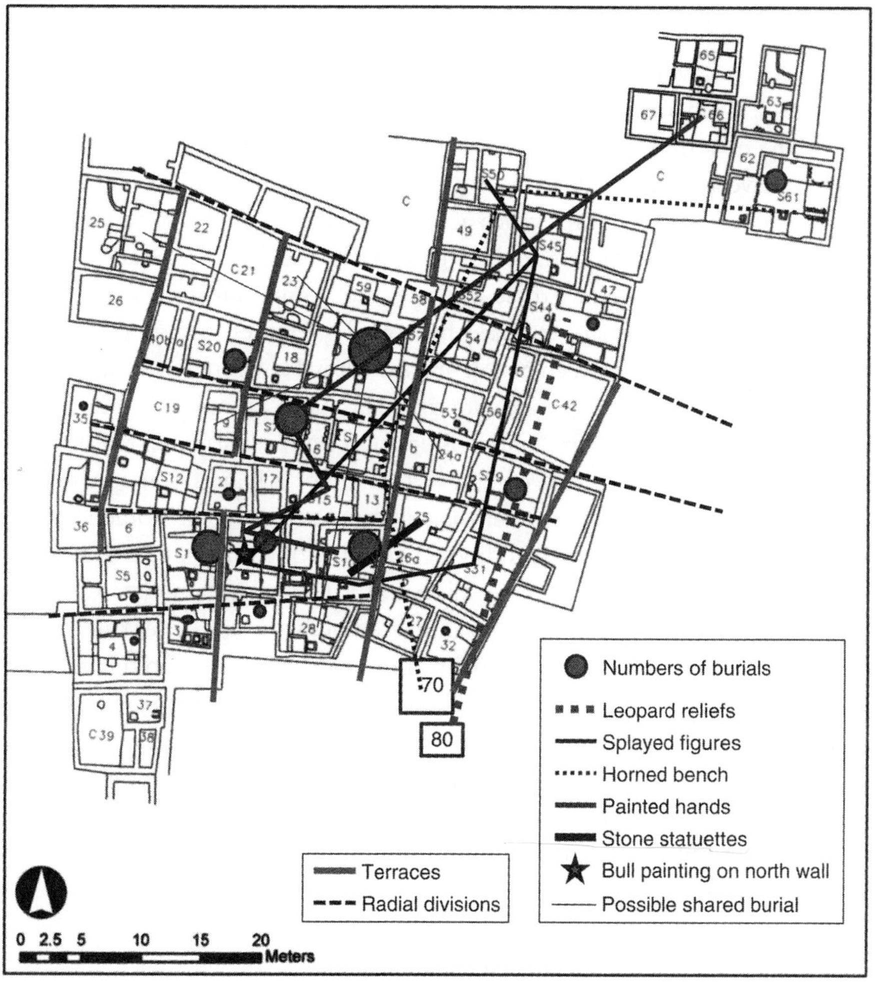

101. **Enclosure and entanglement in the Early Neolithic**
Enclosure and entanglement are visible in the architecture of early towns, like Çatalhöyük in Turkey. Shown here is Level VIb, where archaeologist Ian Hodder has drawn lines connecting houses with similar distinctive features (such as leopard reliefs, and benches with bull horns); the lines do not form any clear patterns but are entangled. As well as materializing enclosure with its rectangular walled structures and houses, Çatalhöyük has yielded one of the world's oldest preserved pieces of woven fabric, a linen cloth that dates to 9,000 years ago.
Source: Hodder, 2012:187. Illustration by Ian Hodder. © John Wiley and Sons. Reproduced with permission from John Wiley and Sons, and courtesy of Ian Hodder.

natural resources in from the wild and domesticating them into a separate human world. That same preference for enclosure led to sedentism as withdrawal from nature, leaving the rest of nature outside as an untamed wilderness. The preference for enclosure is a consequence of being enclosed by clothing, and it constitutes the psychological context for sedentism and agriculture. Only within this context of enclosure could these new adaptations seem comfortable, or make sense subjectively to us.

Complex Clothing and Complex Society

Social complexity is another aspect of these new trends. Hierarchical social structures, together with a decline in egalitarian food-sharing principles, were among the new trends that began to appear after the ice age. Social complexity seems to have accompanied rather than caused the transition to agriculture – and likewise for sedentism. The relevance of clothing is that egalitarian society depends on having intimate personal bonds between people, bonds that are maintained by frequent skin contacts, and these contacts are compromised with complex clothing. When people are enclosed by complex clothes, a basic connection between people – and between people and the natural environment – can be lost.

From this perspective, the development of social complexity follows on from a loss of egalitarian social relationships, and from a collapse of the hunter-gatherer sharing ethos. Social complexity becomes a logical consequence of the death of egalitarianism – rather than a completely new phenomenon that needs its own explanation. An additional factor with complexity is the emergence of new values, notably materialism and a desire to accumulate wealth – behaviors that were largely absent (and often actively suppressed) in simple hunter-gatherer societies. As mentioned above, our attachment to the material of clothing underlies our modern attachment to material things in general. The attachment to clothes becomes generalized to other material possessions, leading ultimately to the rampant materialism in modern societies. Moreover, when people become enclosed by clothes, things can be hidden, whereas not much can be hidden in a naked world. In effect, the viability of egalitarian society may require the openness of nakedness.

CIVILIZATION AS DOUBLE ENCLOSURE

In bringing this book to closure, in linking agriculture and sedentism as two facets of the phenomenon of enclosure, we can see how these two trends coalesced and resulted in the emergence of civilization. It was a case of societies changing when people changed – and people changed with clothing. Specifically, complex clothing was the transformative technology – the technology that transformed humanity.

Civilization can be seen as a complex system that separates and insulates us from the natural environment. Some decades ago, Renfrew described this view of civilization in his seminal tome *The Emergence of Civilisation*. He compared civilization to a space rocket, with people as astronauts:

> ...to a large extent encapsulated, insulated from direct contact with nature... Civilisation is the complex artificial environment of man; it is the insulation created by man, an artefact which mediates between himself and the world of nature.[11]

Once we conceive of civilization in this way as an insular system – and it is no doubt the same for female astronauts – we can comprehend it as the outcome of the two trends, agriculture and sedentism. Each trend serves to enclose us from the natural environment. When these two trends coincided, it created a double enclosure: agriculture as ecological enclosure, and sedentary life as environmental enclosure (reinforced by the architecture of stone walls and buildings). It was like having two layers of clothing, and making the transition from simple to complex clothing. Civilization was no mere shift along some continuum but a truly quantum transition, resulting in a qualitative change. When these two trends came together, starting in Mesopotamia and in northern China, it allowed the human world – reaching all the way from the individual to society, from the city centers out into the surrounding farmlands – to become enclosed effectively for the first time.

Civilization was made possible by agriculture and sedentism, a synergistic collision that catapulted our enclosure into orbit at a newly emergent level. We now risk losing touch with the earthly surface, almost floating above the ground but not quite free, propelled forward by a powerful inertia but still held in strange suspension by an opposing attraction, a kind of sensual gravity that penetrates everything. Yet with the advent of the computer we may finally break loose and head out toward the moon, to live on the lunar surface of a virtual reality where skin is superseded by screen. In this hypermodern world, the analog quality of nature is hidden by the brilliance of its digital display, and the touchscreen is an oxymoron. The electronic revolution adds a new layer and may have more ramifications than the Industrial Revolution, leading to a merging of human and artificial intelligence that transcends our biological existence.[12]

The spacecraft is a fine analogy for civilization, a multilayered vehicle that has transported humanity much further than anyone could have foreseen 5,000 years ago. The question arises as to what powers this wonderful craft. The fuel in question is ultimately psychological, secretive, and in its purest forms, sublimated beyond recognition. Propulsion is produced by an internal combustion of our naked sensuality, a mixture as potentially destructive as it is productive. Enclosure is the fabricated structure that contains, concentrates, and tries to control that volatile mix. The process began not with constructing a spacecraft but with the spacesuit of clothing, which still encapsulates us when we look upon the world with naked eyes, or walk with bare feet upon the surface of the earth.

APPENDIX

DOMESTICATED RESOURCES AND THEIR USES

List of major domesticates (to mid-Holocene) and relative importance of their uses when first domesticated. *Scale:* 0 = absent, 1 = minor, 2 = moderate, 3 = major. For plant taxa, ★ = role as feed for animals domesticated for fibers; for animal taxa, the redundant "animal food" column shows likely commensals in brackets.

Domesticated species	Human food	Animal food	Clothing-related	Other non-comestible
Plant				
Einkorn wheat *(Triticum sp.)*	1	3	1★	0
Emmer wheat *(Triticum sp.)*	3	2	1★	0
Barley *(Hordeum vulgare)*	1	3	1★	0
Rye *(Secale cereale)*	1	3	1★	0
Legumes *(Fabaceae sp.)*	2	3	1★	0
Rice *(Oryza sativa)*	3	1	0	1
Millet *(Panicum, Setaria sp.)*	1	3	1★	0
Soybean *(Glycine max)*	1	3	1★	0
Flax *(Linum usitatissimum)*	1	1	3	1
Beans *(Phaseolus vulgaris)*	3	1	0	0
Squash *(Cucurbita sp.)*	3	2	0	0
Gourd *(Lagenaria siceraria)*	0	0	1	3
Cotton *(Gossypium sp.)*	1	1	3	0
Peppers *(Capsicum sp.)*	2	0	0	1
Sisal hemp *(Agave americana)*	0	0	3	2
Maize *(Zea mays)*	2	3	0	0
Mulberry *(Morus sp.)*	0	0	3	1
Hemp *(Cannabis sativa)*	0	0	3	2
Ramie *(Boehmeria nivea)*	0	0	3	2
Jute *(Corchorus sp.)*	0	0	3	2
Taro *(Colocasia esculenta)*	3	3	0	0
Yams *(Dioscera sp.)*	3	3	0	0
Banana *(Musa acuminata)*	2	2	2	2
Sorghum *(Sorghum bicolor)*	2	3	1★	0
Animal		**(commensal)**		
Dog *(Canis lupus familiaris)*	1	(3)	1	3
Sheep/goat *(Ovis sp./ Capra sp.)*	2	(0)	3	2

(continued)

(*continued*)

Domesticated species		Human food	Animal food	Clothing-related	Other non-comestible
Pig *(Sus sp.)*		1	(3)	0	2
Llama *(Lama glama)*		1	(0)	3	2
Fowl *(Gallus gallus domesticus)*		3	(3)	1	1
Cattle *(Bos taurus)*		3	(0)	2	2
Silkworm *(Bombyx mori)*		0	(0)	3	1
Guinea pig *(Cavia porcellus)*		2	(2)	2	1
Horse *(Equus caballus)*		1	(0)	1	3
Camel *(Camelus bactrianus)*		1	(0)	1	3
Cat *(Felis silvestris catus)*		0	(3)	1	3
Totals	*Plant*	35	40	32	17
	Animal	15	—	18	23
	Total	50	40	50	40

NOTES

Chapter 1

1 *Homo sapiens* appeared by around 300,000 years ago, with a possible pan-African origin extending from northern to southern Africa. The date of around 300,000 years ago derives from fossil and genetic evidence: fossils in Morocco with a blend of modern human and slightly primitive features (Hublin, et al., 2017, pp. 290–291), and a genetic study indicating that Khoe-San (or Khoisan) peoples in southern Africa diverged from ancestral populations between 350,000 and 260,000 years ago (Schlebusch, et al., 2017, p. 654).

2 The few Andamans who remain isolated from the rest of the world are located on North Sentinel Island and are known as the Sentinelese. The Andaman Islands are a territory of India, and access to North Sentinel Island is now restricted by the government to reduce any adverse impacts of external contact. Nevertheless, visitors in recent decades have photographed and videoed the Sentinelese a few times; they often wear colored bands around their waists, which could reflect the fact that visitors have usually encouraged them to cover themselves and accept gifts of cloth, e.g., (Mukerjee, 2003, p. 232). The earliest accounts describe the Andaman Islanders as naked, e.g., (Colebrook, 1807, p. 390), (Temple, 1901, p. 236), and the few items of clothing documented subsequently among some of them (Radcliffe-Brown, 1922, pp. 476–483) may have been adopted in comparatively recent times (Cipriani, 1966, p. 149), (Gilligan, 2010c, p. 28). Genetic studies indicate that the Andaman Islanders have had a long period of comparative isolation from other human groups. They probably migrated to the islands from northeast India around 20,000 years ago at the height of the last ice age, when lower sea levels reduced distances over water between the islands and the Asian continent (Wang, Mitra, Chaudhuri, Palanichamy, Kong, & Zhang, 2011, pp. 120-121).

3 Evolutionary approaches struggle to explain the relatively recent advent of our complex modern lifestyle – and the comparative simplicity of hunter-gatherers, such as the Tasmanian Aborigines (Gilligan, 2016). In its more elegant formulations, social evolutionary theory tackles the question of how evolution has allowed our species to loosen the biological constraints that govern the rest of nature; one such attempt is the work of Dwight W. Read at UCLA (Read, 2012, pp. 178–187).

4 We usually emphasize the evolution of higher intelligence, which may have been favored by a dietary shift to meat-eating and hunting among early hominins; hunting has been linked to the development of tool-use and language and more complex forms of social organization, e.g., (Foley, 2002, pp. 20–24), (Pinker, 2010, p. 8995). However, hunting also occurs in other primates, including chimpanzees (Goodall, 1986, pp. 267–312). Similarly, the manufacture of stone tools can no longer be considered the preserve of our genus: the earliest stone tools occur in eastern Africa around 3.3 million years ago, some 700,000 years before the emergence of *Homo* (Harmand, et al., 2015, p. 314) – and the gap would be longer with a more conservative definition of *Homo* (Tattersall, 2016, p. 8). Even monkeys sometimes make and use stone tools that, if found in hominin archaeological contexts, might easily be mistaken as products of deliberate hominin activity (Proffitt, Luncz, Falótico, Ottoni, de la Torre, & Haslam, 2016, p. 87). Attempts to explain the recent evolutionary success of modern humanity in terms of natural selection and the alleged adaptive advantages of human qualities such as

intelligence and language have proven unsatisfying and, ultimately, unconvincing. We have become effectively unique as a species and this represents a real conundrum. As Foley concedes, the answer cannot be "simply biological" as many of the more significant changes that we associate with human distinctiveness, along with our dramatic evolutionary success, appeared long after the emergence of *Homo sapiens*; hence he sees "a paradox emerging" (Foley, 2002, p. 36). High intelligence may have been a prerequisite for humans to develop civilization and to dominate the planet, but brain size alone does account for our success: "From this perspective, it is easy to imagine that we were predestined to succeed, and that our qualities were those that were required for success… While we are justly proud of our large brains, it is as well to remember that the Neanderthals had brains about the same size as ours, but we are here now, and not them" (Stringer & Andrews, 2011, p. 227). Regarding the preoccupation with food in archaeology, an overemphasis on food is acknowledged by a few paleoanthropologists, such as Clive Finlayson who advocates an alternative emphasis (in his case, the need for water): "Yet most emphasis in human evolutionary studies is on food: what was eaten and how it was procured. Rarely does water enter the discussion" (Finlayson, 2014, p. xii) – to which should be added a neglect of the human need for warmth and clothing.

5 (Gilligan, 2007b, pp. 12–14), (Gilligan, 2010a, pp. 145–146). Theories about the origin of agriculture – and problems with the food assumption – are discussed in later chapters. For instance in the case of animal domestication, zoologist Juliet Clutton-Brock acknowledges that the question of why it happened "when and where it did… has puzzled archaeologists for nearly a century," but nonetheless she reiterates the conventional view that "the causes for the change from hunting to the keeping of tamed livestock" reflect their usefulness as "walking larders" (Clutton-Brock, 2012, p. 23). Issues with archaeological definitions of agriculture are discussed in (Harris, 2007, pp. 18–30), (White J. P., 2011), (Kennedy, 2012, pp. 143-146). Similarly, the definition of domestication is not straightforward: in the context of early agriculture, it must be distinguished from cultivation (which can include the planting of wild crops) and from looser concepts such as resource management (Zeder, 2015, pp. 3191–3193).

6 Graeme Barker at the University of Cambridge notes that while the causal relationship remains unclear, it is clear that "the transition from foraging to farming was as much a social and psychological as an economic and technological process. To change from foraging to farming ultimately involved profound transformations in ways of *thinking* and *being* as well as *doing*" [italics original] (Barker, 2006, p. 385). Clive Gamble, professor of archaeology at the University of Southampton, says we need to look at early agriculture in terms of a more fundamental change in the material relations between humans and the world, which Gamble conceptualizes as a subtle shift from "instruments" to "containers." Sedentism, agriculture, and human domestication reflect an underlying process that "makes containers of us all"; for instance sedentism involved the construction of permanent dwellings (houses) as the focus of human domestication, but Gamble suggests we need to think beyond the obvious importance of this symbolic "container" and consider a host of other "containers," such as clothing (Gamble, 2007, p. 203). Agriculture involved a range of "conceptual" transformations that were associated with an "invention explosion," including innovations such as the weaving of fibers into textile cloth: "new categories of artefacts emerge, new materials are used, new techniques are introduced and new ways to deal with aspects of the material world are 'discovered' in the comparatively short time span of a few thousand years… human-induced generation of new concepts and new relationships (physical, environmental and social) – and thus cultural evolution – takes over from biological evolution" (Read & van der Leeuw, 2008, pp. 1965–1967).

7 Some anthropologists prefer the term forager over hunter-gatherer although these terms tend to be used interchangeably; both denote a foraging economy and also a relatively egalitarian social system, but see (Arnold, Sunell, Nigra, Bishop, Jones, & Bongers, 2016). In terms of economy, a reasonable "working definition" of foraging might be "subsistence

activities entailing negligible control over the gene pool of food resources"; in addition to social organization, a third aspect of the definition of foragers may relate to their "ideology" or "world view" (Panter-Brick, Layton, & Rowley-Conwy, 2001, pp. 3–4). Interestingly, analyses using global data show that variation among hunter-gatherer societies relate most strongly to environmental temperature, although clothing rarely rates a mention (Johnson A. L., 2014, pp. 7–24). In anthropology, there has been an increasing awareness of the great diversity among hunter-gatherer societies and also of their typical interdependence with agricultural and pastoralist societies during the Holocene, resulting in a wariness about making too many generalizations. Robert Kelly, Professor of Anthropology at the University of Wyoming, is a leading critic; he says "the category has reached the end of its useful life in anthropology" (Kelly, 2013, p. 22). At a deeper level, Mark Pluciennik (University of Leicester) critiques the hunter-gatherer concept as historically contingent and loaded with culturally biased ideas about "otherness" (or alterity): "Whether we find the rubric 'hunter-gatherer' and its connotations useful or even essential will depend on what kinds of questions engage us... Thinking about alternative boundaries of alterity may be useful places to start" (Pluciennik, 2014, p. 65).

8 From the outset, archaeology classified societies according to their supposed level of development, based originally on the archaic concept of social evolution as a natural human drive for improvement, or "progress." The term civilization is still encumbered with this old notion of progressive evolution, in contrast to social complexity, which is linked more with the Darwinian view of evolution based on adaptation to the environment. The evolutionary view of prehistoric cultural change – whether based on progress or adaptation – is inherently materialist and was adopted readily by Marxist thinkers, notably by Engels who regarded civilization as "slave labour" of the masses with the state apparatus as the "central link," a "machine for holding down the oppressed, exploited class" (Engels, 1884, pp. 214–215). Archaeological ideas about civilization and social complexity owe much to the work of the Australian prehistorian Vere Gordon Childe, whose definition of civilization was based mainly on these socio-economic aspects and the "urban revolution" (the rise of cities) together with certain material attributes that could be used as archaeological indicators of social complexity (Childe, 1936, p. 157); among the latter Childe listed monuments, writing and some form of science or engineering. The rise of the concept of social complexity (accompanying a decline in use of the term civilization) began during the 1950s and 1960s in the United States. The cultures of the First Americans had been classified by anthropologists according to the complexity of their social and economic structures, leading to a sequence of stages from simple "bands" to larger "tribes" and "chiefdoms," and to highly stratified "state" societies (such as the Incas and Aztecs). The term "complexity" is more compatible with the prevailing evolutionary (as opposed to particularist or "historical") approaches, and it is also more politically correct in that it tends to avoid segregating human societies into categories. Complexity can better accommodate the desired notion that all human societies are essentially equal, varying only in relative terms according to their organizational complexity along a "continuum," and so "all human societies are in some ways complex" (Lourandos, 1997, p. 9). The term "civilization" is rarely used nowadays in anthropology; where it does occur, it equates closely to Childe's ideas about social complexity and the "urban revolution," e.g., (Johnson & Earle, 2000, p. 251).

9 (Angilletta, 2009, p. 1).

10 The difference in cooling between the two hemispheres during the ice ages is due mainly to the greater oceanic area of the southern hemisphere, which acts as a giant thermal buffer. There was also a seasonal difference in the amount of cooling at the LGM, which was much more marked in the northern hemisphere. In the northern hemisphere, summer temperatures on land fell by around 5°C–15°C (with a drop of around 10–20°C in winter) whereas in the southern hemisphere both summer and winter average temperatures fell by only around 2°C–5°C in most areas (Annan & Hargreaves, 2015, p. 6).

11 The word "naked" has two main meanings. Naked refers firstly to the state of being "without clothes" but its second meaning (as defined in the *Concise Oxford English Dictionary*) is

"without the usual covering or protection" (Stevenson & Waite, 2011, p. 950). Therefore, regardless of whether clothes are worn, modern humans are still biologically "naked," lacking the typical layer of fur that provides thermal protection for most mammalian species.

12 (Stringer, 2016, p. 7).

13 One interesting aspect of this problem of heat production by a large brain is that global cooling during the Pleistocene may have facilitated further enlargement of the brain among *Homo* (Naya, Naya, & Lessa, 2016, pp. 70–72).

14 Thermal challenges differ greatly between oceanic and terrestrial environments. On the one hand, oceanic temperatures are highly buffered by the thermal properties of water, so temperature variation is reduced but the density of water means that heat is conducted away from the skin surface twenty-five times faster in water than in air at the same temperature (Dunkin, McLellan, Blum, & Pabst, 2005, p. 1469). As insulation, blubber is far less effective than fur: "a layer of blubber 60–70cm thick has about the same insulating properties as 2cm of effective mammalian fur'(Willmer, Stone, & Johnston, 2005, p. 192). Genetic studies suggest strong adaptive selection pressure for the loss of fur in marine mammals (Chen, Wang, Xu, Zhou, & Yang, 2013, pp. 6–7). For a summary of issues relating to nakedness in mammals and the unusual situation with humans, see (Jablonski, 2010, pp. 44–46).

15 Early use of fire by hominins is reported around 800,000 years ago at the Israeli site of Gesher Benot Ya`aqov (Goren-Inbar, et al., 2004) and at the Spanish site of Cueva Negra (Walker, et al., 2016, pp. 582-585), and possibly 1,000,000 years ago at Wonderwerk Cave in South Africa (Berna, et al., 2012); some evidence for fire at the site of Koobi Fora in Kenya may date as far back as 1,500,000 years ago (Hlubik, Berna, Feibel, Braun, & Harris, 2017, pp. S254–S255). Control of fire was one of the key inventions that allowed hominins to become successful. Richard Wrangham (Professor of Biological Anthropology, Harvard University) has argued that the advent of cooking in particular was a crucial step in making us "human"; he suggests cooking favored the evolution of a larger brain, loss of body fur and more elaborate social networks (Wrangham, 2009, pp. 109–123, 155–183). In particular, cooking may have favored the evolution of cooperative behaviors (Twomey, 2014, p. 96). However, because control of fire was achieved long before the appearance of *Homo sapiens* and since it was utilized by all recent hunter-gatherers including the Tasmanian Aborigines (Gott, 2002), (Gilligan, 2007a, p. 71), the control of fire cannot be regarded as a causal factor in the emergence of modern civilized life.

16 (Ross J., 1831, pp. 100–101, 146) (Gilligan, 2008, pp. 491–494). The colonial imposition of European-style clothing for reasons of modesty and morality – Western notions of morality – represented a fundamental rupture of traditional Aboriginal values and identity. It was not so much the acquisition of routine clothing that mattered so much to them as the loss of habitual nakedness. From their perspective, prior to white settlement, there had been no notion of nakedness: it was a constant state, even when they occasionally wore a cloak to keep warm. The latter held no particular psychological or social significance. To denote a special state of being without a garment made no more sense than for us to have a special term for being without an umbrella, for instance. However, the acquisition of regular body-covering and the imposition of an alien sense of bodily shame had profound connotations. The loss of nakedness involved a loss of ownership of themselves and a loss of their intimate connection with the land, as discussed by Irene Watson, Professor of Law at the University of South Australia: "There are no words that I have come across in our indigenous languages to describe nakedness. Prior to the colonialists' invasion of our territories there was no reflection of our nakedness. The reflection of nakedness came with the other, the clothed colonizing peoples... Nakedness was our identity and culture. What is our culture now? Still nakedness? Yes it is, but it lies suppressed beneath the covering layers of colonialism... This was more than a dispossession of land; it was a dispossession of law, and the disposal of nakedness" (Watson, 1998, p. 2).

17 (Beaglehole, 1955, p. 312).

18 (Brunton, 1998, pp. 97–99). Bark coverings were reportedly used at times, mainly by women and mainly for protection from rain (and often just held over the head). Otherwise,

adult men and women wore no clothes in the Sydney region, besides possum-fur cloaks in the nearby Blue Mountains. The only other garments documented in some early journals and artworks describe a "skirt" worn by girls prior to marriage (which happened at a young age); these garments were "made of possum or kangaroo fur 'twisted into threads' and had a few small uneven 'lines' from five to 12 cm long of the same material hanging down from the centre at the front. The girls wore this waistband until they reached puberty and had a husband (after this it does not appear as if it was replaced by another item)" (Attenbrow, 2010, pp. 107–109). Similar garments that possibly hint at modesty for girls prior to marriage are well-documented in northern Australia, where the garments closely resemble more elaborate skirts worn by young women in coastal Papua New Guinea. The Australian instances likely reflect the cultural influence of these traditional Melanesian garments on the continent (which remained joined to Papua New Guinea until separated by rising sea levels around 8,000 years ago). Despite the lack of reports of these "skirts" in many journal accounts from the Sydney region (including Cook and Banks, who nonetheless described them in northern Australia), such a presence in the Sydney region may result from the southward extension of the northern tradition; no such garments have been described in Tasmania, which was separated from the mainland around 14,000 years ago (Lambeck & Chappell, 2001, pp. 684–685), (Gilligan, 2008, pp. 487, 492).

19 (Darwin, 1839, p. 235). These Fuegians are known as the Yahgan (or Yamana) people who lived on heavily forested islands on the southern side of Beagle Channel. The Yahgan sometimes wore small cloaks, but often they went completely naked: "It is no exaggeration or overstatement to remark that, considering the climate in which they live, this southernmost tribe had less body-covering than any other people in the world... We must add that individuals of both sexes and all ages often went entirely naked... The usual cape worn in summer and winter alike by both men and women was a seal or sea-otter skin. Sometimes two or more were sewn together. In general, however, this garment extended only to the waist and did not completely circle the body" (Lothrup, 1928, pp. 121–123). The nearby Ona (or Selk'nam) people generally wore guanaco cloaks while the Alakaluf (or Kawésqar) wore seal and otter skins, although like the Yahgan, both these groups often went naked (Behnke, Chapman, & Legoupil, 2015, pp. 29–121, 253–261). In Africa we see a similar situation with the San people (a problematic taxonomic category that actually encompasses a diverse group of cultural entities). These mobile hunter-gatherers are often shown as wearing loincloths, but this style of garment was probably foreign, adopted from contact with pastoral and agricultural peoples who spread southwards into their homelands during recent millennia. Early records describe the traditional garment as a loose cape worn across their shoulders, made of antelope skin (called a kaross). The kaross did not provide any routine cover to their genitals, and it was only worn occasionally, to keep them warm; otherwise it served as a rug or blanket (Sparrman, 1785, p. I: 201), (Lee, 1979, p. 124). Aspects of San technology may be traced back 40,000 years judging from archaeological finds at the site of Border Cave in South Africa (d'Errico, et al., 2012, pp. 13215–13218), while genetic studies show the San have the highest genetic diversity of any modern group (Schuster, et al., 2010, pp. 944–945) and so they may be closest to the ancestral populations of all modern-day humans (Henn, et al., 2011, p. 5160). However, it is a mistake to think of the San peoples, or any other recent hunter-gatherers for that matter, as representatives or analogies for prehistoric humans, as though they are living examples of our ancestral state. Analogies from ethnography can be invoked to generate or test hypotheses in archaeology (Politis, 2017, p. 708) but such analogies are "simply devices to stimulate the invention of ideas... a method of hypothesis generation" that should be treated cautiously given the "many problems inherent in the 'ethnographic present' of foragers" (Wobst, 2016, p. 1083).

20 Prehistorians continue to grapple with this issue: even those who claim that the evolution of language and what Robin Dunbar calls a "social brain" allowed humans to develop a capacity to become behaviorally modern, there is the unresolved problem of explaining why humans with this capacity "did relatively little that was modern for their first 100,000 years"

(Gamble, Gowlett, & Dunbar, 2014, pp. 202–203). Renfrew points out that even after unambiguous archaeological evidence becomes discernible by around 40,000 years ago in Europe, "there were few decisive happenings in human existence for another 30,000 years. Hunter-gatherer communities peopled much of the earth... But there were few other profound and long-lasting changes, at any rate when the picture is perceived in very general terms, until the end of the Pleistocene period. Why was this? Why did subsequent change – the cultural trajectory that in many parts of the world later led to the development of complex society – come so slowly?... language itself does not seem to have made all that much difference. Hunter-gatherer societies, with a few exceptions, seem to have been conservative – adaptive certainly, but not often innovative... why is it only in the past ten millennia that we see strikingly new behavior patterns – constructions, innovations, inventions – which are changing the world? That is the sapient paradox" (Renfrew, 2012, pp. 125–127).

21 (Oswalt, 1987, pp. 90–92), (Headrick, 2009, pp. 27–29, 92–96), (Stearns, 2012, pp. 26–32), (Hoffecker, 2017, p. 99). The Industrial Revolution has sometimes been used as an analogy for the agricultural revolution, although textiles are not usually considered as playing any role in the advent of agriculture (Bar-Yosef, 2017, p. 321).

22 (Garfinkel, Klimscha, Shalev, & Rosenberg, 2014, pp. 3–5). One of the first objects made from lead is claimed to be a spindle whorl – also found in Israel, dated to 6,000 years ago (Yahalom-Mack, et al., 2015, p. 6). However, this interpretation of the object as a spindle whorl is problematic, and it may instead be a mace-head (Ben-Yosef, Shamir, & Levy, 2017, pp. 766–767).

23 Plastics were the most significant new material of the twentieth century, and their development was closely interwoven with the advent of synthetic fibers for clothing. The nineteenth-century origins of plastics can be traced to the extraction of artificial textile dyes from coal tar (in the 1850s) and the commercial quest to manufacture artificial substitutes for silk, rubber, and ivory. The first ivory-like plastic (Parkesine) was a cellulose polymer invented in England in 1856 but it proved to be a commercial failure. In 1870 celluloid film was an early by-product of the quest for artificial rubber, while the 1890s witnessed the first artificial silk (Rayon), a cellulose polymer derived mainly from wood pulp. Cellophane was invented in 1908 by a Swiss textile engineer in his attempt to manufacture a waterproof cloth, although the main commercial application of cellophane has been as a food wrapping. Meanwhile in 1907, the first successful ivory-like plastic was an organic resin developed in the US, called Bakelite (Fenichell, 1996, pp. 15–132). Vinyl, a petroleum-based polymer developed in 1926 by the rubber company B. F. Goodrich, was promoted mainly as a waterproof fabric for raincoats and umbrellas; subsequently, as PVC (polyvinyl chloride), it became one of the world's most successful plastics, both in rigid form (used in plastic pipes, cladding, and bottles) and in pliable form as electrical insulation and as imitation leather. In 1930 the Du Pont Corporation also succeeded in manufacturing a synthetic rubber (neoprene), and in 1935 one of its chemists, Wallace Carothers, invented what was marketed as a "miracle fiber," the petroleum-derived polymer called nylon (Gaines, 2002, pp. 35–39). Terylene was the world's first polyester fiber, produced from 1941 by ICI (manufactured as Dacron by Du Pont), and acrylic fibers were produced by Du Pont from 1950. Among the newer fibers is Lycra®, a lightweight stretchable synthetic fiber that has become popular in sportswear, and Gore-Tex®, a polymer membrane that is claimed to be windproof and waterproof but permeable to perspiration. The close historical (and technological) relationship between synthetic fibers and plastics is illustrated by the increasing use of composite materials, mainly carbon fiber and polymer resins. These composite materials find applications in many areas ranging from sports equipment (golf clubs and tennis racquets) to motor vehicles and aircraft. In the aerospace industry, composites are increasingly replacing metals such as aluminum in commercial airframes: 50 percent in the case of the Boeing 787 (first flown in 2009) and 53 percent in the Airbus A350, first flown in 2013 (World Airliner Directory, 2015, pp. 33, 37). Meanwhile, the massive global production of disposable plastics has created a major ecological problem, although many of these plastics can

be recycled. For example, plastic drink bottles are manufactured mainly using PET (polyethylene terephthalate) that is based on polyester fiber. PET bottles are easily recyclable as synthetic fiber for clothing: "China currently takes about 70% of the world's used plastics... Much of that is composed of used PET bottles, almost all of which are processed by the Chinese into polyester fibre. It takes a lot of fabric to clothe a billion people" (Freinkel, 2011, p. 185).

24 The primary significance of clothing in these contact situations between naked peoples and European visitors was apparent in the documented reactions of both the visitors and the locals. For the latter, the clothing of the visitors was typically seen as very strange indeed – as was the fact that the garments concealed the visitors' genitalia from view (Ross, 2008, pp. 87–88). For the locals, "the unsettling way in which the clothing of the strangers encased and hid their bodies raised some questions about their gender and identity which needed to be resolved before a common humanity could be acknowledged. This was particularly true in Aboriginal societies and there are numerous accounts of early European encounters being accompanied by scrutiny or attempted scrutiny of these curious white bodies, with a particular view to establishing their sex. Young beardless Frenchmen on the d'Entrecasteaux and Baudin expeditions were likely to have their genitals felt" (Gascoigne, 2014, pp. 462–463).

25 (Gordon, 2011, p. 6).

26 (Gilligan, 2010c, pp. 17–21).

27 The archaeologist Elizabeth Barber addressed some of these issues in her book *Women's Work*: "Past scholars have generally assumed the history of easily perishable commodities like cloth are unreconstructable, on the ground that there was no evidence... Women's work consisted largely of making perishables – especially food and clothing... Cloth itself, for example, seldom makes it through the millennia except in tiny, hardly recognizable shreds. Until recently excavators tended to throw even those away, assuming they were of no value" (Barber, 1994, pp. 286-287). Textile production in agricultural societies is mainly the work of women, although there are a couple of exceptions where men engage in weaving (Hopi villages in North America, for example, and in some West African communities); in ancient Mesopotamia, analysis of surviving texts shows that woven cloth was a major export commodity that was produced by women (who were often slaves) – 'The product was highly valued; the producers were not' (Nelson, 2004, pp. 43, 85). Two leading archaeologists involved in the study of perishable artifacts – mainly basketry and woven cloth – are Olga Soffer and James Adovasio, who highlight the insidious impact of the gender bias in their book *The Invisible Sex* (Adovasio, Soffer, & Page, 2007, pp. 24–25, 181–192).

28 In his preface to *The Fashion System* for example, Roland Barthes argues that fashion should be granted priority over the physical existence of clothing itself: "It thus seemed unreasonable to place the reality of clothing *before* the discourse on Fashion: true reason would in fact have us proceed from the instituting discourse to the reality which it constitutes" [italics original] (Barthes, 1967, p. xi). For art historians, clothing is primarily "dress" and as such, "the most important aspect of clothing is the way it looks; all other considerations are occasional and conditional" (Hollander, 1978, p. 311). It is crucial, however, to insist on making a distinction between clothing and its social roles in history, which are better subsumed under the terms "dress" or "costume." The French art historian François Boucher made precisely this distinction, which has implications in considering the question of clothing origins: "If one admits that clothing has to do with covering one's body, and costume with the choice of a particular form of garment for a particular use, is it then permissible to deduce that clothing depends primarily on such physical conditions as climate...whereas costume reflects social factors...? Must we also envisage a process of emergence, which might place clothing before costume or costume before clothing?" (Boucher, 1987, p. 9). Roland Barthes hinted at the need to make such a distinction although he ultimately equated clothing with dress and so privileged the social role of "meaning" over the three traditional theories about the origin of clothing – "...as protection against harsh weather, out of modesty for hiding nudity and for ornamentation to get noticed. This is all true. But we must add another function,

which seems to me to be more important: the function of meaning. Man has dressed himself in order to carry out a signifying activity. The wearing of an item of clothing is fundamentally an act of meaning that goes beyond modesty, ornamentation and protection. It is an act of signification and therefore a profoundly social act at the very heart of the dialectic of society" (Barthes, 1966, pp. 90–91). The art historian Michael Carter insists that even when Barthes acknowledged that "protecting" the body from the weather may have been important in the beginning, "any explanation of clothing has to be able to account for the fact that it is social – that is, it is not 'invented' by an individual... If we are set on explaining the origins of clothing, we have to include in that explanation an account of the coming into being of that aspect of the phenomenon that is collective, organized, formal and normative" (Carter, 2003, p. 154). In highlighting the "non-utilitarian" role of clothing, Carter is reluctant to draw a distinction between clothing and dress. With regard to origins, he not only rejects the "tired triumvirate of causes, protection, modesty and decoration" but he also goes beyond Barthes' "linguistic model," which stressed the role of clothing (or dress) as a form of communication. Carter draws a parallel between human dress and Darwin's concept of sexual selection in nature. He sees "self-display" as an inherent, non-utilitarian feature of all living things, an "innate urge held by all living things to present themselves to the world through their appearance... Appearance is for the other but at the same time it is the coming into being of the self. The appearance of an organism is some kind of existential foundation"; the human need for clothing is therefore seen as part of this "compulsory" need for ornamentation and decoration in "an ornamented Nature... something we, as a species, have striven to achieve in our permanently *dressed* condition" [italics original] (Carter, 2013, pp. 9, 40, 50). Hence, to distinguish clothing from dress and to advocate for a separate origin of clothing based on "utility alone" can be misconstrued as challenging this view of dress as fundamental to human existence (Carter, 2017, p. 100).

29 "All societies have customs and taboos which include clothing, and most historians now discount the theory that clothing was originally devised for mere warmth" (Ribeiro, 2003, p. 12). Furthermore, the traditional emphasis on fashion meant that clothing was marginalized by academic historians as a "frivolous and ephemeral characteristic of society"; fortunately, there are encouraging signs that the neglect of clothing generally is being addressed, showing how "textiles and clothing are invested with symbolic meanings which have to be considered... Only then can cloth and clothing be fully recognized for what it is – a powerful cultural enforcer, carrier, enhancer, transmitter and celebrator" (Taylor L., 2002, pp. 2, 64–85, 236); see also (Corrigan, 2008, pp. 155–161), (Loren, 2010, p. 89).

30 In Andersen's story *The Emperor's New Clothes*, the two swindlers proclaimed that their (very expensive) fabric possessed the "amazing quality" of being invisible to anyone who was incompetent or "just stupid"; so as the emperor strode along proudly in the public parade, it took the "innocent voice" of a little child in the crowd to expose its non-existence – "he hasn't got anything on!" (Andersen, 1837, pp. 106, 110).

31 Clothing here is defined according to the definition for clothes given in the *Concise Oxford English Dictionary*, "items worn to cover the body" and for clothing, "clothes collectively" (Stevenson & Waite, 2011, p. 271). Perhaps the most important element in this definition is the word "to," indicating that what distinguishes clothing is the purpose of providing cover (for whatever reasons, such as warmth or modesty). A particular item might be termed clothing in some contexts and not in others. For example in Aboriginal Tasmania, wallaby skins were typically used by women to carry their infants (that is, not as clothing), but in some instances these same skins were worn to cover the body as protection from the cold – in which case they became clothes (Gilligan, 2007c, pp. 8–9). Clothing needs to be distinguished from terms such as "dress" and "costume," which encompass a much broader range of items and also include body modification such as tattooing and scarification (Entwistle, 2000, p. 6), (Ember & Ember, 2015, p. 356). Yet some theorists insist that clothing should not be distinguished from other forms of body decoration, and they argue that the concept of nakedness is a social construct. In this sense, all societies have employed clothing because

the human body is always subject to decoration or modification: "The natural state is, in fact, *unnatural*, if we accept that there have never been human societies in which the body has remained totally unclothed, decorated or adorned" [italics original] (Barcan, 2004, p. 2); see also (Wilson, 2003, pp. 2–3). However, this refers to the broader concept of dress. Clothing is the main form of dress in modern societies – the *Concise Oxford English Dictionary* defines dress primarily in terms of clothes, with decoration a secondary meaning (Stevenson & Waite, 2011, p. 435). Dress, but not clothing, is present in all known human societies (Kaiser, 2012, p. 30), and dress includes a very wide range of items and activities: "our definition of dress as the things we do to the body and the things we put on the body includes even more than clothing or accessories. Our definition encompasses many ways of dressing ourselves. In addition to covering our bodies and applying color to our skins by use of cosmetics, whether paints of powders, we also apply color and through tattoos. We dress by adding scent in using spices, herbs, perfumes, or aftershave lotions and also be eliminating actual or possible body odor when we bathe, shower, or use deodorant" (Eicher & Evenson, 2015, p. 3).

32 In Genesis it was not sexual guilt but disobedience of God's command to refrain from eating the forbidden fruit that led to shame about being naked. There is even a hint that Adam and Eve enjoyed sex without shame before the intervention of the serpent. Nonetheless, the description of the temptation and its consequences – and the phallic imagery of the serpent – is suggestive of sexual pleasure, and the first clothing comprised "girdles" or "skirts" (depending on the translation) that presumably covered their genitalia. To quote from the *Torah* (the Hebrew text which predates the Old Testament), it is said that Adam would "cling to his wife, and they become one flesh. Now the two of them were naked, the man and his wife, and they were not ashamed... So when the woman saw how good to eat the tree's fruit would be, and how alluring to the eyes it was, and how desirable the insight was that the tree would bring, she took some of its fruit and ate; and then she gave some to her man who was with her, and he ate. Then the eyes of both of them were opened, and, realizing that they were naked, they sewed fig leaves together and made themselves skirts" (Anonymous, c. 600 BCE, pp. 24–25). Similarly, the Quran (also Qur'an, or Koran) emphasizes shame as the original cause of clothing, although the Quran later mentions other purposes such as adornment and protection from heat: "Satan whispered to them so as to expose their nakedness... Their nakedness became exposed to them when they had eaten from tree: they began to put together leaves from the Garden to cover themselves... Children of Adam, We have given you garments to cover your nakedness and as adornment for you; the garment of God-consciousness is the best of all garments... do not let Satan seduce you, as he did your parents" (Muhammad, c. 645 CE, pp. 95, 171).

33 (Sinclair, 1991, pp. 6–8). The Epic of Gilgamesh (or more correctly, Gilgameš) has been assembled from many fragmented cuneiform tablets, with overlapping and often disjointed text. A new fragment was recovered from southern Iraq in 2011, adding a more detailed description of the Cedar Forest, where the trees "drip their aromatic sap in cascades" and the forest is described as "a dense jungle inhabited by exotic and noisy fauna... The chatter of monkeys, chorus of cicada, and squawking of many birds formed a symphony (or cacophony) that daily entertained the forest's guardian, Ḫumbaba." Another passage on the new fragment (though only half-lines are preserved on that part) seems to confirm that Enkidu and Ḫumbaba were formerly friends and suggests Ḫumbaba was even looking forward to Enkidu's return, and so "Ḫumbaba's subsequent betrayal by Enkidu, who has brought with him a hostile alien, the king Gilgameš, becomes all the more poignant" (Al-Rawi & George, 2014).

34 The reductionist approach reaches an extreme in sociobiology, illustrated by the work of its leading proponent E. O. Wilson. Based on studies of ant societies, Wilson argues that modern humans evolved to a preeminent position on earth through genetic selection of group-based altruistic behaviors. Making cursory reference to the advent of meat-eating among early hominins and control of fire for cooking at campsites, "the equivalent of nests," Wilson claims that these cooperative social behaviors led to brain expansion in hominins and to the emergence of "innate group-wide morality and a sense of conscience"; according

to Wilson, this process constitutes an "explanation" of how we became a "very special species" (Wilson E. O., 2014, pp. 32–51). In considering the vexing question of human uniqueness, Thomas Suddendorf has critically reviewed the scientific evidence that he summarizes as six main features: intelligence, language, culture, morality, foresight (the ability to perceive future time), and "mind reading" (the ability to perceive the existence of other people's minds). In arguing that humans have indeed evolved to become qualitatively distinct from all other animal species (even from our closest surviving relatives, the chimpanzees), Suddendorf stresses the latter two mental qualities. However, these last two qualities (foresight and mind-reading) may also be present in bonobos and chimpanzees to some extent (de Waal, 2013, pp. 186–187, 204–207). All of our supposedly unique qualities have parallels (if not equivalents) in other species, in terms of these qualities; *Homo sapiens* cannot be viewed scientifically as "qualitatively special" (Gee, 2013, p. 170). Suddendorf grants due emphasis to the biological reality of our animal nature but he concludes, "Reminders of our animal nature are a counterweight to the common view that humans are separate from the natural world, but they should not obscure the fact that we are peculiar indeed. There is no point belittling the extraordinary powers that separate us from other animals nor denying that we are a primate" (Suddendorf, 2013, p. 278). However, while Suddendorf is correct to insist that despite our commonality with other species we have indeed become qualitatively "separate," his attempt to resolve this conundrum still falls short of an adequate explanation. The reason is that even granted the existence of these distinctive human qualities, they could only ever explain how we evolved to become successful hunter-gatherers like the Australian Aborigines. The same limitation applies with social evolutionary theory, even with Read's attempt to resolve the "enigma" of how human culture emerged from biological evolution (Read, 2012, p. 26). This still begs the question of why the possession of culture did not result in all hunter-gatherers developing a modern lifestyle. Similarly, we must be careful to avoid attributing too much to language. For example the linguist Noam Chomsky suggests that the unbounded quality of language makes creative thought possible – and it is this capacity that separates humans from other animals (Chomsky, 2016, pp. 2–25). Yet we cannot assume that language was acquired only recently in human evolution, as Chomsky does, citing the views of paleoanthropologist Ian Tattersall (Tattersall, 2012, pp. 199–225). We also know that recent hunter-gatherers could be very talkative. Likewise, we now suspect that Neanderthals may have had a capacity for symbolic behavior and artistic work; moreover, some precocious signs of these capacities may extend back to *Homo erectus* e.g. (Pike, et al., 2012, p. 1412), (Roebroeks, et al., 2012, p. 1893), (Rodríguez-Vidal, et al., 2014, p. 13302), (Joordens, et al., 2015, p. 230), (Jaubert, et al., 2016, p. 114). The problem is that evolution has made us into successful hunter-gatherers and as such we cannot really be regarded as special or unique (even with language and symbolic behavior), and yet the phenomenon of modern human life is clearly without parallel in the evolutionary history of the world and it has effectively separated us from nature. The paradox arises because this unnatural separation from nature must, by definition (from a scientific perspective), have arisen somehow through natural processes.

Chapter 2

1 (Gilligan, 2010c, pp. 17–21).

2 (Heeres, 1899, p. 81), (Gilligan, 2007d), (Gilligan, 2014, pp. 196–198).

3 (Jablonski, 2010, p. 46), (Dean & Siva-Jothy, 2012, pp. 359–360), (Jablonski & Chaplin, 2012, pp. 8962–8963). In biology, there is a tendency to invent adaptive reasons (or "just so stories") for every physical trait, whereas many traits – including human nakedness – might not have been subject to selection pressure (Koonin, 2016, p. 6).

4 "No-one supposes that the nakedness of the skin is any direct advantage to man, so that his body cannot have been divested of hair through natural selection… The absence of hair on the body is to a certain extent a secondary sexual character; for in all parts of the world women are less hairy than men. Therefore, we may reasonably suspect that this is a character which has been gained through sexual selection" (Darwin, 1871, p. 376).

5 (Quinlan, 2008, p. 232), (Fortunato & Archetti, 2010, p. 154), (Plavcan, 2012, pp. 55–62), (Lukas & Clutton-Brock, 2013, p. 529), (Dunbar, Lehmann, Korstjens, & Gowlett, 2014, pp. 343–352), (Dixson & Rantala, 2016, pp. 884–886), (Lüpold, et al., 2016, p. 535), (Valentova, Varella, Bártová, Štěrbová, & Dixson, 2017, p. 244). Robin Dunbar, for instance, argues that pair-bonding arose quite late in hominin evolution – after 500,000 years ago (Dunbar, 2010, p. 170). In that case, monogamous pair-bonding likely post-dates loss of fur cover – and sexual selection becomes less plausible as an evolutionary reason for nakedness. Sexual selection was developed by Darwin to help explain traits that seemed to contradict his theory of natural selection, traits that appear nonadaptive or, in some cases, maladaptive; in relation to pair-bonding in humans, he was particularly preoccupied with wanting to explain his personal experience of romantic love and monogamy as natural products of evolutionary processes (Richards, 2017, pp. 110–120).

6 (Gould, 2002, pp. 80–81, 1037–1051), (McNamara, 2002, pp. 111–118), (Somel, et al., 2009, pp. 5745–5747), (Somel, Tang, & Khaitovich, 2012, pp. 26–32). Aside from a larger brain size, neoteny would also favor the prolongation of brain plasticity into adulthood, which might enhance the adaptive potential and behavioral flexibility of hominins (Boyd & Silk, 2015, p. 367).

7 (Wheeler P. E., 1984, pp. 93–95), (Wheeler P. E., 1985, pp. 26–27), (Wheeler P. E., 1992, p. 385). Other leading theories about why our ancestors adopted an upright posture include the idea that it helped them to gather fruit from trees or that upright posture freed their hands for carrying things (such as food) and making tools. Wheeler's hypothesis about the cooling advantage is undermined by evidence that our early bipedal ancestors evolved in wooded environments where shade was available (rather than on the open savannah), but it is still considered one of the most plausible hypotheses (e.g., Boyd & Silk, 2015, p. 247). A similar adaptive advantage of having a more vertical surface has been proposed as a cause of the giraffe's long neck and long, thin legs; giraffes also have active sweat glands concentrated in the patched skin areas on their neck, legs, and trunk (Mitchell, van Sittert, Roberts, & Mitchell, 2017, p. 40).

8 (Vignaud, et al., 2002, p. 155), (Haile-Selassie, Suwa, & White, 2004, pp. 1503–1504), (Richmond & Jungers, 2008, pp. 1663–1664), (Lovejoy, Suwa, Spurlock, Asfaw, & White, 2009, p. e5), (White, Ambrose, Suwa, & WoldeGabriel, 2010, p. 3). Early *Homo* may similarly have preferred shady rather than open habitats, judging by the woody plants species identified with fossil hominin remains around two million years ago at a site in Olduvai Gorge, Tanzania (Magill, Ashley, Domínguez-Rodrigo, & Freeman, 2016).

9 (Ruxton & Wilkinson, 2011). The evolutionary origin of nakedness continues to attract plenty of speculative theories (Giles, 2010, p. 330), (Rebora, 2010, p. 19), (Sutou, 2012).

10 (Rogers, Iltis, & Wooding, 2004, p. 107), (Jablonski, 2006, p. 78).

11 (Cerling, et al., 2011, p. 55), (Dávid-Barrett & Dunbar, 2016, pp. 79–80).

12 (Reed, Light, Allen, & Kirchman, 2007, p. 7), (Light & Reed, 2009, p. 386), (Reed, Allen, Toups, Boyd, & Ascunce, 2015, p. 206).

13 (Han, Ma, Chen, Yang, & Chen, 2015, p. 3), (Houghton, 2015, p. 140). Future sea-level projections are subject to considerable uncertainties at the global and local levels; experts disagree, for instance, on the extent of disintegration of the West-Antarctic Ice Sheet (WAIS) and the magnitude of its contribution to a rise in mean sea level (Bakker, Louchard, & Keller, 2017, pp. 340–342).

14 (Ganopolski, Winkelmann, & Schellnhuber, 2016, pp. 201–203).

15 (Petit, et al., 1999, p. 429), (Jouzel, et al., 2007, pp. 794–795), (Bol'shakov & Kuzmin, 2015, pp. 126–127), (Bradley, 2015, pp. 36–46).

16 Oxygen Isotope Stages (OIS) were based mainly on the results from terrestrial ice cores drilled in Greenland and Antarctica, while the term Marine Isotope Stages (MIS) derived from cores drilled into sea sediments. In the marine sediments, the ratio is the reverse of the ice caps (which reflect atmospheric moisture): the heavier oxygen isotope stays in the oceans, and so it increases in the marine record during the colder phases.

17 (Gibbard & Head, 2010, pp. 155–156). There is considerable ambiguity in defining the last interglacial, depending upon which regions and which variables are given priority. Significant disparities (sometimes up to 5,000 years) exist between various isotope records, sea level

changes, and vegetation patterns. Similarly, the last ice age can be defined as commencing with MIS5d or MIS4. In prioritizing temperatures, we should prioritize the polar ice core oxygen isotope records (Greenland and Antarctica) and regard the last ice age as beginning toward the end of MIS5e, between 120,000 and 115,000 years ago. For simplicity in this context, we can loosely designate the last interglacial as a 10,000-year period spanning 130,000 to 120,000 years ago (see, e.g., Bradley, 2015, pp. 212–214). This actually corresponds quite well with the sea level changes (Dutton & Lambeck, 2012, p. 218). For consistency, the last ice age can be designated as beginning around 120,000 years ago; it is now widely considered to have begun toward the end of MIS5e rather than with MIS4 (Otvos, 2015, p. 169).

18 At the global level, the average annual surface air temperature is actually slightly higher in the northern hemisphere than the southern hemisphere, by between 1.2°C and 1.5°C, with summer warmer by around 4.4°C but winter colder by 2.5°C. Most of the average difference is due to the significantly warmer North Atlantic compared to the South Atlantic Ocean, and the colder Antarctica. However, with annual average temperature corrected for elevation, on land the northern hemisphere is still colder by −1.13°C. If both the oceans and Antarctica are excluded, average terrestrial temperatures in regions occupied by humans are significantly lower in the northern hemisphere, with a greater latitudinal temperature difference in the middle latitudes of the northern hemisphere (Feulner, Rahmstorf, Levermann, & Volkwardt, 2013, pp. 7138–7140).

19 (Stuut, Prins, Schneider, Weltje, Jansen, & Postma, 2002, pp. 228–231), (Pichevin, Cremer, Giraudeau, & Bertrand, 2005, p. 88), (McGee, Broecker, & Winckler, 2010, pp. 2342–2348), (Bradley, 2015, pp. 244–248), (Hao, Wang, Oldfield, & Guo, 2015, pp. 2–4), (Potenza, et al., 2016, p. 5), (Wyrwoll, Wei, Lin, Shao, & He, 2016, p. 107). Due to local differences in atmospheric circulation patterns at different altitudes, some sites in Antarctica show the reverse pattern with dust particle size (Delmonte, Petit, Andersen, Basile-Doelsch, Maggi, & Lipenkov, 2004, pp. 430–437). Ideally, not only wind strength but seasonal variation in wind speed should be considered (since stronger winds will lead to more wind chill in winter than in summer); extrapolating from recent meteorological records – where such detailed records are available – may provide some indication of past seasonal variation in wind strength, (e.g., Shulmeister, Kemp, Fitzsimmons, & Gontz, 2016, pp. 1440–1441).

20 (Marlow, Lange, Wefer, & Rosell-Melé, 2000, p. 2289), (Bradley, 2015, pp. 248–258).

21 (Steffensen et al., 2008, p. 683). The rapidity of climate change – whether from cold to warm or vice versa – is probably the most crucial aspect of climate change in terms of threatening the survival of species. For example, a study of extinction patterns in animal species during the second half of the last glacial cycle found most species went extinct at those times of rapid climate swings whereas the coldest period (the LGM) was a time of relative stability that witnessed a lack of extinctions; interestingly, most extinctions occurred during swings from cold to warm conditions – these were generally more rapid than the swings from warm to cold (Cooper, Turney, Hughen, Brook, McDonald, & Bradshaw, 2015, pp. 604–605).

22 (Baldini, Brown, & McElwaine, 2015, p. 1), (Bradley, 2015, pp. 168–172, 263–277), (WAIS Divide Project members, 2015, pp. 662–663).

23 In a Chinese study where a cold spell in winter was defined as two to six days with temperatures below the fifth percentile (a relative measure based on local averages rather than absolute temperatures), cold spells were associated with excess mortality rates between 20 percent and 35 percent (Wang et al., 2016, pp. 5–7).

24 (Kuzmin & Keates, 2018, p. 116).

25 (Osborn, 2004, pp. 13–20), (Osborn, 2014, pp. 47–49).

26 The origin of feathers and flight is one of the most contentious problems in evolution. The evidence favors thermal insulation rather than flight as the adaptive reason for the development of early feathers in the dinosaur ancestors – the only viable alternative seems to be display (Sumida & Brochu, 2000, p. 498). The thermal theory is consistent with the discovery that the scales of reptiles, the feathers of birds, and the hair of mammals are homologous structures that likely reflect shared ancestry (Di-Poï & Milinkovitch, 2016, pp. 1–2).

27 A more realistic index is the apparent temperature (AT) scale devised by Robert Steadman,

which includes not only temperature and wind but also relative humidity and incident solar radiation, as well as proportion of the body clothed. Apparent temperature has been adopted by the Australian Bureau of Meteorology, and it provides a better guide than the wind chill index for the amount of clothing required to maintain thermal comfort – in hot as well as cold environments (Steadman, 1984, pp. 1676–1679).

28 (Rintamäki & Rissanen, 2006, p. 430).

29 (Yoshimura & Iida, 1951, pp. 177–178), (Caplan, 2007, pp. 67–68), (Tsuneishi, 2007, pp. 78–81).

30 In the Swiss system, there are four stages of hypothermia: Stage I (shivering; core temperature 35°C–32°C [95°F–90°F]), Stage II (drowsy, shivering ceases; <32°C–28°C [<90°F–82°F]), Stage III (unconscious, vital signs present; <28°C–24°C, [<82°F–75°F]), and Stage IV (no vital signs; <24°C [<75°F]) (Brown, Brugger, Boyd, & Paal, 2012, p. 1934).

31 (Lim & Duflou, 2008, p. 48), (Dettmeyer, Verhoff, & Schütz, 2014, pp. 207–208).

32 (Golden & Tipton, 2002, p. 55). Experimental studies show that if clothing includes a waterproof jacket, the onset of hypothermia in moderately cold water (12°C [54°F]) is delayed, although swimming endurance is better without clothes (Bowes, Eglin, Tipton, & Barwood, 2016, pp. 763–765).

33 (Hershkowitz, 1977). Major risk factors for frostbite are alcohol and other recreational drug use, serious mental illness, smoking, and (in urban areas) homelessness; the incidence has risen in recent decades due to the increased popularity of winter sports and outdoor pursuits, and breakdown of motor vehicles in remote areas has also become a significant factor (Imray, Grieve, Dhillon, & The Caudwell Xtreme Everest Research Group, 2009, p. 482), (Mohr, Jenabzadeh, & Ahrenholz, 2009, pp. 481–482). The most commonly affected areas of the body are (in descending order) fingers, toes, noses, cheeks, ears, and male genitalia (Hallam, Cubison, Dheansa, & Imray, 2010, p. 1151). Medical conditions increasing the risk include diabetes mellitus, peripheral vascular disease, and thyroid and adrenal diseases (Hutchinson, 2014, p. 1864).

34 (Parsons K., 2014, pp. 355–378).

35 (Orr & Fainer, 1952, p. 191), (Ruff, 1993, pp. 54–55), (Ruff, 2002, pp. 220–227), (Gilligan & Bulbeck, 2007, pp. 81–85). However, even Sherpas who are experienced in climbing at high altitudes can be affected by frostbite (Subedi, Pokharel, Thapa, Bankskota, & Basnyat, 2010, p. 127).

36 (Gilligan, Chandraphak, & Mahakkanukrauh, 2013, pp. 142–143), (Herbenick, Reece, Schick, & Sanders, 2014, p. 96).

37 (Gilligan, 2007a, pp. 15–16).

Chapter 3

1 The type of weave (e.g., plain, twill) also affects the thermal properties of woven fabrics; in general – though there are many weave variations and interactions (such as between the choice of fiber and weave pattern) – plain weaves have greater thermal resistance and lower porosity, making them more suitable in cooler climates (Matusiak & Sikorski, 2011, p. 53), (Ahmed, Ahmad, Afzal, Rasheed, Mohsin, & Ahmad, 2015, pp. 32–33), (Pezzin, 2015, pp. 49–78).

2 (Kwon, Kato, Kawamura, Yanai, & Tokura, 1998), (Hes & Williams, 2011, pp. 132–134), (Pezzin, 2015, pp. 84, 87), (Tang, Chau, Kan, & Fan, 2015). Contemporary fabrics often comprise polyester/cotton yarn blends; due to the differing thermal resistance and moisture transport properties, blends with a higher (e.g., 65%/35%) polyester/cotton ratio are better in colder environments, whereas yarns with higher cotton content are more comfortable in warm and humid climates (Özdemir, 2017, pp. 140–141).

3 (Bradshaw, 2006, pp. 14–17), (Angelova, Georgieva, Reiners, & Kyosev, 2017, pp. 99–100).

4 While still essentially valid, the earlier clo measures have been improved with more sophisticated experimental studies and mathematical modeling (e.g., Tang, He, Shao, & Ji, 2016, p. 570).

5 (White M. J., 2006, p. 559). Warmer furs, such as arctic fox, could have provided high clo values even if the garments were not "tailored" (Hosfield, 2016, p. 662) – but without being fitted, even very warm loose garments are prone to penetration by wind, which is not taken into account with clo values.

6 (Eicher & Evenson, 2015, pp. 158–162).

Chapter 4

1 (Osborn, 2004, pp. 22–23), (Gilligan, 2010c, pp. 39–53), (Osborn, 2014, pp. 48–60).

2 The microscopic study of use-wear traces on Paleolithic tools was pioneered by the Russian archaeologist Sergeĭ Semenov, who identified the multipurpose nature of many tool types and also the working of animal hides as a common function of scraper tools (Semenov, 1964, pp. 82–101). Semenov's influence on archaeology has been enormous (Fullagar, 2000, p. 71).

3 (Hiscock, 1996, pp. 660–664), (Dibble, et al., 2017, pp. 814–821); see also (Walker, 2017, pp. 68–69). While use-wear and residue analyses confirm most tool types were used in multiple ways on different materials, in the Middle-Late Pleistocene the commonest functions identified are woodworking and hide-scraping (Shea, 2017, p. 102).

4 (McNabb & Fluck, 2006, p. 732).

5 (Šajnerová-Dušková, 2007, pp. 28–29).

6 (Falguères, et al., 2016, pp. 9–11).

7 (Lemorini, Stiner, Gopher, Shimelmitz, & Barkai, 2006, pp. 924–925).

8 At Cloggs Cave, archaeologist Josephine Flood suggests that many of the tools were associated with hide-working, and the bone awl was used "for piercing holes in skins" that were sewn together to make large cloaks (Flood, 1974, p. 184). The bone points at NGII (New Guinea II) have use-wear patterns suggesting a function as "perforating implements, consistent with skin-working" (Ossa, Marshall, & Webb, 1995, p. 32). At Devil's Lair the 22,000-year-old bone point was described by archaeologist Charles Dortch as similar to those observed ethnographically to serve various purposes, including "punching holes in skins to be sewn together" (Dortch C. E., 1984, p. 59). Another bone tool – a small triangular bone point – at Devil's Lair is possibly "an awl used in gouging holes in skins," recovered from a layer radiocarbon-dated to between 32,000 and 25,000 years ago (Dortch, 1979, p. 355); Devil's Lair was first visited nearly 50,000 years ago (Turney, et al., 2001, p. 11). The bone point at the Warratyi rock shelter is said to be similar to tools "interpreted elsewhere as having been used for fine needle or awl work on animal skins" (Hamm, et al., 2016, p. 281).

9 (Zhang, Huang, Yuan, Fu, & Zhou, 2010, pp. 516–517), (Li, Chen, & Gao, 2014, p. 68), (Peng, Wang, & Gao, 2014, pp. 16–18), (Song, Li, Wu, Kvavadze, Goldberg, & Bar-Yosef, 2016, p. 142), (Zhang, d'Errico, Backwell, Zhang, Chen, & Gao, 2016, pp. 63–64).

10 (Hoffecker, 2002, p. 118), (Kuzmin & Keates, 2004, p. 142), (Hoffecker, 2005, p. 166), (Kuzmin, 2007, p. 761), (Golovanova, Doronichev, & Cleghorn, 2010, pp. 302–308); at Kostenki 14-II and 15, the bone needles and awls are associated with a lithic industry comprising approximately 40–45 percent end scrapers (Hoffecker, et al., 2010, p. 1086) – a tool form often linked specifically with hide-working (Hoffecker, 2002, p. 123). Some Russian archaeologists have claimed that an eyed needle in Denisova Cave dates from 50,000 years ago, in which case it is not only the world's oldest eyed needle but could have been manufactured by Denisovans rather than by *Homo sapiens* (Siberian Times reporter, 2016). However, the layer (Layer 11) at Denisova Cave with the early eyed needle contains some material derived from multiple occupations between 50,000 and 30,000 years ago. John Hoffecker makes a more cautious assessment and suggests a date for the eyed needle at Denisova Cave around 40,000 years ago, similar to Mezmaiskaya Cave (Hoffecker, 2017, pp. 288, 295–297, 409).

11 (Straus, 2000, p. 48), (Kageyama, et al., 2006, p. 2090); at the early Upper Paleolithic site of Üçağızlı Cave in Turkey dated from 41,000 years ago, where bone awls are found with blade and scraper tools, hide-working is the dominant function identified by use-wear analysis on the stone tools (Kuhn, et al., 2009, pp. 97–102).

12 (Cosgrove & Allen, 2001, p. 413), (Voormolen, 2008, pp. 107–108), (Klein, 2009, pp. 672–673), (Boyd & Silk, 2015, p. 355), (Conard, et al., 2015, p. 11), (Julien, Hardy, Stahlschmidt, Urban, Serangeli, & Conard, 2015, pp. 272–276), (Rots, Hardy, Serangeli, & Conard, 2015, pp. 301–302, 306), (Cueto, Camarós, Castaños, Ontañón, & Arias, 2016, pp. 9–13), (Hoffecker, et al., 2016, p. 319), (Reynard, Discamps, Badenhorst, van Niekerk, & Henshilwood, 2016, pp. 7, 11–12).

Chapter 5

1 (Zhu, et al., 2004, p. 562), (Dennell, 2009, pp. 92–95, 138, 165–185), (Mgeladze, et al., 2011, pp. 592–593), (Blain, Agustí, Lordkipanidze, Rook, & Delfino, 2014, p. 145), (Wei, Huang, Chen, He, Pang, & Wu, 2014, p. 157); the Chinese site of Longgupo (31°N) may date to around 2.2 million years ago (Han, et al., 2017, pp. 80–82).

2 "Therefore, according to the Guadix-Baza record, it seems that hominin presence in the area was strongly influenced by climatic conditions, with the first hominin occurrence taking place only when mild, favourable conditions, both in terms of temperature and humidity, were present. The data reported here clearly support the idea that early human occupation of Europe was strongly constrained by climatic and environmental conditions, rather than by physiography or cultural factors" (Agustí, et al., 2015, pp. 92–93). At present, the archaeological evidence suggests hominins prior to 400,000 years ago could cope only with mild mean winter temperatures between 0°C and +6°C (Hosfield, 2016, pp. 655, 671), (Moncel, Landais, Lebreton, Combourieu-Nebout, Nomade, & Bazin, in press, pp. 12–13).

3 (Parfitt, et al., 2005, pp. 1009–1010), (Parfitt, et al., 2010, pp. 232–233), (Roberts & Grün, 2010, p. 190).

4 (Shen, Gao, & Granger, 2009, p. 200), (Gao, Zhang, Zhang, & Chen, 2017, pp. S271–S275).

5 Compared to the spread of the other main tool technology (bifaces, including hand-axes), it was the increasing presence of tools such "elaborate scrapers" that was probably more important for human survival in Europe, as scrapers were associated with hide-scraping and the likely manufacture of improved clothing to help in "coping with winter cold" (Moncel, Ashton, Lamotte, Tuffreau, Cliquet, & Despriée, 2015, pp. 324–325). At Schöningen (52°N), mean January temperatures are estimated between −4°C and −1°C (Urban & Bigga, 2015, p. 69).

6 (Monnier, 2006, p. 727), (McNabb & Fluck, 2006, p. 732), (White M. J., 2006, p. 559). While eschewing formal tool typologies and favoring Shea's nomenclature, Michael J. Walker's detailed review of southern European sites may similarly suggest some interesting correlations between colder climate phases and the prevalence of scraper tools. Among the various sites, Fontana Ranuccio (central Italy, MIS12) has scrapers; whereas Terra Amata (southern France, MIS11) has pebble and chopper (Lower Paleolithic) tools; Orgnac 3 (southern France, spanning cold phases from MIS10 to MIS8) has side-scrapers, end scrapers, awls, piercers, and burins; Baume Bonne rock-shelter (southern France, MIS10–6) has scrapers, awls, and burins; Grotte du Lazaret (southern France, MIS 6–4) has scrapers; Bau de l'Aubesier (southern France, MIS6) has scrapers and flake-blades (Shea Mode F); Payre (southern France, MIS6) has scrapers; Coupe Gorge (foothills of the French Pyrenees, MIS6) has side-scrapers; Abric Romani (Spanish Catalonia, MIS5d-3) has Mousterian industries with use-wear confirming the processing of hides; and Abri des Canalettes (southern France, MIS4) has side-scrapers, end scrapers, and flake-blades (Walker, 2017, pp. 70–74, 85–102).

7 (Gilligan, 2010c, pp. 42–43), (Monnier & Missal, 2014, pp. 72–77), (Pawlik, Piper, & Mijares, 2014, pp. 142–143), (Hao, Wang, Oldfield, & Guo, 2015, p. 3), (Piper, 2016, p. 35), (Blinkhorn & Petraglia, 2017, pp. S463–S479). Some archaeologists associate blades more with *Homo sapiens*, and scrapers more with Neanderthals (and with other archaic hominins). And indeed there is a strong association of blade industries with *Homo sapiens*, but again this is true mainly in the colder regions – early blade tools are sparse among *Homo sapiens* in warmer regions (Bellwood, 2015, pp. 53–54), (Pawlik, 2015, pp. 183–192). Similarly, many of the early tool industries associated with *Homo sapiens* were scraper industries – as was the case, for instance, in northern Africa, where the toolkits made by biologically modern humans were much the same as the Neanderthal technologies (Dibble, et al., 2013, pp. 195, 207), (Spinapolice & Garcea, 2014, pp. 241–246).

8 Cold conditions due to elevation in the Ethiopian highlands may explain the retreat of *Homo erectus* from the region during the MIS20 glacial phase around 800,000 years ago; today, the average monthly temperature ranges between 16.5°C and 20.5°C (Mussi, Altamura, Bonnefille, De Rita, & Melis, 2016, pp. 259, 266–267).

9 (Sankararaman, Patterson, Li, Pääbo, & Reich, 2012, p. 7). The Denisovans coexisted with Neanderthals and modern humans between around 50,000 to 30,000 years ago (Krause, et al., 2010, p. 896); genetic evidence indicates that they split from a common ancestor with Neanderthals by 600,000 years ago but subsequently interbred with the ancestors of present-day Melanesians and Australian Aborigines (Reich, et al., 2010, p. 1057), (Rasmussen, et al., 2011, p. 97), (Meyer, et al., 2012, p. 223).

10 (Trinkaus, 2005, p. 1523), (Fu, et al., 2014, p. 449), (Xing, Martinón-Torres, Bermúdez de Castro, Wu, & Liu, 2015, p. 224), (Liu, et al., 2015, p. 699), (Hoffecker, Elias, O'Rourke, Scott, & Bigelow, 2016, pp. 66, 70), (Kuzmin & Keates, 2018, pp. 119–120). In China, as Robin Dennell points out, the delay in reaching northern China may be attributable simply to the severe cold: "*H. sapiens* originated in or near the tropics, so it makes sense that the species' initial dispersal was eastwards rather than northwards, where winter temperatures rapidly fell below zero… modern humans were in southern China long before there is evidence for them in northern China and Europe… in Europe… the presence of Neanderthals may have delayed the arrival of modern humans. However, the predominantly colder winter conditions of the enormous landmass between Europe and northern China may better explain the earlier colonization of southern zones" (Dennell, 2015,2015, p. 648). Similarly, winter temperatures in Eastern Europe and Siberia meant that it was an "eyed-needle zone" in terms of clothing requirements for humans (Hoffecker, 2015, pp. 102–103). At Yana, archaeological finds include scrapers and blades, bone awls, eyed needles, possible needle cases, and mammoth-bone beads that may have been sewn onto clothes (Hoffecker, 2017, pp. 299–300).

11 (Hoffecker, 2005, p. 117), (Hoffecker, Elias, O'Rourke, Scott, & Bigelow, 2016, pp. 65–66, 75), (Hoffecker, 2017, pp. 254–265).

12 (Backwell, d'Errico, & Wadley, 2008).

13 (Bar-Yosef & Wang, 2012, pp. 327–330), (Mishra, Chauhan, & Singhvi, 2013, pp. 2, 9–12). On a global scale, the technological complexity of hunter-gatherers – complexity measured in various ways, including the number of technological units, production steps, and hierarchical structures – correlates with occupation of colder environments. The correlation suggests that technological complexity increases in response to the complexity of environmental challenges, including scarcer food resources in colder environments. However, the correlation with low temperature is stronger than the correlation with low food productivity, highlighting how complex clothing was a significant component of the generally increased technological complexity associated with human expansion into high latitudes (Hoffecker & Hoffecker, 2018, pp. 216–219).

Chapter 6

1 "During the period between approximately 160 ka and 20 ka [160,000 and 20,000 years ago] complex technologies, adaptation to hostile environments, engravings, pigments, personal ornaments, formal bone tools and burial practices apparently appear, disappear and reappear in different forms…The discontinuous nature in time and space of this process, and the commonalities found in both hemispheres, indicate that local conditions must have played a role in the emergence, diffusion and the eventual disappearance or continuity of crucial innovations in different regions… This suggests to us that in order to make further progress in this field, we need a research strategy that allows us to model and quantify the link between environment and a particular past cultural adaptation, predict the response of that adaptation to climate change and verify whether the rise and spread of innovations result in an expansion or contraction of the eco-cultural niche of a given population. Assumptions about cognition based on taxonomic affiliation should play no *a priori* role, and the key tools would then be archaeology, palaeoenvironmental studies, climate modelling and methods to integrate results from these disciplines" (d'Errico & Stringer, 2011, pp. 1066–1067). Although d'Errico and Stringer emphasize demographic aspects of responses to climate change, requirements for clothing could provide the missing "link" between climate change and the archaeological evidence.

2 (Brumm & Moore, 2005), (O'Connell & Allen, 2007), (Habgood & Franklin, 2008),

(Gilligan, 2010b), (Mulvaney, 2012), (Hiscock, 2013), (Balme & O'Connor, 2014, p. 164). With regard to clothing, the ancestors of people who first reached Australia from Africa – in the out-of-Africa scenario – likely traveled around the northern rim of the Indian Ocean without straying far beyond the tropics (Bulbeck, 2007, p. 319), and, hence, without needing to wear complex clothes. This is in contrast to the likely entry of humans into the Americas across Beringia, the land bridge between Siberia and Alaska exposed by lower sea levels during the last ice age – or conceivably at the end of the previous ice age, if the claim for a 130,000-year-old site in California is substantiated (Holen, et al., 2017, p. 481). Among the archaeological sites with early evidence for the arrival of humans in Australia is the Madjedbebe rock-shelter (known formerly as Malakunanja II) in Arnhem Land, which was first excavated by archaeologist Johan Kamminga in 1973. Dates from subsequent excavations yielded estimates between 65,000 and 59,000 years ago for the earliest occupation; evidence for the grinding of ochre pigments – used possibly in body painting and other artistic activities – extends to the earliest occupation levels (Clarkson, et al., 2017, p. 309). Iain Davidson, Emeritus Professor of Archaeology at the University of New England, argues that while most of the archaeological signs alleged to indicate a capacity for symbolic thinking were more-or-less absent among the first Australians, the arrival of humans on the continent required construction of sea-worthy watercraft that would not have been possible without such abilities (Davidson, 2014, p. 247). Although inter-island distances were reduced due to lowered sea levels, reaching Australia still meant a minimum of eight sea crossings and one leg of at least 70 km; on East Timor (Timor-Leste), where humans were present by 40,000 years ago, archaeological evidence for fishing (including faunal remains of fast-swimming tuna and sharks) testifies that people were capable of "high levels of planning" (O'Connor, 2015, pp. 215, 221). Decorative items such as beads are more commonly found in late Holocene contexts and were likely unrelated to clothing; for instance, a series of red-colored beads made from shark vertebrae that probably derive from a necklace, found in Arnhem Land in the north of the continent (Wright, Langley, May, Johnston, & Allen, 2016, p. 50).

3 Some of the earliest archaeological evidence for decoration and adornment (such as perforated beads and the use of ochre pigments) has been found in southern Africa during early cold phases of the last glacial cycle, dating from 100,000 years ago (d'Errico & Henshilwood, 2007), (Zilhão, 2007), (Henshilwood, et al., 2011). However, it should not be assumed that ornaments in particular testify to the presence of symbolic or linguistic capacities (Moro Abadía & Nowell, 2015, pp. 968–969). The fluorescence of cave art in ice age Europe has often been seen as indicating a "revolution" in human cognitive and symbolic capacities from around 50,000 years ago, although cave paintings have now been found in Indonesia dating also to 40,000 years ago (Aubert, et al., 2014, p. 225) – demonstrating that these artistic productions were "a worldwide behavioural practice" and "not the isolated cultural invention of specific regional communities" (Taçon, et al., 2014, p. 1062). Richard Klein, Professor of Anthropology at Stanford University, has advocated the "neural hypothesis," arguing that a genetic change occurred around that time that led to a neurological reorganization in the human brain allowing, for instance, modern humans to displace Neanderthals from Europe (Klein & Edgar, 2002, pp. 272–273). Yet these theories about symbolic thinking or our language capacity arising from recent changes in brain structure or function remain "highly speculative and for the most part extremely difficult to evaluate or test in any rigorous way" (Mellars, 2015, p. 15). Following a seminal paper (McBrearty & Brooks, 2000), it is now generally accepted that the first signs of such capacities are witnessed in Africa, and the very earliest signs may coincide with the biological emergence of *Homo sapiens* around 300,000 years ago. For an overview of the evidence and the arguments, see (Mellars, Boyle, Bar-Yosef, & Stringer, 2007). Regardless of when it first emerged, this human capacity for symbolic and artistic behavior is said to signify "a clear gulf between humans and the rest of nature" (McBrearty, 2007, p. 145).

4 (Behnke, Chapman, & Legoupil, 2015, pp. 66–103).

5 (d'Errico, et al., 2009), (d'Errico, Moreno, & Rifkin, 2012, pp. 16055–16056), (Stiner, Kuhn,

& Güleç, 2013, p. 397), (Wei, d'Errico, Vanhaeren, Li, & Gao, 2016, pp. 2–3, 19).

6 (Bader N. O., 1998, pp. 98–100). "There were found about 3000–3500 beads in each burial. The majority of them preserved their original position. Most likely beads were sewn on curried leather, with fur turned inside. On each burial one can trace two coverings of beads, on inner (underwear) and outer clothing... Underwear of all three buried consisted of a high-necked shirt, put on over the head (parka); trousers and high, up to knees, footwear..." (Bader & Bader, 2000, p. 29). Earlier direct carbon-dating of bone collagen from the Sungir skeletons yielded estimated dates between 27,000 and 26,000 years ago (Kuzmin, Burr, Jull, & Sulerzhitsky, 2004, pp. 732–733), (Dobrovolskaya, Richard, & Trinkaus, 2012, p. 100). However, Yaroslav Kuzmin favors a date around 30,000 years ago, with revised estimates for the burials ranging between 35,000 and 30,000 years ago (Kuzmin, van der Plicht, & Sulerzhitsky, 2014, pp. 457–458), (Nalawade-Chavan, McCullagh, & Hedges, 2014). The thousands of decorative beads sewn onto the garments at Sungir were probably a special burial attire, but the presence of underwear was likely an everyday phenomenon by that time (Trinkaus, Buzhilova, Mednikova, & Dobrovolskaya, 2014, p. 26).

7 Although widely referred to as "Venus" figurines, this term originally alluded more to supposed similarities to African "Hottentot" women than to the classical Roman goddess (White R., 2006, pp. 282–283).

8 (Pettitt, Castillejo, Arias, Peredo, & Harrison, 2014, pp. 49–52), (García-Diez, Garrido, Hoffmann, Pettitt, Pike, & Zilhão, 2015, p. 137).

9 In their account of the hand stencils dated to around 27,000 years ago at Cosquer Cave in France, the archaeologists say "it is hard to see why frostbite... would have spared the thumb, which is always intact" (Clottes & Courtin, 1994, p. 67). Similarly Iain Morley at Oxford University favors finger-folding over pathological damage. He regards ritual amputation as the least likely cause and points out that in one case that supposedly favored ritual amputation – a collection of fifty-five hand stencils at Maltravieso with shortened fifth fingers – the original stencils were complete, and the fifth fingers were subsequently painted out. Maltravieso would appear to be a special case as such modification (and consistent involvement of the same digit) is not evident at other sites. However, Morley's only (incorrect) reason for rejecting frostbite as the cause of shortened fingers in the unmodified stencils at other sites is that frostbite would "tend to affect all the fingers simultaneously, rather than different digits selectively... in contrast, the thumb is always complete in the hand silhouettes known..." (Morley, 2007, p. 77).

10 (Gilligan, 2010c, pp. 59–62). Despite the popular misconception of digits dropping off, leprosy can only cause numbness of the nerves, which may then result in accidental damage. Repeated accidental damage can sometimes result in ulcers and infections in fingers (and toes) that may lead to bone resorption and tissue loss. However, leprosy often affects the thumb, and it more typically causes gross deformities – including the classic "claw hand" – which we do not see in the hand stencils (Anderson, 2006, pp. 291–292), (Lastória & de Abreu, 2014, pp. 206, 212). Also, leprosy is more a disease of warm climates. The one medical condition that can mimic frostbite more closely is Raynaud's disease (or Raynaud's phenomenon, since it is not always a distinct disease in itself but can result from various underlying conditions). The symptoms involve constriction of blood vessels, which can be triggered by cold exposure, and it is more prevalent in cold climates. Raynaud's disease also mimics frostbite in that the thumb is usually spared. Although quite common – affecting up to 5 percent of the general population (sometimes more in colder regions) – it is nearly always benign. Raynaud's disease can lead to ulcers in extreme cases but, unlike frostbite, even in these cases Raynaud's disease rarely leads to substantial loss of fingertips or of multiple fingers (Carpentier, Satger, & Poensin, 2006, p. 1027), (Pope, 2007, p. 519), (Prete, Fetone, Favoino, & Perosa, 2014, pp. 656–658), (Plissonneau, Pistorius, Pottier, Aymard, & Planchon, 2015, p. 472), (Poredos & Poredos, 2016, pp. 117–118).

11 (Murphy, zur Nedden, Gostner, Knapp, Recheis, & Seidler, 2003, p. 623). Unlike the situation in hands where the thumb is rarely involved in tissue loss with frostbite, in feet the great toe is not uncommonly affected by frostbite, reflecting its greater length relative to the toes (Hallam, Cubison, Dheansa, & Imray, 2010, p. 1153).

12 (Peterson H. A., 2012, p. 220), (Hutchinson, 2014, pp. 1864–1866). The one exception is found in the Gargas caves; in addition to the thumb being shortened, this stencil is atypical in that it is white (the others employ mainly red or black pigments) and also in the technique, which apparently involved using a brush or pad rather than spraying over the hand (Morley, 2007, p. 77). At the Spanish cave site of Fuente del Trucho, which is dated to between around 30,000 and 25,000 years ago (Hoffmann, et al., 2017, p. 56) there are more than fifty hand stencils and quite a number of small hand stencils with shortened fingers (mainly the fifth), which seem to represent young children; the archaeologists suggest that considering the cold climate of the region in the ice age, "there may have been a real loss of fingers due to frostbite" (Utrilla & Bea, 2015, p. 73).

13 (Taçon, et al., 2014, p. 1058), (Oktaviana, et al., 2016, pp. 34–43).

14 (Walsh, 1979, p. 34), (McDonald, 2008, p. 137), (Dobrez, 2013, p. 288).

15 (Williamson, 2003, pp. 3.8–3.14), (Ducharme & Brajkovic, 2005, pp. 2.3–2.9), (Osczevski & Bluestein, 2005, p. 1457), (Dolez & Vu-Khanh, 2009, pp. 374–388). While hypothermia was a much more serious threat to human survival than frostbite, any loss of finger function due to frostbite "would not have been trivial" (Hosfield, 2017, p. 534).

Chapter 7

1 (Gilligan, 2007d).

2 (Aiello & Wheeler, 2003, pp. 148–150), (Trinkaus, 2011, pp. 461, 466–467), (Walker, Ortega, Parmová, López, & Trinkaus, 2011, p. 10090), (Churchill, 2014, pp. 117–129), (Weaver, Coqueugniot, Golovanova, Doronichev, Maureille, & Hublin, 2016, p. 6474). While Neanderthal body shape and limbs were adapted for conserving rather than losing heat, evidence for their limb segments (proximal versus distal) is less consistent (Collard & Cross, 2017, pp. 169–172).

3 (Nicholson, 2017, pp. 151–152). Neanderthals may also have been limited in their use of fire for warmth: there is evidence for hearths at many Neanderthal sites, but the evidence is less convincing during colder climate phases, which may suggest that while they could use and maintain fire from natural sources (for instance, from lightning strikes), they might not have been capable of making fire (Dibble, Abodolahzadeh, Aldeias, Goldberg, McPherron, & Sandgathe, 2017, pp. S279, S284–S285).

4 (Shaw, Hofmann, Petraglia, Stock, & Gottschall, 2012, pp. 2–4), (Churchill, 2014, pp. 142–149), (Collard, Tarle, Sandgathe, & Allan, 2016, p. 241).

5 (White M. J., 2006, pp. 558–559), (Churchill, 2014, p. 129).

6 (Aiello & Wheeler, 2003, pp. 153–156). Another scenario suggests that Neanderthal population densities were always low, and they may have experienced repeated episodes of regional extinction in the northern zones during the colder phases (Hublin & Roebroeks, 2009, p. 506).

7 (Wales, 2012, pp. 789–793).

8 (Marcott, et al., 2011, p. 13417), (López-García, Blain, Bennàsar, & Daura, 2013, p. 1059). Temperature reconstructions from a cave stalagmite in central China show "remarkable millennial variations" in late MIS3, with H4 having the lowest temperature, around 40,000 to 39,000 years ago (Zhou, et al., 2014, pp. 397–399). The presence of cold-adapted woolly mammoths as far south as the Barcelona region of Spain around 42,000 years ago confirms that late MIS3 witnessed extremely cold conditions even in southern Europe (Álvarez-Lao, Rivals, Sánchez-Hernández, Blasco, & Rosell, 2017, p. 299). Evidence from various sources converges on a date around 40,000 years ago for the disappearance of Neanderthals (Hublin, 2017, p. 10521).

9 (Pichevin, Cremer, Giraudeau, & Bertrand, 2005, p. 88), (Ünal-İmer, et al., 2015, pp. 5–7).

10 Genetic confirmation of interbreeding with Neanderthals includes the *Homo sapiens* mandible (jawbone) found at Oase in Romania, which is dated to between 42,000 and 37,000 years ago. The Oase mandible (from a male, identified as having X and Y chromosomes) has 6–9 percent of its genome derived from Neanderthals; this individual likely had a Neanderthal relative in his family tree as recently as four to six generations back (Fu, et al., 2015, pp. 217–218).

11 (Trinkaus & Zilhão, 2002, pp. 507–512). Neanderthals may have managed to survive to as late as 28,000 years ago in Gibraltar (Finlayson, et al., 2008, p. 69), but doubts have

been raised about the reliability of most radiocarbon dates indicating a very late survival of Neanderthals in southern Iberia (Wood, Barroso-Ruíz, Caparrós, Jordá Pardo, & Galván Santos, 2013, pp. 2784–2785). Prior to their disappearance – currently dated to around 40,000 years ago – there was a likely overlap of between 3,000 and 5,000 years with incoming modern humans (Higham, et al., 2014, p. 308). Genetic studies indicate there was interbreeding between Neanderthals and modern humans, although this seems to have started earlier, outside of Europe (Fu, et al., 2014, p. 448). Even in eastern Eurasia, fossil crania with distinctive Neanderthal traits have been found in Henan Province, central China, dated to between 125,000 and 105,000 years ago during the last interglacial (Li, et al., 2017, p. 971).

12 (Ruebens, McPherron, & Hublin, 2015, p. 83).Besides the Châtelperronian, another tool industry with blades, awls, and ornaments that was once widely considered to be a product of Neanderthals is the Uluzzian, which occurred in Italy and Greece between 45,000 and 40,000 years ago, although its connection with Neanderthals is now considered doubtful (Douka, et al., 2014, pp. 7–11), (Zilhão, Banks, d'Errico, & Gioia, 2015, p. 34), (Hoffecker, 2017, p. 287). Neanderthals, however, are identified as the hominin present at one of the key French sites (the Grotte du Renne) where a fully Upper Paleolithic toolkit includes blades and bone awls (Welker, et al., 2016, p. 11166).

13 (Soressi, et al., 2013, pp. 14187–14188).

14 (Bar-Yosef, 2002, pp. 373–375), (Baykara, Mentzer, Stiner, Asmerom, Güleç, & Kuhn, 2015, pp. 416–425). Steven Kuhn, using the early Upper Paleolithic site of Üçağızlı I in southern Turkey as a case study, argues that while local variations and trends at particular sites may be instructive and amenable to local causal explanatory processes, the widespread general trend toward blades should be viewed as an "emergent" phenomenon that may require a higher "order of explanation" (Kuhn S. L., 2013, pp. 208–209).

15 (Huber, et al., 2006, p. 508), (Sánchez-Goñi, Landais, Fletcher, Naughton, Desprat, & Duprat, 2008, pp. 1140–1149), (Menviel, Timmermann, Friedrich, & England, 2013, pp. 66–72).

16 One of the debated sites where ornaments (and other artifacts such as bone awls) may have moved downwards into Neanderthal levels is at the Grotte du Renne, at Arcy-sur-Cure in France; this site does, however, have one of the earliest directly dated bone awls in Europe, around 42,000 years ago – which presumably associates the awl with Neanderthals (Higham, et al., 2010, p. 20238). At least as early as 250,000 to 200,000 years ago (corresponding to the MIS7 interglacial), Neanderthals were using red ochre at a site in The Netherlands; the site also has scraper tools that were probably used on animal hides to make simple clothing (Roebroeks, et al., 2012, p. 1892).

17 (Burdukiewicz, 2014, p. 404), (Rodríguez-Vidal, et al., 2014, p. 13303).

18 (Gilligan, 2014); technological parallels between Neanderthals and Tasmanians in the last ice age show "a degree of similarity that cannot simply be explained away" (Cosgrove, Pike-Tay, & Roebroeks, 2014, p. 188).

19 (Gilligan, 2007e).

20 (Fullagar, 1986, pp. 348–350). Bone awls also appear in cooler southern parts of mainland Australia during the LGM (Gilligan, 2010b, p. 55); a bone point found in northwest Australia dated to more than 45,000 years ago was probably used not as an awl but as a decorative nose bone (Langley, O'Connor, & Aplin, 2016, p. 208).

21 (Cosgrove & Allen, 2001, p. 399); "the archaeological record of Late Pleistocene Tasmanians, the most southerly peoples at the time, resonated with the European Mousterian… with its prevalence of scrapers and the absence of blades" (Cosgrove, Pike-Tay, & Roebroeks, 2014, p. 188).

22 (Gilligan, 2007a, p. 102).

23 The simplicity of Tasmanian technology at the time of European contact is at odds with the general trend for the diversity and complexity of hunter-gatherer toolkits to increase with latitude, a global pattern that has been attributed to greater risks and costs associated with food procurement in higher-latitude environments (Torrence, 2001, p. 80) – to which can be added the need for more thermally effective clothing (Hoffecker, 2017, pp. 99, 254–264), (Hoffecker & Hoffecker, 2018, pp. 204–208, 216–219). Debate about the apparent simplification of Tasmanian technology after the ice age has sometimes suggested that the Tasmanians were

disadvantaged by their isolation and were a population in decline; for a discussion of some of the key issues see (Hiscock, 2008, pp. 136–144) and for the relevance of clothing, see (Gilligan, 2016).

Chapter 8

1 (Johnson & McBrearty, 2010, p. 198).

2 (Backwell & d'Errico, 2003, pp. 260–262), (Backwell, d'Errico, & Wadley, 2008, p. 1567). Bone tools (made mainly from horse and bison long bones) are also documented around 300,000 years ago at Schöningen in Germany, where they were used as hammers and for knapping stone tools, and also possibly as hide-polishers (van Kolfschoten, Parfitt, Serangeli, & Bello, 2015, pp. 233–256), (Julien, Hardy, Stahlschmidt, Urban, Serangeli, & Conard, 2015, pp. 12–19). Evidence for the working of animal bones to make tools is reported also from Qesem Cave in Israel between 400,000 and 300,000 years ago (Zupancich, et al., 2016, pp. 2–6).

3 (Grömer, Rösel-Mautendorfer, & Reschreiter, 2014, pp. 138–139).

4 (Bonilla, Durden, Eremeeva, & Dasch, 2013, pp. 1–4).

5 (Toups, Kitchen, Light, & Reed, 2011, p. 30), (Reed, Allen, Toups, Boyd, & Ascunce, 2015, pp. 204–205).

6 (Kittler, Kayser, & Stoneking, 2004).

7 John Shea notes that scrapers become more common in the Middle Pleistocene, and blades – tools that provide more cutting edge – become common in the Late Pleistocene. However, while he acknowledges the climate changes, Shea alludes to conventional interpretations, which generally involve notions of increasing efficiency and portability. For instance, in the case of increasing tool retouch in northern (colder) zones, he suggests this could reflect reduced access to raw materials due to snow cover, while enhanced portability could be favored because people had to traverse larger territories to extract resources in the colder environments (Shea, 2017, pp. 63–75, 97–98, 107).

8 Debate continues about the origin of the Hobbit, *Homo floresiensis*, a species which may have evolved as a dwarfed form of local East Asian *Homo erectus* or possibly from early African hominins, such as *Homo habilis* or even Australopithecines, although the former seems more likely (Westaway, Durband, & Lambert, 2015, pp. 255–256), (van den Bergh, et al., 2016, p. 247). Either way, the Hobbit raises questions about the cognitive and behavioral capacities required for wide dispersal, given that Flores has not been connected to Asia by land since at least the Early Pliocene, around five million years ago (Argue, Donlon, Groves, & Wright, 2006, p. 374), (Stringer, 2014, p. 429). The question of whether the Hobbit encountered Denisovans or *Homo sapiens* remains open (Sutikna, et al., 2016, p. 368), although a recent conference paper reports discovery of a pair of 46,000 year-old human teeth in the Liang Bua cave which raises the possibility that the arrival of *Homo sapiens* led to the Hobbit's extinction around 50,000 years ago (Sutikna, et al., 2016, p. 232). The stone tools made by the Hobbit were predominantly simple flakes, although there were some large blades, microblades and stone perforators (Morwood, et al., 2004, pp. 1089–1091); see also (Brumm, et al., 2006, pp. 627–628). As Shea says, the changes in stone tool production seen among *Homo sapiens* during the latter part of the Pleistocene "contrast starkly with the lack of change among stone tools made by *Homo floresiensis*" (Shea, 2017, p. 138).

9 For example, end-scrapers made on blades "are common in lithic assemblages from colder regions, such as northern Eurasia and North America. Not all endscrapers were necessarily used for hide-scraping, of course, but hide-scraping is among the most consistent function [sic] inferred for these artefacts from microwear evidence… Endscrapers and blades are relatively uncommon in lithic assemblages from the tropical targets of Late Pleistocene human dispersal, Sahul and South America" (Shea, 2017, pp. 133–134). Similarly, on the Indian subcontinent, the advent of scraper and then blade industries – though perhaps less well-defined than in colder northern regions, without many bone awls and with no reported eyed needles, for instance – closely mirrors the major climate trends in the Late Pleistocene (Blinkhorn & Petraglia, 2017, pp. S467–S475).

10 In Africa the Lower, Middle, and Upper Paleolithic are called the Early, Middle, and Late Stone Ages. Another global classification was proposed by Grahame Clark in 1969; see (Foley, 2002, pp. 25–29), (Shea, 2017, p. 28).

In Clark's system of six modes in tool development, the key steps with clothing would be mode 3 (simple clothing, with scrapers) and mode 4 (complex clothing, with blades). John Shea has proposed a more sophisticated system (modes A-I) that is also more complicated (though perhaps more realistic), in which the major clothing steps correspond broadly to his modes D1 and G2; as Shea remarks, "archaeological lithic systematics are a mess, and they have been so for a very long time" (Shea, 2013, pp. 152–157, 175); see also (Walker, 2017, pp. 21–27). At a more fundamental level, there are issues involved in making these kind of sweeping generalizations that link the shapes of tools to different functions or purposes, and also the extent to which archaeological tool assemblages defined on the basis of relative tool frequencies should be regarded as reliable reflections of past human behaviors (Dibble, et al., 2017, pp. 838–840). Nonetheless, there are some striking trends in tool morphology associated with exposure of hominins to colder environments. One example is the increasing prevalence of formal blade tools in the European Upper Paleolithic, a trend that existing approaches struggle to explain: "Systematic prismatic blade production is one of the most conspicuous derived features of the European Upper Paleolithic stone tool evidence. Blades vary in number and in how they were made, but few Upper Paleolithic assemblages lack evidence for prismatic blade production... Blades are simply elongated flakes knapped from unifacial hierarchical cores in response to various selective pressures. These pressures might have included tabular raw materials, the need to boost cutting edge recovery rates, tool standardization, portability, accommodations to hafting, or other circumstances... Sometimes, a prismatic blade is just a stone tool" (Shea, 2017, p. 107).

Chapter 9

1 (Wang, et al., 2007, pp. 968–969), (Chinta & Gujar, 2013, pp. 814–815). Dealing with the moisture problem involves resolving a contradiction: garments need to be simultaneously waterproof (impermeable to external moisture) and yet permeable to internal moisture from perspiration – and recent technological advances in textile technology may lead to more practical solutions (Mukhopadhyay & Midha, 2016, p. 226), (Ju, Shi, Deng, Liang, Kang, & Cheng, 2017, p. 32156).

2 (Li Y., 2005, pp. 235–247), (Rossi, 2009, pp. 5–12), (Song G., 2009, pp. 20–29), (Choudhury, Majumdar, & Datta, 2011, pp. 37–39), (Hes & Williams, 2011, pp. 114–122). The challenge of simultaneously covering the body while maximizing comfort in warm environments becomes most acute in the case of protective garments (e.g., heat-resistant garments for firefighters, bullet-proof garments for security, and the more impermeable garments required for chemical protection); sweat production and environmental humidity are critical factors limiting their use, hence the need to improve permeability to water vapor (Rossi, 2005, p. 237). Poor permeability to sweat is, rather paradoxically, a significant cause of heat stress with immersion suits designed to prevent cold stress in water (Zhang & Song, 2014, pp. 293–294). Similarly, moisture management is a crucial consideration in designing garments for outdoor workers in hot climates; e.g., construction workers in Hong Kong during summer, when air temperatures can rise to 35°C and relative humidity often reaches 95 percent (Chan, Guo, Wong, Li, Sun, & Han, 2016, pp. 489–493). Efforts to solve the challenge of warm weather clothing include nanotechnology, where micropores in the fabric allow body heat and perspiration to diffuse through a material that is transparent to mid-infrared (IR) radiation but opaque to visible light – hence retaining visual cover whilst effectively conducting heat and moisture from the body surface (Hsu, et al., 2016, pp. 1020–1022). Even with light textile clothing (~1.0 clo value), air temperatures above 30°C can lead to a failure of evaporative cooling due to clothing vapor resistance, resulting in heat stress and a potentially lethal rise in core (rectal) temperature above 38°C (d'Ambrosio Alfano, Palella, Riccio, & Malchaire, 2016, pp. 243–244). In terms of subjective thermal comfort with clothes, sweating is a dominant factor that affects comfort in warm conditions, especially with increasing levels of physical activity (Bhatia & Malhotra, 2016, pp. 5–7), (Wang & Hu, 2016, p. 133). The adverse effect of environmental humidity on body cooling is striking: in one study, when relative humidity increased from 20 percent to

80 percent, heat dissipation by sweat evaporation dropped by nearly a third, from 20.0 W to 14.0 W (Tang, He, Shao, & Ji, 2016, pp. 579–580).

3 In the Americas for instance, aridity in the Late Pleistocene was followed by a more humid climate between 11,000 and 8,000 years ago in the Rocky Mountains region (Shuman & Serravezza, 2017, pp. 71–72), and similarly in the Amazon basin (Fontes, et al., 2017, pp. 172–173). Illustrating the massive change in moisture levels, speleothem records in the Amazon basin show that precipitation during the LGM was only 58 percent compared to the present, climbing to 142 percent in the mid-Holocene (Wang, et al., 2017, pp. 204–206). While the transition to moister conditions was a widespread global trend, in a few regions there was reduced precipitation. One example is central Asia, where the early Holocene remained dry, in contrast to wetter conditions in southern and most of eastern Asia (Long, et al., 2017, pp. 26–28).

4 (deMenocal, et al., 2000, pp. 353–355), (Steffensen, et al., 2008, pp. 682–683), (Liu, et al., 2014, p. E3504), (Roy, Quiroz-Jiménez, Chávez-Lara, Sánchez-Zavala, Pérez-Cruz, & Muthu Sankar, 2014, pp. 582–586), (Rawat, Gupta, Sangode, Srivastava, & Nainwal, 2015, pp. 174–179), (Shanahan, et al., 2015, pp. 141–142), (Lasher, Axford, McFarlin, Kelly, Osterberg, & Berkelhammer, 2017, pp. 51–53), (Lecavalier, et al., 2017, pp. 5953–5954), (Mangerud & Svendsen, 2018, pp. 76–78).

5 (Levy, 2017, pp. 64–65).The excavation of Göbekli Tepe in the 1990s was led by the archaeologist Klaus Schmidt of the German Archaeological Institute in Istanbul. The stone pillars at Göbekli Tepe are arranged in circles, carved with animal shapes and abstract figures – and with a few humans too, wearing loincloths. Schmidt interpreted the site as a ritual center, built by local teams of mobile hunter-gatherers who were on the verge of domesticating crops and animals around 11,000 years ago. In his view, the significance of the site lies in the implication that settled village life and agriculture could only start after people had already acquired novel ways of perceiving the world – the transitions need to be understood as happening "not only through economic or ecological reasons" (Schmidt, 2000, p. 49). Fox bones are among the commonest faunal remains at Göbekli Tepe (along with wild gazelle, cattle, and sheep, including mouflon); plant remains include wild cereals (wheat, barley, and rye). With the fox remains, there is a bias in skeletal elements – a relatively high frequency of paw bones – suggesting that the fox was exploited for its pelt (Peters & Schmidt, 2004, p. 207).

6 (Ghaddar & Ghali, 2009, pp. 131–135), (Epstein, et al., 2013, p. 873), (Wang, Gao, Kuklane, & Holmér, 2013, pp. 572–573). Animal hides are not entirely impervious to moisture: leather for example – which is still generally preferred over fabric for shoes due to its durability – has superior moisture permeability compared, for instance, to shoes made from rubber (Irzmańska, 2016, p. 78). However, with regard to garments for covering the body in warm environments, experimental studies demonstrate that woven materials confer significant advantages over non-woven materials. For instance, jackets designed for fire fighters using leather and Gore-Tex® show that in terms of measured physiological parameters and subjective reports of comfort (e.g., heat and moisture perception), woven materials are clearly superior (Hocke, Strauss, & Nocker, 2000, pp. 294–295).

7 (Davis & Bishop, 2013, pp. 701–704), (Naebe, Yu, McGregor, Tester, & Wang, 2013), (Chen, Chen, & Wang, 2014). For instance, whereas wool has a water vapor permeability of nearly 40 percent, the figure for animal furs is around 5 percent and some – such as buffalo hide – are almost impermeable (Hes, 2008, pp. 164–166).

8 (Kuzmin, 2010, p. 254). The distribution of cold-adapted woolly mammoths (and woolly rhinoceros) extended south into Spain around 42,000 years ago during late MIS3 (Álvarez-Lao, Rivals, Sánchez-Hernández, Blasco, & Rosell, 2017, pp. 293–295); woolly mammoths also survived until nearly 5,000 years ago on St. Paul Island, a remnant of the Bering Land Bridge 450km off the coast of Alaska (Graham, et al., 2016). The advantage of linen cloth (for bedding as well as garments) in the warm Egyptian climate reflects the fiber properties: flax fibers absorb moisture easily but have low heat retention, so compared to most other textile fibers, linen soaks up more perspiration but remains relatively cool to touch (Rast-Eicher, 2016, p. 89).

9 (O'Sullivan, et al., 2016, p. 3).
10 (Kvavadze, et al., 2009), (Hardy, et al., 2013, pp. 27–29), (Rast-Eicher, 2016, p. 91).
11 (Soffer, 2004, pp. 410–412), (Adovasio, Soffer, Illingworth, & Hyland, 2014, p. 333).
12 (Conard, 2009, p. 250).
13 (Soffer, Adovasio, & Hyland, 2000, p. 520), (White R., 2006, p. 288).
14 (Jolie, Lynch, Geib, & Adovasio, 2011).
15 (Bar-Yosef, 1985, pp. 8–10), (Reade & Potts, 1993, p. 102), (Hodder, 2013, p. 1), (Tung, 2013, p. 4). Linen threads have been preserved from 10,000 years ago in the southern Levant, in the Murabba'at caves (Shamir, 2015, p. 16).
16 (Adovasio, Andrews, Hyland, & Illingworth, 2001, pp. 41–44, 75), (Kuzmin, Keally, Jull, Burr, & Klyuev, 2012, pp. 329–331), (Connolly, Barker, Fowler, Hattori, Jenkins, & Cannon, 2016, p. 494), (Piqué, Romero, Palomo, Tarrús, Terradas, & Bogdanovic, 2018, pp. 265–266).
17 (Liu & Chen, 2012, p. 154), (Zhang, et al., 2016, p. 3).

Chapter 10

1 For instance, while demonstrating the value of niche construction theory (NCT) in modeling the transition to agriculture, Melinda Zeder does not directly address this question of why the onset of agriculture was delayed until 12,000 years ago (Zeder, 2016, p. 341).
2 (Diamond, 2002, p. 700). In the Levant, evidence indicates that hunter-gatherers adapted successfully to a series of upheavals in climate and food resources at the end of the last ice age, which makes it hard to attribute agricultural origins in the region to any failure of foraging strategies (Rosen & Rivera-Collazo, 2012, pp. 3641–3644).
3 (Unaipon, 2001, p. 17). Even in the Western Desert of Australia for example, "over the course of an average foraging bout (just under 3 hours), a single forager can very reliably supply daily food requirements for two to three people" (Bird, Bird, Codding, & Taylor, 2016, p. S68).
4 (Bowles, 2011, p. 4763).
5 "Declining health and increasing 'risk' through the archaeological sequences in question are both very widespread and very commonly recognized... Skeletal markers of health and risk, ethnographic studies, and extrapolated patterns of epidemiology all demonstrate that the health of human populations (measured in stature) and the quality of nutrition commonly declined as hunter-gatherers moved toward agriculture, while the frequency of stress episodes, infection, disease, and exposure to parasites all increased... I consider the hypothesis of generally declining health associated with the approach to and adoption of farming economies one of the more robust general arguments about prehistory" (Cohen, 2009, p. 592). Cohen's view is supported, for instance, by isotope analyses of skeletal material comparing hunter-gatherer to agricultural populations, e.g., (Tsutaya, 2017, p. 554).
6 In much of Africa, Asia, and Europe, hunter-gatherer populations resisted agriculture, and the ultimate spread of agriculture was due more to invasion by expanding agricultural populations than the adoption of agriculture by local foragers (Bellwood, 2017, p. 34), (Smith B., in press, pp. 3–6).
7 (Hayden, Canuel, & Shanse, 2013, pp. 126–131).
8 (Ryder, 2005, p. 125). Nevertheless, it is still often said that wild sheep could not have been domesticated for wool: "It is accepted that this wild ancestor was not domesticated for wool, for wild sheep have none" (Breniquet, 2014, p. 59).
9 "There is absolutely no doubt that a great deal of knowledge has been accumulated of the archaeological record during critical time periods and from critical locations where major changes occurred... On the other hand there has been little progress in the character of arguments about such changes. I hope that this will change in the near future" (Binford, 2002, p. 235). Similarly: "The simple fact is that we do not yet have a good grasp on the causes for the origins of agriculture. The how and why of the Neolithic transition remain among the more intriguing questions in human prehistory. There is as yet no single accepted theory for the origins of agriculture – rather, there is a series of ideas and suggestions that do not quite resolve the question...The phantom of causality floated at the edge of our deliberations... always there but not often addressed. This transition from hunting to farming poses one of the most intriguing questions about the human past and one of the most difficult to answer... Are there general causes? The almost

simultaneous development of agriculture in so many different places is not simple coincidence" (Price & Bar-Yosef, 2011, pp. S168–S171). Price says that while new evidence from places such as Papua New Guinea certainly adds to our knowledge, it still leaves fundamental questions unanswered: "The future of archaeological research is exciting in part because it will involve the continuing resolution of this issue. At the same time, we still do not understand why these changes were initiated, nor why agriculture expanded to become the preeminent mode of human subsistence across the globe. Answers to these mysteries may require completely new questions..." (Price, 2009, p. 6428). While Bar-Yosef tends to favor a food-based motive in the contexts of sedentism, ecological changes, social changes and population growth, he admits that the "most difficult [question] is why it happened after more than two or three million years of human evolution" (Bar-Yosef, 2017, p. 297). As Ian Hodder remarks in relation to Southwest Asia (though his observation applies more generally), "It is remarkable that despite many decades of research there remains little consensus about the causes of the agricultural revolution..." (Hodder, 2018, p. 156).

10 They continue: "It is completely remarkable that the process of domesticating plants and animals appears to have taken place separately and independently in a number of areas at about the same time. Given the long prehistory of our species, why should the transition to agriculture happen within such a brief period, a few thousand years in a span of more than 6 million years of human existence? An important and dramatic shift in the trajectory of human adaptation would seem to demand general explanation" (Price & Bar-Yosef, 2011, pp. S169–S172). Others, however, are inclined to argue the opposite and downplay the many parallels in different regions, saying that the quest for a "prime mover" or any "simple cause-effect relation" is misguided and instead we should adopt a "multifactorial" approach that emphasizes local interactions between climate, demographic, social, and cognitive factors (Vigne, 2015, p. 139).

11 (Bellwood, 2017, p. 32).

12 Population pressure has also been invoked as a cause of technological change and complexity during the Paleolithic, but again the evidence suggests that "population size probably was not the main driver of change and stability during the Palaeolithic" (Collard, Vaesen, Cosgrove, & Roebroeks, 2016, p. 9). One exception in the case of agriculture is the claim for evidence of population growth preceding the transition to agriculture in eastern North America around 5,000 years ago (Weitzel & Codding, 2016, p. 5).

13 (Cohen, 2009, p. 591).

14 "I would argue, however, that storage is, in effect, a 'low-ranking' means of avoiding risk compared to mobility, broad dietary variety, effective sharing mechanisms, and the potential use of broad-spectrum foraging as a buffer against shortages..." (Cohen, 2009, p. 593).

15 (Hayden, 2009, p. 600).

16 (Hayden, 2001, p. 571), (Hayden, Canuel, & Shanse, 2013, pp. 139–141).

17 (Hayden, 2011, pp. 82–83).

18 The plant species used to make the twisted fibers were not identifiable (Nadel, Danin, Werker, Schick, Kislev, & Stewart, 1994, pp. 454–455). The evidence for year-round sedentism at Ohalo II is based on the remains of plants and animals from different seasons and the presence of rodent commensals (house mice and rats); it is suggested that people at Ohalo II were experimenting with plant cultivation and using sickle blades to harvest barley and wheat, but this agricultural experiment ultimately "failed" (Snir, et al., 2015, pp. 4, 7–8).

19 (Vigne, 2015, p. 132).

20 (Larson, et al., 2012, p. 8891), (Freedman, et al., 2014, p. 8), (Drake, Coquerelle, & Colombeau, 2015, pp. 5–6), (Skoglund, Ersmark, Palkopoulou, & Dalén, 2015, pp. 3–4). Some claims for dog domestication prior to 16,000 years ago are based on skeletal signs that are not diagnostic and may be found within the range of variation for wolf populations (Perri, 2016, p. 3). Genetic evidence currently points to all domestic dogs (including feral dogs such as the Dingo in Australia) descending from the Gray Wolf or its immediate ancestor; while the location of initial domestication is in doubt (and there may have been multiple independent locations), dog domestication probably began more than 20,000 years ago (Jackson, et al., 2017, p. 207).

21 (Hu, et al., 2014, p. 119).

22 (Sætre, et al., 2012), (Xiang, et al., 2014, p. 17567), (Yang, et al., 2015, pp. 5–6); the

evidence for chicken domestication in northern China as early as 10,000 years ago is not widely accepted (Eda, Lu, Kikuchi, Li, Li, & Yuan, 2016).

23 Resistance to the spread of agriculture is well-documented in northern Europe after the end of the last ice age, in Mesolithic societies. These societies were based economically on hunting, gathering, and fishing, but they had "a degree of sedentism and organisational complexity not normally associated with hunter-gatherer communities"; in southern Scandinavia, "farming appears to have been rejected symbolically and in practice," but the Mesolithic lifestyle gradually succumbed to "a process of prehistoric 'encapsulation,' whereby hunter-gatherer communities are marginalized and impoverished by encroaching farming settlement" (Zvelebil, 2008, pp. 35, 57). In southern China around 5,000 years ago, local communities such as Xincun (near Hong Kong) evidently favored a relatively easy lifestyle based on exploiting plants such as the sago palm and banana (the latter not necessarily for food), and the people were apparently not eager to adopt labor-intensive rice cultivation (Yang, et al., 2013, pp. 6–7). Another example of a mixed Meso-Neolithic economy is the Vietnamese site of Rach Nui (50km south of Ho Chi Minh City), where people around 3,500 years ago engaged in a forager economy that relied heavily on collecting wild plant foods, hunting wild animals (including crocodiles), and fishing, in addition to having pigs and a couple of crops (millet and rice); perforated ceramic discs that were likely spindle whorls suggest the use of textile clothing, although the materials woven (possibly wild plant fibers) are not known (Oxenham, et al., 2015, pp. 324–333). On the Korean peninsula, the transition from Mesolithic to Neolithic economies based on rice cultivation around 3,400 years ago was complex, with rice often slow to appear; sedentism may have favored the eventual adoption of intensive rice cultivation, which was associated with the presence of spindle whorls at archaeological sites (Kwak, 2017, pp. 69, 77–78, 101).

24 (Sellato, 2006, pp. 153–160), (Barker & Janowski, 2011, pp. 11–12). The transition to agriculture among hunter-gatherers entails a profound psychological change, including a loss of "immediate engagement" with nature and the emergence of "concealment" (Naveh & Bird-David, 2014, pp. 76–89).

Chapter 11

1 Zeder's list of fifteen domestication centers (with the main domesticates) is 1: Eastern North America (chenopod, squash, sunflower, knotweed, maygrass), 2: Southwest US (turkeys), 3: Mesoamerica (maize, squash, beans, turkeys), 4: northern Peru/Ecuador (squash, lima beans), 5: Amazonia (manioc, yams, peanuts, Muscovy duck), 6: Andes (oca, potato, quinoa, amaranth, llama, alpaca, guinea pig), 7: sub-Saharan Africa (pearl millet, sorghum, African rice), 8: Horn of Africa/Nile Valley (asses, teff), 9: Near East (wheat, barley, lentils, peas, sheep, goats, taurine cattle, pigs), 10: Central Asia (horses, golden hamster), 11: South Asia (browntop millet, water buffalo, zebu cattle), 12: North China (foxtail and broomcorn millet), 13: South Asia/Southeast Asia (rice, chickens), 14: Japan (barnyard millet, mung bean, burdock), 15: New Guinea (banana, yams, taro); her list omits major domesticated fiber crops such as maguey, hemp, flax and cotton (Zeder, 2017, p. 10).

2 (Zeder, 2011, p. S230).

3 (Ryder, 1960, pp. 395–406), (Ryder, 1962), (Ryder, 1964, pp. Plate LVIb, 293–294), (Bruford & Townsend, 2006, pp. 308–311); primitive sheep are characterized by a "coarser fleece" and a "moulting coat" like that of the ancestral mouflon (Chessa, et al., 2009, p. 534). Similarly, Soay sheep – descended from a feral population on an island off the coast of Scotland – shed their wool coat annually, and the wool can be plucked from tame sheep; the quantity of wool tends to increase if the sheep are kept after the second year (Ryder, 1971, pp. 183–185), (Clutton-Brock & Pemberton, 2004, pp. 1–4). In recent decades, with a decline in demand for wool, there has been a trend in the UK toward breeding sheep that shed wool annually without shearing, which has a number of advantages including reduced susceptibility to blowfly strike and also avoiding the labor costs of shearing (Conington, Collins, & Dwyer, 2010, p. 87), (Matika, Bishop, Pong-Wong, Riggio, & Headon, 2013, pp. 242–243).

4 (Frangipane, et al., 2009, pp. 6–20), (Russell, 2010, pp. 270–273), (Levy & Gilead, 2012,

p. 131), (Saña & Tornero, 2012, pp. 80–81), (Laurito, Lemorini, & Perilli, 2014, pp. 155–162), (Becker, et al., 2016, pp. 104–109). The concept of the Secondary Products Revolution was developed by English archaeologist Andrew Sherratt in the 1980s and relates mainly to developments subsequent to the emergence of agriculture, highlighting the advent of the plough and milking as well as wool production. In relation to wool, however, Sherratt's model specifically claims that wool was not involved in the initial domestication of sheep and goats – or ovocaprids: "secondary features of domesticated ovocaprids – notably the development of wool in sheep – allowed a new range of uses for these animals in providing fibres suitable for textiles... These features were not part of the original complex of plant and animal domestication... where these features can be dated, it is apparent that they only appear five millennia or so after the beginnings of agriculture... The textile fibre which became most important in the Old World, wool, was not present in the first four to five millennia after the initial domestication of the sheep" (Sherratt, 1981, pp. 261–262, 282). Subsequent archaeological research into the Secondary Products Revolution reiterates the common assertion that wool could not have been a factor in the Early Neolithic because "sheep were unlikely to be woolly in this period" (Marciniak, 2011, p. 121).

5 (Arbuckle & Atici, 2013, pp. 224, 230–232), (Stiner, et al., 2014, p. 8408). Likewise with goats – and similar to other sites where the mortality profile "does not indicate selective culling for meat" – at one Israeli site, only around 40 percent of goats were culled by thirty-six months, which is "significantly lower than predicted by the classic models for a herd optimized for meat production" (Sapir-Hen, Dayan, Khalaily, & Munro, 2016, p. 13).

6 (Saña & Tornero, 2012, p. 87); other studies have looked at the slaughter patterns to highlight the likely significance of another product of sheep and goats as living animals – namely, milk, e.g., (Makarewicz, 2013).

7 At Abu Hureyra, where rye appears to have been the first domesticated cereal, the archaeologists point out that its straw would have been useful for thatching and bedding and "would one day also prove useful as fodder for domestic herbivores"; they note too that lentils and barley accompany rye prior to the domestication of wheat (Hillman, Hedges, Moore, Colledge, & Pettitt, 2001, pp. 387–388).

8 (Charles, 2007, pp. 44–47), (Hayden, Canuel, & Shanse, 2013, p. 125). Grapes were first domesticated for wine somewhat later in the Neolithic, by around 7,000 years ago in the southern Caucasus region between the Caspian and Black Seas (Myles, et al., 2011, pp. 3533–3534).

9 (Court, Webb-Ware, & Hides, 2010, p. 44), (Van Os, Mintline, DeVries, & Tucker, 2017, pp. 71–72).

10 (Lösch, Grupe, & Peters, 2006, pp. 188–190); see also (Murray M. A., 2009, pp. 256–261), (Makarewicz & Tuross, 2012, pp. 501–502).

11 (Harlan, 1967, p. 198).

12 (Kislev, Weiss, & Hartmann, 2004, p. 2694), (Abbo, Zezak, Zehavi, Schwartz, Lev-Yadun, & Gopher, 2013, p. 2100), (Ladizinsky & Abbo, 2015, p. 23).

13 (Bar-Yosef, et al., 2011), (Fu Y.-B., 2011, p. 1120), (Andersson Strand, 2012, p. 24). A genetic study suggests that oil rather than fiber was the reason for its initial cultivation; however, the reduced use of flax for fiber in historical times following the more widespread cultivation of cotton (especially from the seventeenth century) may have affected its genetic diversity and hence the results of the analysis (Allaby, Peterson, Merriwether, & Fu, 2005, p. 64). The recovery of fine linen fabrics, which are dated fairly close in time to its likely domestication, suggests that fiber was an important resource from the outset. In any case, "the available archaeological evidence clearly suggests that flax belongs to the first group of grain crops that started agriculture in the Levant" (Zohary, Hopf, & Weiss, 2012, p. 106). Experimental studies show that extracting useful quantities of fiber is reasonably easy with wild flax, and suggest that domestication of flax was a deliberate process aimed at maximizing fiber production (Abbo, Zezak, Lev-Yadun, Shamir, Friedman, & Gopher, 2015, pp. 57–62). While possible evidence for linen (flax) thread on a wooden comb dating to 10,000 years ago cannot be substantiated, many indirect lines of evidence (such as textile imprints on clay, and bone weaving tools) point to advanced

textile-weaving activities in the region during the transition to agriculture (Boyd B., 2018, p. 254).

14 (Langgut, Yahalom-Mack, Lev-Yadun, Kremer, Ullman, & Davidovich, 2016, p. 981).

15 (Giner, 2012, p. 44); wooden tools used to weave textiles are generally not preserved in the archaeological record until recent millennia, e.g., (Daragan, Gleba, & Buravchuk, 2016).

16 (Yang, et al., 2012, p. 3729), (Liu, Bestel, Shi, Song, & Chen, 2013), (Song, Li, Wu, Kvavadze, Goldberg, & Bar-Yosef, 2016).

17 (Larson, et al., 2010, p. 7686), (Xiang, et al., 2014, p. 17567), (Barnes, 2015, pp. 101–102), (Shelach-Lavi, 2015, p. 54), (Zheng, Crawford, Jiang, & Chen, 2016, p. 5), (Zuo, et al., 2017, pp. 6488–6489). The Taiwanese archaeologist K. C. Chang wondered whether food crops might have played only a "minor role" in the oriental transition to agriculture (Chang K. C., 1970, p. 180), and recent evidence lends support to this view: "These first domesticates, including rice, millets, soybean, dogs, and pigs, played rather minor roles for a few millennia before becoming dominant staples or major sources of protein in the subsistence system, during the middle Neolithic (ca. 5000–3000 BC) or even later" (Liu & Chen, 2012, p. 121).

18 (Pechenkina, Ambrose, Xiaolin, & Benfer, 2005, pp. 1184–1185), (Barton, Newsome, Chen, Wang, Guilderson, & Bettinger, 2009, pp. 5525–5526), (Guo, Hu, Zhu, Zhou, Wang, & Richards, 2011, pp. 524–525), (Lanehart, et al., 2011, pp. 2176–2179).

19 (Zhang, et al., 2016, p. 155).

20 (Lu, et al., 2009, p. 7371), (Chi & Hung, 2012, pp. 21–24), (Sun, 2013, p. 566), (Buckley & Boudot, 2017, p. 2), (Tao, Wang, & Yu, 2017, p. 111), (Zhao, et al., 2017, pp. 362–365). Spindle whorls occur commonly in the early Hemudu and Yangshao Neolithic cultures, from 7,500 and 7,000 years ago, respectively (Zhao, 2004, p. 63), (Ebrey, 2010, p. 16), (Hui & Jia, 2016, p. 336). Furthermore, "the absence of spindle-whorls (in the archaeological record, for example) does not necessarily imply the absence of yarn for weaving: for example, abacá fibres used in the southern Philippines are processed into yarn and woven into cloth without any spinning or twisting. Ramie is normally twisted into yarn, but may also be used as flat, untwisted strips on occasions" (Buckley, 2017, p. 278).

21 (Cai, et al., 2011, p. 900), (Betts, Jia, & Dodson, 2014, pp. 165–166), (Dodson, et al., 2014, p. 3).

22 (Bergfjord & Holst, 2010, p. 1195).

23 (Liu & Chen, 2012, p. 154), (Li, Wang, Tian, Liao, & Bae, 2014, p. 187), (Shelach-Lavi, 2015, p. 92), (Liao & Yang, 2016, p. 110), (Buckley, 2017, p. 278).

24 (Good, 2002, pp. 9–10), (Gong, Li, Gong, Yin, & Zhang, 2016, p. 8), (Zhang, et al., 2016, p. 6).

25 (Singh, 2008, pp. 102–107), (Good, Kenoyer, & Meadow, 2009, p. 464), (Fuller, 2011, pp. S350–S351).

26 (Moulherat, Tengberg, Haquet, & Mille, 2002, pp. 1394, 1397–1400), (Zohary, Hopf, & Weiss, 2012, p. 108); doubts have been raised by textile fiber expert Antoinette Rast-Eicher about the identification of the 8,000-year-old fibers in Pakistan as cotton (Rast-Eicher, 2016, p. 73).

27 (Fuller, 2006, pp. 178–182), (Singh, 2008, pp. 107–122, 163).

Chapter 12

1 (Pickersgill, 2007, pp. 928–929).

2 (Smith B. D., 2001, p. 1325), (Piperno, Ranere, Holst, Iriarte, & Dickau, 2009, p. 5023), (Bitocchi, et al., 2012, pp. E793-E794), (Kistler, et al., 2014, p. 2938), (Vallebueno-Estrada, et al., 2016, p. 14154).

3 (Somerville, Nelson, & Knudson, 2010, p. 133), (Azúa, Padilla, Galicia, & Roldán, 2013, pp. 572–574), (Somerville, Sugiyama, Manzanilla, & Schoeninger, 2016, p. 16).

4 (Larson & Fuller, 2014, p. 126), (Sugiyama, Somerville, & Schoeninger, 2015, pp. 6–10).

5 (Scheffler, Hirth, & Hasemann, 2012, pp. 603–607), (Figueredo, Casas, Colunga-GarcíaMarín, Nassar, & González-Rodríguez, 2014, p. 2), (Figueredo, Casas, González-Rodríguez, Nassar, Colunga-GarcíaMarín, & Rocha-Ramírez, 2015, pp. 2–3).

6 (Evans, 1990, pp. 118–128), (Stark, Heller, & Ohnersorgen, 1998), (Feinman, 2006, pp. 270–272), (Anderies, Nelson, & Kinzig, 2008, pp. 416–418), (Ardren, Manahan, Wesp, & Alonso, 2010, pp. 276–285), (Carpenter, Feinman, & Nicholas, 2012, pp. 395–396).

7 (Coppens d'Eeckenbrugge & Lacape, 2014, p. 2).

8 (Splitstosser, Dillehay, Wouters, & Claro, 2016, p. 1) Genetic studies of the Mexican and South American cotton varieties point to people selecting strains with longer fibers (Chaudhary, Hovav, Flagel, Mittler, & Wendel, 2009, pp. 6–7). The antiquity of weaving technology in the region is attested by fragments of woven rush – probably matting – dated to 11,000 years ago at the site of Huaca Prieta (Dillehay, et al., 2017, p. 11).

9 (Perry, et al., 2007, pp. 986–987), (Piperno & Dillehay, 2008, pp. 19623–19626), (Haas, Creamer, Mesía, Goldstein, Reinhard, & Rodríguez, 2013, p. 4948). As for maize, it seems to have become significant in human diets and economies around 2,000 years ago (Lambert, Gagnon, Billman, Katzenberg, Carcelén, & Tykot, 2012, pp. 160–161). The evidence "suggests that maize was present in Ecuador and Peru at a fairly early time, but that it was not a major component of diets. If it had been important it would be in evidence in many forms with cobs, stems, and leaves in abundance, but it simply is not. Maize did not become a staple crop in the Central Andes until well after Chavín, and at present it is only clearly a major dietary component in parts of the Inca Empire. Irrigation and monument building in Peru and other regions thus developed without maize as an essential or even an important ingredient" (Quilter, 2014, p. 92).

10 (Dillehay, et al., 2012, p. 56).

11 These fishing communities along the coast of the Atacama Desert were using fishing nets made from cotton as early as 7,000 to 5,000 years ago (Disspain, Ulm, Santoro, Carter, & Gillanders, 2017, p. 432).

12 (Quilter, Bernardino Ojeda, Pearsall, Sandweiss, Jones, & Wing, 1991, pp. 281–282), (Haas & Creamer, 2006, pp. 753–755), (Shady Solís, 2006, pp. 50–63).

13 (Moseley, 2006, p. 78); early agricultural sites in coastal Peru had "fields of cotton with scant comestibles" (Sandweiss, Shady Solís, Moseley, Keefer, & Ortloff, 2009, p. 1359).

14 (Wheeler, Chikhi, & Bruford, 2006, pp. 335–338), (Bonavia, 2008, pp. 205–206), (Clutton-Brock, 2012, p. 128), (Dillehay, et al., 2012, p. 68), (Wheeler, 2012, pp. 7–11).

15 "Camelid fleece is not a secondary product. In Eurasia, the wool of sheep has been regarded as a 'new use' or a 'secondary product' that was only exploited later in the history of domesticated sheep… In contrast, the fleece of vicuña and guanaco was spun as soon as human groups began to occupy sites in the South-Central Andes. In the Andes, a fabric-making tradition developed that relied heavily on camelid fibre. The domestication of the South American camelids was not a prerequisite for that development"; moreover clothing was as biologically important as food in these climates, and wool explains why people kept camelids alive rather than killing them for meat: "The situation is different with fleece, which can be harvested from camelids while they are still alive. Clothing is arguably of equal importance to food in order to sustain human life in the South-Central Andes, especially at high altitude, where climate variability is extreme" (Dransart, 2002, pp. 236–238).

16 (Mengoni Goñalons & Yacobaccio, 2006, p. 239).

17 (Wheeler, 2005, p. 4).

18 (Finucane, Maita Agurto, & Isbell, 2006, pp. 1772–1774), (Kellner & Schoeninger, 2008, p. 240), (Stanish, et al., 2010, pp. 525–528), (Clutton-Brock, 2012, p. 129), (Dantas, Figueroa, & Laguens, 2014, pp. 155–161), (Labarca & Gallardo, 2015, pp. 67–69), (Szpak, Millaire, White, Lau, Surette, & Longstaffe, 2015, pp. 454–458).

19 (Iriarte, 2007, pp. 169–180), (Isendahl, 2011, pp. 460–464), (Clement, et al., 2015, pp. 2–5).

20 (Roosevelt, 1991, pp. 51, 59), (Rossetti, Góes, & de Toledo, 2009, pp. 38–39).

21 (Smith B. D., 2006, p. 12228), (Fritz, 2007, pp. 203–205), (Smith B. D., 2009, pp. 6562–6566), (Smith B. D., 2011b, pp. S478-S482), (Mueller, Fritz, Patton, Carmody, & Horton, 2017, pp. 1–4). Maize cultivation had spread from Mexico and was well-established in the southwest of the U.S. by 4,000 years ago (Merrill, et al., 2009, p. 21020), little more than 1,000 km from the western edge of the agricultural center in eastern North America where maize was cultivated from around 2,200 years ago. With squash, debate about whether squash spread into eastern North America from Mexico has been reignited by genetic research on the bee that pollinates domesticated squash. Until the arrival of the honey bee with Europeans in the 1600's, domesticated squash plants depended on this particular bee species for

their reproduction. The reason for considering the possibility of a diffusion of squash from Mexico is that the bee originated in Mexico and must have somehow spread from Mexico to eastern North America, most likely via the Midwest where, perhaps, the bee survived on wild squash plants (López-Uribe, Cane, Minckley, & Danforth, 2016, pp. 2–7).

22 (Adovasio, Andrews, Hyland, & Illingworth, 2001, pp. 41–44, 75), (Carocci, 2010, pp. 6–19), (Solazzo, et al., 2011, pp. 1424–1426), (Adovasio & Pedler, 2016, p. 209).

23 (Whitford, 1941, pp. 17–18), (Heckenberger, Petersen, King, & Basa, 1996, p. 65), (Petersen, 1996, p. 114), (Thompson & Jakes, 2005, p. 138), (Adovasio, Soffer, Illingworth, & Hyland, 2014, pp. 338–339), (Turner, 2014, pp. 404–411).

24 (Smith B. D., 2011b, p. S482); on the contrary, there are those who defend the need for general theories – they argue that "the retreat from theory and the embrace of particularism are not only unwarranted but also counterproductive" (Gremillion, Barton, & Piperno, 2014, p. 6172). As mentioned earlier, there is a claim that population growth triggered the transition to agriculture in eastern North America, although the same analysis found signs of population growth in the region during the early Holocene – without any agricultural transition (Weitzel & Codding, 2016, p. 5).

25 "These Pacific Coast people do not fit any of the classic anthropological models devised to explain the evolutionary progression from simple, mobile hunter-gatherers to larger, sedentary, and more complex agrarian societies... Although technically they are hunter-gatherers, many Native California communities exhibited traits more typically associated with well-developed agrarian societies. That is, they enjoyed sizeable population densities, had relatively sedentary villages, amassed significant quantities of stored food and goods, and maintained complex political and religious organizations... None of this makes sense according to theoretical models about the rise of agriculture that are predicated on either population pressure or socioeconomic competition, or that view agriculture as an outgrowth of experimentation by complex hunter-gatherers in areas of diverse and rich food supplies..." (Lightfoot & Parrish, 2009, pp. 3–5).

26 (Smith B. D., 2011b, pp. S472, S477, S482).

27 (Champlain (de), 1619, p. 284); see also (Heiser, 1976, pp. 34–35). There are some poorly documented claims that the fibers from sunflower stalks were used to make textiles, including ropes and even fabrics (Keoke & Porterfield, 2002, p. 253), (Vizgirdas & Rey-Vizgirdas, 2006, p. 203), (Tull, 2013, p. 51).

28 (Pickersgill, 2007, p. 926), (Applegate, 2008, p. 501), (Thompson & Simon, 2008, p. 170), (Tiedemann & Jakes, 2006, pp. 294–297), (Claassen, 2015, p. 100), (Borders & Lee-Mäder, 2014, p. 10), (Kozen & Netravali, 2015, p. 168).

29 "The Chickasaws are known to have revered the eagle, the white swan, and turkey. Man lived in the middle world and the birds in the above world. Man can't fly, but he admired the birds soaring in the sky – messengers to the creator god in the sky. Thus, bird feathers were sacred symbols with special meaning that took special care... The Chickasaws believed that sacred feathers lose power when touched to the earth – the middle world. Such an error would be judged 'bad medicine' and bad luck to follow." (Perry R., 2008, pp. 5–6).

30 (Pearlstein, 2010, pp. 91–93), (Rawlings & Driver, 2010, pp. 2434, 2439–2440), (Speller, et al., 2010, p. 2811), (Cooper, Lupo, Matson, Lipe, Smith, & Richards, 2016, p. 16).

Chapter 13

1 Sorghum was cultivated in Africa between 5,500 and 5,000 years ago, in eastern Sudan (Winchell, Stevens, Murphy, Champion, & Fuller, 2017, pp. 675–681).

2 (di Lernia, 2001, pp. 416–429), (Akraim, Milad, Abdulkarim, & Ganem, 2008), (Clutton-Brock, 2012, p. 49).

3 (Marshall F., 2007, pp. 375, 380–384), (Decker, et al., 2014, p. 5).

4 (Stevenson & Dee, 2016).

5 (Vogel-Eastwood, 2000), (Romer, 2012, pp. 3–17), (Linseele, et al., 2014, pp. 8–9).

6 (Magnavita, 2008, p. 246), (Kriger, 2009, pp. 107–125), (Horsburgh & Rhines, 2010, pp. 2906–2907), (Hamilton-Dyer, 2012, p. 251), (Orton, Mitchell, Klein, Steele, & Horsburgh, 2013, pp. 115–116), (Magee, 2014, pp. 203–213), (Chritz, Marshall, Zagal, Kirera, & Cerling, 2015, pp. 3676–3677).

7 (Hildebrand, 2007, pp. 285–289); see also (Neumann & Hildebrand, 2009, p. 355).

8 (Denham, Golson, & Hughes, 2004, pp. 277–286), (Denham, 2007, pp. 79–90), (Golson, 2007, pp. 110–122), (Denham, Golson, & Hughes, 2017, pp. 194–196).

9 (Fullagar, Field, Denham, & Lentfer, 2006, p. 612), (Summerhayes, et al., 2010, p. 80). The spread of agricultural peoples from China and Taiwan across island Southeast Asia was associated with the spread of textile weaving. Diagnostic spindle whorls (similar to those found in the 7,500 year-old Hemudu culture of the lower Yangtze River basin) are dated from 3,500 years ago in the Philippines (Cameron & Mijares, 2006, pp. 6–7). With taro, the corms first have to be cooked, although the leaves and stem are fine as fodder. In parts of Vietnam, taro is the main feed crop for pigs (Toan & Preston, 2010). Besides banana, Papua New Guinea may be the center of domestication for a number of other important crops, including sugarcane and sago. Sugarcane is used widely by farmers as pig fodder, while the sago palm yields useful fibers for textiles (from the leaves) as well as edible starch from the stem. These local crops were displaced around 300 years ago by the arrival of the sweet potato (first domesticated in tropical America), and sweet potato also became popular as pig fodder. However, the use of crops as pig fodder is not relevant to the earliest agriculture in the highlands, as pigs did not arrive in the region until around 3,000 years ago. The arrival of pigs and pottery was associated with the Lapita cultural complex that accompanied the expansion of agricultural Austronesian populations into the Pacific from Southeast Asia (Spriggs, 2001, pp. 238–241), (Gaffney, et al., 2015, pp. 2–3), (Skoglund, et al., 2016, p. 512). The long-standing debate about the earliest pigs in Papua New Guinea has only recently been resolved (Denham, 2004, pp. 614–616), (Golson, 2007, p. 114), (Denham, 2011, p. S389), (O'Connor, Barham, Aplin, Dobney, Fairbairn, & Richards, 2011, pp. 12, 20).

10 The fruits of wild bananas "are full of hard seeds roughly the size of lead shot, with little or no pulp" (Kennedy J., 2009b, p. 195).

11 (Appell-Warren, 2013, p. 591), (Kozen & Netravali, 2015, pp. 168–169).

12 "This may imply that the Harappan experiment with banana cultivation in Sindh vanished when that urban civilization collapsed... It is also possible that Harappan cultivation was focused on producing a raw material such as paper or fiber rather than fruit... The possibility of Harappan banana cultivation (2500–1900 B.C.) provides tantalizing hints that there may be some hidden prehistory of banana dispersal yet to be unearthed in some parts of South Asia, but the balance of evidence, especially from historical linguistics, suggests that the main introduction of edible bananas was some 2000 years later. This leads us to hypothesize that the Kot Diji *Musa*-type phytoliths may relate to cultivation of a Musaceae for raw material (fiber)...This remains to be tested through finds of fiber" (Fuller & Madella, 2009, pp. 337–346).

13 (Kennedy J., 2009a, p. 180); see also (Mohapatra, Mishra, & Sutar, 2010, pp. 326–327).

14 (de Langhe, 2009, p. 276). Similarly: "Those non-culinary uses may originally have been what attracted humans to exploit and domesticate it rather than its food value... It therefore follows that initial human selection was not necessarily towards the cultivation of seedless bananas, but in time the banana developed parthenocarpy and the seeds were suppressed, making the fruit more appetizing" (Castillo & Fuller, 2017, p. 3).

15 (Leahy, 1991, pp. 23, 71, 128, 151), (Heider, 1997, pp. 60–62), (Herdt, 2006, pp. 95–112), (Hardy, 2008, pp. 274–277), (Bolton & Tarisesei, 2010, pp. 479–481), (Burt, 2010, p. 491), (Lewis-Harris, 2010, p. 461), (Mel, 2010, p. 455), (Kamel, 2015, p. 23), (Kleiner, 2016, p. 1112).

16 (Prentice, Hope, Maryunani, & Peterson, 2005, p. 111), (Batra, 2007, p. 492).

17 Archaeological evidence confirms that humans were present in the highlands prior to the LGM, for instance at the site of Kosipe (elevation 2,000 m) by around 40,000 years ago (White, Crook, & Ruxton, 1970, p. 160), (Summerhayes, et al., 2010, p. 78), and people occupied highland valleys during the LGM (Fairbairn, Hope, & Summerhayes, 2006, p. 381).

18 (Hope & Haberle, 2005, pp. 543–547), (Reeves, et al., 2013, p. 27), (Hill B., 2015); temperatures in the highlands during the LGM may have fallen to as low as $-5°C$, at the very limit for modern humans without clothes (Summerhayes & Ford, 2014, p. 222).

19 (Gilligan, 2010a, pp. 149–152). In discussing the absence of agriculture in Aboriginal Australia,

archaeologist Josephine Flood points out that Australia possessed potential plant and animal domesticates. And although there was contact with agricultural peoples to the north, she says Aboriginal people "saw nature as their garden, a resource that didn't need cultivation or improvement" and their traditional values were probably incompatible with agriculture (Flood, 2006, pp. 20–24).

20 (Gerritsen, 2008, pp. 32–38).

21 (Denham, Donohue, & Booth, 2009, p. 644).

22 (McNiven, Crouch, Richards, Sniderman, Dolby, & Gunditj Mirring Traditional Owners Aboriginal Corp, 2015, pp. 44, 54–55), (Bird, Bird, Codding, & Taylor, 2016, p. 10). So-called firestick farming among foragers probably began early in hominin evolution, and so it is unlikely to be relevant to the relatively recent origins of agriculture (Gowlett, Brink, Caris, Hoare, & Rucina, 2017, p. S215). Even chimpamzees, while not known to actively promote burning, are known to exploit natural bushfires and take advantage of the feeding opportunities that are found in burned landscapes (Pruetz & Herzog, 2017, pp. S344–S348).

23 (Gerritsen, 2008, pp. 113–118), (Gammage, 2011, pp. 281–304), (Pascoe, 2014, pp. 19–71, 115–123); see also (Keen, 2004, pp. 83–127), (White J. P., 2011, pp. 88–89).

24 (Pascoe, 2014, p. 156).

25 Technically, elephants have not been domesticated: they are often raised (and can be bred) in captivity, like tigers and chimpanzees, but they are not considered a domesticated species (Clutton-Brock, 2012, p. 88), (Zeder, 2016, p. 328).

Chapter 14

1 (Harris, 2007, pp. 21–26), (Zeder, 2015, pp. 3191–3195).

2 (Denham, 2007, p. 101). For an example of a locally contingent explanatory model (in this case, the agricultural transition in Thailand), which makes no mention of the fundamental issues and no attempt at global comparisons, see (Marwick, Van Vlack, Conrad, Shoocongdej, Thongcharoenchaikit, & Kwak, 2017, p. 12).

3 (Harris, 2007, p. 26).

4 (Zeder, 2015, pp. 3196–3197), (Zeder, 2016, p. 338).

Chapter 15

1 (Bocquet-Appel & Bar-Yosef, 2008, pp. 4–5), (Bocquet-Appel, 2011, p. 560). Availability of suitable weaning foods is not necessarily related to the duration of breastfeeding (McKerracher, Collard, Altman, Sellen, & Nepomnaschy, 2017, p. 620).

2 (Gray, et al., 1990, p. 27), (McNeilly, 2001, p. 587). The hormonal mechanism for suppression of ovulation involves GnRH (from the pituitary gland) and higher prolactin levels, which result mainly from intense nipple stimulation (Riordan & Wambach, 2010, pp. 707–714), (Labbok, 2015, pp. 917–923), (Lawrence & Lawrence, 2016, pp. 688–697).

3 (Plomley & Piard-Bernier, 1993, p. 300).

4 The natural duration of breastfeeding for humans is probably at least three to four years, considering that chimpanzees, for instance, wean at age five to six; data for hunter-gatherers like the San and Hadza (who traditionally wore little or no clothes) correspond to this prediction, with figures of 49 and 45 months, respectively (Kennedy G. E., 2005, pp. 125–129), (Jay, 2009, pp. 164–165), (Humphries, 2010, pp. 454–456), (Blurton Jones, 2016, pp. 50–51). Isotope studies of archaeological skeletal samples indicate a fairly consistent pattern of earlier weaning in agricultural communities compared to hunter-gatherers, e.g., (Pearson, Hedges, Molleson, & Özbek, 2010, pp. 453–455), (Oelze, Siebert, Nicklisch, Meller, Dresely, & Alt, 2011, p. 276). The trend for early weaning may have been less pronounced in some Mesolithic societies such as in California and in the Jomon of Japan (Eerkens, Berget, & Bartelink, 2011, pp. 3107–3109), (Eerkens & Bartelink, 2013, pp. 480–481), although an estimate of around two years was found for the Mesolithic Okhotsk culture in northern Japan (Tsutaya & Ishida, 2015, p. 551). In contrast, even recent mobile hunter-gatherers in southern Argentina were weaning infants at around age five years (Tessone, García Guraieb, Goñi, & Panarello, 2015, p. 112). Weaning practices among pastoralist groups may be intermediate between hunter-gatherers and sedentary agriculturalists: among pastoralists in north central Eurasia around 4,000 years ago, weaning began at age six months and was complete by four years (Miller, Hanks, Judd, Epimakhov, & Razhev, 2017, pp. 417–418).

5 Together with the commercial promotion of artificial milk formulas, there are various problems like mastitis and engorgement that can discourage breastfeeding (Bergmann, Bergmann, von Weizsäcker, Berns, Henrich, & Dudenhausen, 2014). Yet one of the main disincentives among women (at least in contemporary industrial societies) is psychological discomfort, especially with breastfeeding in public (Amir, 2014), (Mulready-Ward & Hackett, 2014). Contributing to this anxiety is the sexuality of nipple stimulation (which is what causes milk secretion). For example, brain imaging research using functional MRI (fMRI) scans has shown that nipple stimulation activates the same brain regions as stimulation of the clitoris and vagina (Komisaruk, Wise, Frangos, Liu, Allen, & Brody, 2011, pp. 2825–2828). Surveys reveal that while breastfeeding their infants, most women experience sexual arousal ("pleasurable contractions in the uterine region") and around 10 percent have orgasms (Levin, 2006, pp. 240–241), (Josephs, 2015, p. 1063). So far, the sexuality of breastfeeding has slipped safely beneath the public radar – for obvious reasons. However, the sexual qualities of breastfeeding and the role of shame and guilt in causing early weaning (and preventing breastfeeding) are acknowledged in the medical profession: "The erotic response to nursing the infant has no significance in terms of being normal or abnormal. The decline in breastfeeding because of feelings of shame, modesty, embarrassment, and distaste has been reported and interpreted as indicating that breastfeeding is viewed as a forbidden sexual activity... Major changes in the number of women who breastfeed may not be possible until society can accept the breast in its relationship to nurturing the infant and as an object of less sexual ambivalence" (Lawrence & Lawrence, 2016, p. 705).

Chapter 16

1 (Doumani & Frachetti, 2012, pp. 376–377).

2 (Bar-Yosef & Wang, 2012, p. 330), (Wu, et al., 2012, pp. 1698–1699).

3 (Tchernov, 1991, pp. 156–157), (Snir, et al., 2015, p. 4). While the increased presence of rodents and sparrows at archaeological sites is commonly cited as evidence of sedentism, this evidence should be treated cautiously (Tangri & Wyncoll, 1989, p. 91) and considered in the context of additional signs such as architectural features and food storage; the house mouse (*Mus musculus*) seems the most promising commensal marker of sedentism (Belmaker & Brown, 2016, p. 40). In the Levant, house mice occur as commensals in sedentary Natufian hunter-gatherer campsites from 15,000 years ago (Weissbrod, et al., 2017, p. 4101).

4 (Outram, et al., 2009, p. 1333), (Warmuth, et al., 2012, p. 8203).

5 (Naumann, 2000, pp. 11, 57), (Matsui & Kanehara, 2006, p. 271), (Zvelebil, 2008, p. 35), (Crawford, 2011, p. S335). Another example of a sedentary Mesolithic community is the large coastal Inuit settlement at Point Hope, Alaska, which developed from AD 500 with an economy based on hunting sea mammals; the only domesticated animals these people had were their dogs, used mainly for transport (Hoffecker, 2005, p. 137).

6 (Arnold, Sunell, Nigra, Bishop, Jones, & Bongers, 2016).

7 While chest infections were the main cause of death among Tasmanians in the settlement, there was a "general despondency among them" and on his departure from Flinders Island in 1839, the commandant George Robinson said: "It would be impossible to describe the gloom that pervades at the present time the whole of these poor people..." (Plomley, 1987, pp. 99, 111).

8 For a summary of the issues with sedentism see (Marshall Y., 2006). In terms of causes, some archaeologists argue in favor of resource abundance rather than population pressure as the main cause (Hayden, 2000, p. 111). Others suggest that while resource abundance was a necessary (though not sufficient) precondition for sedentism, the "mobility ethos" of hunter-gatherers – their psychological preference for mobility – existed only because they had to move around to get food; in this scenario, population growth and consequent "group packing" made mobility more problematic and hence led to sedentism (Kelly, 2013, pp. 104–113).

Chapter 17

1 (Renfrew, 2012, p. 126).

2 Exceptions to the rule did occur: in some cases, incoming agricultural settlers reverted to

hunting and gathering, as was the case, for instance, with rice cultivation at the site of Khok Phanom Di in Thailand 4,000 years ago (Higham C. F., 2017, p. 18).

3 (Lourandos, 1997, pp. 305–323), (Mulvaney & Kamminga, 1999, pp. 271, 303–309), (Hiscock, 2008, pp. 252–253), (Pardoe, 2014, p. 115).

4 "My argument has been, first, that the concept of sedentism as currently employed in Levantine prehistory is not nuanced enough for analysis of the nature of the evidence we see before us...This was not some kind of evolutionary change... rather the introduction of new traditions of acting and ways of being in the world." (Boyd, 2006, pp. 171–174). While variations in the incidence of commensal species such as mice and rats may suggest that Natufian sedentism was spatially and temporally varied (Weissbrod, Kaufman, Nadel, Yeshurun, & Weinstein-Evron, 2013, pp. 708–710), the architectural and other archaeological signs of sedentism are found within the context of an exclusively hunter-gatherer rather than an agricultural economy (Yeshurun, Bar-Oz, & Weinstein-Evron, 2014, pp. 31–32). Angkor Wat in Thailand, on the other hand, was constructed within a complex agricultural landscape, and while many of its structures functioned for water management, other features, such as the recently discovered "rectilinear spirals," seem to defy any explanation (Fletcher, Evans, Pottier, & Rachna, 2015, p. 1398). At a more pragmatic level, the need for caution with interpreting archaeological signs of sedentism is illustrated by the 8,000-year-old stone circles on Rosemary Island in northwest Australia, which are described by the archaeologists as "house structures" built by mobile foragers (McDonald & Berry, 2017, pp. 32–34, 41).

5 (Bellwood, 2005, pp. 19–43); Bellwood states, "In fact, we do not know exactly why farming began anywhere in the world... It is also not absolutely clear whether it was connected with the production of more food for humans (and domesticated animals), with the need for fibers for clothing and cordage, or with both" (Bellwood, 2013, p. 81). Over the years, some have said that maybe fiber production was more important than food production. Among them was the American geographer Carl Sauer who wrote extensively on agricultural origins. He was particularly impressed by the evidence in eastern Asia for the "multi-purpose" role of early crops – "especially as sources of fiber" – and he went so far as to postulate that producing food for humans was "perhaps not the most important reason for bringing plants under cultivation" (Sauer, 1952, p. 27). In fact from the beginning, textiles were traditionally considered a definitive part of the Neolithic package. When Sir John Lubbock first coined the term "Neolithic" in the nineteenth century, he included textiles as one of its main features. The first Neolithic sites to be identified were Swiss lake dwellings exposed by low water levels in the 1850s. Numerous cloth artifacts were preserved in the water-logged conditions, along with bones of domesticated animals (cattle, sheep, goats, pigs, and dogs). Lubbock noted that ceramic spindle whorls for spinning textile fibers were "abundant," and he described one such whorl found attached to its wooden spindle, with thread still wound around it (Lubbock, 1890, p. 196). Likewise Gordon Childe, the leading archaeologist of the early twentieth century who coined the phrase "neolithic revolution," regarded textiles as a key feature (Childe, 1936, pp. 106–107). And returning to eastern Asia, recent discoveries in China have led archaeologists there to suggest that once we allow for the taphonomic bias, textiles were probably present from the onset of agriculture: "looms, needles, spindle whorls, weights, cordage, and weaving impressions on ceramics have been unearthed increasingly from several early Holocene archaeological sites... we propose that the occurrence of textiles in China might accompany the origin of agriculture" (Zhang, et al., 2016, p. 6).

6 (Ingold, 2008, pp. 1796–1797), (Smith B. D., 2011a, pp. 837–838), (Smith B. D., 2011b, p. S482), (Gilligan, in press). Many years ago Gordon Childe had similarly suggested that his "neolithic revolution" required a "radical change" in the human "attitude" to the natural environment (Childe, 1936, p. 74). With regard to how niche construction theory relates to the advent of agriculture, see (Zeder, 2016).

7 "In this respect it is very striking that the Kelabit farmers and Penan foragers of Borneo, whilst both in reality depending heavily on foraging for much of their diet, are unanimous in believing that there is a significant

gulf – psychological and cosmological as much as practical – between their respective ways of life. Penan life involves living in close spiritual association with the forest, and rejecting the implications of rice-growing. Kelabit life involves... a clear separation between the world of humans and that of the forest through the creation of the rice fields along with the variety of symbolic structures... They constantly, every day, make the choice to construct a different way of life, based on rice. So these two societies share many similarities in their place on the spectrum between foraging and farming, both relying heavily on the wild, yet have entirely separate world-views. There is the same profound psychological difference between people within similarly overlapping forms of subsistence in tropical Australia and New Guinea... Rice, then, ushered in a different way of conceiving of the relationship between people and the rest of the natural world" (Barker & Janowski, 2011, p. 9).

8 This is quite a radical suggestion, namely, that changes in psychological processes – located ultimately within the individual and operating over the relatively brief timescale of human lives – could exert a formative influence over the much longer archaeological timescales of human prehistory. In archaeology, the very different timescales of human lives and human evolution mean that processes operating over one timescale are generally considered to be necessarily different, with hierarchies of explanation involved that generally preclude such a connection between short-term and long-term causal relationships. Traditionally, the loss of temporal resolution with increasing timescales leads to short-term processes becoming almost irrelevant, reduced to epiphenomena that cannot have causal status in the long term. Conversely, the longer timescales opened up by archaeology can reveal the operation of long-term processes that are essentially invisible within the short timespans of individual lives. The potential influence of psychological processes – quite distinct from social processes that are conventionally considered to transcend the individual and so be capable of influencing long-term evolutionary trends – is one implication of what Geoff Bailey terms "time perspectivism" – an appreciation of how the treatment of time itself in archaeology (and how it affects what we are prepared to consider) needs to be better understood (Bailey, 2008, pp. 15–16).

9 (Hodder, 1990, pp. 283–296), (Hodder, 2007, pp. 106–107, 114–116). Domestication as a concept is inherently dualistic, an "anthropocentric nature/culture dualism" and, in the case of animal domestication, "a distinction between wild animal nature and human culture, placing animals ontologically in a place where they are always constitutively outside the human" (Boyd B., 2017, p. 306).

10 (Hodder, 2012, pp. 158–216).

11 Renfrew specifically considers the role of textile production in the material and economic developments associated with the emergence of civilization in the Aegean region, although he sees textiles as just one element and grants priority to metallurgy (Renfrew, 1972, pp. 13, 351–354, 491). For an overview of the archaeological approaches to social complexity (where state societies correspond broadly to civilization) – and also for a note on the neglected role of the individual – see (Renfrew & Bahn, 2016, pp. 179–232, 503–506).

12 This predicted transition is known as the technological "singularity," resulting in a transcendence of intelligence and consciousness over material existence (Kurzweil, 2005, p. 389). Yet whether or not it does result in such a profound and unparalleled alteration in human existence, the computer revolution will very likely lead to a qualitative transformation: "The Industrial Revolution ushered in humanity's first machine age... Now comes the second machine age. Computers and other digital advances are doing for mental power – the ability to use our brains to understand and shape our environments – what the steam engine and its descendants did for muscle power. They're allowing us to blow past previous limitations and taking us into new territory... What they're enabling is something without precedent... we are at an inflection point – the early stages of a shift as profound as that brought about by the Industrial Revolution" (Brynjolfsson & McAfee, 2014, pp. 6–7, 250–251). "These resources will provide high-resolution, full-immersion visual-auditory virtual reality at any time. We will also have augmented reality with displays overlaying the real world... technology will provide fully immersive, totally convincing virtual reality... your brain will experience the

synthetic signals just as it would real ones... a panoply of virtual worlds to explore. Some will be re-creations of real places; others will be fanciful environments that have no counterpart in the physical world. Some, indeed, would be impossible, perhaps because they violate the laws of physics. We will be able to visit these virtual places and have any kind of interaction with other real, as well as simulated, people (of course, ultimately there won't be a clear distinction between the two), ranging from business negotiations to sensual encounters" (Kurzweil, 2005, pp. 313–314). With regard to the latter, sexual contacts are increasingly shifting into cyberspace and, ultimately, it is envisioned that virtual bodies ("data suits") will be capable of generating erotic tactile sensations (Jütte, 2000, p. 334). Yet as philosopher Alan Cholodenko says, this potential fusion of the human with the digital threatens a qualitative transition, not a mere expansion or substitution but an "erasure" of the human, and a new form of enclosure: "a disintegration of the human, the human become the simulation clone... in the passage of the upper case 'I' of the self into the lower case 'i' of the iPod, iPhone, iPad, etc... the computer (re)programmes the human as computer, as computer-human, as cyborg... each person now inhabits a universe as cocoon, a pod of one's own... that cocoon, that pod, that clone, becomes not only 'body' but 'mind', the very self" (Cholodenko, 2015, pp. 37–38). An alternative view – which may illustrate the real danger – denies any difference and does not "treat the digital as a 'lossy' approximation of the analog"; the physical world is not privileged as the only real and so virtual worlds are merely "additional realities" (Boellstorff, 2016, p. 395).

REFERENCES

Abbo, S., Zezak, I., Lev-Yadun, S., Shamir, O., Friedman, T., & Gopher, A. (2015). Harvesting wild flax in the Galilee, Israel and extracting fibers: bearing on Near Eastern plant domestication. *Israel Journal of Plant Sciences, 62*, 52–64.

Abbo, S., Zezak, I., Zehavi, Y., Schwartz, E., Lev-Yadun, S., & Gopher, A. (2013). Six seasons of wild pea harvest in Israel: bearing on Near Eastern plant domestication. *Journal of Archaeological Science, 40*, 2095–2100.

Adovasio, J. M., Andrews, R. L., Hyland, D. C., & Illingworth, J. S. (2001). Perishable industries from the Windover bog: an unexpected window into the Florida Archaic. *North American Archaeologist, 22*, 1–90.

Adovasio, J. M., & Pedler, D. (2016). *Strangers in a New Land: What Archaeology Reveals About the First Americans*. Buffalo, NY: Firefly.

Adovasio, J. M., Soffer, O., Illingworth, J. S., & Hyland, D. C. (2014). Perishable fiber artefacts and Paleoindians: new implications. *North American Archaeologist, 35*, 331–352.

Adovasio, J. M., Soffer, O., & Page, J. (2007). *The Invisible Sex: Uncovering the True Roles of Women in Prehistory*. New York: HarperCollins / Smithsonian Books.

Agustí, J., Blain, H.-A., Lozano-Fernández, I., Piñero, P., Oms, O., Furió, M., et al. (2015). Chronological and environmental context of the first hominin dispersal into Western Europe: the case of Barranco León (Guadix-Baza Basin, SE Spain). *Journal of Human Evolution, 87*, 87–94.

Ahmed, S., Ahmad, F., Afzal, A., Rasheed, A., Mohsin, M., & Ahmad, N. (2015). Effect of weave structure on thermo-physiological properties of cotton fabrics. *Autex Research Journal, 15*, 30–34.

Aiello, L. C., & Wheeler, P. (2003). Neanderthal thermoregulation and the glacial climate. In T. H. van Andel, & W. Davies (Eds.), *Neanderthals and Modern Humans in the European Landscape during the Last Glaciation: Archaeological Results of the Stage 3 Project* (pp. 147–166). Cambridge: Macdonald Institute for Archaeological Research.

Akraim, F., Milad, I. S., Abdulkarim, A. A., & Ganem, M. (2008). Wool characteristics of Libyan Barbary sheep in north-eastern Libya: I. Fibre diameter and staple length. *Livestock Research for Rural Development, 20*, 118.

Allaby, R. G., Peterson, G. W., Merriwether, D. A., & Fu, Y.-B. (2005). Evidence for the domestication history of flax (*Linum usitatissimum* L.) from genetic diversity of the *sad2* locus. *Theoretical and Applied Genetics, 112*, 58–65.

Al-Rawi, F. N., & George, A. R. (2014). Back to the Cedar Forest: the beginning and end of Tablet V of the standard Babylonian Epic of Gilgameš. *Journal of Cuneiform Studies, 66*, 69–90.

Álvarez-Lao, D. J., Rivals, F., Sánchez-Hernández, C., Blasco, R., & Rosell, J. (2017). Ungulates from Teixoneres Cave (Moiá, Barcelona, Spain): presence of cold-adapted elements in NE Iberia during the MIS3. *Palaeogeography, Palaeoclimatology, Palaeoecology, 466*, 287–302.

Amir, L. H. (2014). Breastfeeding in public: "You can do it?" *International Breastfeeding Journal, 9*, 187.

Anderies, J. M., Nelson, B. A., & Kinzig, A. P. (2008). Analyzing the impact of agave cultivation on famine risk in arid Pre-Hispanic northern Mexico. *Human Ecology, 36*, 409–422.

Andersen, H. C. (1837). *The Emperor's New Clothes (Kejserens nye Klæder)*. Translated by Diana Crone Frank and Jeffrey Frank. In *The Stories of Hans Christian Andersen*, pp. 105–110. Durham, NC: Duke University Press, 2005.

Anderson, G. A. (2006). The surgical management of deformities of the hand in leprosy. *Bone and Joint Journal, 88-B*, 290–294.

Andersson Strand, E. (2012). The textile chaîne opératoire: using a multidisciplinary approach to textile archaeology with a focus on the ancient Near East. *Paléorient, 38*(1–2), 21–40.

Angelova, R., Georgieva, E., Reiners, P., & Kyosev, Y. (2017). Selection of clothing for a cold environment by predicting thermophysiological comfort limits. *Fibres and Textiles in Eastern Europe, 25*(1), 95–101.

Angilletta, M. J. (2009). *Thermal Adaptation: A Theoretical and Empirical Synthesis*. Oxford: Oxford University Press.

Annan, J. D., & Hargreaves, J. C. (2015). A perspective on model-data surface temperature comparison at the Last Glacial Maximum. *Quaternary Science Reviews, 107*, 1–10.

Anonymous. (c. 600 BCE). *The Torah: A Modern Commentary*. Edited by W. Gunther Plaut and David E. S. Stein. Revised edition. New York: Union for Reform Judaism, 2005.

Appell-Warren, L. P. (2013). The Philippines. In J. Condra (Ed.), *Encyclopedia of National Dress: Traditional Clothing Around the World* (pp. 585–593). Santa Barbara, CA: ABC-CLIO.

Applegate, D. (2008). Woodland period. In D. Pollack (Ed.), *The Archaeology of Kentucky: An Update* (pp. 339–604). Volume 1. Frankfort, KY: Kentucky Heritage Council.

Arbuckle, B. S., & Atici, L. (2013). Initial diversity in sheep and goat management in neolithic south-western Asia. *Levant, 45*, 219–235.

Ardren, T., Manahan, T. K., Wesp, J. K., & Alonso, A. (2010). Cloth production and economic intensification in the area surrounding Chichen Itza. *Latin American Antiquity, 21*, 274–289.

Argue, D., Donlon, D., Groves, C. P., & Wright, R. V. (2006). *Homo floresiensis*: microcephalic, pygmoid, *Australopithecus*, or *Homo*? *Journal of Human Evolution, 51*, 360–374.

Arnold, J. E., Sunell, S., Nigra, B. T., Bishop, K. J., Jones, T., & Bongers, J. (2016). Entrenched disbelief: complex hunter-gatherers and the case for inclusive cultural evolutionary thinking. *Journal of Archaeological Method and Theory, 23*, 448–499.

Attenbrow, V. (2010). *Sydney's Aboriginal Past: Investigating the Archaeological and Historical Records*. Second edition. Sydney: UNSW Press.

Aubert, M., Brumm, A., Ramli, M., Sutikna, T., Saptomo, E. W., Hakim, B., et al. (2014). Pleistocene cave art from Sulawesi, Indonesia. *Nature, 514*, 223–227.

Azúa, R. V., Padilla, A. B., Galicia, B. R., & Roldán, G. P. (2013). The dog in the Mexican archaeozoological record. In C. M. Götz, & K. F. Emery (Eds.), *The Archaeology of Mesoamerican Animals* (pp. 557–582). Atlanta, GA: Lockwood Press.

Backwell, L., & d'Errico, F. (2003). Additional evidence on the early hominid bone tools from Swartkrans with reference to spatial distribution of lithic and organic artefacts. *South African Journal of Science, 99*, 259–267.

Backwell, L., d'Errico, F., & Wadley, L. (2008). Middle Stone Age bone tools from the Howiesons Poort layers, Sibudu Cave, South Africa. *Journal of Archaeological Science, 35*, 1566–1580.

Bader, N. O. (1998). Clothes reconstruction based on the grave material. In N. O. Bader (Ed.), *Upper Palaeolithic Site Sungir (Graves and Environment)* (pp. 83–114). Moscow: Nauchny Mir (Scientific World).

Bader, O. N., & Bader, N. O. (2000). Upper Palaeolithic site Sunghir. In T. I. Alexeeva, & N. O. Bader (Eds.), *Homo Sungirensis. Upper Palaeolithic Man: Ecological and Evolutionary Aspects of the Investigation* (pp. 21–29). Moscow: Nauchny Mir (Scientific World).

Bailey, G. (2008). Time perspectivism: origins and consequences. In S. Holdaway, & L. Wandsnider (Eds.), *Time in Archaeology: Time Perspectivism Revisited* (pp. 13–30). Salt Lake City, UT: University of Utah Press.

Bakker, A. M., Louchard, D., & Keller, K. (2017). Sources and implications of deep uncertainties surrounding sea-level projections. *Climate Change*, *140*, 339–347.

Baldini, J. U., Brown, R. J., & McElwaine, J. N. (2015). Was millennial scale climate change during the last glacial triggered by explosive volcanism? *Scientific Reports*, *5*, 17442.

Balme, J., & O'Connor, S. (2014). Early modern humans in Island Southeast Asia and Sahul: adaptive and creative societies with simple lithic industries. In R. Dennell, & M. Porr (Eds.), *Southern Asia, Australia and the Search for Human Origins* (pp. 164–174). New York: Cambridge University Press.

Barber, E. W. (1994). *Women's Work: The First 20,000 Years. Women, Cloth, and Society in Early Times.* New York: W. W. Norton & Company.

Barcan, R. (2004). *Nudity: A Cultural Anatomy.* Oxford: Berg.

Barker, G. W. (2006). *The Agricultural Revolution in Prehistory: Why did Foragers become Farmers?* Oxford: Oxford University Press.

Barker, G. W., & Janowski, M. (2011). Why cultivate? Anthropological and archaeological approaches to foraging-farming transitions in Southeast Asia. In G. W. Barker, & M. Janowski (Eds.), *Why Cultivate? Anthropological and Archaeological Approaches to Foraging-Farming Transitions in Southeast Asia* (pp. 1–16). Cambridge: McDonald Institute for Archaeological Research.

Barnes, G. L. (2015). *Archaeology of East Asia: The Rise of Civilization in China, Korea and Japan.* Oxford: Oxbow Books.

Barthes, R. G. (1966). Fashion and the social sciences (La mode et les sciences humaines). In A. Stafford, & M. Carter (Eds.), *The Language of Fashion* (pp. 85–91). Translated by Andy Stafford. London: Bloomsbury, 2013.

Barthes, R. G. (1967). *The Fashion System (Système de la Mode).* Translated by Matthew Ward and Richard Howard. Berkeley, CA: University of California Press, 1990.

Barton, L., Newsome, S. D., Chen, F.-H., Wang, H., Guilderson, T. P., & Bettinger, R. L. (2009). Agricultural origins and the isotopic identity of domestication in northern China. *Proceedings of the National Academy of Sciences USA*, *106*, 5523–5528.

Bar-Yosef, O. (1985). *A Cave in the Desert: Nahal Hemar, 9,000-Year-Old Finds.* Jerusalem: The Israel Museum.

Bar-Yosef, O. (2002). The upper paleolithic revolution. *Annual Review of Anthropology*, *31*, 363–393.

Bar-Yosef, O. (2017). Multiple origins of agriculture in Eurasia and Africa. In M. Tibayrenc, & F. J. Ayala (Eds.), *On Human Nature: Biology, Psychology, Ethics, Politics, Religion* (pp. 297–331). London: Academic Press.

Bar-Yosef, O., Belfer-Cohen, A., Mesheviliani, T., Jakeli, N., Bar-Oz, G., Boaretto, E., et al. (2011). Dzudzuana: an Upper Palaeolithic cave site in the Caucasus foothills (Georgia). *Antiquity*, *85*, 331–349.

Bar-Yosef, O., & Wang, Y. (2012). Paleolithic archaeology in China. *Annual Review of Anthropology*, *41*, 319–335.

Batra, S. K. (2007). Other long vegetable fibers: abaca, banana, sisal, henequen, flax, ramie, hemp, sunn, and coir. In M. Lewin (Ed.), *Handbook of Fiber Chemistry* (pp. 453–520). Third edition. Boca Raton, FL: CRC.

Baykara, İ., Mentzer, S. M., Stiner, M. C., Asmerom, Y., Güleç, E. S., & Kuhn, S. L. (2015). The Middle Paleolithic occupations of Üçağızlı II Cave (Hatay, Turkey): geoarcheological and archeological perspectives. *Journal of Archaeological Science: Reports*, *4*, 409–426.

Beaglehole, J. C. (Ed.). (1955). *The Journals of Captain James Cook on his Voyages of Discovery. Four Volumes. I: The Voyage of the Endeavour 1768–1771.* Cambridge: Hakluyt Society / Cambridge University Press.

Becker, C., Benecke, N., Grabundžija, A., Küchelmann, H.-C., Pollock, S., Schier, W., et al. (2016). The textile revolution: research into the origin and spread of wool production between the Near East and central Europe. *eTopoi: Journal for Ancient Studies, Special Volume 6*, 102–148.

Behnke, M. P., Chapman, A., & Legoupil, D. (2015). *The Lost Tribes of Tierra del Fuego: Selk'nam, Yamana, Kawésqar [L'esprit des Hommes de la Terre de Feu: Selk'nam, Yamana, Kawésqar].* (C. Barthe, & X. Barral, Eds.) Photographs by Martin Gusinde. Translated by

Ruth Sharman. London: Thames and Hudson.

Bellwood, P. (2005). *First Farmers: The Origins of Agricultural Societies*. Boston, MA: Blackwell.

Bellwood, P. (2013). Neolithic migrations: food production and population expansion. In P. Bellwood (Ed.), *The Global Prehistory of Human Migration* (pp. 79–86). Oxford: Wiley Blackwell.

Bellwood, P. (2015). Migration and the origins of *Homo sapiens*. In Y. Kaifu, M. Izuho, T. Goebel, H. Sato, & A. Ono (Eds.), *Emergence and Diversity of Modern Human Behavior in Paleolithic Asia* (pp. 51–58). College Station, TX: Texas A&M University Press.

Bellwood, P. (2017). Early agriculture in world perspective. In J. Golson, T. Denham, P. Hughes, P. Swadling, & J. Muke (Eds.), *Ten Thousand Years of Cultivation at Kuk Swamp in the Highlands of Papua New Guinea* (pp. 29–37). Canberra: ANU Press.

Belmaker, M., & Brown, A. B. (2016). A new look at "on mice and men": should commensal species be used as a universal indicator of early sedentism? In N. Marom, R. Yeshurun, L. Weissbrod, & G. Bar-Oz (Eds.), *Bones and Identity: Zooarchaeological Approaches to Reconstructing Social and Cultural Landscapes in Southwest Asia* (pp. 25–43). Oxford: Oxbow.

Ben-Yosef, E., Shamir, O., & Levy, J. (2017). On early metallurgy and textile-production technologies in the southern Levant: a response to Langgut et al. (2016). *Antiquity*, *91*, 765–776.

Bergfjord, C., & Holst, B. (2010). A procedure for identifying textile bast fibres using microscopy: flax, nettle/ramie, hemp and jute. *Ultramicroscopy*, *110*, 1192–1197.

Bergmann, R. L., Bergmann, K. E., von Weizsäcker, K., Berns, M., Henrich, W., & Dudenhausen, J. W. (2014). Breastfeeding is natural but not always easy: intervention for common medical problems of breastfeeding mothers — a review of the scientific evidence. *Journal of Perinatal Medicine*, *42*, 9–18.

Berna, F., Goldberg, P., Horwitz, L. K., Brink, J., Holt, S., Bamford, M., et al. (2012). Microstratigraphic evidence of in situ fire in the Acheulean strata of Wonderwerk Cave, Northern Cape province, South Africa. *Proceedings of the National Academy of Sciences USA*, *109*, E1215-E1220.

Betts, A. V., Jia, P. W., & Dodson, J. (2014). The origins of wheat in China and potential pathways for its introduction: a review. *Quaternary International*, *348*, 158–168.

Bhatia, D., & Malhotra, U. (2016). Thermophysiological wear comfort of clothing: an overview. *Journal of Textile Science and Engineering*, *6*(2), 1000250.

Binford, L. R. (2002). *In Pursuit of the Past: Decoding the Archaeological Record*. With a new Afterword. Berkeley, CA: University of California Press.

Bird, D. W., Bird, R. B., Codding, B. F., & Taylor, N. (2016). A landscape architecture of fire: cultural emergence and ecological pyrodiversity in Australia's Western Desert. *Current Anthropology*, *57* (Suppl. 13), S65-S79.

Bitocchi, E., Nanni, L., Bellucci, E., Rossi, M., Giardini, A., Zeuli, S., et al. (2012). Mesoamerican origin of the common bean (*Phaseolus vulgaris* L.) is revealed by sequence data. *Proceedings of the National Academy of Sciences USA*, *109*, E788–E796.

Blain, H.-A., Agustí, J., Lordkipanidze, D., Rook, L., & Delfino, M. (2014). Paleoclimatic and paleoenvironmental context of the Early Pleistocene hominins from Dmanisi (Georgia, Lesser Caucasus) inferred from the herpetofaunal assemblage. *Quaternary Science Reviews*, *105*, 136–150.

Blinkhorn, J., & Petraglia, M. D. (2017). Environments and cultural change in the Indian subcontinent. *Current Anthropology*, *58* (*Suppl. 17*), S463–S479.

Blurton Jones, N. G. (2016). *Demography and Evolutionary Ecology of Hadza Hunter-Gatherers*. Cambridge: Cambridge University Press.

Bocquet-Appel, J.-P. (2011). When the world's population took off: the springboard of the Neolithic Demographic Transition. *Science*, *333*, 560–561.

Bocquet-Appel, J.-P., & Bar-Yosef, O. (2008). Prehistoric demography in a time of globalization. In J.-P. Bocquet-Appel, & O. Bar-Yosef (Eds.), *The Neolithic Demographic Transition and its Consequences* (pp. 1–10). New York: Springer.

Boellstorff, T. (2016). For whom the ontology turns: theorizing the digital real. *Current Anthropology*, *57*, 387–407.

Bol'shakov, V. A., & Kuzmin, Y. V. (2015). Comment on "Quaternary glaciations: from observations to theories" by D. Paillard [Quat. Sci. Rev. 107 (2015), 11–24]. *Quaternary Science Reviews*, *120*, 126–128.

Bolton, L., & Tarisesei, J. (2010). Dress of Vanuatu. In M. Marnard (Ed.), *Berg Encyclopedia of World Dress and Fashion. Volume 7: Australia, New Zealand, and the Pacific Islands* (pp. 479–483). Oxford: Berg.

Bonavia, D. (2008). *The South American Camelids (Los Camélidos Sudamericanos: Una Introducción a su Estudio)*. Translated by Javier Flores Espinoza. Expanded and corrected edition. Los Angeles, CA: Cotsen Institute of Archaeology, UCLA.

Bonilla, D. L., Durden, L. A., Eremeeva, M. E., & Dasch, G. A. (2013). The biology and taxonomy of head and body lice – implications for louse-borne disease prevention. *PLoS Pathogens*, *9*, e1003724.

Borders, B., & Lee-Mäder, E. (2014). *Milkweeds: A Conservation Practitioner's Guide. Plant Ecology, Seed Production Methods, and Habitat Restoration Opportunities*. Portland, OR: Xerces Society for Invertebrate Conservation.

Boucher, F. (1987). *A History of Costume in the West (Histoire du Costume en Occident)*. Second edition, with additional chapter by Yvonne Deslandres. Translated by John Ross. London: Thames and Hudson.

Bowes, H., Eglin, C. M., Tipton, M. J., & Barwood, M. J. (2016). Swim performance and thermoregulatory effects of wearing clothing in a simulated cold-water survival situation. *European Journal of Applied Physiology*, *116*, 759–767.

Bowles, S. (2011). Cultivation of cereals by the first farmers was not more productive than foraging. *Proceedings of the National Academy of Sciences USA*, *108*, 4760–4765.

Boyd, B. (2006). On 'sedentism' in the later Epipalaeolithic (Natufian) Levant. *World Archaeology*, *38*, 164–178.

Boyd, B. (2017). Archaeology and human-animal relations: thinking through anthropocentrism. *Annual Review of Anthropology*, *46*, 299–316.

Boyd, B. (2018). Ecologies of fiber-work: animal technologies and invisible craft practices in prehistoric Southwest Asia. *Quaternary International*, 468, 250–261.

Boyd, R., & Silk, J. B. (2015). *How Humans Evolved*. Seventh edition. New York: W. W. Norton & Company.

Bradley, R. S. (2015). *Paleoclimatology: Reconstructing Climates of the Quaternary*. Oxford: Elsevier.

Bradshaw, V. (2006). *The Building Environment: Active and Passive Control Systems*. Third edition. New York: John Wiley & Sons.

Breniquet, C. (2014). The archaeology of wool in early Mesopotamia: sources, methods, perspectives. In C. Breniquet, & C. Michel (Eds.), *Wool Economy in the Ancient Near East and the Aegean: From the Beginnings of Sheep Husbandry to Institutional Textile Industry* (pp. 52–78). Oxford: Oxbow.

Brown, D. J., Brugger, H., Boyd, J., & Paal, P. (2012). Accidental hypothermia. *New England Journal of Medicine*, *367*, 1930–1938.

Bruford, M. W., & Townsend, S. J. (2006). Mitochondrial DNA diversity in modern sheep: implications for domestication. In M. A. Zeder, D. G. Bradley, E. Emshwiller, & B. D. Smith (Eds.), *Documenting Domestication: New Genetic and Archaeological Paradigms* (pp. 306–316). Berkeley, CA: University of California Press.

Brumm, A., Aziz, F., van den Bergh, G. D., Morwood, M. J., Moore, M. W., Kurniawan, I., et al. (2006). Early stone technology on Flores and its implications for *Homo floresiensis*. *Nature*, *441*, 624–628.

Brumm, A., & Moore, M. W. (2005). Symbolic revolutions and the Australian archaeological record. *Cambridge Archaeological Journal*, *15*, 157–175.

Brunton, P. (Ed.). (1998). *The Endeavour Journal of Joseph Banks: The Australian Journey*. Sydney: Angus & Robertson.

Brynjolfsson, E., & McAfee, A. (2014). *The Second Machine Age: Work, Progress, and Prosperity in a Time of Brilliant Technologies*. New York: W. W. Norton & Company.

Buckley, C. D. (2017). Looms, weaving and the Austronesian expansion. In A. Acri, R. Blench, & A. Landmann (Eds.), *Spirits and Ships: Cultural Transfers in Early Monsoon Asia* (pp. 273–324). Singapore: ISEAS.

Buckley, C. D., & Boudot, E. (2017). The evolution of an ancient technology. *Royal Society Open Science*, *4*, 170208.

Bulbeck, D. (2007). Where river meets sea: a parsimonious model for *Homo sapiens* colonization of the Indian Ocean rim and Sahul. *Current Anthropology*, *48*, 315–321.

Burdukiewicz, J. M. (2014). The origin of symbolic behavior of middle palaeolithic humans: recent controversies. *Quaternary International*, *326–327*, 398–405.

Burt, B. (2010). Body ornaments of Solomon Islands. In M. Marnard (Ed.), *Berg Encyclopedia of World Dress and Fashion. Volume 7: Australia, New Zealand, and the Pacific Islands* (pp. 488–492). Oxford: Berg.

Cai, D., Tang, Z., Yu, H., Han, L., Ren, X., Zhao, X., et al. (2011). Early history of Chinese sheep indicated by ancient DNA analysis of Bronze Age individuals. *Journal of Archaeological Science*, *38*, 896–902.

Cameron, J., & Mijares, A. S. (2006). Report on an analysis of spindle whorl from Callao Cave, Peñablanca, northern Luzon, Philippines. *Hukay*, *9*, 5–13.

Caplan, A. L. (2007). The ethics of evil: the challenge and lessons of Nazi medial experiments. In W. R. Lafleur, G. Böhme, & S. Shimazono (Eds.), *Dark Medicine: Rationalizing Unethical Medical Research* (pp. 63–72). Bloomington, IN: Indiana University Press.

Carocci, M. (2010). Clad with the 'hair of trees': a history of Native American Spanish Moss textile industries. *Textile History*, *41*, 3–27.

Carpenter, L. B., Feinman, G. M., & Nicholas, L. M. (2012). Spindle whorls from El Palmillo: economic implications. *Latin American Antiquity*, *23*, 381–400.

Carpentier, P. H., Satger, B., & Poensin, D. (2006). Incidence and natural history of Raynaud phenomenon: a long-term follow-up (14 years) of a random sample from the general population. *Journal of Vascular Surgery*, *44*, 1023–1028.

Carter, M. (2003). *Fashion Classics from Carlyle to Barthes*. Oxford: Berg.

Carter, M. (2013). *Overdressed: Barthes, Darwin and the Clothes that Speak*. Sydney: Puncher & Wattmann.

Carter, M. (2017). *Being Prepared: Aspects of Dress and Dressing*. Sydney: Puncher & Wattmann.

Castillo, C., & Fuller, D. Q. (2017). Bananas: the spread of a tropical forest fruit as an agricultural staple. In J. Lee-Thorp, & M. A. Katzenberg (Eds.), *The Oxford Handbook of the Archaeology of Diet*. Oxford: Oxford University Press / Oxford Handbooks Online.

Cerling, T. E., Wynn, J. G., Andanje, S. A., Bird, M. I., Korir, D. K., Levin, N. E., et al. (2011). Woody cover and hominin environments in the past 6 million years. *Nature*, *476*, 51–56.

Champlain (de), S. (1619). *Voyages and Discoveries in New France from the Year 1615 to the End of the Year 1618 (Voyages et descouvertures faites en la Nouvelle France, depuis l'anné 1615, jusques à la fin de l'année 1618 par le Sieur de Champlain)*. In 'Voyages of Samuel de Champlain 1604–1608' (pp. 261–361). Translated by Charles Pomeroy Otis, edited by W. L. Grant. New York: Charles Scribner's Sons, 1907.

Chan, A. P., Guo, Y. P., Wong, F. K., Li, Y., Sun, S., & Han, X. (2016). The development of anti-heat stress clothing for construction workers in hot and humid weather. *Ergonomics*, *59*, 479–495.

Chang, K. C. (1970). The beginnings of agriculture in the Far East. *Antiquity*, *40*, 175–185.

Charles, M. (2007). East of Eden? A consideration of neolithic crop spectra in the eastern Fertile Crescent and beyond. In S. Colledge, & J. Conolly (Eds.), *The Origins and Spread of Domestic Plants in Southwest Asia and Europe* (pp. 37–51). San Francisco, CA: Left Coast Press.

Chaudhary, B., Hovav, R., Flagel, L., Mittler, R., & Wendel, J. F. (2009). Parallel expression evolution of oxidative stress-related genes in fiber from wild and domesticated diploid and polyploid cotton (Gossypium). *BMC Genomics, 10*, 378.

Chen, T.-H., Chen, W.-P., & Wang, M.-J. J. (2014). The effect of air permeability and water vapor permeability of cleanroom clothing on physiological responses and wear comfort. *Journal of Occupational and Environmental Hygiene, 11*, 366–376.

Chen, Z., Wang, Z., Xu, S., Zhou, K., & Yang, G. (2013). Characterization of hairless (Hr) and FGF5 genes provides insights into the molecular basis of hair loss in cetaceans. *BMC Evolutionary Biology, 13*, 34.

Chessa, B., Pereira, F., Arnaud, F., Amorim, A., Goyache, F., Mainland, I., et al. (2009). Revealing the history of sheep domestication using retrovirus integrations. *Science, 324*, 532–536.

Chi, Z., & Hung, H.-c. (2012). Later hunter-gatherers in southern China, 18 000–3000 BC. *Antiquity, 86*, 11–29.

Childe, V. G. (1936). *Man Makes Himself.* London: Watts & Company.

Chinta, S. K., & Gujar, P. D. (2013). Significance of moisture management for high performance textile fabrics. *International Journal of Innovative Research in Science, Engineering and Technology, 2*, 814–819.

Cholodenko, A. (2015). "Computer says no", or: the erasure of the human. In B. Buckley, & J. Conomos (Eds.), *Erasure: The Spectre of Cultural Memory* (pp. 31–47). Faringdon: Libri.

Chomsky, N. (2016). *What Kind of Creatures Are We?* New York: Columbia University Press.

Choudhury, A. K., Majumdar, P. K., & Datta, C. (2011). Factors affecting comfort: human physiology and the role of clothing. In G. Song (Ed.), *Improving Comfort in Clothing* (pp. 3–60). Cambridge: Woodhead.

Chritz, K. L., Marshall, F. B., Zagal, M. E., Kirera, F., & Cerling, T. E. (2015). Environments and trypanosomiasis risks for early herders in the later Holocene of the Lake Victoria basin, Kenya. *Proceedings of the National Academy of Sciences USA, 112*, 3674–3679.

Churchill, S. E. (2014). *Thin on the Ground: Neandertal Biology, Archeology, and Ecology.* Oxford: Wiley Blackwell.

Cipriani, L. (1966). *The Andaman Islanders.* New York: Frederick A. Praeger.

Claassen, C. (2015). *Beliefs and Rituals in Archaic Eastern North America: An Interpretive Guide.* Tuscaloosa, AL: University of Alabama Press.

Clarkson, C., Jacobs, Z., Marwick, B., Fullagar, R., Wallis, L., Smith, M., et al. (2017). Human occupation of northern Australia by 65,000 years ago. *Nature, 547*, 306–310.

Clement, C. R., Denevan, W. N., Heckenberger, M. J., Junqueira, A. B., Neves, E. G., Teixeira, W. G., et al. (2015). The domestication of Amazonia before European conquest. *Proceedings of the Royal Society B, 282*, 20150813.

Clottes, J., & Courtin, J. (1994). *The Cave Beneath the Sea: Paleolithic Images at Cosquer (La Grotte Cosquer: Peintures et Gravures de la Caverne Engloutie).* Translated by Marilyn Garner. New York: Harry N. Abrams, 1996.

Clutton-Brock, J. (2012). *Animals as Domesticates: A World View through History.* East Lansing, MI: Michigan State University Press.

Clutton-Brock, T. H., & Pemberton, J. M. (2004). Individuals and populations. In T. H. Clutton-Brock, & J. M. Pemberton (Eds.), *Soay Sheep: Dynamics and Selection in an Island Population* (pp. 1–16). Cambridge: Cambridge University Press.

Cohen, M. N. (2009). Rethinking the origins of agriculture. *Current Anthropology, 50*, 591–595.

Colebrook, R. H. (1807). On the Andaman Islands. *Asiatic Researches, 4*, 385–394.

Collard, M., & Cross, A. (2017). Thermoregulation in *Homo erectus* and the Neanderthals: a reassessment using a segmented model. In A. Marom, & E. Hovers (Eds.), *Human Paleontology and Prehistory: Contributions in Honor of Yoel Rak* (pp. 161–174). Cham: Springer.

Collard, M., Tarle, L., Sandgathe, D., & Allan, A. (2016). Faunal evidence for a difference in the thermal effectiveness of modern human and Neanderthal clothing. *Journal of Anthropological Archaeology, 44*, 235–246.

Collard, M., Vaesen, K., Cosgrove, R., & Roebroeks, W. (2016). The empirical case against the 'demographic turn' in palaeolithic archaeology. *Philosophical Transactions of The Royal Society B, 371*, 20150242.

Conard, N. J. (2009). A female figurine from the basal Aurignacian of Hohle Fels Cave in southwestern Germany. *Nature, 459*, 248–252.

Conard, N. J., Serangeli, J., Böhner, U., Starkovich, B. M., Miller, C. E., Urban, B., et al. (2015). Excavations at Schöningen and paradigm shifts in human evolution. *Journal of Human Evolution, 89*, 1–17.

Conington, J., Collins, J., & Dwyer, C. (2010). Selection for easier managed sheep. *Animal Welfare, 19* (Suppl. 1), 83–92.

Connolly, T. J., Barker, P., Fowler, C. S., Hattori, E. M., Jenkins, D. L., & Cannon, W. J. (2016). Getting beyond the point: textiles of the Terminal Pleistocene/Early Holocene in the northwestern Great Basin. *American Antiquity, 81*, 490–514.

Cooper, A., Turney, C., Hughen, K. A., Brook, B. W., McDonald, H. G., & Bradshaw, C. J. (2015). Abrupt warming events drove Late Pleistocene Holarctic megafaunal turnover. *Science, 349*, 602–606.

Cooper, C., Lupo, K., Matson, R. G., Lipe, W., Smith, C. I., & Richards, M. P. (2016). Short-term variability of diet at Basketmaker II Turkey Pen Ruins, Utah: insights from bulk and single amino acid isotope analysis of hair. *Journal of Archaeological Science: Reports, 5*, 10–18.

Coppens d'Eeckenbrugge, G., & Lacape, J.-M. (2014). Distribution and differentiation of wild, feral, and cultivated populations of perennial upland cotton (*Gossypium hirsutum* L.) in Mesoamerica and the Caribbean. *PLoS ONE, 9*, e107458.

Corrigan, P. (2008). *The Dressed Society: Clothing, the Body and Some Meanings of the World*. London: Sage.

Cosgrove, R., & Allen, J. (2001). Prey choice and hunting strategies in the Late Pleistocene: evidence from southwest Tasmania. In A. Anderson, I. Lilley, & S. O'Connor (Eds.), *Histories of Old Ages: Essays in Honour of Rhys Jones* (pp. 397–429). Canberra: Pandanus Books, Australian National University.

Cosgrove, R., Pike-Tay, A., & Roebroeks, W. (2014). Tasmanian archaeology and reflections on modern human behaviour. In R. Dennell, & M. Porr (Eds.), *Southern Asia, Australia and the Search for Human Origins* (pp. 175–188). New York: Cambridge University Press.

Court, J., Webb-Ware, J., & Hides, S. (2010). *Sheep Farming for Meat and Wool*. Melbourne: CSIRO.

Crawford, G. W. (2011). Advances in understanding early agriculture in Japan. *Current Anthropology, 52* (Suppl. S4), S331–S345.

Cueto, M., Camarós, E., Castaños, P., Ontañón, R., & Arias, P. (2016). Under the skin of a lion: unique evidence of upper paleolithic exploitation and use of cave lion (*Panthera spelaea*) from the Lower Gallery of La Garma (Spain). *PLoS ONE, 11*, e0163591.

d'Ambrosio Alfano, F. R., Palella, B. I., Riccio, G., & Malchaire, J. (2016). On the effect of thermophysical properties of clothing on the heat strain predicted by PHS model. *Annals of Occupational Hygiene, 60*, 231–251.

Dantas, M., Figueroa, G. G., & Laguens, A. (2014). Llamas in the cornfield: prehispanic agro-pastoral system in the southern Andes. *International Journal of Osteoarchaeology, 24*, 149–165.

Daragan, M., Gleba, M., & Buravchuk, O. (2016). "Pandora's Box": a textile tool set from a Scythian burial in Ukraine. In J. Ortiz, C. Alfaro, L. Turell, & M. J. Martínez (Eds.), *Textiles, Basketry and Dyes in the Ancient Mediterranean World* (pp. 57–61). Valencia: Universitat de València.

Darwin, C. R. (1839). *Journal of Researches into the Geology and Natural History of the Various Countries Visited by H.M.S. Beagle, under the Command of Captain Fitzroy, R.N. from 1832 to 1836*. London: Henry Colburn.

Darwin, C. R. (1871). *The Descent of Man, and Selection in Relation to Sex*. In two volumes. Volume II. London: John Murray.

Dávid-Barrett, T., & Dunbar, R. (2016). Bipedality and hair loss in human evolution revisited: the impact of altitude and activity scheduling. *Journal of Human Evolution, 94*, 72–82.

Davidson, I. (2014). It's the thought that counts: unpacking the package of behaviour of the first people of Australia and its adjacent islands. In R. Dennell, & M. Porr (Eds.), *Southern Asia, Australia and the Search for Human Origins* (pp. 243–256). New York: Cambridge University Press.

Davis, J.-K., & Bishop, P. A. (2013). Impact of clothing on exercise in the heat. *Sports Medicine, 43*, 695–706.

de Langhe, E. A. (2009). Relevance of banana seeds in archaeology. *Ethnobotany Research and Applications, 7*, 271–281.

de Waal, F. B. (2013). *The Bonobo and the Atheist.* New York: W. W. Norton & Company.

Dean, I., & Siva-Jothy, M. T. (2012). Human fine body hair enhances ectoparasite detection. *Biology Letters, 8*, 358–361.

Decker, J. E., McKay, S. D., Rolf, M. M., Kim, J. W., Molina Alcalá, A., Sonstegard, T. S., et al. (2014). Worldwide patterns of ancestry, divergence, and admixture in domesticated cattle. *PLoS Genetics, 10*, e1004254.

Delmonte, B., Petit, J. R., Andersen, K. K., Basile-Doelsch, I., Maggi, V., & Lipenkov, V. Y. (2004). Dust size evidence for opposite regional atmospheric circulation changes over east Antarctica during the last glacial transition. *Climate Dynamics, 23*, 427438.

deMenocal, P., Ortiz, J., Guilderson, T., Adkins, J., Sarnthein, M., Baker, l., et al. (2000). Abrupt onset and termination of the African Humid Period: rapid climate responses to gradual insolation forcing. *Quaternary Science Reviews, 19*, 347–361.

Denham, T. (2004). The roots of agriculture and aboriculture in New Guinea: looking beyond Austronesian expansion, neolithic packages and indigenous origins. *World Archaeology, 36*, 610–620.

Denham, T. (2007). Early to mid-Holocene plant exploitation in New Guinea: towards a contingent interpretation of agriculture. In T. Denham, J. Iriarte, & L. Vrydaghs (Eds.), *Rethinking Agriculture: Archaeological and Ethnoarchaeological Perspectives* (pp. 78–108). San Francisco, CA: Left Coast Press.

Denham, T. (2011). Early agriculture and plant domestication in New Guinea and island Southeast Asia. *Current* Anthropology *52* (Suppl. S4), S379–S395.

Denham, T., Donohue, M., & Booth, S. (2009). Horticultural experimentation in northern Australia reconsidered. *Antiquity, 83*, 634–648.

Denham, T., Golson, J., & Hughes, P. (2004). Reading early agriculture at Kuk Swamp, Wahgi Valley, Papua New Guinea: the archaeological features (Phases 1–3). *Proceedings of the Prehistoric Society, 70*, 259–297.

Denham, T., Golson, J., & Hughes, P. (2017). Phase 1: the case for 10,000-year-old agriculture at Kuk. In J. Golson, T. Denham, P. Hughes, P. Swadling, & J. Muke (Eds.), *Ten Thousand Years of Cultivation at Kuk Swamp in the Highlands of Papua New Guinea* (pp. 187–200). Canberra: ANU Press.

Dennell, R. (2009). *The Palaeolithic Settlement of Asia.* New York: Cambridge University Press.

Dennell, R. (2015). *Homo sapiens* in China 80,000 years ago. *Nature, 526*, 647–648.

d'Errico, F., Backwell, L., Villa, P., Degano, I., Lucejko, J. J., Bamford, M. K., et al. (2012). Early evidence of San material culture represented by organic artifacts from Border Cave, South Africa. *Proceedings of the National Academy of Sciences USA, 109*, 13214–13219.

d'Errico, F., & Henshilwood, C. S. (2007). Additional evidence for bone technology in the Southern African Middle Stone Age. *Journal of Human Evolution, 52*, 142–163.

d'Errico, F., Moreno, R. G., & Rifkin, R. F. (2012). Technological, elemental and colorimetric analysis of an engraved ochre fragment from the Middle Stone Age levels of Klasies River Cave 1, South Africa. *Journal of Archaeological Science, 39*, 942–952.

d'Errico, F., & Stringer, C. B. (2011). Evolution, revolution or saltation scenario for the emergence of modern cultures? *Philosophical Transactions of the Royal Society B, 366*, 1060–1069.

d'Errico, F., Vanhaeren, M., Barton, N., Bouzouggar, A., Mienis, H., Richter, D., et al. (2009). Additional evidence on the use of personal ornaments in the Middle Paleolithic of North Africa. *Proceedings of the National Academy of Sciences USA*, *106*, 16051–16056.

Dettmeyer, R. B., Verhoff, M. A., & Schütz, H. F. (2014). *Forensic Medicine: Fundamentals and Perspectives*. Heidelberg: Springer.

di Lernia, S. (2001). Dismantling dung: delayed use of food resources among early Holocene foragers of the Libyan Sahara. *Journal of Anthropological Archaeology*, *20*, 408–441.

Diamond, J. (2002). Evolution, consequences and future of plant and animal domestication. *Nature*, *418*, 700–707.

Dibble, H. L., Abodolahzadeh, A., Aldeias, V., Goldberg, P., McPherron, S. P., & Sandgathe, D. M. (2017). How did hominins adapt to Ice Age Europe without fire? *Current Anthropology*, *58* (Suppl. S16), S278–S287.

Dibble, H. L., Aldeias, V., Jacobs, Z., Olszewski, D. I., Rezek, Z., Lin, S. C., et al. (2013). On the industrial attributions of the Aterian and Mousterian of the Maghreb. *Journal of Human Evolution*, *64*, 194–210.

Dibble, H. L., Holdaway, S. J., Lin, S. C., Braun, D. R., Douglass, M. J., Iovita, R., et al. (2017). Major fallacies surrounding stone artefacts and assemblages. *Journal of Archaeological Method and Theory*, *24*, 813–851.

Dillehay, T. D., Bonavia, D., Goodbred, S., Pino, M., Vasquez, V., Tham, T. R., et al. (2012). Chronology, mound-building and environment at Huaca Prieta, coastal Peru, from 13 700 to 4000 years ago. *Antiquity*, *86*, 48–70.

Dillehay, T. D., Goodbred, S., Pino, M., Vásquez Sánchez, V. F., Tham, T. R., Adovasio, J., et al. (2017). Simple technologies and diverse food strategies of the Late Pleistocene and Early Holocene at Huaca Prieta, coastal Peru. *Science Advances*, *3*, e1602778.

Di-Poï, N., & Milinkovitch, M. C. (2016). The anatomical placode in reptile scale morphogenesis indicates shared ancestry among skin appendages in amniotes. *Science Advances*, *2*, e1600708.

Disspain, M. C., Ulm, S., Santoro, C. M., Carter, C., & Gillanders, B. M. (2017). Pre-Columbian fishing on the coast of the Atacama Desert, northern Chile: an investigation of fish size and species distribution using otoliths from Camarones Punta Norte and Caleta Vitor. *Journal of Island and Coastal Archaeology*, *12*, 428–450.

Dixson, B. J., & Rantala, M. J. (2016). The role of facial and body hair distribution in women's judgements of men's sexual attractiveness. *Archives of Sexual Behavior*, *45*, 877–889.

Dobrez, P. (2013). The case for hand stencils and prints as proprio-performative. *Arts*, *2*, 273–327.

Dobrovolskaya, M., Richard, M.-P., & Trinkaus, E. (2012). Direct radiocarbon dates for the Mid Upper Paleolithic (eastern Gravettian) burials from Sunghir, Russia. *Bulletins et Mémoires de la Société d'Anthropologie de Paris*, *24*, 96–102.

Dodson, J., Dodson, E., Banati, R., Li, X., Atahan, P., Hu, S., et al. (2014). Oldest directly dated remains of sheep in China. *Scientific Reports*, *4*, 7170.

Dolez, P. I., & Vu-Khanh, T. (2009). Gloves for protection from cold weather. In J. Williams (Ed.), *Textiles for Cold Weather Apparel* (pp. 374–398). Cambridge: Woodhead.

Dortch, C. E. (1979). 33,000 year old stone and bone artefacts from Devil's Lair, Western Australia. *Records of the Western Australian Museum*, *7*, 329–367.

Dortch, C. E. (1984). *Devil's Lair, A Study in Prehistory*. Perth: Western Australian Museum.

Douka, K., Higham, T. F., Wood, R., Boscato, P., Gambassini, P., Karkanas, P., et al. (2014). On the chronology of the Uluzzian. *Journal of Human Evolution*, *68*, 1–13.

Doumani, P. N., & Frachetti, M. D. (2012). Bronze Age textile evidence in ceramic impressions: weaving and pottery technology among mobile pastoralists of central Eurasia. *Antiquity*, *86*, 368–382.

Drake, A. G., Coquerelle, M., & Colombeau, G. (2015). 3D morphometric analysis of fossil canid skulls contradicts the suggested domestication of dogs during the late paleolithic. *Scientific Reports*, *5*, 8289.

Dransart, P. Z. (2002). *Earth, Water, Fleece and Fabric: An Ethnography and Archaeology of*

Andean Camelid Herding. New York: Routledge.

Ducharme, M. B., & Brajkovic, D. (2005). *Guidelines on the Risk and Time to Frostbite during Exposure to Cold Winds*. Paris: NATO Research and Technology Organisation.

Dunbar, R. I. (2010). Deacon's dilemma: the problem of pair-bonding in human evolution. In R. I. Dunbar, C. Gamble, & J. Gowlett (Eds.), *Social Brain, Distributed Mind* (pp. 155–175). Proceedings of The British Academy, 158. Oxford: Oxford University Press.

Dunbar, R. I., Lehmann, J., Korstjens, A. H., & Gowlett, J. A. (2014). The road to modern humans: time budgets, fission-fusion sociality, kinship and the division of labour in hominin evolution. In R. I. Dunbar, C. Gamble, & J. A. Gowlett (Eds.), *Lucy to Language: The Benchmark Papers* (pp. 333–355). Oxford: Oxford University Press.

Dunkin, R. C., McLellan, W. A., Blum, J. E., & Pabst, D. A. (2005). The ontogenic changes in the thermal properties of blubber from Atlantic bottlenose dolphin *Tursiops truncatus*. *Journal of Experimental Biology*, *208*, 1469–1480.

Dutton, A., & Lambeck, K. (2012). Ice volume and sea level during the last interglacial. *Science*, *337*, 216–219.

Ebrey, P. B. (2010). *The Cambridge Illustrated History of China*. Second edition. New York: Cambridge University Press.

Eda, M., Lu, P., Kikuchi, H., Li, Z., Li, F., & Yuan, J. (2016). Reevaluation of early Holocene chicken domestication in northern China. *Journal of Archaeological Science*, *67*, 25–31.

Eerkens, J. W., & Bartelink, E. J. (2013). Sex-biased weaning and early childhood diet among middle Holocene hunter-gatherers in central California. *American Journal of Physical Anthropology*, *152*, 471–483.

Eerkens, J. W., Berget, A. G., & Bartelink, E. J. (2011). Estimating weaning and early childhood diet from serial micro-samples of dentin collagen. *Journal of Archaeological Science*, *38*, 3101–3111.

Eicher, J. B., & Evenson, S. L. (2015). *The Visible Self: Global Perspectives on Dress, Culture, and Society*. Fourth edition. New York: Fairchild.

Ember, C. R., & Ember, M. R. (2015). *Cultural Anthropology*. Fourteenth edition. Boston, MA: Pearson.

Engels, F. (1884). *The Origin of the Family, Private Property and the State, in the Light of the Researches of Lewis H. Morgan (Der Ursprung der Familie, des Privateigenthums und des Staats. Im Anschluss an Lewis H. Morgan's Forschungen)*. Translated by Alick West. London: Penguin Books, 2010.

Entwistle, J. (2000). *The Fashioned Body: Fashion, Dress and Modern Social Theory*. Cambridge: Polity Press.

Epstein, Y., Heled, Y., Ketko, I., Muginshtein, J., Yanovich, R., Druyan, A., et al. (2013). The effect of air permeability characteristics of protective garments on the induced physiological strain under exercise-heat stress. *Annals of Occupational Hygiene*, *7*, 866–874.

Evans, S. T. (1990). The productivity of maguey terrace agriculture in central Mexico during the Aztec period. *Latin American Antiquity*, *1*, 117–132.

Fairbairn, A. S., Hope, G. S., & Summerhayes, G. R. (2006). Pleistocene occupation of New Guinea's highland and subalpine environments. *World Archaeology*, *38*, 371–386.

Falguères, C., Richard, M., Tombret, O., Shao, Q., Bahain, J. J., Gopher, A., et al. (2016). New ERS/U-series dates in Yabrudian and Amudian layers at Qesem Cave, Israel. *Quaternary International*, *398*, 6–12.

Feinman, G. M. (2006). The economic underpinnings of Prehispanic Zapotec civilization: small-scale production, economic interdependence, and market exchange. In J. Marcus, & C. Stanish (Eds.), *Agricultural Strategies* (pp. 255–280). Los Angeles, CA: Cotsen Institute of Archaeology, UCLA.

Fenichell, S. (1996). *Plastic: The Making of a Synthetic Century*. New York: HarperCollins.

Feulner, G., Rahmstorf, S., Levermann, A., & Volkwardt, S. (2013). On the origin of the surface air temperature difference between the hemispheres in Earth's present-day climate. *Journal of Climate*, *26*, 7136–7150.

Figueredo, C. J., Casas, A., Colunga-GarcíaMarín, P., Nassar, J. M., & González-Rodríguez, A.

(2014). Morphological variation, management and domestication of 'maguey alto' (*Agave inaequidens*) and 'maguey manso' (*A. hookeri*) in Michoacán, México. *Journal of Ethnobiology and Ethnomedicine, 10*, 66.

Figueredo, C. J., Casas, A., González-Rodríguez, A., Nassar, J. M., Colunga-García-Marín, P., & Rocha-Ramírez, V. (2015). Genetic structure of coexisting wild and managed agave populations: implications for the evolution of plants under domestication. *AoB PLANTS, 7*, plv 114.

Finlayson, C. (2014). *The Improbable Primate: How Water Shaped Human Evolution*. Oxford: Oxford University Press.

Finlayson, C., Fa, D. A., Espejo, F. J., Carrión, J. S., Finlayson, G., Pacheco, F. G., et al. (2008). Gorham's Cave, Gibraltar – the persistence of a Neanderthal population. *Quaternary International, 181*, 64–71.

Finucane, B., Maita Agurto, P., & Isbell, W. H. (2006). Human and animal diet at Conchopata, Peru: stable isotope evidence for maize agriculture and animal management practices during the Middle Horizon. *Journal of Archaeological Science, 33*, 1766–1776.

Fletcher, R., Evans, D., Pottier, C., & Rachna, C. (2015). Angkor Wat: an introduction. *Antiquity, 89*, 1388–1401.

Flood, J. (1974). Pleistocene Man at Cloggs Cave: his tool kit and environment. *Mankind, 9*, 175–188.

Flood, J. (2006). *The Original Australians: Story of the Aboriginal People*. Sydney: Allen & Unwin.

Foley, R. A. (2002). Parallel tracks in time: human evolution and archaeology. In B. Cunliffe, W. Davies, & C. Renfrew (Eds.), *Archaeology: The Widening Debate* (pp. 3–42). Oxford: Oxford University Press.

Fontes, D., Cordeiro, R. C., Martins, G. S., Behling, H., Turcq, B., Sifeddine, A., et al. (2017). Paleoenvironmental dynamics in South Amazonia, Brazil, during the last 35,000 years inferred from pollen and geochemical records of Lago do Saci. *Quaternary Science Reviews, 173*, 161–180.

Fortunato, L., & Archetti, M. (2010). Evolution of monogamous marriage by maximization of inclusive fitness. *Journal of Evolutionary Biology, 23*, 149–156.

Frangipane, M., Andersson Strand, E., Laurito, R., Möller-Weiring, S., Nosch, M.-L., Rast-Eicher, A., et al. (2009). Arslantepe, Malatya (Turkey): textiles, tools and imprints of fabrics from the 4th to the 2nd millennium BCE. *Paléorient, 35*(1), 5–29.

Freedman, A. H., Gronau, I., Schweizer, R. M., Vecchyo, D. O.-D., Han, E., Silva, P. M., et al. (2014). Genome sequencing highlights the dynamic early history of dogs. *PLoS Genetics, 10*, e1004016.

Freinkel, S. (2011). *Plastic: A Toxic Love Story*. Boston, MA: Houghton Mifflin Harcourt.

Fritz, G. J. (2007). Keepers of Louisiana's levees: early mound builders and forest managers. In T. Denham, J. Iriarte, & L. Vrydaghs (Eds.), *Rethinking Agriculture: Archaeological and Ethnoarchaeological Perspectives* (pp. 189–209). San Francisco, CA: Left Coast Press.

Fu, Q., Hajdinjak, M., Moldovan, O. T., Constantin, S., Mallick, S., Skoglund, P., et al. (2015). An early modern human from Romania with a recent Neanderthal ancestor. *Nature, 524*, 216–219.

Fu, Q., Li, H., Moorjani, P., Jay, F., Slepchenko, S. M., Bondarev, A. A., et al. (2014). Genome sequence of a 45,000-year-old modern human from western Siberia. *Nature, 514*, 445–449.

Fu, Y.-B. (2011). Genetic evidence for early flax domestication with capsular dehiscence. *Resources and Crop Evolution, 58*, 1119–1128.

Fullagar, R. (1986). *Use-wear and Residues on Stone Tools: Functional Analysis and its Application to Two Southeastern Australian Archaeological Assemblages*. PhD thesis. Melbourne: La Trobe University.

Fullagar, R. (2000). In honour of S. A. Semenov: archaeology, use wear and technology. *Lithic Technology, 25*, 71–72.

Fullagar, R., Field, J., Denham, T., & Lentfer, C. (2006). Early and mid Holocene tool-use and processing of taro (*Colocasia esculenta*), yam (*Dioscorea* sp.) and other plants at Kuk Swamp in the highlands of Papua New Guinea. *Journal of Archaeological Science, 33*, 595–614.

Fuller, D. Q. (2006). Silence before sedentism and the advent of cash-crops: a status report on early agriculture in South Asia from plant domestication to the development of political economies (with an excursus on the problem of semantic shift among millets and rice). In T. Osada, & N. Hase (Eds.), *Proceedings of the Pre-Symposium of RIHN and 7th ESCA Harvard-Kyoto Roundtable* (pp. 175–213). Kyoto: Research Institute for Humanity and Nature.

Fuller, D. Q. (2011). Finding plant domestication in the Indian subcontinent. *Current Anthropology, 52* (Supp. S4), S347–S362.

Fuller, D. Q., & Madella, M. (2009). Banana cultivation in South Asia and East Asia: a review of the evidence from archaeology and linguistics. *Ethnobotany Research and Applicationns, 7*, 333–351.

Gaffney, D., Summerhayes, G. R., Ford, A., Scott, J. M., Denham, T., Field, J., et al. (2015). Earliest pottery on New Guinea mainland reveals Austronesian influences in highland environments 3000 years ago. *PLoS ONE, 10*, e0134497.

Gaines, A. G. (2002). *Wallace Carothers and the Story of Du Pont Nylon*. Newark, NJ: Mitchell Lane.

Gamble, C. S. (2007). *Origins and Revolutions: Human Identity in Earliest Prehistory*. Cambridge: Cambridge University Press.

Gamble, C. S., Gowlett, J., & Dunbar, R. (2014). *Thinking Big: How the Evolution of Social Life Shaped the Human Mind*. New York: Thames & Hudson.

Gammage, W. L. (2011). *The Biggest Estate on Earth: How Aborigines Made Australia*. Sydney: Allen & Unwin.

Ganopolski, A., Winkelmann, R., & Schellnhuber, H. J. (2016). Critical insolation-CO2 relation for diagnosing past and future glacial inception. *Nature, 529*, 200–203.

Gao, X., Zhang, S., Zhang, Y., & Chen, F. (2017). Evidence of hominin use and maintenance of fire at Zhoukoudian. *Current Anthropology, 58* (Suppl. S16), S267–S277.

García-Diez, M., Garrido, D., Hoffmann, D. L., Pettitt, P. B., Pike, A. W., & Zilhão, J. (2015). The chronology of hand stencils in European palaeolithic rock art: implications of new U-series results from El Castillo Cave (Cantabria, Spain). *Journal of Anthropological Sciences, 93*, 135–152.

Garfinkel, Y., Klimscha, F., Shalev, S., & Rosenberg, D. (2014). The beginning of metallurgy in the southern Levant: a late 6th millennium CalBC copper awl from Tel Tsaf, Israel. *PLoS ONE, 9*, e92591.

Gascoigne, J. (2014). *Encountering the Pacific in the Age of The Enlightenment*. New York: Cambridge University Press.

Gee, H. (2013). *The Accidental Species: Misunderstandings of Human Evolution*. Chicago, IL: University of Chicago Press.

Gerritsen, R. (2008). *Australia and the Origins of Agriculture*. BAR International Series 1874. Oxford: Archaeopress.

Ghaddar, N., & Ghali, K. (2009). Designing for ventilation in cold weather apparel. In J. Williams (Ed.), *Textiles for Cold Weather Apparel* (pp. 131–151). Cambridge: Woodhead.

Gibbard, P. L., & Head, M. J. (2010). The newly-ratified definition of the Quaternary System/Period and redefinition of the Pleistocene Series/Epoch, and comparison of proposals advanced prior to formal ratification. *Episodes, 33*, 152–158.

Giles, J. (2010). Naked love: the evolution of human hairlessness. *Biological Theory, 5*, 326–336.

Gilligan, I. (2007a). *Another Tasmanian Paradox: Clothing and Thermal Adaptations in Aboriginal Australia*. BAR International Series 1710. Oxford: Archaeopress.

Gilligan, I. (2007b). Clothing and farming origins: the Indo-Pacific evidence. *Journal of Indo-Pacific Archaeology (formerly Bulletin of the Indo-Pacific Prehistory Association), 27*, 12–21.

Gilligan, I. (2007c). Clothing and modern human behaviour: prehistoric Tasmania as a case study. *Archaeology in Oceania, 42*, 102–111.

Gilligan, I. (2007d). Neanderthal extinction and modern human behaviour: the role of climate change and clothing. *World Archaeology, 39*, 419–514.

Gilligan, I. (2007e). Resisting the cold in ice age Tasmania: thermal environment and settlement strategies. *Antiquity, 81*, 555–568.

Gilligan, I. (2008). Clothing and climate in Aboriginal Australia. *Current Anthropology, 49*, 487–495.

Gilligan, I. (2010a). Agriculture in Aboriginal Australia: why not? *Journal of Indo-Pacific Archaeology (formerly Bulletin of the Indo-Pacific Prehistory Association), 30*, 145–156.

Gilligan, I. (2010b). Clothing and modern human behaviour in Australia. *Journal of Indo-Pacific Archaeology (formerly Bulletin of the Indo-Pacific Prehistory Association), 30*, 54–69.

Gilligan, I. (2010c). The prehistoric development of clothing: archaeological implications of a thermal model. *Journal of Archaeological Method and Theory, 17*, 15–80.

Gilligan, I. (2014). Clothing and modern human behaviour: The challenge from Tasmania. In R. Dennell, & M. Porr (Eds.), *Southern Asia, Australia and the Search for Human Origins* (pp. 189–199). New York: Cambridge University Press.

Gilligan, I. (2016). Comment. 'The evolution of cultural complexity: not by the treadmill alone', Andersson, C. and Read, D. *Current Anthropology, 57*, 276–277.

Gilligan, I. (in press). Clothing. In T. K. Shackelford, & V. Weekes-Shakelford (Eds.), *Encyclopedia of Evolutionary Psychological Science*. Heidelberg: Springer.

Gilligan, I., & Bulbeck, D. (2007). Environment and morphology in Australian Aborigines: a re-analysis of the Birdsell database. *American Journal of Physical Anthropology, 134*, 75–91.

Gilligan, I., Chandraphak, S., & Mahakkanukrauh, P. (2013). Femoral neck-shaft angle in humans: variation relating to climate, clothing, lifestyle, sex, age and side. *Journal of Anatomy, 223*, 133–151.

Giner, C. A. (2012). Textiles from the Pre-Pottery Neolithic site of Tell Halula (Euphrates Valley, Syria). *Paléorient, 38*(1–2), 41–54.

Golden, F., & Tipton, M. (2002). *Essentials of Sea Survival*. Champaign, IL: Human Kinetics.

Golovanova, L. V., Doronichev, V. B., & Cleghorn, N. E. (2010). The emergence of bone-working and ornamental art in the Causasian Upper Palaeolithic. *Antiquity, 84*, 299–320.

Golson, J. (2007). Unravelling the story of early plant exploitation in highland Papua New Guinea. In T. Denham, J. Iriarte, & L. Vrydaghs (Eds.), *Rethinking Agriculture: Archaeological and Ethnoarchaeological Perspectives* (pp. 109–125). San Francisco, CA: Left Coast Press.

Gong, Y., Li, L., Gong, D., Yin, H., & Zhang, J. (2016). Biomolecular evidence of silk from 8,500 years ago. *PLoS ONE, 11*, e0168042.

Good, I. L. (2002). The archaeology of early silk. *Textile Society of America Symposium Proceedings, 388*, 7–15.

Good, I. L., Kenoyer, J. M., & Meadow, R. H. (2009). New evidence for early silk in the Indus civilization. *Archaeometry, 51*, 457–466.

Goodall, J. (1986). *The Chimpanzees of Gombe: Patterns of Behavior*. Boston, MA: The Belknap Press of Harvard University Press.

Gordon, B. (2011). *Textiles: The Whole Story*. London: Thames & Hudson.

Goren-Inbar, N., Alperson, N., Kislev, M. E., Simchoni, O., Melamed, Y., Ben-Nun, A., et al. (2004). Evidence of hominin control of fire at Gesher Benot Ya`aqov, Israel. *Science, 304*, 725–727.

Gott, B. (2002). Fire-making in Tasmania: absence of evidence is not evidence of absence. *Current Anthropology, 43*, 650–656.

Gould, S. J. (2002). *The Structure of Evolutionary Theory*. Boston, MA: The Belknap Press of Harvard University Press.

Gowlett, J. A., Brink, J. S., Caris, A., Hoare, S., & Rucina, S. M. (2017). Evidence of burning from bushfires in Southern and East Africa and its relevance to hominin evolution. *Current Anthropology, 58* (Suppl. S16), S206–S216.

Graham, R. W., Belmecheri, S., Choy, K., Culleton, B. J., Davies, L. J., Frose, D., et al. (2016). Timing and causes of mid-Holocene mammoth extinction on St. Paul Island, Alaska. *Proceedings of the National Academy of Sciences USA, 113*, 9310–9314.

Gray, R. H., Campbell, O. M., Apelo, R., Eslami, S. S., Zacur, H., Ramos, R. M., et al. (1990). Risk of ovulation during lactation. *The Lancet, 335*, 25–29.

Gremillion, K. J., Barton, L., & Piperno, D. R. (2014). Particularism and the retreat from theory in the archaeology of agricultural origins. *Proceedings of the National Academy of Sciences USA*, *111*, 6171–6177.

Grömer, K., Rösel-Mautendorfer, H., & Reschreiter, H. (2014). Out of the dark... New textile finds from Hallstatt. In S. Bergerbrant, & S. H. Fossøy (Eds.), *A Stitch in Time: Essays in Honour of Lise Bender Jørgensen* (pp. 129–144). Gothenburg: Humanities Department, Gothenburg University.

Guo, Y., Hu, Y. W., Zhu, J. Y., Zhou, M., Wang, C. S., & Richards, M. P. (2011). Stable carbon and nitrogen isotope evidence of human and pig diets at the Qinglongquan site, China. *Science China (Earth Sciences)*, *54*, 519–527.

Haas, J., & Creamer, W. (2006). Crucible of Andean civilization: the Peruvian coast from 3000 to 1800 BC. *Current Anthropology*, *47*, 745–775.

Haas, J., Creamer, W., Mesía, L. H., Goldstein, D., Reinhard, K., & Rodríguez, C. V. (2013). Evidence for maize (*Zea mays*) in the Late Archaic (3000–1800 B.C.) in the Norte Chico region of Peru. *Proceedings of the National Academy of Sciences USA*, *110*, 4945–4949.

Habgood, P. J., & Franklin, N. R. (2008). The revolution that didn't arrive: a review of Pleistocene Sahul. *Journal of Human Evolution*, *55*, 187–222.

Haile-Selassie, Y., Suwa, G., & White, T. D. (2004). Late Miocene teeth from Middle Awash, Ethiopia, and early hominid dental evolution. *Science*, *303*, 1503–1505.

Hallam, M.-J., Cubison, T., Dheansa, B., & Imray, C. (2010). Managing frostbite. *British Medical Journal*, *341*, 1151–1156.

Hamilton-Dyer, S. (2012). Camel, domestication of the. In N. A. Silberman (Ed.), *The Oxford Companion to Archaeology. Volume 1* (pp. 250–252). Second edition. Oxford: Oxford University Press.

Hamm, G., Mitchell, P., Arnold, L. G., Prideaux, G. J., Questiaux, D., Spooner, N. A., et al. (2016). Cultural innovation and megafauna interaction in the early settlement of arid Australia. *Nature*, *539*, 280–283.

Han, F., Bahain, J.-J., Deng, C., Boëda, É., Hou, Y., Wei, G., et al. (2017). The earliest evidence of hominid settlement in China: combined electron spin resonance and uranium series (ESR/U series) dating of mammalian fossil teeth from Longgupo cave. *Quaternary International*, *434*, 75–83.

Han, G., Ma, Z., Chen, N., Yang, J., & Chen, N. (2015). Coastal sea level projections with improved accounting for vertical land motion. *Scientific Reports*, *5*, 16085.

Hao, Q., Wang, L., Oldfield, F., & Guo, Z. (2015). Extra-long interglacial in northern hemisphere during MISs 15–13 arising from limited extent of Arctic ice sheets in glacial MIS 14. *Scientific Reports*, *5*, 12103.

Hardy, B. L., Moncel, M.-H., Daujeard, C., Fernandez, P., Béarez, P., Desclaux, E., et al. (2013). Impossible Neanderthals? Making string, throwing projectiles and catching small game during Marine Isotope Stage 4 (Abri du Maras, France). *Quaternary Science Reviews*, *82*, 23–40.

Hardy, K. (2008). Prehistoric string theory: how twisted fibres helped to shape the world. *Antiquity*, *82*, 271–280.

Harlan, J. R. (1967). A wild wheat harvest in Turkey. *Archaeology*, *20*, 197–201.

Harmand, S., Lewis, J. E., Feibel, C. S., Lepre, C. J., Prat, S., Lenoble, A., et al. (2015). 3.3-million-year-old stone tools from Lomekwi 3, West Turkana, Kenya. *Nature*, *521*, 310–315.

Harris, D. R. (2007). Agriculture, cultivation and domestication: exploring the conceptual framework. In T. Denham, J. Iriarte, & L. Vrydaghs (Eds.), *Rethinking Agriculture: Archaeological and Ethnoarchaeological Perspectives* (pp. 16–35). San Francisco, CA: Left Coast Press.

Hayden, B. D. (2000). On territorality and sedentism. *Current Anthropology*, *41*, 109–111.

Hayden, B. D. (2001). The dynamics of wealth and poverty in the transegalitarian societies of Southeast Asia. *Antiquity*, *75*, 571–581.

Hayden, B. D. (2009). The proof is in the pudding: feasting and the origins of domestication. *Current Anthropology*, *50*, 597–601.

Hayden, B. D. (2011). Rice: the first Asian luxury food? In G. W. Barker, & M. Janowski (Eds.),

Why Cultivate? Anthropological and Archaeological Approaches to Foraging-Farming Transitions in Southeast Asia (pp. 75–93). Cambridge: McDonald Institute for Archaeological Research.

Hayden, B. D., Canuel, N., & Shanse, J. (2013). What was brewing in the Natufian? An archaeological assessment of brewing technology in the Epipaleolithic. *Journal of Archaeological Method and Theory*, *20*, 102–150.

Headrick, D. R. (2009). *Technology: A World History*. Oxford: Oxford University Press.

Heckenberger, M. J., Petersen, J. B., King, F. B., & Basa, L. A. (1996). Fiber industries from the Boucher site: an early Woodland cemetery in northwestern Vermont. In J. B. Petersen (Ed.), *A Most Indispensable Art: Native Fiber Industries from Eastern North America* (pp. 50–72). Knoxville, TN: University of Tennessee Press.

Heeres, J. E. (1899). *The Part Borne by the Dutch in the Discovery of Australia 1606–1765 [Het Aadeel der Nederlanders in de Ontdekking van Australië 1606–1765]*. Leiden: E. J. Brill / London: Luzac & Co.

Heider, K. G. (1997). *Grand Valley Dani: Peaceful Warriors*. Third edition. San Francisco, CA: Wadsworth.

Heiser, C. B. (1976). *The Sunflower*. Norman, OK: University of Oklahoma Press.

Henn, B. M., Gignoux, C. R., Jobin, M., Granka, J. M., Macpherson, J. M., Kidd, J. M., et al. (2011). Hunter-gatherer genomic diversity suggests a southern African origin for modern humans. *Proceedings of the National Academy of Sciences USA*, *108*, 5154–5162.

Henshilwood, C. S., d'Errico, F., van Niekerk, K. L., Coquinot, Y., Jacobs, Z., Lauritzen, S.-E., et al. (2011). A 100,000-year-old ochre-processing workshop at Blombos Cave, South Africa. *Science*, *334*, 219–222.

Herbenick, D., Reece, M., Schick, V., & Sanders, S. A. (2014). Erect penile length and circumference dimensions of 1,661 sexually active men in the United States. *Journal of Sexual Medicine*, *11*, 93–101.

Herdt, G. (2006). *The Sambia: Ritual, Sexuality, and Change in Papua New Guinea*. Second edition. San Francisco, CA: Wadsworth.

Hershkowitz, M. (1977). Penile frostbite, an unforeseen hazard of jogging. *The New England Journal of Medicine*, *296*, 178.

Hes, L. (2008). Analysing the thermal properties of animal furs for the production of artifical furs. In A. Abbott, & M. Ellison (Eds.), *Biologically Inspired Textiles* (pp. 150–167). Cambridge: Woodhead.

Hes, L., & Williams, J. (2011). Laboratory measurement of thermo-physiological comfort. In G. Song (Ed.), *Improving Comfort in Clothing* (pp. 114–137). Cambridge: Woodhead.

Higham, C. F. (2017). First farmers in mainland Southeast Asia. *Journal of Indo-Pacific Archaeology*, *41*, 13–21.

Higham, T., Douka, K., Wood, R., Bronk Ramsey, C., Brock, F., Basell, L., et al. (2014). The timing and spatiotemporal patterning of Neanderthal disappearance. *Nature*, *512*, 306–309.

Higham, T., Jacobi, R., Julien, M., David, F., Basell, L., Wood, R., et al. (2010). Chronology of the Grotte du Renne (France) and implications for the context of ornaments and human remains within the Châtelperronian. *Proceedings of the National Academy of Sciences USA*, *107*, 20234–20239.

Hildebrand, E. A. (2007). A tale of two tuber crops: how attributes of enset and yams may have shaped prehistoric human-plant interactions in southwest Ethiopia. In T. Denham, J. Iriarte, & L. Vrydaghs (Eds.), *Rethinking Agriculture: Archaeological and Ethnoarchaeological Perspectives* (pp. 273–298). San Francisco, CA: Left Coast Press.

Hill, B. (2015). Reports of deaths in PNG as El Nino hits. *The Sydney Morning Herald, October 16* (No. 55,541), 21.

Hillman, G., Hedges, R., Moore, A., Colledge, S., & Pettitt, P. (2001). New evidence of late glacial cereal cultivation at Abu Hureyra on the Euphrates. *The Holocene*, *11*, 383–393.

Hiscock, P. (1996). Transformations of upper palaeolithic implements in the Dabba industry from Haua Fteah (Libya). *Antiquity*, *90*, 657–664.

Hiscock, P. (2008). *Archaeology of Ancient Australia*. New York: Routledge.

Hiscock, P. (2013). The human colonization of Australia. In P. Bellwood (Ed.), *The Global Prehistory of Human Migration* (pp. 55–60). Oxford: Wiley Blackwell.

Hlubik, S., Berna, F., Feibel, C., Braun, D., & Harris, J. W. (2017). Researching the nature of fire at 1.5 Mya on the site of FxJj20 AB, Koobi Fora, Kenya, using high-resolution spatial analysis and FTIR spectrometry. *Current Anthropology*, *58* (Suppl. S16), S243-S257.

Hocke, M., Strauss, L., & Nocker, W. (2000). Fire fighter garment with non textile insulation. In K. Kuklane, & I. Holmér (Eds.), *Ergonomics of Protective Clothing* (pp. 293–295). Stockholm: Arbetslivsinstitutet.

Hodder, I. (1990). *The Domestication of Europe: Structure and Contingency in Neolithic Societies*. Oxford: Blackwell.

Hodder, I. (2007). Çatalhöyük in the context of the Middle Eastern Neolithic. *Annual Review of Anthropology*, *36*, 105–120.

Hodder, I. (2012). *Entangled: An Archaeology of the Relationships between Humans and Things*. Oxford: Wiley-Blackwell.

Hodder, I. (2013). 2013 season review. *Çatal News*, *20*, 1.

Hodder, I. (2018). Things and the slow Neolithic: the Middle Eastern transformation. *Journal of Archaeological Method and Theory*, 25, 155–177.

Hoffecker, J. F. (2002). The Eastern Gravettian "Kostenki Culture" as an Arctic adaptation. *Anthropological Papers of the University of Alaska, NS*, *2*, 115–136.

Hoffecker, J. F. (2005). *A Prehistory of the North: Human Settlement of the Higher Latitudes*. New Brunswick, NJ: Rutgers University Press.

Hoffecker, J. F. (2015). Review. Stratum Plus: Культурная антропология и археология (Stratum Plus: Cultural Anthropology and Archaeology): the paleolithic issues. *PaleoAnthropology*, *2015*, 101–104.

Hoffecker, J. F. (2017). *Modern Humans: Their African Origin and Global Dispersal*. New York: Columbia University Press.

Hoffecker, J. F., Elias, S. A., O'Rourke, D. H., Scott, G. R., & Bigelow, N. H. (2016). Beringia and the global dispersal of modern humans. *Evolutionary Anthropology*, *25*, 64–78.

Hoffecker, J. F., & Hoffecker, I. T. (2018). The structural and functional complexity of hunter-gatherer technology. *Journal of Archaeological Method and Theory*, 25, 202–225.

Hoffecker, J. F., Holliday, V. T., Anikovich, M. V., Dudin, A. E., Platonova, N. I., Popov, V. V., et al. (2016). Kostenki 1 and the early Upper Paleolithic of Eastern Europe. *Journal of Archaeological Science: Reports*, 5, 307–326.

Hoffecker, J. F., Kuz'mina, I. E., Syromyatnikova, E. V., Anikovich, M. V., Sinitsyn, A. A., Popov, V. V., et al. (2010). Evidence for kill-butchery events of early Upper Paleolithic age at Kostenki, Russia. *Journal of Archaeological Science*, *37*, 1073–1089.

Hoffmann, D. L., Utrilla, P., Bea, M., Pike, A. W., García-Diez, M., Zilhão, J., et al. (2017). U-series dating of palaeolithic rock art at Fuente del Trucho (Aragón, Spain). *Quaternary International*, *432*, 50–58.

Holen, S. R., Deméré, T. A., Fisher, D. C., Fullagar, R., Paces, J. B., Jefferson, G. T., et al. (2017). A 130,000-year-old archaeological site in southern California, USA. *Nature*, *544*, 479–483.

Hollander, A. H. (1978). *Seeing Through Clothes*. Revised edition. New York: Viking Penguin.

Hope, G. S., & Haberle, S. G. (2005). The history of the human landscapes of New Guinea. In A. Pawley, R. Attenborough, J. Golson, & R. Hide (Eds.), *Papuan Pasts: Cultural, Linguistic and Biological Histories of Papuan-speaking Peoples*. Canberra: Pacific Linguistics, Research School of Pacific and Asian Studies, Australian National University.

Horsburgh, K. A., & Rhines, A. (2010). Genetic characterization of an archaeological sheep assemblage from South Africa's Western Cape. *Journal of Archaeological Science*, *37*, 2906–2910.

Hosfield, R. (2016). Walking in a winter wonderland? Strategies for Early and Middle Pleistocene survival in midlatitude Europe. *Current Anthropology*, 57, 653–682.

Hosfield, R. (2017). Clothing and hypothermia as limitations for midlatitude hominin settlement during the Pleistocene. A reply to Gilligan. *Current Anthropology*, *58*, 534.

Houghton, J. T. (2015). *Global Warming: The Complete Briefing*. Fifth edition. Cambridge: Cambridge University Press.

Hsu, P.-C., Song, A. Y., Catrysse, P. B., Liu, C., Peng, Y., Xie, J., et al. (2016). Radiative human body cooling by nanoporous polyethylene textile. *Science*, *353*, 1019–1023.

Hu, Y., Hu, S., Wang, W., Wu, X., Marshall, F. B., Chen, X., et al. (2014). Earliest evidence for commensal processes of cat domestication. *Proceedings of the National Academy of Sciences USA*, *111*, 116–120.

Huber, C., Leuenberger, M., Spahni, R., Flückiger, J., Schwander, J., Stocker, T. F., et al. (2006). Isotope calibrated Greenland temperature record over Marine Isotope Stage 3 and its relation to CH4. *Earth and Planetary Science Letters*, *243*, 504–519.

Hublin, J.-J. (2017). The last Neanderthal. *Proceedings of the National Academy of Sciences USA*, *114*, 10520–10522.

Hublin, J.-J., Ben-Ncer, A., Bailey, S. E., Freidline, S. E., Neubauer, S., Skinner, M. M., et al. (2017). New fossils from Jebel Irhoud, Morocco and the pan-African origin of Homo sapiens. *Nature*, *546*, 289–292.

Hublin, J.-J., & Roebroeks, W. (2009). Ebb and flow or regional extinctions? On the character of Neandertal occupation of northern environments. *Comptes Rendus Palevol*, *8*, 503–509.

Hui, S., & Jia, X. (2016). Envisioning fibre in the cultural heritage of Hangzhou, China. In J. Jefferies, D. W. Conroy, & H. Clark (Eds.), *The Handbook of Textile Culture* (pp. 335–348). London: Bloomsbury.

Humphries, L. T. (2010). Weaning behaviour in human evolution. *Seminars in Cell & Developmental Biology*, *21*, 453–461.

Hutchinson, R. L. (2014). Frostbite of the hand. *Journal of Hand Surgery (America)*, *39*, 1863–1868.

Imray, C. H., Grieve, A., Dhillon, S., & The Caudwell Xtreme Everest Research Group. (2009). Cold damage to the extremities: frostbite and non-freezing cold injuries. *Postgraduate Medical Journal*, *85*, 481–488.

Ingold, T. (2008). Bindings against boundaries: entanglements of life in an open world. *Environment and Planning A*, *40*, 1796–1810.

Iriarte, J. (2007). New perspectives on plant domestication and the development of agriculture in the New World. In T. Denham, J. Iriarte, & L. Vrydaghs (Eds.), *Rethinking Agriculture: Archaeological and Ethnoarchaeological Perspectives* (pp. 167–188). San Francisco, CA: Left Coast Press.

Irzmańska, E. (2016). The microclimate in protective fire fighter footwear: foot temperature and air temperature and relative humidity. *Autex Research Journal*, *16*, 75–79.

Isendahl, C. (2011). The domestication and early spread of manoic (*Manihot esculenta* Crantz): a brief synthesis. *Latin American Antiquity*, *22*, 452–468.

Jablonski, N. G. (2006). *Skin: A Natural History*. With a new preface by the author. Berkeley, CA: University of California Press, 2013.

Jablonski, N. G. (2010). The naked truth. *Scientific American*, *302*(2), 42–49.

Jablonski, N. G., & Chaplin, G. (2012). Human skin pigmentation as an adaptation to UV radiation. *Proceedings of the National Academy of Sciences USA*, *107*, 8962–8968.

Jackson, S. M., Groves, C. P., Fleming, P. J., Aplin, K. P., Eldridge, M. D., Gonzalez, A., et al. (2017). The wayward dog: is the Australian native dog or Dingo a distinct species? *Zootaxa*, *4317*, 201–224.

Jaubert, J., Verheyden, S., Genty, D., Soulier, M., Cheng, H., Blamart, D., et al. (2016). Early Neanderthal constructions deep in Bruniquel Cave in southwestern France. *Nature*, *534*, 111–115.

Jay, M. (2009). Breastfeeding and weaning behaviour in archaeological populations: evidence from the isotopic analysis of skeletal remains. *Childhood in the Past*, *2*, 163–178.

Johnson, A. L. (2014). Exploring adaptive variation among hunter-gatherers with Binford's frames of reference. *Journal of Archaeological Science*, *22*, 1–42.

Johnson, A. W., & Earle, T. (2000). *The Evolution of Human Societies: From Foraging Group to Agrarian State*. Stanford, CA: Stanford University Press.

Johnson, C. R., & McBrearty, S. (2010). 500,000 year old blades from the Kapthurin Formation, Kenya. *Journal of Human Evolution, 58*, 193–200.

Jolie, E. A., Lynch, T. F., Geib, P. R., & Adovasio, J. M. (2011). Cordage, textiles, and late Pleistocene peopling of the Andes. *Current Anthropology, 52*, 285–296.

Joordens, J. C., d'Errico, F., Wesselingh, F. P., Munro, S., de Vos, J., Wallinga, J., et al. (2015). *Homo erectus* at Trinil on Java used shells for tool production and engraving. *Nature, 518*, 228–231.

Josephs, L. (2015). How children learn about sex: a cross-species and cross-cultural analysis. *Archives of Sexual Behavior, 44*, 1059–1069.

Jouzel, J., Masson-Delmotte, V., Cattani, O., Dreyfus, G., Falourd, S., Hoffmann, G., et al. (2007). Orbital and millennial Antarctic climate variability over the past 800,000 years. *Science, 317*, 793–796.

Ju, J., Shi, Z., Deng, N., Liang, Y., Kang, W., & Cheng, B. (2017). Designing waterproof breathable material with moisture unidirectional transport characteristics based on a TPU/TBAC tree-like and TPU nanofiber double-layer membrane fabricated by electrospinning. *RSC Advances, 7*, 32155–32163.

Julien, M.-A., Hardy, B., Stahlschmidt, M., Urban, B., Serangeli, J., & Conard, N. J. (2015). Characterizing the lower paleolithic bone industry from Schöningen 12 II: a multi-proxy study. *Journal of Human Evolution, 89*, 264–286.

Jütte, R. (2000). *A History of the Senses: From Antiquity to Cyberspace (Geschichte der Sinne: Von der Antike bis zum Cyberspace)*. Translated by James Lynn. Boston, MA: Polity Press, 2005.

Kageyama, M., Laîné, A., Abe-Ouchi, A., Braconnot, P., Cortijo, E., Crucifix, M., et al. (2006). Last Glacial Maximum temperatures over the North Atlantic, Europe and western Siberia: a comparison between PMIP models, MARGO sea-surface temperatures and pollen-based reconstructions. *Quaternary Science Reviews, 25*, 2082–2102.

Kaiser, S. B. (2012). *Fashion and Cultural Studies*. London: Berg.

Kamel, F. (2015). Bilum meri - bilum woman. In N. Wilson (Ed.), *Plumes and Pearlshells: Art of the New Guinea Highlands* (pp. 23–25). Sydney: Art Gallery of New South Wales.

Keen, I. (2004). *Aboriginal Economy and Society: Australia at the Threshold of Colonisation*. Melbourne: Oxford University Press.

Kellner, C. M., & Schoeninger, M. J. (2008). Wari's imperial influence on local Nasca diet: the stable isotope evidence. *Journal of Anthropological Archaeology, 27*, 226–243.

Kelly, R. L. (2013). *The Lifeways of Hunter-Gatherers: The Foraging Spectrum*. Second edition. Cambridge: Cambridge University Press.

Kennedy, G. E. (2005). From the ape's dilemma to the weanling's dilemma: early weaning and its evolutionary context. *Journal of Human Evolution, 48*, 123–145.

Kennedy, J. (2009a). Bananas and people in the homeland of genus *Musa*: not just pretty fruit. *Ethnobotany Research and Applications, 7*, 179–197.

Kennedy, J. (2009b). Bananas: towards a revised prehistory. In A. S. Fairbairn, & E. Weiss (Eds.), *From Foragers to Farmers: Papers in Honour of Gordon C. Hillman* (pp. 190–204). Oxford: Oxbow Books.

Kennedy, J. (2012). Agricultural systems in the tropical forest: a critique framed by tree crops of Papua New Guinea. *Quaternary International, 249*, 140–150.

Keoke, E. D., & Porterfield, K. M. (2002). *Encyclopedia of American Indian Contributions to the World: 15,000 Years of Inventions and Innovations*. New York: Checkmark Books.

Kislev, M. E., Weiss, E., & Hartmann, A. (2004). Impetus for sowing and the beginnings of agriculture: ground collecting of wild cereals. *Proceedings of the National Academy of Sciences USA, 101*, 2692–2695.

Kistler, L., Montenegro, Á., Smith, B. D., Gifford, J. A., Green, R. E., Newsom, L. A., et al. (2014). Transoceanic drift and the domestication of African bottle gourds in the Americas. *Proceedings of the National Academy of Sciences USA, 111*, 2937–2941.

Kittler, R., Kayser, M., & Stoneking, M. (2004). Erratum. Molecular evolution of *Pediculus humanus* and the origin of clothing. *Current Biology*, *14*, 2309.

Klein, R. G. (1973). *Ice-Age Hunters of the Ukraine*. Third edition. Chicago: University of Chicago Press.

Klein, R. G. (2009). *The Human Career: Human Biological and Cultural Origins*. Third edition. Chicago, IL: University of Chicago Press.

Klein, R. G., & Edgar, B. (2002). *The Dawn of Human Culture*. New York: John Wiley.

Kleiner, F. S. (2016). *Gardner's Art Through The Ages. Book F: Non-Western Art Since 1300*. Fifteenth edition. Boston, MA: Cengage.

Komisaruk, B. R., Wise, N., Frangos, E., Liu, W.-C., Allen, K., & Brody, S. (2011). Women's clitoris, vagina, and cervix mapped on the sensory cortex: fMRI evidence. *Journal of Sexual Medicine*, *8*, 2822–2830.

Koonin, E. V. (2016). Splendor and misery of adaptation, or the importance of neutral null for understanding evolution. *BMC Biology*, *14*, 114.

Kozen, F. H., & Netravali, A. N. (2015). Cellulose fibers: a brief review. In A. N. Netravali, & C. M. Pastore (Eds.), *Sustainable Composites: Fibers, Resins and Applications*. Lancaster, PA: DEStech.

Krause, J., Fu, Q., Good, J. M., Viola, B., Shunkov, M. V., Derevianko, A. P., et al. (2010). The complete mitochondrial DNA genome of an unknown hominin from southern Siberia. *Nature*, *464*, 894–897.

Kriger, C. E. (2009). 'Guinea cloth': production and consumption of cotton textiles in West Africa before and during the Atlantic slave trade. In G. Riello, & P. Parthasarathi (Eds.), *The Spinning World: A Global History of Cotton Textiles, 1200–1850* (pp. 105–126). Oxford: Oxford University Press.

Kuhn, S. L. (2013). Questions of complexity and scale in explantions for cultural transitions in the Pleistocene: a case study from the early upper paleolithic. *Journal of Archaeological Method and Theory*, *20*, 194–211.

Kuhn, S. L., Stiner, M. C., Güleç, E., Özer, I., Yılmaz, H., Baykara, I., et al. (2009). The early Upper Paleolithic occupations at Üçağızlı Cave (Hatay, Turkey). *Journal of Human Evolution*, *56*, 87–113.

Kurzweil, R. (2005). *The Singularity is Near: When Humans Transcend Biology*. New York: Penguin Books.

Kuzmin, Y. V. (2007). Chronological framework of the Siberian paleolithic: recent achievements and future directions. *Radiocarbon*, *49*, 757–766.

Kuzmin, Y. V. (2010). Extinction of the woolly mammoth (*Mammuthus primigenius*) and woolly rhinoceros (*Coelodonta antiquitatis*) in Eurasia: review of chronological and environmental issues. *Boreas*, *39*, 247–261.

Kuzmin, Y. V., Burr, G. S., Jull, A. J., & Sulerzhitsky, L. D. (2004). AMS 14C age of the Upper Palaeolithic skeletons from Sungir site, Central Russian Plain. *Nuclear Instruments and Methods in Physics Research B*, *223–224*, 731–734.

Kuzmin, Y. V., Keally, C. T., Jull, A. J., Burr, G. S., & Klyuev, N. A. (2012). The earliest surviving textiles in East Asia from Chertovy Vorota Cave, Primorye Province, Russian Far East. *Antiquity*, *86*, 325–337.

Kuzmin, Y. V., & Keates, S. G. (2004). Comment on "Colonization of northern Eurasia by modern humans: radiocarbon chronology and environment" by P. M. Dolukhanov, A. M. Shukurov, P. E. Tasasov and G. I. Zaitseva. Journal of Archaeological Science 29, 593–606 (2002). *Journal of Archaeological Science*, *31*, 141–143.

Kuzmin, Y. V., & Keates, S. G. (2018). Siberia and neighboring regions in the Last Glacial Maximum: did people occupy northern Eurasia at that time? *Archaeological and Anthropological Sciences*, 10, 111–124.

Kuzmin, Y. V., van der Plicht, J., & Sulerzhitsky, L. D. (2014). Puzzling radiocarbon dates for the Upper Paleolithic site of Sungir (Central Russian Plain). *Radiocarbon*, *56*, 451–459.

Kvavadze, E., Bar-Yosef, O., Belfer-Cohen, A., Boaretto, E., Jakeli, N., Matskevich, Z., et al. (2009). 30,000-year-old wild flax fibers. *Science*, *325*, 1359.

Kwak, S. (2017). *The Hunting Farmers: Understanding Ancient Human Subsistence in the Central Part of the Korean Peninsula during the Late Holocene*. Oxford: Archaeopress.

Kwon, A., Kato, M., Kawamura, H., Yanai, Y., & Tokura, H. (1998). Physiological significance of hydrophilic and hydrophobic textile materials during intermittent exercise in humans under the influence of warm ambient temperature with and without wind. *European Journal of Applied Physiology and Occupational Physiology*, *78*, 487–493.

Labarca, R., & Gallardo, F. (2015). The domestic camelids (Cetartiodactyla: Camelidae) from the Middle Formative cemetery of Topater 1 (Atacama Desert, northern Chile): osteometric and palaeopathological evidence of cargo animals. *International Journal of Osteoarchaeology*, *25*, 61–73.

Labbok, M. H. (2015). Postpartum sexuality and the Lactational Amenorrhea Method for contraception. *Clinical Obstetrics & Gynecology*, *58*, 915–927.

Ladizinsky, G., & Abbo, S. (2015). *The Search for Wild Relatives of Cool Season Legumes*. Cham: Springer.

Lambeck, K., & Chappell, J. (2001). Sea level change through the last glacial cycle. *Science*, *292*, 679–686.

Lambert, P. M., Gagnon, C. M., Billman, B. R., Katzenberg, M. A., Carcelén, J., & Tykot, R. H. (2012). Bone chemistry at Cerro Orega: a stable isotope perspective on the development of a regional economy in the Moche Valley, Peru during the Early Intermediate period. *Latin American Antiquity*, *23*, 144–166.

Lanehart, R. E., Tykot, R. H., Underhill, A. P., Luan, F., Yu, H., Fang, H., et al. (2011). Dietary adaptation during the Longshan period in China: stable isotope analyses at Liangchengzhen (southeastern Shandong). *Journal of Archaeological Science*, *38*, 2171–2181.

Langgut, D., Yahalom-Mack, N., Lev-Yadun, S., Kremer, E., Ullman, M., & Davidovich, U. (2016). The earliest Near Eastern wooden spinning implements. *Antiquity*, *90*, 973–990.

Langley, M. C., O'Connor, S., & Aplin, K. (2016). A >46,000-year-old kangaroo bone implement from Carpenter's Gap 1 (Kimberley, northwest Australia). *Quaternary Science Reviews*, *154*, 199–213.

Larson, G., & Fuller, D. Q. (2014). The evolution of animal domestication. *Annual Review of Ecology, Evolution, and Systematics*, *45*, 115–136.

Larson, G., Karlsson, E. K., Perri, A., Webster, M., Ho, S. Y., Peters, J., et al. (2012). Rethinking dog domestication by integrating genetics, archaeology, and biogeography. *Proceedings of the National Academy of Sciences USA*, *109*, 8878–8883.

Larson, G., Liu, R., Zhao, X., Yuan, J., Fuller, D., Barton, L., et al. (2010). Patterns of East Asian pig domestication, migration, and turnover revealed by modern and ancient DNA. *Proceedings of the National Academy of Sciences USA*, *107*, 7686–7691.

Lasher, G. E., Axford, Y., McFarlin, J. M., Kelly, M. A., Osterberg, E. C., & Berkelhammer, M. B. (2017). Holocene temperatures and isotopes of precipitation in northwest Greenland recorded in lacustrine organic materials. *Quaternary Science Reviews*, *170*, 45–55.

Lastória, J. C., & de Abreu, M. A. (2014). Leprosy: review of the epidemiological, clinical, and etiopathogenic aspects - Part 1. *Anais Brasileiros de Dermatologia*, *89*, 205–218.

Laurito, R., Lemorini, C., & Perilli, A. (2014). Making textiles at Arslantepe, Turkey, in the 4th and 3rd Millennia BC. Archaeological data and experimantal archaeology. In C. Breniquet, & C. Michel (Eds.), *Wool Economy in the Ancient Near East and the Aegean: From the Beginnings of Sheep Husbandry to Institutional Textile Industry* (pp. 151–168). Oxford: Oxbow.

Lawrence, R. A., & Lawrence, R. M. (2016). *Breastfeeding: A Guide for the Medical Profession*. Eighth edition. Philadelphia, PA: Elsevier.

Leahy, M. J. (1991). *Explorations into Highland New Guinea, 1930–1935*. Edited by Douglas E. Jones. Tuscaloosa, AL: University of Alabama Press.

Lecavalier, B. S., Fisher, D. A., Milne, G. A., Vinther, B. M., Tarasov, L., Huybrechts, P., et al. (2017). High Arctic Holocene temperature record from the Agassiz ice cap and Greenland ice sheet evolution. *Proceedings of the National Academy of Sciences USA*, *114*, 5952–5957.

Lee, R. B. (1979). *The !Kung San: Men, Women, and Work in a Foraging Society*. Cambridge: Cambridge University Press.

Lemorini, C., Stiner, M. C., Gopher, A., Shimelmitz, R., & Barkai, R. (2006). Use-wear analysis of an Amudian laminar assemblage from the Acheuleo-Yabrudian of Qesem Cave, Israel. *Journal of Archaeological Science, 33*, 921–934.

Levin, R. J. (2006). The breast/nipple/areola complex and human sexuality. *Sexual and Relationship Therapy, 21*, 237–249.

Levy, J. (2017). Sartorial vestments in the southern Levant: headwear, footwear, girdles, sashes and shrouds, 15,000–5,900 BP cal. In S. Gonen, & A. Ronen (Eds.), *Suyanggae and Her Neighbours in Haifa, Israel* (pp. 60–79). Oxford: Archaeopress.

Levy, J., & Gilead, I. (2012). Spinning in the 5th millennium in the southern Levant: aspects of the textile economy. *Paléorient, 38*(1–2), 127–139.

Lewis-Harris, J. A. (2010). Textiles and dress of the Motu Koita people. In M. Maynard (Ed.), *Berg Encyclopedia of World Dress and Fashion. Volume 7: Australia, New Zealand, and the Pacific Islands* (pp. 460–464). Oxford: Berg.

Li, D., Wang, W., Tian, F., Liao, W., & Bae, C. J. (2014). The oldest bark cloth beater in southern China (Dingmo, Bubing basin, Guangxi). *Quaternary International, 354*, 184–189.

Li, F., Chen, F.-y., & Gao, X. (2014). "Modern behaviors" of ancient populations at Shuidonggou Locality 2 and their implications. *Quaternary International, 347*, 66–73.

Li, Y. (2005). Perceptions of temperature, moisture and comfort in clothing during environmental transients. *Ergonomics, 48*, 234–248.

Li, Z.-Y., Wu, X.-J., Zhou, L.-P., Liu, W., Gao, X., Nian, X.-M., et al. (2017). Late Pleistocene archaic human crania from Xuchang, China. *Science, 355*, 969–972.

Liao, J., & Yang, X. (2016). Study on the evolution of grass cloth. *Asian Social Science, 12*(6), 109–115.

Light, J. E., & Reed, D. L. (2009). Multigene analysis of phylogenetic relationships and divergence times of primate sucking lice (Phthiraptera: Anoplura). *Molecular Phylogenetics and Evolution, 50*, 376–390.

Lightfoot, K. G., & Parrish, O. (2009). *California Indians and Their Environment: An Introduction.* Berkeley, CA: University of California Press.

Lim, C., & Duflou, J. (2008). Hypothermia fatalities in a temperate climate: Sydney, Australia. *Pathology, 40*, 46–51.

Linseele, V., Van Neer, W., Thys, S., Phillipps, R., Cappers, R., Wendrich, W., et al. (2014). New archaeozoological data from the Fayum "Neolithic" with a critical assessment of the evidence for early stock keeping in Egypt. *PLoS ONE, 9*, e108517.

Liu, L., Bestel, S., Shi, J., Song, Y., & Chen, X. (2013). Paleolithic human exploitation of plant foods during the last glacial maximum in North China. *Proceedings of the National Academy of Sciences USA, 110*, 5380–5385.

Liu, L., & Chen, X. (2012). *The Archaeology of China: From the Late Paleolithic to the Early Bronze Age*. New York: Cambridge University Press.

Liu, W., Martinón-Torres, M., Cai, Y.-j., Xing, S., Tong, H.-w., Pei, S.-w., et al. (2015). The earliest unequivocally modern humans in southern China. *Nature, 526*, 696–700.

Liu, Z., Zhu, J., Rosenthal, Y., Zhang, X., Otto-Bliesner, B. L., Timmermann, A., et al. (2014). The Holocene temperature conundrum. *Proceedings of the National Academy of Sciences USA, 111*, E3501-E3505.

Long, H., Shen, J., Chen, J., Tsukamoto, S., Yang, L., Cheng, H., et al. (2017). Holocene moisture variations over the arid central Asia revealed by a comprehensive sand-dune record from the central Tian Shan, NW China. *Quaternary Science Reviews, 174*, 13–32.

López-García, J. M., Blain, H. -A., Bennàsar, M., & Daura, J. (2013). Heinrich event 4 characterized by terrestrial proxies in southwestern Europe. *Climate of the Past, 9*, 1053–1064.

López-Uribe, M. M., Cane, J. H., Minckley, R. L., & Danforth, B. N. (2016). Crop domestication facilitated rapid geographical expansion of a specialist pollinator, the squash bee *Peponapis pruinosa*. *Proceedings of the Royal Society B, 283*, 20160443.

Loren, D. D. (2010). *The Archaeology of Clothing and Bodily Adornment in Colonial America*. Gainesville, FL: University Press of Florida.

Lösch, S., Grupe, G., & Peters, J. (2006). Stable isotopes and dietary adaptations in humans and animals at Pre-Pottery Neolithic Nevalı Çori, southeast Anatolia. *American Journal of Physical Anthropology*, *131*, 181–193.

Lothrup, S. K. (1928). *The Indians of Tierra del Fuego*. New York: Museum of the American Indian. Reprint. Buenos Aires: Zagier & Urrity, 2002.

Lourandos, H. (1997). *Continent of Hunter-Gatherers: New Perspectives in Australian Prehistory*. Cambridge: Cambridge University Press.

Lovejoy, C. O., Suwa, G., Spurlock, L., Asfaw, B., & White, T. D. (2009). The pelvis and femur of *Ardipithecus ramidus*: the emergence of upright walking. *Science*, *326*, 71.

Lu, H., Zhang, J., Liu, K.-b., Wu, N., Li, Y., Zhou, K., et al. (2009). Earliest domestication of common millet (*Panicum miliaceum*) in East Asia extended to 10,000 years ago. *Proceedings of the National Academy of Sciences USA*, *106*, 7367–7372.

Lubbock, J. (1890). *Pre-Historic Times, as Illustrated by Ancient Remains and the Manners and Customs of Modern Savages*. Fifth edition. New York: D. Appleton and Company.

Lukas, D., & Clutton-Brock, T. H. (2013). The evolution of social monogamy in mammals. *Science*, *341*, 526–530.

Lüpold, S., Manier, M. K., Puniamoorthy, N., Schoff, C., Starmer, W. T., Luepold, S. H., et al. (2016). How sexual selection can drive the evolution of costly sperm ornamentation. *Nature*, *533*, 535–538.

Magee, P. (2014). *The Archaeology of Prehistoric Arabia: Adaptation and Social Formation from the Neolithic to the Iron Age*. New York: Cambridge University Press.

Magill, C. R., Ashley, G. M., Domínguez-Rodrigo, M., & Freeman, K. H. (2016). Dietary options and behavior suggested by plant biomarker evidence in an early human habitat. *Proceedings of the National Academy of Sciences USA*, *113*, 2874–2879.

Magnavita, S. (2008). The oldest textiles from sub-Saharan West Africa: woolen facts from Kissi, Burkina Faso. *Journal of African Archaeology*, *6*, 243–257.

Makarewicz, C. A. (2013). More than meat: diversity in caprine harvesting strategies and the emergence of complex production systems during the Late Pre-Pottery Neolithic B. *Levant*, *45*, 236–261.

Makarewicz, C. A., & Tuross, N. (2012). Finding fodder and tracking transhumance: isotopic detection of goat domestication processes in the Near East. *Current Anthropology*, *53*, 495–505.

Mangerud, J., & Svendsen, I. (2018). The Holocene Thermal Maximum around Svalbard, Arctic North Atlantic; molluscs show early and exceptional warmth. *The Holocene*, 28, 65–83.

Marciniak, A. (2011). The Secondary Products Revolution: empirical evidence and its current zooarchaeological critique. *Journal of World Prehistory*, *24*, 117–130.

Marcott, S. A., Clark, P. U., Padman, L., Klinkhammer, G. P., Springer, S. R., Liu, Z., et al. (2011). Ice-shelf collapse from subsurface warming as a trigger for Heinrich events. *Proceedings of the National Academy of Sciences USA*, *108*, 13415–13419.

Marlow, J. R., Lange, C. B., Wefer, G., & Rosell-Melé, A. (2000). Upwelling intensification as part of the Pliocene-Pleistocene climate transition. *Science*, *290*, 2288–2291.

Marshall, F. (2007). African pastoral perspectives on domestication of the donkey: a first synthesis. In T. Denham, J. Iriarte, & L. Vrydaghs (Eds.), *Rethinking Agriculture: Archaeological and Ethnoarchaeological Perspectives* (pp. 371–407). San Francisco, CA: Left Coast Press.

Marshall, Y. (2006). Introduction: adopting a sedentary lifeway. *World Archaeology*, *38*, 153–163.

Marwick, B., Van Vlack, H. G., Conrad, C., Shoocongdej, R., Thongcharoenchaikit, C., & Kwak, S. (2017). Adaptations to sea level change and transitions to agriculture at Khao Toh Chong rockshelter, peninsular Thailand. *Journal of Archaeological Science*, *77*, 94–108.

Matika, O., Bishop, S. C., Pong-Wong, R., Riggio, V., & Headon, D. J. (2013). Genetic factors controlling wool shedding in a composite Easycare sheep flock. *Animal Genetics, 44*, 742–749.

Matsui, A., & Kanehara, M. (2006). The question of prehistoric plant husbandry during the Jomon period in Japan. *World Archaeology, 38*, 259–273.

Matusiak, M., & Sikorski, K. (2011). Influence of the structure of woven fabrics on their thermal insulation properties. *Fibres and Textiles in Eastern Europe, 19*(5), 46–53.

McBrearty, S. (2007). Down with the revolution. In P. Mellars, K. Boyle, O. Bar-Yosef, & C. Stringer (Eds.), *Rethinking the Human Revolution: New Behavioural and Biological Perspectives on the Origin and Dispersal of Modern Humans* (pp. 133–151). Cambridge: McDonald Institute for Archaeological Research.

McBrearty, S., & Brooks, A. S. (2000). The revolution that wasn't: a new interpretation of the origin of modern human behavior. *Journal of Human Evolution, 39*, 453–563.

McDonald, J. (2008). *Dreamtime Superhighway: Sydney Basin Rock Art and Prehistoric Information Exchange*. Canberra: ANU Press.

McDonald, J., & Berry, M. (2017). Murujuga, northwestern Australia: when arid hunter-gatherers became coastal foragers. *Journal of Island and Coastal Archaeology, 12*, 24–43.

McGee, D., Broecker, W. S., & Winckler, G. (2010). Gustiness: the driver of glacial dustiness? *Quaternary Science Reviews, 29*, 2340–2350.

McKerracher, L., Collard, M., Altman, R. M., Sellen, D., & Nepomnaschy, P. A. (2017). Energy-related influences on variation in breastfeeding duration among indigenous Maya women from Guatemala. *American Journal of Physical Anthropology, 162*, 616–626.

McNabb, J., & Fluck, H. (2006). Comment. The Lower/Middle Paleolithic periodization in Western Europe: an evaluation, Gillaine F. Monnier. *Current Anthropology, 47*, 731–732.

McNamara, K. J. (2002). Sequential hypermorphosis: stretching ontogeny to the limit. In N. Minugh-Purvis, & K. J. McNamara (Eds.), *Human Evolution Through Developmental Change* (pp. 102–121). Baltimore, MD: John Hopkins University Press.

McNeilly, A. S. (2001). Lactational control of reproduction. *Reproduction, Fertility and Development, 13*, 583–590.

McNiven, I. J., Crouch, J., Richards, T., Sniderman, K., Dolby, N., & Gunditj Mirring Traditional Owners Aboriginal Corp. (2015). Phased redevelopment of an ancient Gunditjmara fish trap over the past 800 years: Muldoons Trap Complex, Lake Condah, southwestern Victoria. *Australian Archaeology, 81*, 44–58.

Mel, M. A. (2010). Bilas: dressing the body in Papua New Guinea. In M. Maynard (Ed.), *Berg Encyclopedia of World Dress and Fashion. Volume 7: Australia, New Zealand, and the Pacific Islands* (pp. 415–459). Oxford: Berg.

Mellars, P. (2015). Some key issues in the emergence and diversity of "modern" human behavior. In Y. Kaifu, M. Izuho, T. Goebel, H. Sato, & A. Ono (Eds.), *Emergence and Diversity of Modern Human Behavior in Paleolithic Asia* (pp. 3–22). College Station, TX: Texas A&M University Press.

Mellars, P., Boyle, K., Bar-Yosef, O., & Stringer, C. (Eds.). (2007). *Rethinking the Human Revolution: New Behavioural and Biological Perspectives on the Origin and Dispersal of Modern Humans*. Cambridge: McDonald Institute for Archaeological Research.

Mengoni Goñalons, G. L., & Yacobaccio, H. D. (2006). The domestication of South American camelids: a view from the south-central Andes. In M. A. Zeder, D. G. Bradley, E. Emshwiller, & B. D. Smith (Eds.), *Documenting Domestication: New Genetic and Archaeological Paradigms* (pp. 228–244). Berkeley, CA: University of California Press.

Menviel, L., Timmermann, A., Friedrich, T., & England, M. H. (2013). Hindcasting the continuum of Dansgaard-Oeschger variability: mechanisms, patterns and timing. *Climate of the Past, 10*, 63–77.

Merrill, W. L., Hard, R. J., Mabry, J. B., Fritz, G. J., Adams, K. R., Roney, J. R., et al.

(2009). The diffusion of maize to the southwestern United States and its impact. *Proceedings of the National Academy of Sciences USA, 106*, 21019–21026.

Meyer, M., Kircher, M., Gansauge, M.-T., Li, H., Racimo, F., Mallick, S., et al. (2012). A high-coverage genome sequence from an archaic Denisovan individual. *Science, 338*, 222–226.

Mgeladze, A., Lordkipanidze, D., Moncel, M.-H., Despriee, J., Chagelishvili, R., Nioradze, M., et al. (2011). Hominin occupations at the Dmanisi site, Georgia, southern Caucasus: raw materials and technical behaviours of Europe's first hominins. *Journal of Human Evolution, 60*, 571–596.

Miller, A. V., Hanks, B. K., Judd, M., Epimakhov, A., & Razhev, D. (2017). Weaning practices among pastoralists: new evidence of infant feeding patterns from Bronze Age Eurasia. *American Journal of Physical Anthropology, 162*, 409–422.

Mishra, S., Chauhan, N., & Singhvi, A. K. (2013). Continuity of microblade technology in the Indian subcontinent since 45 ka: implications for the dispersal of modern humans. *PLoS ONE, 8*, e69280.

Mitchell, G., van Sittert, S., Roberts, D., & Mitchell, D. (2017). Body surface area and thermoregulation in giraffes. *Journal of Arid Environments, 145*, 35–42.

Mohapatra, D., Mishra, S., & Sutar, N. (2010). Banana and its by-product utilization: an overview. *Journal of Scientific and Industrial Research, 69*, 323–329.

Mohr, W. J., Jenabzadeh, K., & Ahrenholz, D. H. (2009). Cold injury. *Hand Clinics, 25*, 481–496.

Moncel, M.-H., Ashton, N., Lamotte, A., Tuffreau, A., Cliquet, D., & Despriée, J. (2015). The early Acheulian of north-western Europe. *Journal of Anthropological Archaeology, 40*, 302–331.

Moncel, M.-H., Landais, A., Lebreton, V., Combourieu-Nebout, N., Nomade, S., & Bazin, L. (in press). Linking environmental changes with human occupations between 900 and 400 ka in western Europe. *Quaternary International.*

Monnier, G. F. (2006). The Lower/Middle Paleolithic periodization in Western Europe: an evaluation. *Current Anthropology, 47*, 709–744.

Monnier, G. F., & Missal, K. (2014). Another Mousterian debate? Bordian facies, chaîne opératoire technocomplexes, and patterns of lithic variability in the western European Middle and Upper Pleistocene. *Quaternary International, 350*, 59–83.

Morley, I. (2007). New questions of old hands: outlines of human representation in the palaeolithic. In C. Renfrew, & I. Morley (Eds.), *Image and Imagination: A Global Prehistory of Figurative Representation* (pp. 69–81). Cambridge: McDonald Institute for Archaeological Research.

Moro Abadía, O., & Nowell, A. (2015). Palaeolithic personal ornaments: historical development and epistemological challenges. *Journal of Archaeological Method and Theory, 22*, 952–979.

Morwood, M. J., Soejono, R. P., Roberts, R. G., Sutikna, T., Turney, C. S., Westaway, K. E., et al. (2004). Archaeology and age of a new hominin from Flores in eastern Indonesia. *Nature, 431*, 1087–1091.

Moseley, M. E. (2006). Preceramic civilization in coastal Peru: revolutionary data, pioneering interpretations. *Review of Archaeology, 27*, 72–81.

Moulherat, C., Tengberg, M., Haquet, J.-F., & Mille, B. (2002). First evidence of cotton at Neolithic Mehrgarh, Pakistan: analysis of mineralized fibres from a copper bead. *Journal of Archaeological Science, 29*, 1393–1401.

Mueller, N. G., Fritz, G. J., Patton, P., Carmody, S., & Horton, E. T. (2017). Growing the lost crops of eastern North America's original agricultural system. *Nature Plants, 3*, 17092.

Muhammad. (c. 645 CE). *The Qur'an.* Translated by M. A. S. Abdel Haleem. Corrected edition. Oxford: Oxford University Press, 2010.

Mukerjee, M. (2003). *The Land of Naked People: Encounters with Stone Age Islanders.* New York: Houghton Mifflin.

Mukhopadhyay, A., & Midha, V. K. (2016). Waterproof breathable fabrics. In A. R.

Horrocks, & S. C. Anand (Eds.), *Handbook of Technical Textiles, Volume 2: Technical Textile Applications* (pp. 27–55). Second edition. Cambridge: Woodhead.

Mulready-Ward, C., & Hackett, M. (2014). Perception and attitudes: breastfeeding in public in New York City. *Journal of Human Lactation, 30*, 195–200.

Mulvaney, J. (2012). Human cognition: the Australian evidence. *Antiquity, 86*, 915–921.

Mulvaney, J., & Kamminga, J. (1999). *Prehistory of Australia*. Sydney: Allen & Unwin.

Murphy, W. A., zur Nedden, D., Gostner, P., Knapp, R., Recheis, W., & Seidler, H. (2003). The Iceman: discovery and imaging. *Radiology, 226*, 614–629.

Murray, M. A. (2009). Questions of continuity: fodder and fuel use in Bronze Age Egypt. In A. S. Fairbairn, & E. Weiss (Eds.), *From Foragers to Farmers: Papers in Honour of Gordon C. Hillman* (pp. 254–267). Oxford: Oxbow Books.

Mussi, M., Altamura, F., Bonnefille, R., De Rita, D., & Melis, R. T. (2016). The environment of the Ethiopian highlands at the Mid Pleistocene Transition: fauna, flora and hominins in the 850–700 ka sequence of Gombore II (Melka Kunture). *Quaternary Science Reviews, 149*, 259–268.

Myles, S., Boyko, A. R., Owens, C. L., Brown, P. J., Grassi, F., Aradhya, M., et al. (2011). Genetic structure and domestication history of the grape. *Proceedings of the National Academy of Sciences USA, 108*, 3530–3535.

Nadel, D., Danin, A., Werker, E., Schick, T., Kislev, M. E., & Stewart, K. (1994). 19,000-year-old twisted fibres from Ohalo II. *Current Anthropology, 35*, 451–458.

Naebe, M., Yu, Y., McGregor, B. A., Tester, D., & Wang, X. (2013). The effect of humidity and temperature on Wool ComfortMeter assessment of single jersey wool fabrics. *Textile Research Journal, 83*, 83–89.

Nalawade-Chavan, S., McCullagh, J., & Hedges, R. (2014). New hydroxyproline radiocarbon dates from Sungir, Russia, confirm early mid Upper Palaeolithic burials in Eurasia. *PLoS ONE, 9*, e76896.

Naumann, N. (2000). *Japanese Prehistory: The Material and Spiritual Culture of the Jōmon Period*. Wiesbaden: Harrassowitz.

Naveh, D., & Bird-David, N. (2014). How persons become things: economic and epistemological changes among Nayaka hunter-gatherers. *Journal of the Royal Anthropological Institute, 20*, 74–92.

Naya, D. E., Naya, H., & Lessa, E. P. (2016). Brain size and thermoregulation during the evolution of the genus *Homo*. *Comparative Biochemistry and Physiology, Part A, 191*, 66–73.

Nelson, S. M. (2004). *Gender in Archaeology: Analyzing Power and Prestige*. Second edition. Washington, DC: AltaMira Press.

Neumann, K., & Hildebrand, E. (2009). Early banana in Africa: the state of the art. *Ethnobotany Research and Applications, 7*, 353–362.

Nicholson, C. M. (2017). Eemian paleoclimate zones and Neandethal landscape-use: a GIS model of settlement patterning during the last interglacial. *Quaternary International, 438* (Part B), 144–157.

O'Connell, J. F., & Allen, J. (2007). Pre-LGM Sahul (Pleistocene Australia-New Guinea) and the archaeology of early modern humans. In P. Mellars, K. Boyle, O. Bar-Yosef, & C. Stringer (Eds.), *Rethinking the Human Revolution: New Behavioural and Biological Perspectives on the Origin and Dispersal of Modern Humans* (pp. 395–410). Cambridge: McDonald Institute for Archaeological Research.

O'Connor, S. (2015). Crossing the Wallace Line: the maritime skills of the earliest colonists in the Wallacean Archipelago. In Y. Kaifu, M. Izuho, T. Goebel, H. Sato, & A. Ono (Eds.), *Emergence and Diversity of Modern Human Behavior in Paleolithic Asia* (pp. 214–224). College Station, TX: Texas A&M University Press.

O'Connor, S., Barham, A., Aplin, K., Dobney, K., Fairbairn, A., & Richards, M. (2011). The power of paradigms: examining the evidential basis for Early to Mid-Holocene pigs and pottery in Melanesia. *Journal of Pacific Archaeology, 2*(2), 1–25.

Oelze, V. M., Siebert, A., Nicklisch, N., Meller, H., Dresely, V., & Alt, K. W. (2011). Early neolithic diet and animal husbandry: stable isotope evidence from three Linearbandkeramik (LBK) sites in central Germany. *Journal of Archaeological Science, 38*, 270–279.

Oktaviana, A. A., Bulbeck, D., O'Connor, S., Hakim, B., Suryatman, Wibowo, U. P., et al. (2016). Hand stencils with and without narrowed fingers at two new rock art sites in Sulawesi, Indonesia. *Rock Art Research, 33*, 32–48.

Orr, K. D., & Fainer, D. C. (1952). Cold injuries in Korea during winter of 1950–51. *Miltary Medicine, 31*, 177–220.

Orton, J., Mitchell, P., Klein, R., Steele, T., & Horsburgh, K. A. (2013). An early date for cattle from Namaqualand, South Africa: implications for the origins of herding in southern Africa. *Antiquity, 87*, 108–120.

Osborn, A. J. (2004). Adaptive responses of Paleoindians to cold stress on the periglacial northern Great Plains. In G. M. Crothers (Ed.), *Hunters and Gatherers in Theory and Archaeology* (pp. 10–47). Carbondale, IL: Southern Illinois University Press.

Osborn, A. J. (2014). Eye of the needle: cold stress, clothing, and sewing technology during the Younger Dryas Cold Event in North America. *American Antiquity, 79*, 45–68.

Osczevski, R., & Bluestein, M. (2005). The new wind chill equivalent temperature chart. *Bulletin of the American Meteorological Society, 86*, 1453–1458.

Ossa, P., Marshall, B., & Webb, C. (1995). New Guinea II Cave: a Pleistocene site on the Snowy River, Victoria. *Archaeology in Oceania, 30*, 22–35.

O'Sullivan, N. J., Teasdale, M. D., Mattiangeli, V., Maixner, F., Pinhasi, R., Bradley, D. G., et al. (2016). A whole mitachondria analysis of the Tyrolean Iceman's leather provides insights into the animal sources of Copper Age clothing. *Scientific Reports, 6*, 31279.

Oswalt, W. H. (1987). Technological complexity: the Polar Eskimos and the Tareumiut. *Arctic Anthropology, 24*(2), 82–98.

Otvos, E. G. (2015). The last interglacial stage: definitions and marine highstand, North America and Eurasia. *Quaternary International, 383*, 158–173.

Outram, A. K., Stear, N. A., Bendrey, R., Olsen, S., Kasparov, A., Zaibert, V., et al. (2009). The earliest horse harnessing and milking. *Science, 323*, 1332–1335.

Oxenham, M. F., Piper, P. J., Bellwood, P., Bui, C. H., Nguyen, K. T., Nguyen, Q. M., et al. (2015). Emergence and diversification of the Neolithic in southern Vietnam: insights from coastal Rach Nui. *Journal of Island and Coastal Archaeology, 10*, 309–338.

Özdemir, H. (2017). Thermal comfort properties of clothing fabrics woven with polyester/cotton blend yarns. *Autex Research Journal, 17*, 135–141.

Panter-Brick, C., Layton, R. H., & Rowley-Conwy, P. (2001). Lines of enquiry. In C. Panter-Brick, R. H. Layton, & P. Rowley-Conwy (Eds.), *Hunter-Gatherers: An Interdisciplinary Perspective* (pp. 1–11). Cambridge: Cambridge University Press.

Pardoe, C. (2014). Conflict and territoriality in Aboriginal Australia: evidence from biology and ethnography. In M. W. Allen, & T. L. Jones (Eds.), *Violence and Warfare among Hunter-Gatherers* (pp. 112–132). San Francisco, CA: Left Coast Press.

Parfitt, S. A., Ashton, N. M., Lewis, S. G., Abel, R. L., Coope, G. R., Field, M. H., et al. (2010). Early Pleistocene human occupation at the edge of the boreal zone in northwest Europe. *Nature, 466*, 229–233.

Parfitt, S. A., Barendregt, R. W., Breda, M., Candy, I., Collins, M. J., Coope, G. R., et al. (2005). The earliest record of human activity in northern Europe. *Nature, 438*, 1008–1012.

Parsons, K. (2014). *Human Thermal Environments: The Effects of Hot, Moderate, and Cold Environments on Human Health, Comfort, and Performance.* Third edition. Boca Raton, FL: CRC Press.

Pascoe, B. (2014). *Dark Emu, Black Seeds: Agriculture or Accident?* Broome: Magabala Books Aboriginal Corporation.

Pawlik, A. F. (2015). Detecting traits of modern behavior through microwear analysis: a case study from the Philippine terminal Pleistocene. In Y. Kaifu, M. Izuho, T. Goebel, H.

Sato, & A. Ono (Eds.), *Emergence and Diversity of Modern Human Behavior in Paleolithic Asia* (pp. 182–198). College Station, TX: Texas A&M University Press.

Pawlik, A. F., Piper, P. J., & Mijares, A. S. (2014). Modern humans in the Philippines: colonization, subsistence and new insights into behavioural complexity. In R. Dennell, & M. Porr (Eds.), *Southern Asia, Australia and the Search for Human Origins* (pp. 135–147). New York: Cambridge University Press.

Pearlstein, E. (2010). Restoring provenance to a Native American feather blanket. *Museum Management and Curatorship*, *25*, 87–105.

Pearson, J. A., Hedges, R. E., Molleson, T. I., & Özbek, M. (2010). Exploring the relationship between weaning and infant mortality: an isotope case study from Aşıklı Höyük and Çayönü Tepesi. *American Journal of Physical Anthropology*, *143*, 448–457.

Pechenkina, E. A., Ambrose, S. H., Xiaolin, M., & Benfer, R. A. (2005). Reconstructing northern Chinese Neolithic subsistence practices by isotopic analysis. *Journal of Archaeological Science*, *32*, 1176–1189.

Peng, F., Wang, H., & Gao, X. (2014). Blade production of Shuidonggou Locality 1 (northwest China): a technological perspective. *Quaternary International*, *347*, 12–20.

Perri, A. (2016). A wolf in dog's clothing: initial dog domestication and Pleistocene wolf variation. *Journal of Archaeological Science*, *68*, 1–4.

Perry, L., Dickau, R., Zarrillo, S., Holst, I., Pearsall, D. M., Piperno, D. R., et al. (2007). Starch fossils and the domestication and dispersal of chili peppers (*Capsicum* spp. L.) in the Americas. *Science*, *315*, 986–988.

Perry, R. (2008). *The Turkey Feather Cape: My Creation from Beyond History*. Lincoln, NE: iUniverse.

Peters, J., & Schmidt, K. (2004). Animals in the symbolic world of Pre-Pottery Neolithic Göbekli Tepe, south-eastern Turkey: a preliminary assessment. *Anthropozoologica*, *39*(1), 179–218.

Petersen, J. B. (1996). Fiber industries from northern New England: ethnicity and technological traditions during the Woodland period. In J. B. Petersen (Ed.), *A Most Indispensable Art: Native Fiber Industries from Eastern North America*. Knoxville, TN: University of Tennessee Press.

Peterson, H. A. (2012). *Physeal Injury Other Than Fracture*. Heidelberg: Springer.

Petit, J. R., Jouzel, J., Raynaud, D., Barkov, N. I., Barnola, J.-M., Basile, I., et al. (1999). Climate and atmospheric history of the past 420,000 years from the Vostok ice core. *Nature*, *399*, 429–436.

Pettitt, P., Castillejo, A. M., Arias, P., Peredo, O., & Harrison, R. (2014). New views on old hands: the context of stencils in El Castillo and La Garma caves (Cantabria, Spain). *Antiquity*, *88*, 47–63.

Pezzin, A. (2015). *Thermo-physiological Comfort Modelling of Fabrics and Garments*. PhD thesis. Turin: Politecnico di Torino.

Pichevin, L., Cremer, M., Giraudeau, J., & Bertrand, P. (2005). A 190 ky record of lithogenic grain-size on the Namibian slope: forging a tight link between past wind-strength and coastal upwelling dynamics. *Marine Geology*, *218*, 81–96.

Pickersgill, B. (2007). Domestication of plants in the Americas: insights from Mendelian and molecular genetics. *Annals of Botany*, *100*, 925–940.

Pike, A. W., Hoffmann, D. L., García-Diez, M., Pettitt, P. B., Alcolea, J., De Balbín, R., et al. (2012). U-series dating of paleolithic art in 11 caves in Spain. *Science*, *336*, 1409–1413.

Pinker, S. A. (2010). The cognitive niche: coevolution of intelligence, sociality, and language. *Proceedings of the National Academy of Sciences USA*, *107*, 8993–8999.

Piper, P. J. (2016). Human cultural, technological and adaptive changes from the end of the Pleistocene to the mid-Holocene in Southeast Asia. In M. Oxenham, & H. R. Buckley (Eds.), *The Routledge Handbook of Bioarchaeology in Southeast Asia and the Pacific Islands* (pp. 24–44). New York: Routledge.

Piperno, D. R., & Dillehay, T. D. (2008). Starch grains on human teeth reveal early broad crop diet in northern Peru. *Proceedings of the*

National Academy of Sciences USA, 105, 19622–19627.

Piperno, D. R., Ranere, A. J., Holst, I., Iriarte, J., & Dickau, R. (2009). Starch grain and phytolith evidence for early ninth millennium B.P. maize from the Central Balsas River Valley, Mexico. *Proceedings of the National Academy of Sciences USA, 106,* 5019–5024.

Piqué, R., Romero, S., Palomo, A., Tarrús, J., Terradas, X., & Bogdanovic, I. (2018). The production and use of cordage at the early neolithic site of La Draga (Banyoles, Spain). *Quaternary International*, 468, 262–270.

Plavcan, J. M. (2012). Sexual size dimorphism, canine dimorphism, and male-male competition in primates: where do humans fit in? *Human Nature, 23,* 45–67.

Plissonneau, D. P., Pistorius, M. A., Pottier, P., Aymard, B., & Planchon, B. (2015). Cold climate could be an etiologic factor involved in Raynaud's phenomenon physiopathology: epidemiological investigation from 954 consulations in general practice. *International Angiology, 34,* 467–474.

Plomley, N. J. (1987). *Weep in Silence: A History of the Flinders Island Aboriginal Settlement.* Hobart: Blubber Head Press.

Plomley, N. J., & Piard-Bernier, J. (1993). *The General: The Visits of the Expedition Led by Bruny D'Entrecasteaux to Tasmanian Waters in 1792 and 1793.* Launceston: Queen Victoria Museum.

Pluciennik, M. (2014). Historical frames of reference for 'hunter-gatherers'. In V. Cummings, P. Jordan, & M. Zvelebil (Eds.), *The Oxford Handbook of The Archaeology and Anthropology of Hunter-Gatherers* (pp. 55–68). Oxford: Oxford University Press.

Politis, G. G. (2017). The role and place of ethnoarchaeology in current archaeological debate. *World Archaeology, 48,* 705–709.

Pope, J. E. (2007). The diagnosis and treatment of Raynaud's phenomenon. *Drugs, 67,* 517–525.

Poredos, P., & Poredos, P. (2016). Raynaud's syndrome - a neglected disease. *International Angiology, 35,* 117–121.

Potenza, M. A., Albani, S., Delmonte, B., Villa, S., Sanvito, T., Paroli, B., et al. (2016). Shape and size constraints on dust optical properties from the Dome C ice core, Antarctica. *Scientific Reports, 6,* 28162.

Prentice, M. L., Hope, G. S., Maryunani, K., & Peterson, J. A. (2005). An evaluation of snowline data across New Guinea during the last major glaciation, and area-based glacier snowlines in the Mt. Jaya region of Papua, Indonesia, during the Last Glacial Maximum. *Quaternary International, 138–139,* 93–117.

Prete, M., Fetone, M. C., Favoino, E., & Perosa, F. (2014). Raynaud's phenomenon: from molecular pathogenesis to therapy. *Autoimmunity Reviews, 13,* 655–667.

Price, T. D. (2009). Ancient farming in eastern North America. *Proceedings of the National Academy of Sciences USA, 106,* 6427–6428.

Price, T. D., & Bar-Yosef, O. (2011). The origins of agriculture: new data, new ideas. *Current Anthropology, 52* (Suppl. S4), S163-S174.

Proffitt, T., Luncz, L. V., Falótico, T., Ottoni, E. B., de la Torre, I., & Haslam, M. (2016). Wild monkeys flake stone tools. *Nature, 539,* 85–88.

Pruetz, J. D., & Herzog, N. M. (2017). Savanna chimpanzees at Fongoli, Senegal, navigate a fire landscape. *Current Anthropology, 58 (Suplement S16),* S337-S350.

Quilter, J. (2014). *The Ancient Central Andes.* New York: Routledge.

Quilter, J., Bernardino Ojeda, E., Pearsall, D. M., Sandweiss, D. H., Jones, J. G., & Wing, E. S. (1991). Subsistence economy of El Paraíso, an early Peruvian site. *Science, 252,* 277–283.

Quinlan, R. J. (2008). Human pair-bonds: evolutionary functions, ecological variation, and adaptive development. *Evolutionary Anthropology, 17,* 227–238.

Radcliffe-Brown, A. R. (1922). *The Andaman Islanders.* New York: The Free Press.

Rasmussen, M., Guo, X., Wang, Y., Lohmueller, K. E., Rasmussen, S., Albrechtsen, A., et al. (2011). An Aboriginal Australian genome reveals separate human dispersals into Asia. *Science, 334,* 94–98.

Rast-Eicher, A. (2016). *Fibres: Microscopy of Archaeological Textiles and Furs.* Budapest: Archaeolingua.

Rawat, S., Gupta, A. K., Sangode, S. J., Srivastava, P., & Nainwal, H. C. (2015). Late Pleistocene-Holocene vegetation and Indian summer monsoon record from the Lahaul, northwest Himalaya, India. *Quaternary Science Reviews*, *114*, 167–181.

Rawlings, T. A., & Driver, J. C. (2010). Paleodiet of domestic turkey, Shields Pueblo (5MT3807), Colorado: isotopic analysis and its implications for care of a household domesticate. *Journal of Archaeological Science*, *37*, 2433–2441.

Read, D. W. (2012). *How Culture Made Us Human: Primate Social Evolution and the Formation of Human Societies*. San Francisco, CA: Left Coast Press.

Read, D. W., & van der Leeuw, S. (2008). Biology is only part of the story... *Philosophical Transactions of the Royal Society B*, *363*, 1959–1968.

Reade, W. J., & Potts, D. T. (1993). New evidence for late third millennium linen from Tell Abraq, Umm Al-Qaiwain, UAE. *Paléorient*, *19*(2), 99–106.

Rebora, A. (2010). Lucy's pelt: when we became hairless and how we managed to survive. *International Journal of Dermatology*, *49*, 17–20.

Reed, D. L., Allen, J. M., Toups, M. A., Boyd, B. M., & Ascunce, M. S. (2015). The study of primate evolution from a lousy perspective. In S. Morand, B. R. Krasnov, & D. T. Littlewood (Eds.), *Parasite Diversity and Diversification: Evolutionary Ecology Meets Phylogenetics* (pp. 202–214). Cambridge: Cambridge University Press.

Reed, D. L., Light, J. E., Allen, J. M., & Kirchman, J. J. (2007). Pair of lice lost or parasites regained: the evolutionary history of anthropoid primate lice. *BMC Biology*, *5*(7), 1–11.

Reeves, J. M., Barrows, T. T., Cohen, T. J., Kiem, A. S., Bostock, H. C., Fitzsimmons, K. E., et al. (2013). Climate variability over the last 35,000 years recorded in marine and terrestrial archives in the Australian region: an OZ-INTIMATE compilation. *Quaternary Science Reviews*, *74*, 21–34.

Reich, D., Green, R. E., Kircher, M., Krause, J., Patterson, N., Durand, E. Y., et al. (2010). Genetic history of an archaic hominin group from Denisova Cave in Siberia. *Nature*, *468*, 1053–1060.

Renfrew, C. (1972). *The Emergence of Civilisation: The Cyclades and the Aegean in the Third Millennium B.C.* London: Methuen.

Renfrew, C. (2012). Towards a cognitive archaeology: material engagement and the early development of society. In I. Hodder (Ed.), *Archaeological Theory Today* (pp. 124–145). Second edition. Cambridge: Polity Press.

Renfrew, C., & Bahn, P. (2016). *Archaeology: Theories, Methods and Practice*. Seventh edition. London: Thames & Hudson.

Reynard, J. P., Discamps, E., Badenhorst, S., van Niekerk, K., & Henshilwood, C. S. (2016). Subsistence strategies in the southern Cape during the Howiesons Poort: taphonomic and zooarchaeological analyses of Klipdrift Shelter, South Africa. *Quaternary International*, *404* (Part B), 2–19.

Ribeiro, A. (2003). *Dress and Morality*. Second edition. Oxford: Berg.

Richards, E. (2017). *Darwin and the Making of Sexual Selection*. Chicago, IL: University of Chicago Press.

Richmond, B. G., & Jungers, W. L. (2008). *Orrorin tugenensis* femoral morphology and the evolution of hominin bipedalism. *Science*, *319*, 1662–1665.

Rintamäki, H., & Rissanen, S. (2006). Heat strain in cold. *Industrial Health*, *44*, 427–432.

Riordan, J., & Wambach, K. (2010). *Breastfeeding and Human Lactation*. Fourth edition. Boston, MA: Jones and Bartlett.

Roberts, A. P., & Grün, R. (2010). Early human northerners. *Nature*, *466*, 189–190.

Rodríguez-Vidal, J., d'Errico, F., Pacheco, F. G., Blasco, R., Rossell, J., Jennings, R. P., et al. (2014). A rock engraving made by Neanderthals in Gibraltar. *Proceedings of the National Academy of Sciences USA*, *111*, 13301–13306.

Roebroeks, W., Sier, M. J., Nielsen, T. K., De Loecker, D., Parés, J. M., Arps, C. E., et al. (2012). Use of red ochre by early Neandertals. *Proceedings of the National Academy of Sciences USA*, 109, 1889–1894.

Rogers, A. R., Iltis, D., & Wooding, S. (2004). Genetic variation at the MCIR locus and the time since loss of human body hair. *Current Anthropology*, *45*, 105–108.

Romer, J. (2012). *A History of Ancient Egypt: From the First Farmers to the Great Pyramid*. New York: St. Martin's Press, 2013.

Roosevelt, A. C. (1991). *Moundbuilders of the Amazon: Geophysical Archaeology on Marajo Island, Brazil*. San Diego, CA: Academic Press.

Rosen, A. M., & Rivera-Collazo, I. (2012). Climate change, adaptive cycles, and the persistence of foraging economies during the late Pleistocene/Holocene transition in the Levant. *Proceedings of the National Academy of Sciences USA*, *109*, 3640–3645.

Ross, J. (1831). Recollections, of a short excursion to Lake Echo in March, 1823. In *An Account of the Colony of Van Dieman's Land in 1830, With a Descriptive Itinerary of the Country* (pp. 85–122). London: George Cowie & Co.

Ross, R. (2008). *Clothing: A Global History. Or, The Imperialists' New Clothes*. Cambridge: Polity Press.

Rossetti, D. d., Góes, A. M., & de Toledo, P. M. (2009). Archaeological mounds in Marajó Island in northern Brazil: a geological perspective integrating remote sensing and sedimentology. *Geoarchaeology*, *24*, 22–41.

Rossi, R. (2005). Interactions between protection and thermal comfort. In R. A. Scott (Ed.), *Textiles for Protection* (pp. 233–260). Cambridge: Woodhead.

Rossi, R. (2009). Comfort and thermoregulatory requirements in cold weather clothing. In J. Williams (Ed.), *Textiles for Cold Weather Apparel* (pp. 3–18). Cambridge: Woodhead.

Rots, V., Hardy, B. L., Serangeli, J., & Conard, N. J. (2015). Residue and microwear analyses of the stone artefacts from Schöningen. *Journal of Human Evolution*, *89*, 298–308.

Roy, P. D., Quiroz-Jiménez, J. D., Chávez-Lara, C. M., Sánchez-Zavala, J. L., Pérez-Cruz, L. L., & Muthu Sankar, G. (2014). Humid Pleistocene-Holocene transition and early Holocene in sub-tropical northern Mexico and possible Gulf of California forcing. *Boreas*, *43*, 577–587.

Ruebens, K., McPherron, S. J., & Hublin, J.-J. (2015). On the local Mousterian origin of the Châtelperronian: integrating typo-technological, chronostratigraphic and contextual data. *Journal of Human Evolution*, *86*, 55–91.

Ruff, C. B. (1993). Climatic adaptation and hominid evolution: the thermoregulatory imperative. *Evolutionary Athropology*, *2*, 53–60.

Ruff, C. B. (2002). Variation in human body size and shape. *Annual Review of Anthropology*, *31*, 211–232.

Russell, A. (2010). *Retracing the Steppes: A Zooarchaeological Analysis of Changing Subsistence Patterns in the Late Neolithic at Tell Sabi Abyad, Northern Syria, c. 6900 to 5900 BC*. PhD thesis. Leiden: Leiden University.

Ruxton, G. D., & Wilkinson, D. M. (2011). Avoidance of overheating and selection for both hair loss and bipedality in hominins. *Proceedings of the National Academy of Sciences USA*, *108*, 20965–20969.

Ryder, M. L. (1960). A study of the coat of the mouflon *Ovis Musimon* with special reference to seasonal change. *Proceedings of the Zoological Society of London (now Journal of Zoology)*, *135*, 387–408.

Ryder, M. L. (1962). The origin of felt-making and spinning. *Antiquity*, *36*, 304.

Ryder, M. L. (1964). The origin of spinning. *Antiquity*, *38*, 293–294.

Ryder, M. L. (1971). Wool growth cycles in Soay sheep. *Journal of Agricultural Science*, *76*, 183–197.

Ryder, M. L. (2005). The human development of different fleece-types in sheep and its association with the development of textile crafts. In F. Pritchard, & J. P. Wild (Eds.), *Northern Archaeological Textiles* (pp. 122–128). Oxford: Oxbow.

Sætre, G.-P., Riyahi, S., Aliabadian, M., Hermansen, J. S., Hogner, S., Olsson, U., et al. (2012). Single origin of human commensalism in the house sparrow. *Journal of Evolutionary Biology*, *25*, 788–796.

Šajnerová-Dušková, A. (2007). *Tools of the Mammoth Hunters: The Application of Use-Wear Analysis on the Czech Upper Palaeolithic Chipped Industry*. BAR International Series 1645. Oxford: Archaeopress.

Saña, M., & Tornero, C. (2012). Use of animal fibres during the Neolithisation in the Middle Euphrates Valley: an archaeozoological approach. *Paléorient, 38*(1–2), 79–91.

Sánchez-Goñi, M., Landais, A., Fletcher, W. J., Naughton, F., Desprat, S., & Duprat, J. (2008). Contrasting impacts of Dansgaard-Oeschger events over a western European latitudinal transect modulated by orbital parameters. *Quaternary Science Reviews, 27*, 1136–1151.

Sandweiss, D. H., Shady Solís, R., Moseley, M. E., Keefer, D. K., & Ortloff, C. R. (2009). Environmental change and economic development in coastal Peru between 5,800 and 3,600 years ago. *Proceedings of the National Academy of Sciences USA, 106*, 1359–1363.

Sankararaman, S., Patterson, N., Li, H., Pääbo, S., & Reich, D. (2012). The date of interbreeding between Neandertals and modern humans. *PLoS Genetics, 8*, e1002947.

Sapir-Hen, L., Dayan, T., Khalaily, H., & Munro, N. D. (2016). Human hunting and nascent animal management at Middle Pre-Pottery Neolithic Yiftah'el, Israel. *PLoS ONE, 11*, e0156964.

Sauer, C. O. (1952). *Agricultural Origins and Dispersals*. New York: American Geographical Society.

Scheffler, T. E., Hirth, K. G., & Hasemann, G. (2012). The El Gigante rockshelter: preliminary observations on an early to late Holocene occupation in southern Honduras. *Latin American Antiquity, 23*, 597–610.

Schlebusch, C. M., Malmström, H., Günther, T., Sjödin, P., Coutinho, A., Edlund, H., et al. (2017). Southern African ancient genomes estimate modern human divergence to 350,000 to 260,000 years ago. *Science*, 358, 652–655.

Schmidt, K. (2000). Göbekli Tepe, southeastern Turkey: a preliminary report on the 1995–1999 excavations. *Paléorient, 26*(1), 45–54.

Schuster, S. C., Miller, W., Ratan, A., Tomsho, L. P., Giardine, B., Kasson, L. R., et al. (2010). Complete Khoisan and Bantu genomes from southern Africa. *Nature, 463*, 943–947.

Sellato, B. (2006). Bark-clothes in East Kalimantan. In M. C. Howard (Ed.), *Bark-cloth in Southeast Asia* (pp. 153–263). Bangkok: White Lotus.

Semenov, S. A. (1964). *Prehistoric Technology: An Experimental Study of the Oldest Tools and Artefacts from Traces of Manufacture and Wear*. Translated by M. W. Thomas. London: Cory, Adams and Mackay.

Shady Solís, R. (2006). America's first city? The case of Late Archaic Caral. In W. H. Isbell, & H. Silverman (Eds.), *Andean Archaeology III: North and South* (pp. 28–66). New York: Springer.

Shamir, O. (2015). Textiles from the Chalcolithic Period, Early and Middle Bronze Age in the southern Levant. *Archaeological Textiles Review, 57*, 12–25.

Shanahan, T. M., McKay, N. P., Hughen, K. A., Overpeck, J. T., Otto-Bliesner, B., Heil, C. W., et al. (2015). The time-transgressive termination of the African Humid Period. *Nature Geoscience, 8*, 140–144.

Shaw, C. N., Hofmann, C. L., Petraglia, M. D., Stock, J. T., & Gottschall, J. S. (2012). Neandertal humeri may reflect adaptation to scraping tasks, but not spear thrusting. *PLoS ONE, 7*, e40349.

Shea, J. J. (2013). Lithic modes A-I: a new framework for describing global-scale variation in stone tool technology illustrated with evidence from the east Mediterranean Levant. *Journal of Archaeological Method and Theory, 20*, 151–186.

Shea, J. J. (2017). *Stone Tools in Human Evolution: Behavioral Differences Among Technological Primates*. New York: Cambridge University Press.

Shelach-Lavi, G. (2015). *The Archaeology of Early China: From Prehistory to the Han Dynasty*. New York: Cambridge University Press.

Shen, G., Gao, X., & Granger, D. E. (2009). Age of Zhoukoudian *Homo erectus* determined with 26Al/10Be burial dating. *Nature, 458*, 198–200.

Sherratt, A. (1981). Plough and pastoralism: aspects of the secondary products revolution. In I. Hodder, G. Isaac, & N. Hammond (Eds.), *Pattern of The Past: Studies in Honour of David Clarke* (pp. 261–305). Cambridge: Cambridge University Press.

Shulmeister, J., Kemp, J., Fitzsimmons, K. E., & Gontz, A. (2016). Constant wind regimes during the Last Glacial Maximum and early Holocene: evidence from Little Llangothlin Lagoon, New England Tablelands, eastern Australia. *Climate of the Past, 12*, 1435–1444.

Shuman, B. M., & Serravezza, M. (2017). Patterns of hydroclimatic change in the Rocky Mountains and surrounding regions since the last glacial maximum. *Quaternary Science Reviews, 173*, 58–77.

Siberian Times reporter. (2016). World's oldest needle found in Siberian Cave that stitches together human history. *Siberian Times*, 23 August 2016.

Sinclair, A. (1991). *The Naked Savage*. London: Sinclair-Stevenson.

Singh, U. (2008). *A History of Ancient and Early Medieval India: From the Stone Age to the 12th Century*. Patparganj: Dorling Kindersley.

Skoglund, P., Ersmark, E., Palkopoulou, E., & Dalén, L. (2015). Ancient wolf genome reveals an early divergence of domestic dog ancestors and admixture into high-latitude breeds. *Current Biology, 25*, 1–5.

Skoglund, P., Posth, C., Sirak, K., Spriggs, M., Valentin, F., Bedford, S., et al. (2016). Genomic insights into the peopling of the southwest Pacific. *Nature, 538*, 510–513.

Smith, B. D. (2001). Documenting plant domestication: the consilience of biological and archaeological approaches. *Proceedings of the National Academy of Sciences USA, 98*, 1324–1326.

Smith, B. D. (2006). Eastern North America as an independent centre of plant domestication. *Proceedings of the National Academy of Sciences USA, 103*, 12223–12228.

Smith, B. D. (2009). Initial formation of an indigenous crop complex in eastern North America at 3800 B.P. *Proceedings of the National Academy of Sciences USA, 106*, 6561–6566.

Smith, B. D. (2011a). General patterns of niche construction and the management of 'wild' plant and animal resources by small-scale pre-industrial societies. *Philosophical Transactions of the Royal Society B, 366*, 836–848.

Smith, B. D. (2011b). The cultural context of plant domestication in eastern North America. *Current Anthropology, 52* (Suppl. S4), S471-S484.

Smith, B. (in press). The last hunter-gatherers of China and Africa: a life amongst pastoralists and farmers. *Quaternary International.*

Snir, A., Nadel, D., Groman-Yaroslavski, I., Melamed, Y., Sternberg, M., Bar-Yosef, O., et al. (2015). The origin of cultivation and proto-weeds, long before neolithic farming. *PLoS ONE, 10*, e0131422.

Soffer, O. (2004). Recovering perishable technologies through use wear on tools: preliminary evidence for Upper Paleolithic weaving and net making. *Current Anthropology, 45*, 407–413.

Soffer, O., Adovasio, J. M., & Hyland, D. C. (2000). The "Venus" figurines: textiles, basketry, gender, and status in the Upper Paleolithic. *Current Anthropology, 41*, 511–537.

Solazzo, C., Heald, S., Ballard, M. W., Ashford, D. A., DePriest, P. T., Koestler, R. J., et al. (2011). Proteomics and Coast Salish blankets: a tale of shaggy dogs? *Antiquity, 85*, 1418–1432.

Somel, M., Franz, H., Yan, Z., Lorenc, A., Guo, S., Giger, T., et al. (2009). Transcriptional neoteny in the human brain. *Proceedings of the National Academy of Sciences USA, 106*, 5743–5748.

Somel, M., Tang, L., & Khaitovich, P. (2012). The role of neoteny in human evolution: from genes to phenotype. In H. Hirai, H. Imai, & Y. Go (Eds.), *Post-Genome Biology of Primates* (pp. 23–41). Tokyo: Springer.

Somerville, A. D., Nelson, B. A., & Knudson, K. J. (2010). Isotopic investigation of pre-Hispanic macaw breeding in northwest

Mexico. *Journal of Anthropological Archaeology, 29*, 125–135.

Somerville, A. D., Sugiyama, N., Manzanilla, L. R., & Schoeninger, M. J. (2016). Animal management at the ancient metropolis of Teotihuacan, Mexico: stable isotope analysis of Leporid (Cottontail and Jackrabbit) bone mineral. *PLoS ONE, 11*, e0159982.

Song, G. (2009). Thermal insulation properties of textiles and clothing. In J. Williams (Ed.), *Textiles for Cold Weather Apparel* (pp. 19–32). Cambridge: Woodhead.

Song, Y., Li, X., Wu, X., Kvavadze, E., Goldberg, P., & Bar-Yosef, O. (2016). Bone needle fragment in LGM from the Shizitan site (China): archaeological evidence and experimental study. *Quaternary International, 400*, 140–148.

Soressi, M., McPherron, S. P., Lenoir, M., Dogandžić, T., Goldberg, P., Jacobs, Z., et al. (2013). Neandertals made the first specialized bone tools in Europe. *Proceedings of the National Academy of Sciences USA, 110*, 14186–14190.

Sparrman, A. (1785). *A Voyage to the Cape of Good Hope, towards the Antarctic Polar Circle, and Round the World: but chiefly into the Country of the Hottentots and Caffres, from the Year 1772, to 1776 (Resa till Goda Hopps-Udden, Södra Pol-Kretsen och omkring jordklotet, samt til Hottentott- och Caffer-landen, åren 1772-76)*. Translated by Charles Rivington Hopson. In two volumes. London: G. G. J. and J. Robinson.

Speller, C. F., Kemp, B. M., Wyatt, S. D., Monroe, C., Lipe, W. D., Arndt, U. M., et al. (2010). Ancient mitochondrial DNA analysis reveals complexity of indigenous North American turkey domestication. *Proceedings of the National Academy of Sciences USA, 107*, 2807–2812.

Spinapolice, E. E., & Garcea, E. A. (2014). Aterian lithic technology and settlement system in the Jebel Gharbi, north-western Libya. *Quaternary International, 350*, 241–253.

Splitstosser, J. C., Dillehay, T. D., Wouters, J., & Claro, A. (2016). Early pre-Hispanic use of indigo blue in Peru. *Science Advances, 2*, e1501623.

Spriggs, M. (2001). Who cares what time it is? The importance of chronology in Pacific archaeology. In A. Anderson, I. Lilley, & S. O'Connor (Eds.), *Histories of Old Ages: Essays in Honour of Rhys Jones* (pp. 237–249). Canberra: Pandanus Books, Australian National University.

Stanish, C., de la Vega, E., Moseley, M. E., Williams, P. R., Chávez, J. C., Vining, B., et al. (2010). Tiwanaku trade patterns in southern Peru. *Journal of Anthropological Archaeology, 29*, 524–532.

Stark, B. L., Heller, L., & Ohnersorgen, M. A. (1998). People with cloth: Mesoamerican economic change from the perspective of cotton in south-central Veracruz. *Latin American Antiquity, 9*, 7–36.

Steadman, R. G. (1984). A universal scale of Apparent Temperature. *Journal of Climate and Applied Meteorology, 23*, 1674–1687.

Stearns, P. N. (2012). *The Industrial Revolution in World History*. Fourth edition. Boulder, CO: Westview Press.

Steffensen, J. P., Andersen, K. K., Bigler, M., Clausen, H. B., Dahl-Jensen, D., Fischer, H., et al. (2008). High-resolution Greenland ice core data show abrupt climate change happens in a few years. *Science, 321*, 680–684.

Stevenson, A., & Dee, M. W. (2016). Confirmation of the world's oldest garment: the Tarkhan dress. *Antiquity, 90*(349), Project Gallery (online).

Stevenson, A., & Waite, M. (Eds.). (2011). *Concise Oxford English Dictionary*. Twelfth edition. Oxford: Oxford University Press.

Stiner, M. C., Buitenhuis, H., Duru, G., Kuhn, S. L., Mentzer, S. M., Munro, N. D., et al. (2014). A forager-herder trade-off, from broad-spectrum hunting to sheep management at Aşıklı Höyük, Turkey. *Proceedings of the National Academy of Sciences USA, 111*, 8404–8409.

Stiner, M. C., Kuhn, S. L., & Güleç, E. (2013). Early Upper Paleolithic shells beads at Üçağızlı Cave I (Turkey): technology and the socioeconomic context of ornament life-histories. *Journal of Human Evolution, 64*, 380–398.

Straus, L. G. (2000). A quarter-century of research on the Solutrean of Vasco-Cantabria,

Iberia and beyond. *Journal of Anthropological Research, 56*, 39–58.

Stringer, C. (2014). Small remains still pose big problems. *Nature, 514*, 427–429.

Stringer, C. (2016). The origin and evolution of *Homo sapiens. Philosophical Transactions of The Royal Society B, 371*, 20150237.

Stringer, C., & Andrews, P. (2011). *The Complete World of Human Evolution*. Second edition. London: Thames & Hudson.

Stuut, J.-B. W., Prins, M. A., Schneider, R. R., Weltje, G. J., Jansen, J. H., & Postma, G. (2002). A 300-kyr record of aridity and wind strength in southwestern Africa: inferences from grain-size distributions of sediments on Walvis Ridge, SE Atlantic. *Marine Geology, 180*, 221–233.

Subedi, B. H., Pokharel, J., Thapa, R., Bankskota, N., & Basnyat, B. (2010). Frostbite in a Sherpa. *Wilderness and Environmental Medicine, 21*, 127–129.

Suddendorf, T. (2013). *The Gap: The Science of What Separates Us from Other Animals*. New York: Basic Books.

Sugiyama, N., Somerville, A. D., & Schoeninger, M. J. (2015). Stable isotopes and zooarchaeology at Teotihuacan, Mexico reveal earliest evidence of wild carnivore management in Mesoamerica. *PLoS ONE, 10*, e0135635.

Sumida, S. S., & Brochu, C. A. (2000). Phylogenetic context for the origin of feathers. *American Zoologist, 40*, 486–503.

Summerhayes, G. R., & Ford, A. (2014). Late Pleistocene colonisation and adaptation in New Guinea: implications for modelling modern human behaviour. In R. Dennell, & M. Porr (Eds.), *Southern Asia, Australia and the Search for Human Origins* (pp. 213–227). New York: Cambridge University Press.

Summerhayes, G. R., Leavesley, M., Fairbairn, A., Mandui, H., Field, J., Ford, A., et al. (2010). Human adaptation and plant use in highland New Guinea 49,000 to 44,000 years ago. *Science, 330*, 78–81.

Sun, G. (2013). Recent research on the Hemudu culture and the Tianluoshan site. In A. P. Underhill (Ed.), *A Companion to Chinese Archaeology* (pp. 555–573). Oxford: Wiley-Blackwell.

Sutikna, T., Tocheri, M. W., Faith, J. T., Jatmiko, Awe, R. D., Meijer, H. J., et al. (2016). Modern humans on Flores by 46,000 years ago: new evidence from Liang Bua [abstract]. *Proceedings of the European Society for the Study of Human Evolution, 5*, 232.

Sutikna, T., Tocheri, M. W., Morwood, M. J., Saptomo, E. W., Jatmiko, Awe, R. D., et al. (2016). Revised stratigraphy and chronology for *Homo floresiensis* at Liang Bua in Indonesia. *Nature, 532*, 366–369.

Sutou, S. (2012). Hairless mutation: a driving force of humanization from a human-ape common ancestor by enforcing upright walking while holding a baby with both hands. *Genes to Cells, 17*, 264–272.

Szpak, P., Millaire, J.-F., White, C. D., Lau, G. F., Surette, F., & Longstaffe, F. J. (2015). Origins of prehispanic camelid wool textiles from the north and central coasts of Peru traced by carbon and nitrogen isotopic analyses. *Current Anthropology, 56*, 449–459.

Taçon, P. S., Tan, N. H., O'Connor, S., Xueping, J., Gang, L., Curnoe, D., et al. (2014). The global implications of the early surviving rock art of greater Southeast Asia. *Antiquity, 88*, 1050–1064.

Tang, K. P., Chau, K. H., Kan, C. W., & Fan, J. T. (2015). Characterizing the transplanar and in-plane water transport properties of fabrics under different sweat rates: forced flow water transport tester. *Scientific Reports, 5*, 17012.

Tang, Y., He, Y., Shao, H., & Ji, C. (2016). Assessment of comfortable clothing thermal resistance using a multi-scale human thermoregulatory model. *International Journal of Heat and Mass Transfer, 98*, 568–583.

Tangri, D., & Wyncoll, G. (1989). Of mice and men: is the presence of commensal animals in archaeological sites a positive correlate of sedentism? *Paléorient, 15*(2), 85–94.

Tao, Y., Wang, Q., & Yu, W. (2017). Study on the origins of textile materials on the basis of analysis of related hard relics from Chinese excavations. *Fibres and Textiles in Eastern Europe, 25*(1), 108–112.

Tattersall, I. (2012). *Masters of the Planet: The Search for Our Human Origins*. New York: Palgrave Macmillan.

Tattersall, I. (2016). The genus *Homo*. *Inference: International Review of Science*, *2*(1), 1–9.

Taylor, L. (2002). *The Study of Dress History*. Manchester: Manchester University Press.

Tchernov, E. (1991). Of mice and men. Biological markers for long-term sedentism; a reply. *Paléorient*, *17*(1), 153–160.

Temple, R. C. (1901). An unpublished XVIII century document about the Andamans. *Indian Antiquary*, *30*, 232–238.

Tessone, A., García Guraieb, S., Goñi, R. A., & Panarello, H. O. (2015). Isotopic evidence of weaning in hunter-gatherers from the late Holocene in Lake Salitroso, Patagonia, Argentina. *American Journal of Physical Anthropology*, *158*, 105–115.

Thompson, A. J., & Jakes, K. A. (2005). Textile evidence for Ohio Hopewell burial practices. *Southeastern Archaeology*, *24*, 137–141.

Thompson, A. J., & Simon, M. (2008). An analysis of textile fragments from the Janey B. Goode site. *Midcontinental Journal of Archaeology*, *33*, 155–181.

Tiedemann, E. J., & Jakes, K. A. (2006). An exploration of prehistoric spinning technology: spinning efficiency and technology transition. *Archaeometry*, *48*, 293–307.

Toan, N. H., & Preston, T. R. (2010). Taro as a local feed resource for pigs in small scale household condition. *Livestock Research for Rural Development*, *22*(8), 152.

Torrence, R. (2001). Hunter-gatherer technology: macro- and microscale approaches. In C. Panter-Brick, R. H. Layton, & P. Rowley-Conwy (Eds.), *Hunter-Gatherers: An Interdisciplinary Perspective* (pp. 73–98). Cambridge: Cambridge University Press.

Toups, M. A., Kitchen, A., Light, J. E., & Reed, D. L. (2011). Origin of clothing lice indicates early clothing use by anatomically modern humans in Africa. *Molecular Biology and Evolution*, *28*, 29–32.

Trinkaus, E. (2005). Anatomical evidence for the antiquity of human footwear use. *Journal of Archaeological Science*, *32*, 1515–1526.

Trinkaus, E. (2011). The postcranial dimensions of the La Chapelle-aux-Saints 1 Neandertal. *American Journal of Physical Anthropology*, *145*, 461–468.

Trinkaus, E., Buzhilova, A. P., Mednikova, M. B., & Dobrovolskaya, M. V. (2014). *The People of Sunghir: Burials, Bodies, and Behavior in the Earlier Upper Paleolithic*. Oxford: Oxford University Press.

Trinkaus, E., & Zilhão, J. (2002). Phylogenetic implications. In J. Zilhão, & E. Trinkaus (Eds.), *Portrait of the Artist as a Child: The Gravettian Human Skeleton from the Abrigo do Lagar Velho and its Archeological Context* (pp. 497–518). Lisbon: Instituto Português de Arqueologia.

Tsuneishi, K.-i. (2007). Unit 731 and the human skulls discovered in 1989: physicians carrying out organized crimes. In W. R. Lafleur, G. Böhme, & S. Shimazono (Eds.), *Dark Medicine: Rationalizing Unethical Medical Research* (pp. 73–84). Bloomington, IN: Indiana University Press.

Tsutaya, T. (2017). Post-weaning diet in archaeological human populations: a meta-analysis of carbon and nitrogen stable isotope ratios of child skeletons. *American Journal of Physical Anthropology*, *164*, 546–557.

Tsutaya, T., & Ishida, H. (2015). Weaning age in an expanding population: stable carbon and nitrogen isotope analysis of infant feeding practices in the Okhotsk culture (5th-13th centuries AD) in northern Japan. *American Journal of Physical Anthropology*, *157*, 544–555.

Tull, D. (2013). *Edible and Useful Plants of the Southwest: Texas, New Mexico, and Arizona*. Revised edition. Austin, TX: University of Texas Press.

Tung, B. (2013). 2013 excavations overview: north area. *Çatal News*, *20*, 4.

Turner, N. J. (2014). *Ancient Pathways, Ancestral Knowledge: Ethnobotany and Ecological Wisdom of Indigenous Peoples of Northwestern North America*. Volume I: The History and Practice of Indigenous Plant Knowledge. Montreal: McGill-Queen's University Press.

Turney, C. S., Bird, M. I., Fifield, L. K., Roberts, R. G., Smith, M., Dortch, C. E., et al. (2001). Early human occupation at Devil's Lair, southwestern Australia 50,000 years ago. *Quaternary Research, 55*, 3–13.

Twomey, T. (2014). How domesticating fire facilitated the evolution of human cooperation. *Biology and Philosophy, 29*, 89–99.

Unaipon, D. (2001). *Legendary Tales of the Australian Aborigines*. Edited by Stephen Muecke and Adam Shoemaker. Melbourne: Miegunyah Press.

Ünal-İmer, E., Shulmeister, J., Zhao, J.-X., Uysal, I. T., Feng, Y.-X., Nguyen, A. D., et al. (2015). An 80 kyr-long continuous speleothem record from Dim Cave, SW Turkey with paleoclimatic implications for the eastern Mediterranean. *Scientific Reports, 5*, 13560.

Urban, B., & Bigga, G. (2015). Environmental reconstruction and biostratigraphy of late Middle Pleistocene lakeshore deposits at Schöningen. *Journal of Human Evolution, 89*, 57–70.

Utrilla, P., & Bea, M. (2015). Fuente del Trucho, Huesca (Spain): reading interaction in palaeolithic art. In P. Bueno-Ramírez, & P. G. Bahn (Eds.), *Prehistoric Art as Prehistoric Culture: Studies in Honour of Professor Rodrigo de Balbín-Behrmann* (pp. 69–77). Oxford: Archaeopress.

Valentova, J. V., Varella, M. A., Bártová, K., Štěrbová, Z., & Dixson, B. J. (2017). Mate preferences and choices for facial and body hair in heterosexual women and homosexual men: influence of sex, population, homogamy, and imprinting-like effect. *Evolution and Human Behavior, 38*, 241–248.

Vallebueno-Estrada, M., Rodríguez-Arévalo, I., Rougon-Cardoso, A., Martínez González, J., Cook, A. G., Montiel, R., et al. (2016). The earliest maize from San Marcos Tehuacán is a partial domesticate with genomic evidence of inbreeding. *Proceedings of the National Academy of Sciences USA, 113*, 14151–14156.

van den Bergh, G. D., Kaifu, Y., Kurniawan, I., Kono, R. T., Brumm, A., Setiyabudi, E., et al. (2016). *Homo floresiensis*-like fossils from the early Middle Pleistocene of Flores. *Nature, 534*, 245–248.

van Kolfschoten, T., Parfitt, S. A., Serangeli, J., & Bello, S. M. (2015). Lower Paleolithic bone tools from the 'Spear Horizon' at Schöningen (Germany). *Journal of Human Evolution, 89*, 226–263.

Van Os, J. M., Mintline, E. M., DeVries, T. J., & Tucker, C. B. (2017). Motivation of naïve feedlot cattle to obtain grain and individual responses to novelty. *Applied Animal Behaviour Science, 197*, 68–74.

Vignaud, P., Duringer, P., Mackaye, H. T., Likius, A., Blondel, C., Boisserie, J.-R., et al. (2002). Geology and palaeontology of the Upper Miocene Toros-Menalla hominid locality, Chad. *Nature, 418*, 152–155.

Vigne, J.-D. (2015). Early domestication and farming: what should we know or do for a better understanding? *Anthropozoologica, 50*(2), 123–150.

Vizgirdas, R. S., & Rey-Vizgirdas, E. M. (2006). *Wild Plants of the Sierra Nevada*. Reno, NV: University of Nevada Press.

Vogel-Eastwood, G. (2000). Textiles. In P. T. Nicholson, & I. Shaw (Eds.), *Ancient Egyptian Materials and Technology*. Cambridge: Cambridge University Press.

Voormolen, B. (2008). *Ancient Hunters, Modern Butchers: Schöningen 13II-4, a Kill-Butchery Site Dating from the Northwest European Lower Palaeolithic*. PhD thesis. Leiden: University of Leiden.

WAIS Divide Project members. (2015). Precise interpolar phasing of abrupt climate change during the last ice age. *Nature, 520*, 661–665.

Wales, N. (2012). Modeling Neanderthal clothing using ethnographic analogues. *Journal of Human Evolution, 63*, 781–795.

Walker, M. J. (2017). *Palaeolithic Pioneers: Behaviour, Abilities, and Activity of Early Homo in European Landscapes around the Western Mediterranean Basin ~1.3–0.05 Ma*. Oxford: Archaeopress.

Walker, M. J., Anesin, D., Angelucci, D. E., Avilés-Fernández, A., Berna, F., Buitrago-López, A. T., et al. (2016). Combustion at the late Early Pleistocene site of Cueva Negra del Estrecho del Río Quípar (Murcia, Spain). *Antiquity, 90*, 571–589.

Walker, M. J., Ortega, J., Parmová, K., López, M. V., & Trinkaus, E. (2011). Morphology, body proportions, and postcranial hypertrophy of a female Neandertal from the Sima de las Palomas, southeastern Spain. *Proceedings of the National Academy of Sciences USA*, *108*, 10087–10091.

Walsh, G. L. (1979). Mutilated hands or signal stencils? A consideration of irregular hand stencils from central Queensland. *Australian Archaeology*, *9*, 33–41.

Wang, F., Gao, C., Kuklane, K., & Holmér, I. (2013). Effects of various protective clothing and thermal environments on heat strain of unacclimated men: the PHS (predicted heat strain) model revisited. *Industrial Health*, *51*, 266–274.

Wang, H., & Hu, S. (2016). Experimental study on thermal sensation of people in moderate activities. *Building and Environment*, *100*, 127–134.

Wang, H.-W., Mitra, B., Chaudhuri, T. K., Palanichamy, M. G., Kong, Q.-P., & Zhang, Y.-P. (2011). Mitochondrial DNA evidence supports northeast Indian origin of the aboriginal Andamanese in the late Paleolithic. *Journal of Genetics and Genomics*, *38*, 117–122.

Wang, L., Liu, T., Hu, M., Zeng, W., Zhang, Y., Rutherford, S., et al. (2016). The impact of cold spells on mortality and effect modification by cold spell characteristics. *Scientific Reports*, *6*, 38380.

Wang, S. X., Li, Y., Tokura, H., Hu, J. Y., Han, Y. X., Kwok, Y. L., et al. (2007). Effect of moisture management on functional performance of cold protective clothing. *Textile Research Journal*, *77*, 968–980.

Wang, X., Edwards, L. R., Auler, A. S., Cheng, H., Kong, X., Wang, Y., et al. (2017). Hydroclimate changes across the Amazon lowlands over the past 45,000 years. *Nature*, *541*, 204–207.

Warmuth, V., Eriksson, A., Bower, M. A., Barker, G., Barrett, E., Hanks, B. K., et al. (2012). Reconstructing the origin and spread of horse domestication in the Eurasian steppe. *Proceedings of the National Academy of Sciences USA*, *109*, 8202–8206.

Watson, I. (1998). Naked peoples: rules and regulations. *Law. Text. Culture*, *4*(1), 1–17.

Weaver, T. D., Coqueugniot, H., Golovanova, L. V., Doronichev, V. B., Maureille, B., & Hublin, J.-J. (2016). Neonatal postcrania from Mezmaiskaya, Russia, and Le Moustier, France, and the development of Neandertal body form. *Proceedings of the National Academy of Sciences USA*, *113*, 6472–6477.

Wei, G., Huang, W., Chen, S., He, C., Pang, L., & Wu, Y. (2014). Paleolithic culture of Longgupo and its creators. *Quaternary International*, *354*, 154–161.

Wei, Y., d'Errico, F., Vanhaeren, M., Li, F., & Gao, X. (2016). An early instance of upper palaeolithic personal ornamentation from China: the freshwater shell bead from Shuidonggou 2. *PLoS ONE*, *11*, e0155847.

Weissbrod, L., Kaufman, D., Nadel, D., Yeshurun, R., & Weinstein-Evron, M. (2013). Commensalism: was it truly a Natufian phenomenon? Recent contributions from ethnoarcheology and ecology. In O. Bar-Yosef, & F. R. Valla (Eds.), *Natufian Foragers in the Levant: Terminal Pleistocene Social Changes in Western Asia* (pp. 699–717). Ann Arbor, MI: International Monographs in Prehistory.

Weissbrod, L., Marshall, F. B., Valla, F. R., Khalaily, H., Bar-Oz, G., Auffray, J.-C., et al. (2017). Origins of house mice in ecological niches created by settled hunter-gatherers in the Levant 15,000 y ago. *Proceedings of the National Academy of Sciences USA*, *114*, 4099–4104.

Weitzel, E. M., & Codding, B. F. (2016). Population growth as a driver of initial domestication in Eastern North America. *Royal Society Open Science*, *3*, 160319.

Welker, F., Hajdinjak, M., Talamo, S., Jaouen, K., Dannemann, M., David, F., et al. (2016). Palaeoproteomic evidence identifies archaic hominins associated with the Châtelperronian at the Grotte du Renne. *Proceedings of the National Academy of Sciences USA*, *113*, 11162–11167.

Westaway, M. C., Durband, A., & Lambert, D. (2015). Human evolution in Sunda and Sahul and the continuing contributions of Professor Colin Groves. In A. M. Behie, & M. F. Oxenham (Eds.), *Taxonomic Tapestries: The*

Threads of Evolutionary, Behavioural and Conservation Research (pp. 249–276). Canberra: ANU Press.

Wheeler, J. C. (2005). Pre-conquest alpaca and llama breeding. *The Camelid Quarterly, December 2005*, 1–5.

Wheeler, J. C. (2012). South American camelids - past, present and future. *Journal of Camelid Science*, 5, 1–24.

Wheeler, J. C., Chikhi, L., & Bruford, M. W. (2006). Genetic analysis of the origins of domestic South American Camelids. In M. A. Zeder, D. G. Bradley, E. Emshwiller, & B. D. Smith (Eds.), *Documenting Domestication: New Genetic and Archaeological Paradigms* (pp. 329–341). Berkeley, CA: University of California Press.

Wheeler, P. E. (1984). The evolution of bipedality and the loss of functional body hair in hominids. *Journal of Human Evolution, 13*, 91–98.

Wheeler, P. E. (1985). The loss of functional body hair in Man: the influence of thermal environment, body form and bipedality. *Journal of Human Evolution, 14*, 23–28.

Wheeler, P. E. (1992). The influence of the loss of functional body hair on the water budgets of early hominids. *Journal of Human Evolution, 23*, 379–388.

White, J. P. (2011). Revisiting the 'Neolithic problem' in Australia. *Records of the Western Australian Museum,* Suppl., *79*, 86–92.

White, J. P., Crook, K. A., & Ruxton, B. P. (1970). Kosipe: a Late Pleistocene site in the Papuan highlands. *Proceedings of the Prehistoric Society, 36*, 152–170.

White, M. J. (2006). Things to do in Doggerland when you're dead: surviving OIS3 at the northwestern-most fringe of Middle Palaeolithic Europe. *World Archaeology, 38*, 547–575.

White, R. (2006). The women of Brassempouy: a century of research and interpretation. *Journal of Archaeological Method and Theory, 13*, 251–304.

White, T. D., Ambrose, S. H., Suwa, G., & WoldeGabriel, G. (2010). Response to comment on the paleoenvironment of *Ardipithecus ramidus*. *Science, 328*, 1105.

Whitford, A. C. (1941). *Textile Fibers Used in Eastern Aboriginal North America.* Anthropological Papers of The American Museum of Natural History, Volume XXXVIII, Part I. New York: American Museum of Natural History.

Williamson, S. P. (2003). *Report on Wind Chill Temperature and Extreme Heat Indices: Evaluation and Improvement Projects.* Washington, DC: National Oceanic and Atmospheric Administration.

Willmer, P., Stone, G., & Johnston, I. (2005). *Environmental Physiology of Animals.* Second edition. Oxford: Blackwell.

Wilson, E. (2014). *Adorned in Dreams: Fashion and Modernity.* Second edition. London: I. B. Tauris.

Wilson, E. O. (2014). *The Meaning of Human Existence.* New York: W. W. Norton & Company.

Winchell, F., Stevens, C. J., Murphy, C., Champion, L., & Fuller, D. Q. (2017). Evidence for sorghum domestication in fourth millennium BC eastern Sudan. *Current Anthropology, 58*, 673–683.

Wobst, H. M. (2016). The analogy generation game. *Antiquity, 90*, 1083–1084.

Wood, R. E., Barroso-Ruíz, C., Caparrós, M., Jordá Pardo, J. F., & Galván Santos, B. (2013). Radiocarbon dating casts doubt on the late chronology of the middle to upper palaeolithic transition in southern Iberia. *Proceedings of the National Academy of Sciences USA, 110*, 2781–2786.

World Airliner Directory. (2015). *Flight International, 188*(5515), 30–39.

Wrangham, R. W. (2009). *Catching Fire: How Cooking Made Us Human.* New York: Basic Books.

Wright, D., Langley, M. C., May, S. K., Johnston, I. G., & Allen, L. (2016). Painted shark vertebrae beads from the Djawumbu-Madjawarrnja complex, western Arnhem Land. *Australian Archaeology, 82*, 43–54.

Wu, X., Zhang, C., Goldberg, P., Cohen, D., Pan, Y., Arpin, T., et al. (2012). Early pottery at 20,000 years ago in Xianrendong Cave, China. *Science, 336*, 1696–1700.

Wyrwoll, K.-H., Wei, J., Lin, Z., Shao, Y., & He, F. (2016). Cold surges and dust events: establishing the link between the East Asian Winter Monsoon and the Chinese loess record. *Quaternary Science Reviews*, *149*, 102–108.

Xiang, H., Gao, J., Yu, B., Zhou, H., Cai, D., Zhang, Y., et al. (2014). Early Holocene chicken domestication in northern China. *Proceedings of the National Academy of Sciences USA*, *111*, 17564–17569.

Xing, S., Martinón-Torres, M., Bermúdez de Castro, J. M., Wu, X., & Liu, W. (2015). Hominin teeth from the early Late Pleistocene site of Xujiayao, northern China. *American Journal of Physical Anthropology*, *156*, 224–240.

Yahalom-Mack, N., Langgut, D., Dvir, O., Tirosh, O., Eliyahu-Behar, A., Erel, Y., et al. (2015). The earliest lead object in the Levant. *PLoS ONE*, *10*, e0142948.

Yang, X., Barton, H. J., Wan, Z., Li, Q., Ma, Z., Li, M., et al. (2013). Sago-type palms were an important plant food prior to rice in southern subtropical China. *PLoS ONE*, *8*, e63148.

Yang, X., Fuller, D. Q., Huan, X., Perry, L., Li, Q., Li, Z., et al. (2015). Barnyard grasses were processed with rice around 10000 years ago. *Scientific Reports*, *5*, 16251.

Yang, X., Wan, Z., Perry, L., Lu, H., Wang, Q., Zhao, C., et al. (2012). Early millet use in northern China. *Proceedings of the National Academy of Sciences USA*, *109*, 3726–3730.

Yeshurun, R., Bar-Oz, G., & Weinstein-Evron, M. (2014). Intensification and sedentism in the terminal Pleistocene Natufian sequence of el-Wad Terrace (Israel). *Journal of Human Evolution*, *70*, 16–35.

Yoshimura, H., & Iida, T. (1951). Studies on the reactivity of skin vessels to extreme cold. Part II: factors governing the individual difference of the reactivity, or the resistance against frostbite. *Japanese Journal of Physiology*, *2*, 177–185.

Zeder, M. A. (2011). The origins of agriculture in the Near East. *Current Anthropology*, *52* (Suppl. S4), S221-S235.

Zeder, M. A. (2015). Core questions in domestication research. *Proceedings of the National Academy of Sciences USA*, *112*, 3191–3198.

Zeder, M. A. (2016). Domestication as a model system for niche construction theory. *Evolutionary Ecology*, *30*, 325–348.

Zeder, M. A. (2017). Domestication as a model system for the extended evolutionary synthesis. *Interface Focus*, *7*, 20160133.

Zhang, H., & Song, G. (2014). Performance of immersion suits: a literature review. *Journal of Industrial Textiles*, *44*, 288–306.

Zhang, J., Lu, H., Sun, G., Flad, R., Wu, N., Huan, X., et al. (2016). Phytoliths reveal the earliest fine reedy textile in China at the Tianluoshan site. *Scientific Reports*, *6*, 18664.

Zhang, J.-F., Huang, W.-W., Yuan, B.-Y., Fu, R.-Y., & Zhou, L.-P. (2010). Optically stimulated luminescence dating of cave deposits at the Xiaogushan prehistoric site, northeastern China. *Journal of Human Evolution*, *59*, 514–524.

Zhang, S., d'Errico, F., Backwell, L. R., Zhang, Y., Chen, F., & Gao, X. (2016). Ma'anshan cave and the origin of bone tool technology in China. *Journal of Archaeological Science*, *65*, 57–69.

Zhang, Y., Gao, X., Pei, S., Chen, F., Niu, D., Xu, X., et al. (2016). The bone needles from Shuidonggou locality 12 and implications for human subsistence behaviors in North China. *Quaternary International*, *400*, 149–157.

Zhao, F., Wang, Y., Luo, Q., Long, B., Zhang, B., Xia, Y., et al. (2017). The earliest evidence of pattern looms: Han Dynasty tomb models from Chengdu, China. *Antiquity*, *91*, 360–374.

Zhao, J. (2004). The early Yangshao settlement at Dadiwan, Qin'an County, Gangsu Province (translated by Li Xinwei). *Chinese Archaeology*, *4*, 63–70.

Zheng, Y., Crawford, G. W., Jiang, L., & Chen, X. (2016). Rice domestication revealed by reduced shattering of archaeological rice from the Lower Yangtze valley. *Scientific Reports*, *6*, 28136.

Zhou, H., Zhao, J.-x., Feng, Y., Chen, Q., Mi, X., Shen, C.-C., et al. (2014). Heinrich event 4 and Dansgaard/Oeschger events 5–10 recorded by high-resolution speleothem oxygen isotope data from central China. *Quaternary Research*, *82*, 394–404.

Zhu, R. X., Potts, R., Xie, F., Hoffman, K. A., Deng, C. L., Shi, C. D., et al. (2004). New evidence on the earliest human presence at high northern latitudes in northeast Asia. *Nature*, *431*, 559–562.

Zilhão, J. (2007). The emergence of ornaments and art: an archaeological perspective on the origins of "behavioral modernity." *Journal of Archaeological Research*, *15*, 1–54.

Zilhão, J., Banks, W. E., d'Errico, F., & Gioia, P. (2015). Analysis of site formation and assemblage integrity does not support attribution of the Uluzzian to modern humans at Grotta del Cavallo. *PLoS ONE*, *10*, e0131181.

Zohary, D., Hopf, M., & Weiss, E. (2012). *Domestication of Plants in the Old World: The Origin and Spread of Domesticated Plants in South-West Asia, Europe, and the Mediterranean Basin*. Fourth edition. Oxford: Oxford University Press.

Zuo, X., Lu, H., Jiang, L., Zhang, J., Yang, X., Huan, X., et al. (2017). Dating rice remains through phytolith carbon-14 study reveals domestication at the beginning of the Holocene. *Proceedings of the National Academy of Sciences USA*, *114*, 6486–6491.

Zupancich, A., Nunziante-Cesaro, S., Blasco, R., Rosell, J., Cristiani, E., Venditti, F., et al. (2016). Early evidence of stone tool use in bone working activities at Qesem Cave, Israel. *Scientific Reports*, *6*, 37686.

Zvelebil, M. (2008). Innovating hunter-gatherers: the mesolithic in the Baltic. In G. Bailey, & P. Spikins (Eds.), *Mesolithic Europe* (pp. 18–59). Cambridge: Cambridge University Press.

INDEX